DATE DUE

MAR 2 4 2010	
MAR 2 6 2014	
MAY 0 1 2014	

BRODART, CO.

Cat. No. 23-221-003

GAY MARRIAGE: *For Better or for Worse?*

GAY MARRIAGE: *For Better or for Worse?*

WHAT WE'VE LEARNED FROM THE EVIDENCE

William N. Eskridge, Jr.   *Darren R. Spedale*

OXFORD
UNIVERSITY PRESS

2006

OXFORD
UNIVERSITY PRESS

Oxford University Press, Inc., publishes works that further
Oxford University's objective of excellence
in research, scholarship, and education.

Oxford   New York
Auckland   Cape Town   Dar es Salaam   Hong Kong   Karachi
Kuala Lumpur   Madrid   Melbourne   Mexico City   Nairobi
New Delhi   Shanghai   Taipei   Toronto

With offices in
Argentina   Austria   Brazil   Chile   Czech Republic   France   Greece
Guatemala   Hungary   Italy   Japan   Poland   Portugal   Singapore
South Korea   Switzerland   Thailand   Turkey   Ukraine   Vietnam

Published by Oxford University Press, Inc.
198 Madison Avenue, New York, New York 10016

www.oup.com

Oxford is a registered trademark of Oxford University Press

Library of Congress Cataloging-in-Publication Data
Eskridge, William N.
Gay marriage : for better or for worse? : what we've learned from the
evidence / William N. Eskridge, Jr. and Darren R. Spedale.
    p. cm.
Includes bibliographical references.
ISBN-13 978-0-19-518751-9
ISBN 0-19-518751-2
1. Gay couples—Legal status, laws, etc.—United States.   2. Same-sex
marriage—Law and legislation—United States.   3. Gay couples—Legal
status, laws, etc.—Scandinavia.   4. Same-sex marriage—Law and
legislation—Scandinavia.   I. Spedale, Darren R.   II. Title.
K699.E85 2006
346.01'68—dc22   2005027132

9 8 7 6 5 4 3 2 1

Printed in the United States of America
on acid-free paper

Darren Spedale dedicates this book to those members

of his family who have always been there for him—

his parents, Daniel and Iris Spedale,

and his aunt, Adele Rifkin.

William Eskridge dedicates this book to the married couple

to whom he owes the most—his parents, William Nichol

and the late Elizabeth Beckwith DeJarnette Eskridge.

ACKNOWLEDGMENTS

First and foremost, the research in this book could not have been conducted without the assistance of many kind and generous people in
Scandinavia who have been involved with the partnership laws over the
years, and who have had particularly important stories to tell. Bent Hansen
and Steffen Jensen in particular have been instrumental in this research,
and in helping us locate the right sources and persons to contact. We would
also like to make a very special thanks to Landsforeningen for Bøsser og
Lesbiske (the National Organization for Gays and Lesbians, LBL) for all
of their members' time, help and support, and for making LBL's resources
available for the completion of this project. We also thank the following
people in Scandinavia for sharing their personal perspectives and experiences relating to the partnership laws, which were critical in the development of this project. In Denmark: Axel Axgil, Wilhem von Rosen, Henning
Bech, Ivan Larsen, Margrete Auken, Uffe Østergaard, Per Kleis, Torben
Lund, Jann Sjursen and Jonna Waage. In Norway: Kjell Erik Øie and Gro
Lindstad. In Sweden: Stig-Åke Petersson. In Iceland: Gudni Baldursson
and Lana Eddudottir. In Finland: Hannele Lehtikuusi, whose memory this
book honors. Countless others in Scandinavia helped in this research, and
to them we extend our deepest appreciation.

We also thank all of the couples who graciously opened their homes to
our interviews, and were willing to share their personal stories as couples
who have entered into registered partnerships. While some couples' stories
are not used in this publication, this book could not have come to fruition
without the help of each and every one of them. We also extend our gratitude to Michael McConnell and Jack Baker for their comments and insight,
and to Ken Bronson for putting us in touch with these American pioneers.

We owe a tremendous debt to a number of scholars and intellectuals, and
none greater than that owed to three law professors who reviewed our manuscript for Oxford University Press: Nan Hunter of Brooklyn Law School, Andy
Koppelman of Northwestern University School of Law (twice), and Sylvia Law
of New York University School of Law (also twice).

We also benefited from workshop presentations of particular chapters,
or portions of chapters, in this book at Princeton University, Yale Law
School, the Department of Psychology of Yale University, the New York
University School of Law, the University of Florida School of Law, Brooklyn Law School, and the University of Minnesota School of Law, as well as
the Lesbian and Gay Legal Studies Group convened by Nan Hunter in New

York City. Participants in those workshops gave us useful feedback, and we particularly appreciate the comments of Michelle Adams, Matthew Coles, Suzanne Goldberg, Julie Goldscheid, Elizabeth Hillman, Marianne LaFrance, Arthur Leonard, Steven Macedo, Marc Poirier, Vicki Schultz, and Edward Stein.

Associate Judge and Ombudsman Hans Ytterberg, of Sweden's Office of Ombudsman against Discrimination on Grounds of Sexual Orientation, provided us with much of the demographic as well as registered partnership data we report for Sweden. Chapter 5 of this book draws on an article we published with Judge Ytterberg: "Nordic Bliss? Scandinavian Registered Partnerships and the Same-Sex Marriage Debate," *Issues in Legal Scholarship* 5 (2004): Article 1, available at www.bepress.com/ils/issue5/article1. Turid Noack, a researcher on family law at Statistics Norway, provided us with additional guidance.

We were fortunate to work with excellent research assistants during the time they were students at the Yale Law School. We thank Michael Gottlieb, C. J. Mahoney, Rebecca Marcuse, Sheila Nagaraj, David Newman, Darsana Srinivasan, Bree Grossi Wilde, and Robert Yablon.

Gene Coakley and other experts in the Yale Law School Library greatly facilitated our research. Gene and Scott Matheson made it their business to teach our research assistants some fine points of legal research. Patricia Page of the Yale Law School not only assisted our research in critical ways but also developed most of the figures and charts used in the book; Robert Yablon developed the remainder. We also thank the Benay Brothers, Aaron and Matthew, for lending their creative talents to our title.

Perhaps not least, we owe a great debt to scholars who have joined the same-sex marriage debate in a serious way, especially those scholars who have provided empirical support for their arguments. One of the most insightful and rigorous of these new empiricists is Dr. M. V. Lee Badgett, Research Director for the Institute for Gay and Lesbian Strategic Studies. We have also learned much from Dr. Kathleen Kiernan's modeling of family-formation patterns in Europe, Maggie Gallagher's factual reports and argumentation on her website (www.marriagedebate.com), and Stanley Kurtz's on-line articles maintaining that same-sex partnerships have contributed to the decline of different-sex marriage in Scandinavia. Although we dispute Mr. Kurtz's work, in particular, we appreciate that it has been reasoned, intellectually adventurous, and influential.

For Darren Spedale, this book represents the culmination of many years' research on the Scandinavian partnership laws, which was begun a decade ago. Over this lengthy period of time, there have been many wonderful persons who have made this experience possible. I would like to first and foremost thank my parents, Daniel and Iris Spedale, and my aunt, Adele Rifkin, without whose constant support none of this would have been possible. I would also like to thank the Dushman family (Rebecca, Charles, Rory, Brad, Ashley and Brittany) for their presence and support, and my close friends, Carol Mozell in particular, whose encouragement on this project over the years has been invaluable.

In addition, I would like to extend my sincerest thanks to the Fulbright Foundation for their financial, academic, and social support during my two-year stay in Denmark, and in particular Marie Mønsted and Barbara Lehman for all their help. Critical research support was also provided by the Lonnie Martin Jr. Living Trust and the Markowski-Leach Scholarship Fund. My gratitude also goes to Professor Linda Nielsen, my academic sponsor at the University of Copenhagen; to Bruce Payne and William Reppy at Duke University, and to Evan Wolfson at Freedom to Marry, for advancing my interests in this research; and to Tone Fanger, who helped me to Danish fluency in a fraction of the time I would have thought possible.

William Eskridge expresses his appreciation to his boss at the Yale Law School, Dean Harold H. Koh, who not only provided funds for our under-compensated research assistants, but also supported my summer research and writing for this project. The Reading Group of the Gay and Lesbian Attorneys of Washington (DC) provided critical personal support as well as intellectual feedback for my work on this as well.

CONTENTS

GAY MARRIAGE: *For Better or for Worse?*

Toward a Brave New World

Jean Luscher and Diana Skovgaard, an American-Danish couple who have entered into a registered partnership in Denmark.

Born in 1942, Michael McConnell grew up in Norman, Oklahoma, surrounded by the graceful architecture and intellectual atmosphere of the state university. A bookish, clean-cut boy whose career aspiration was to be a librarian, Michael also had a deeper aspiration: to find his soul mate. He kept the latter aspiration secret because he knew from an early age that this special someone would not be one of the shapely coeds he saw around the campus of the University of Oklahoma—instead, it would be another man.

While Norman was a college town, Michael knew that it was also a strict Baptist community where homosexuality was unmentionable. Thus, while he was able to come to terms with being gay, Michael lived in constant fear of exposure. His fears were confirmed by the experience of Joe Clem, his high school friend and classmate at the University. Because he was a personable jock, Joe believed he could get away with dropping his mask of heterosexuality on occasion. After all, it was the 1960s, and many college students were exploring new sexual freedoms. One night Joe went out drinking with his frat buddies. With some alcohol in his system, his mask began to slip off. "Soon, things escalated out of control as they called Joe a 'faggot,'" Michael recalls. "Later, he awoke on a deserted road outside Norman, a bloody mess, barely able to walk."[1]

Joe Clem never reported this crime to the police, for in Oklahoma, the homosexual was an *outlaw* in every sense of the term. First, there was no likelihood that the police would act against gay-bashers. Even as a victim of private violence or discrimination, the homosexual was a "person excluded from the benefit of the law, or deprived of its protection." Indeed, Joe himself might have ended up in jail if the police got involved. As a serial violator of the Oklahoma statute making consensual sodomy a felony, the homosexual was a criminal, a "lawless" person. Yet, despite his occasional openness with a few friends, what Joe most feared was public exposure. From the perspective of both the police and his fraternity brothers, and perhaps even Joe's own parents and neighbors, the homosexual was "a wild beast" (the third dictionary definition of "outlaw" in 1961). The homosexual was understood, in that era, to be subhuman, vicious, and predatory.[2]

Despite the oppressive atmosphere and Joe Clem's frightening experience, Michael held out hope that he could find a normal romantic relationship with another man. After a lengthy period of longing in silence while earning his master's degree in library science, his secret aspiration was finally realized on Halloween night in 1966. While he was attending a party in a creaky, run-down barn outside of Norman, a friend introduced him to Richard John (Jack) Baker, also twenty-four years old, a dashing field engineer who was working in Oklahoma City. As if a spell were cast on this Halloween night, there was an instant connection between the shy librarian, who had rarely been outside the state, and the brash engineer, who had served in the Air Force and done a tour of duty in Vietnam. Soon thereafter these young men became entangled in one another's lives, and quickly became soul mates. On March 10, 1967, Michael's twenty-fifth birthday, Jack asked Michael to join him as a committed life partner. "Michael accepted the proposal but on one condition. He insisted that someday, some way, they would marry legally."[3]

This romantic gesture had a fairy-tale quality for the two men who wanted to live "happily ever after," but in Oklahoma, that seemed unlikely. Yet two years after Jack's marriage proposal, the Stonewall riots in New York City foreshadowed a sea change in the social status of homosexuals. Thousands of gays and lesbians marched out of their closets and challenged their outlaw status. Lesbian and gay activists insisted that the state should no longer treat them as presumptive criminals and should, instead, treat them the same as it treated straight citizens. Caught up in the excitement of this new movement, Baker and McConnell applied for a marriage license in 1970.

Their marriage application made history in the United States, and triggered a public discussion that has lasted more than thirty years: Should the state allow gay and lesbian couples to enjoy the legal benefits, duties, and sanction of civil marriage? At first, state officials and most Americans simply denied the possibility of same-sex marriage. It is a contradiction in terms, they declared, for marriage has generally been limited to one man and one woman throughout Western history. Indeed, this was the only reason given by state authorities who denied Baker and McConnell's and similar marriage petitions.[4] Such *definitional* objections were the main reasons that clerks, legislators, and judges rejected same-sex marriage claims in the 1970s and 1980s.[5] Despite these rejections by the government, lesbians and gay men continued to stream out of their closets, and many of them formed committed relationships and even families with children, defying the notion that homosexual marriage was a contradiction in terms.

Yet the United States was not the only country in which the debate over same-sex marriage was taking place. Even as early as the mid-1960s, a few years before the Stonewall riots, gays and lesbians in Denmark and elsewhere in Scandinavia began their public campaign for the right to marry. Taking advantage of the progressive political atmosphere that had been spawned by the student revolution of the late 1960s, gays and lesbians in Denmark challenged the oppressiveness of the closet and argued that they were deserving of equal treatment of their relationships.

Over the course of two decades, national debate over same-sex legal unions took place in Denmark, Sweden, and eventually the other Nordic nations as well. Proponents for marriage equality found themselves facing the same objections to same-sex marriage that were closing the door on same-sex marriage in the United States. Nevertheless, in 1989, Denmark made world history by enacting a law granting (almost) all of the rights of marriage to same-sex couples. These new unions were called *registered partnerships*.[6] One of us (Spedale) spent two years in Denmark in the late 1990s, researching the effects of this legislation and the lessons it provides, and recording the stories of same-sex couples living in registered partnerships.[7]

While thousands of Danes would "tie the knot" under this historic legislation over the next decade, citizens from other nations would take advantage of the Danish law as well, including American citizens. Born in 1962 and raised in Buffalo, New York, Jean Luscher was taught at a young age that one of the greatest joys in a girl's life is to marry a man and raise children in a loving marriage—not unlike the lessons a child would learn in Norman, Oklahoma. In high school, Jean played soccer and spent a great deal of her time studying, leaving little time for dating. Because she was a politically active student, she had many male friends, but she was never sexually engaged until she was a student at Bryn Mawr College, the tony women's school near Philadelphia's Main Line. Her first female sexual encounter was initiated by a jogging partner—and Jean realized soon thereafter that her earlier aspiration for a husband would never satisfy her. She became active in the lesbian community, and soon settled into her self-identification as a lesbian. After graduating from college, Luscher lived for a year in Germany, before pursuing a master's degree and later a Ph.D. in German studies at Indiana University.

During her graduate work, Jean won a Fulbright scholarship to study in Denmark for two years. In 1991, during the course of her Fulbright research, Luscher met Diane Skovgaard during a lesbian meet-and-greet at Pan, Copenhagen's largest gay disco. They hit it off instantly, and soon thereafter became lovers. After several years of dating, much of it long-distance, Jean and Diane in 1995 decided to register as partners under the 1989 Danish law.[8]

Luscher and Skovgaard's partnership, or "marriage," as they (and most other Scandinavians) consider it, poses real-life challenges to definitional arguments against same-sex marriage. The Danish law helped trigger a new generation of petitions for same-sex marriage in the United States and elsewhere in Europe, but opponents batted them aside with a new generation of arguments against same-sex marriage. Although homosexuals were no longer the outlaw class they were in the 1950s, many Americans still considered homosexuality immoral or diseased (or both). Homo-anxious Americans (including Jean Luscher's mother) worried that same-sex marriage would constitute a state *stamp of approval* for relationships they considered fundamentally wrong. The most popular argument against same-sex marriage in the 1990s, however, was that it would undermine *real marriage,* thereby harming ordinary Americans and, especially, children. This *defense-of-marriage* objection maintains that same-sex marriage would fundamentally change the institution, reinforcing the malign effects of previous liberalizations. Married couples now tend to understand marriage as an institution providing pleasure and self-fulfillment, a departure from traditional understandings of marriage as an institution fostering altruism and child-rearing. By severing the last link between marriage and procreation, many traditionalists believe, state recognition of same-sex unions or marriages will destroy the best features of this cherished institution.[9]

The public debates surrounding the Danish Registered Partnership Act often mirrored the arguments that have been made in America. Some Danes accepted the definitional or stamp-of-approval arguments as a matter of religious faith or even prejudice, but the main reason publicly advanced against legal unions was the defense-of-marriage objection. Although many Danes and their legislators agreed with this objection, most did not—or felt that its force was outweighed by the advantages of creating a state institution recognizing and reinforcing the commitments same-sex couples were anxious to make. All the other Scandinavian countries have adopted a model almost identical to the Danish law, always over definitional, stamp-of-approval, and defense-of-marriage objections such as those suggested here. Other European countries have created their own institutions for same-sex unions. The Netherlands, Belgium, and Spain have now recognized same-sex marriages, as has Canada.[10]

Like Jean Luscher and Diana Skovgaard, other same-sex couples who have entered into a legal union in Scandinavia have generally considered it a very positive experience. Couple after couple told us how "marriage" changed their lives in beneficial ways they had not anticipated.[11] Luscher and Skovgaard found that registering as partners made their complicated dual careers much easier to manage, while at the same time opening up new opportunities to Jean in particular. Many couples found that registered partnership added an additional element of commitment to their relationship, while others found that their public declaration of legal commitment also strengthened their relationships with extended families, friends, and coworkers, giving them support and enriching the lives of everyone. Jean's family in the United States, for example, has welcomed Diana as part of the family, just as Diana's son and family have welcomed Jean in Denmark. Indeed, there is even evidence suggesting that same-sex marriages or partnership equivalents harbor benefits that will attach to the greater society.[12]

There is another side to the Scandinavian story, however. Some outside observers believe that the happiness that registered partnership has brought to Jean Luscher has come at a tremendous social cost—in their words, the "end of marriage." Stanley Kurtz, a Research Fellow at the Hoover Institution of Stanford University, has produced a series of empirical claims, mainly based upon publicly available data from Scandinavia, supporting the defense-of-marriage objection. Because lesbian and gay couples can now register as partners, and in effect "get married," Kurtz says younger Scandinavians have simply given up on marriage and are now raising children outside of marriage. This Scandinavian twist on the defense-of-marriage argument has become the factual backbone of the Republican Party's campaign for a Federal Marriage Amendment, espoused not only by leading politicians like Senator Rick Santorum but also by such important conservative intellectuals as former judge Robert Bork. The conservative reading of the Scandinavian experience has also been picked up by local traditionalists' grassroots campaigns seeking to amend state statutes and constitutions to head off same-sex marriage in their jurisdictions—and to guarantee that Massachusetts same-sex marriages, Vermont or Connecticut civil unions, and California domestic partnerships will not be given recognition either.[13]

These traditionalists' reading of the Scandinavian experience raises some empirical issues. Has same-sex marriage accelerated the social trend, apparent as early as the 1970s in Denmark and Sweden, toward cohabitation rather than marriage? Has it had an effect on the divorce rates of the Scandinavian countries? On the marital birth rate? The Scandinavian experience also poses broader normative questions about marriage and the state's proper role in molding it. Does expanding civil marriage rights and duties to lesbian and gay couples *fundamentally* alter the goals and norms of marriage? Does same-sex marriage reinforce other legal changes in the institution, such as no-fault divorce and state tolerance of cohabitation arrangements? Or does same-sex marriage send a different cultural message, that the procommitment norm is applicable to lesbian and gay couples? Many gay and, especially, lesbian couples are raising children within their partnered unions in Scandinavia. Has legal recognition of their partnerships affected the lives of their children? Of children generally?[14]

Reaching beyond the demographic effects of registered partnerships, we ask what lessons Scandinavia offers for the politics of the same-sex marriage debate in the United States and elsewhere. Some of the lessons are pertinent to the defenders of "traditional" marriage, public figures like Senator Santorum and Judge Bork, as well as scholars such as Kurtz. Bork, in particular, says that it is straight couples who have almost destroyed marriage in this country, sacrificing its altruistic commitment-based features so that they will have a wider array of pleasure-seeking choices. But, like other traditionalists, Bork says that same-sex marriage would be the last straw, ending any chance of saving marriage.[15] Are cultural conservatives like Bork in fact saving traditional marriage from complete collapse by opposing same-sex marriage? What effect does their opposition, thus far quite successful, have on marriage and on religious faith in this country? Are there other strategies they should be following?

Traditional family values Americans, like Bork, also need to consider the social fact that there are now more (perhaps much more) than half a million committed lesbian and gay couples in the United States. They have established households and are participants in their communities; a surprisingly large percentage of these are households of color.[16] More than a fourth of these households are raising children. From a profamily point of view, what should be society's or the state's stance toward those households? Those children?

Same-sex marriages—as well as registered partnerships and civil unions—are part of a brave new world of family law that is now beyond the complete control of either churches or gay rights advocates. The contours of that world, outlined in our epilogue, will reflect a different kind of choice regime for couples, increasingly including same-sex couples. For the last generation, Western countries have been moving toward a *menu* approach, where couples can opt for the legal regime that best fits the level of commitment they want to undertake. In such a brave new world, marriage becomes one of several options. Is this a world where the romance of traditional marriage will come to an end? Like Robert Bork and Stanley Kurtz, couples such as Michael McConnell and Jack Baker, and Jean Luscher and Diana Skovgaard, certainly hope not.

CHAPTER 1

The Evolving Same-Sex Marriage Debate in the United States

Michael McConnell and Jack Baker.

R ecall librarian Michael McConnell and engineer Jack Baker, the two men who fell in love on All Hallows Eve. In 1968, the couple moved to Kansas, where Jack worked as a DuPont engineer and Michael as an acquisitions librarian. Always politically active, Jack decided to pursue a law degree, which Michael encouraged. The University of Minnesota's prestigious School of Law accepted him. Jack moved to Minneapolis and enrolled in September 1969; accepting an offer to work at the university's library, Michael followed early in 1970. Most first-year law students spend the entire year poring through highly detailed law books and competing for grades that would earn them top law firm jobs. But Jack's first year coincided with the fermenting of gay liberation that followed the Stonewall riots of June 1969. Jack joined the campus gay activist group, Fight Repression of Erotic Expression (FREE), and worked within the university to advance an antidiscrimination policy. But he had not forgotten his promise to Michael that they would find a way to be legally married. So Jack also found time to research Minnesota marriage law, which provided that any two "persons" could apply for a marriage license.[1]

A practicing Catholic, Baker brought McConnell to religious services at the university's Newman Center chapel. One Sunday, they asked the priest, Reverend William Hunt, "Do you feel that if two people give themselves in love to each other and want to grow together with mutual understanding, that Jesus would be open to such a union if the people were of the same sex?" After thinking for a moment, Reverend Hunt said, "Yes, in my opinion, Christ would be open." Elated by the reverend's response, the couple purchased wedding rings and planned a religious ceremony. Baker and McConnell appeared at the Hennepin County Courthouse on May 18, 1970, to apply for a marriage license. Upon hearing their request, Clerk of the Court Gerald Nelson stared blankly at the couple for a moment, and realized he had no idea what to do with this couple. He asked County Attorney George Scott for a legal opinion. On May 22, Scott opined that Minnesota law did not authorize a marriage license for a same-sex couple. The common law treated marriage as only different-sex, and Minnesota's divorce and other marriage-related laws explicitly regulated only relations between a "husband" and a "wife." To approve the license, he concluded, "would be to result in an undermining or destruction of the entire legal concept of our family structure in all areas of law."[2]

Most people agreed with Scott. Only a handful of Americans, and not many gay ones, could even conceive of, much less endorse, marriage between two men in 1970. Most devout Catholics, fundamentalist Protestants, and orthodox Jews found *homosexual* marriage an affront to their religious beliefs, and many radical feminists and queers were highly critical of *marriage* of any kind. But Baker and McConnell were firmly committed, not only to one another but to the notion of *full formal equality* for lesbians, gay men, and bisexuals—a principle requiring state recognition of gay marriages. Theirs was not an idea whose time had come, however. Baker and McConnell were never legally married. McConnell lost his job because of the scandalous publicity. In the 1980s, gay rights attorneys turned to issues like sodomy reform and job discrimination, where there was some chance of persuading mainstream America to recognize some rights for homosexuals. Although overwhelming numbers of lesbians and gay men said they favored state recognition of their unions as marriages, the issue seemed politically and legally unattainable.

In 1989, Denmark surprised Americans of all orientations by enacting a law creating marriage-like *registered partnerships* for same-sex couples, and reports of the first couples to tie the knot in Copenhagen's Town Hall were carried by media outlets from around the world. Although the leading gay legal advocacy organizations believed full marriage equality remained politically unattainable in the United States, the Danish law inspired several committed lesbian and gay couples to petition anew, repeating Baker and McConnell's arguments for same-sex marriage. At the dawn of the new millennium, civil unions came to Vermont, followed by legal recognition of same-sex marriages in the Netherlands, Belgium, Massachusetts, Spain, and Canada. Has the time finally come for Baker and McConnell's idea?

The answer remains unclear. Lesbian and gay Americans, their friends, and their families strongly support same-sex marriage, while a larger number of traditional family value Americans are dead set against it. Yet a significant number of Americans remain open-minded. From their point of view, any big change in public policy must be justified, and its risks carefully evaluated. This middle group is the primary audience for writers about the same-sex marriage issue, including the authors of this book. In this chapter, we shall introduce this audience to the evolution of the same-sex marriage debate and to the argument that has recently caught the attention of thoughtful Americans: Has the legal recognition of same-sex partnerships in other countries had positive consequences for citizens in those countries?

Visions of Equality and the Same-Sex Marriage Debate within the Lesbian and Gay Community

The gay-liberal argument for same-sex marriage primarily rests upon the norm of *formal equality:* The state ought to accord the same legal options for committed same-sex couples that different-sex couples now enjoy, including the rights and duties entailed in civil marriage. Although almost all lesbian, gay, bisexual, and transgendered (LGBT) Americans agree that the state should not discriminate against or exclude them from state institutions, they do not all support same-sex marriage. Gay-radicals, for example, believe in *transformative equality:* a culture that has denigrated and randomly persecuted gender-benders and sexual minorities must itself change if these unfairly disadvantaged groups are to assume their rightful place as equal citizens; marriage is a prominent part of such an oppressive society. Hence LGBT people should seek new forms of legal recognition rather than assimilate into a questionable form.

Gay People as a Minority Group: The Liberal Right to Same-Sex Marriage

For most of the twentieth century, LGBT people not only were socially and legally disapproved but were witch-hunted and disciplined by local and military police, civil service agencies, school boards, and universities. Fearful homosexuals not only hid their sexual identities but lied about them. Most of them married persons of the opposite sex. But even marriage was a closet the antihomosexual gendarmerie sometimes penetrated. For example, an FBI investigation of "Mr. and Mrs. David Warren" turned up a lesbian couple (Thelma Jane Walker and Marieta Cook) who had obtained a marriage license in 1947. In the homophobic period after World War II, this was no longer an odd curiosity; it was a crime against society. The couple were reportedly charged with criminal perjury.[3]

In part *because of* such persecution, this era gave rise to tentative discussions about same-sex marriage. Huddled together in the shadows of the law, otherwise dissimilar people called one another brother and sister (or girlfriend) because of their shared sexual orientation. Aggressive state discrimination helped establish "homosexuals" as a socially coherent "minority" group. Like Jews and African Americans, homosexuals were marked as a denigrated group on the basis of a trait that some of them considered irrelevant to their ability to form productive relationships and contribute to society. In 1950, Harry Hay's prospectus for the first ongoing "homophile" group, the Mattachine Society, explicitly made this analogy and asserted that homosexuals, like people of color, were entitled to civil and political rights against state discrimination.[4]

Also viewing homosexuals as a minority group, Donald Webster Cory's book *The Homosexual in America* (1951) urged state recognition of lesbian and gay unions. "Is it possible or desirable for two young people of the same sex to be in love with each other, just as a man is in love with a woman; to show the same affection and interest, to offer the same loyalty, to form a union as permanent?" Admittedly, the author was ambivalent. Although the homosexual's "deepgoing shame" and men's "promiscuity" undermined the possibility of lasting unions, society and law bear much of the responsibility for their impermanence.[5] Many homosexuals yearned for committed relationships with other men, and Cory gently suggested that "society recognize and sanction marriages in which both 'bride' and 'groom' are of the same sex."[6]

E. W. Saunders wrote in 1953 that any serious effort to attain rights for homosexuals must advocate marriage rights, but he admitted that marriage was not then a "prominent" item in the homophile agenda.[7] Job discrimination and police harassment were more relevant to the lives of the gay men who set that agenda. In 1959, the Daughters of Bilitis (DOB) conducted a survey of more than 250 lesbians and gay men in California. Seventy-two percent of the lesbians were in a sexual relationship, as were 46 percent of the men. Most of the male relationships lasted fewer than five years, while most of the lesbian ones lasted four years or more. For sociological reasons, same-sex marriage was a more prominent issue for DOB than for Mattachine in the fifties and sixties.[8]

In the 1960s, an increasing but still tiny number of homosexuals living in the gay meccas celebrated their relationships in "weddings," with all the bells and whistles of a marriage. As the *Ladder* (the DOB's official journal) noted, these weddings had no legal effect, and "the homosexual marriage must be maintained only through the mutual love and devotion of those involved."[9] Several years later, however, the journal published a piece on the "Economics of Gay Marriage," with financial and legal planning tips for the lesbian couple who wanted to "live happily ever after."[10] Martha Shelley, the president of DOB New York, observed that lesbian marriage was a topic of great interest among DOB members—some of them quite skeptical. "Personally, I refuse to enter an agreement which binds me to have sex with one and only one person, which gives that person jurisdiction over my friendships and finances." A reader from Cleveland objected that the key to marriage is mutual commitment, a human good that is liberating more than confining.[11] This exchange suggested that same-sex marriage was not only an important topic within lesbian communities but also one that was being discussed with sophistication and a critical eye.

Accepting Hay's view that gay people were an unfairly persecuted minority, most of the young homophile leaders of the 1960s favored complete formal equality. Among them were the San Franciscans José Sarrìa, Del Martin, and Phyllis Lyon; Frank Kameny, Lilli Vincenz, and Jack Nichols in Washington, D.C.; Philadelphia's Barbara Gittings and Clark Polak; and New York's Dick Leitsch. In February 1966, the First National Planning Conference of Homophile Organizations resolved: "Homosexual American citizens should have precise equality with all other citizens before the law and are entitled to social and economic equality of opportunity." Implicitly, this would have included same-sex marriage.[12]

But there was little specific discussion of same-sex marriage as a legal right until the late 1960s. In *Loving v. Virginia* (1967), the Supreme Court struck down laws refusing to recognize different-race marriages. The Court reasoned that marriage is a fundamental right of citizenship that cannot be denied because of the different races of the partners. From this ruling, homophile leaders concluded that, if social prejudice were not enough to support traditional marriage discrimination because of the race of the partners, why should it be sufficient to support traditional discrimination because of their sex?[13]

New York's Stonewall riots transformed the feisty but tiny homophile movement into a mass-mobilized gay rights movement. Knowledge of homo-resistance at the Stonewall Inn on the night of June 26–27, 1969, inspired thousands of lesbians, gay men, and bisexuals to come out of their closets and openly proclaim erotic love for persons of the same sex. Some of these couples publicly appropriated the conventions of marriage. Reverend Troy Perry, the founder of the gay-friendly Metropolitan Community Church, performed three dozen same-sex marriages in Los Angeles during the first six months of 1970. Some couples went further. Three months after Baker and McConnell applied for a marriage license in Hennepin County, Minnesota, Tracy Knight and Marjorie Ruth Jones (a mother of three) applied for a marriage license in Jefferson County, Kentucky.[14]

Baker and McConnell sued Clerk of the Court Nelson on the ground that denying them a marriage license is unconstitutional. (In November, Knight and Jones filed a similar lawsuit.) After the Minnesota courts dismissed these claims in 1971, Michael Wetherbee of the Minnesota American Civil Liberties Union (ACLU) filed an appeal with the U.S. Supreme Court. "At first, the question and the proposed relationship may well appear bizarre—especially to heterosexuals," he conceded, but that first impulse "provides us with some measure of the continuing impact on our society of prejudice against non-heterosexuals." Indeed, "the relationship contemplated is neither grotesque nor uncommon."[15] Wetherbee's brief for Baker and McConnell argued that it was presumptively unconstitutional for the state to discriminate. Such bars denied lesbian and gay couples their fundamental right to marry that had been recognized for different-race couples in *Loving*. The marriage bar was more than an abstract discrimination, for it effectively denied such couples the important property and economic rights that accompany spousehood as a matter of law. In a final parallel to *Loving*, Wetherbee maintained that the state's discrimination deployed a suspicious classification, namely, the sex or gender of the partners.[16]

By 1971, therefore, the framework for a gay-liberal case for same-sex marriage in the United States was in place. Lesbians, gay men, and bisexuals are a minority group unfairly subject to private prejudice and state discrimination. Like racial minorities, sexual minorities are good citizens who do not deserve this kind of disrespectful treatment. Under the equal protection clause of the U.S. Constitution, they are entitled to the same rights as straight Americans. Among those are the right to marry the person one falls in love with. Lesbians such as Knight and Jones, and gay men such as

Baker and McConnell, wanted the romantic symbolism as well as legal benefits associated with marriage, and they wanted to undertake the legal as well as social duties of marriage. A neutral state that treats all its citizens with respect must recognize such marriages and certainly cannot refuse to do so because of social prejudice.

Liberals versus Radicals: The Marriage Debate within the LGBT Community

In the 1960s, it was radical to argue, as Frank Kameny did (and José Sarrìa had before him), that "Gay is good." Apart from that, however, the Harvard-educated Kameny was a good old-fashioned, ACLU liberal. (In 1961, he was a founding member of the National Capital Area chapter of the ACLU.) Such gay-liberals accepted the basic institutions of American society—marriage and the family, the market system, and the mechanisms of representative democracy—and argued that gay people should have equal access to those institutions. All of these institutions had their problems, but the role of the liberal was to work for reform within the assumptions of the system. By the end of the 1960s, younger thinkers demanded more radical social change. The LGBT persons most energized by Stonewall and most likely to come out of the closet were baby boomers influenced by Marxist, feminist, and other radical theories. These were the people, including marriage critic Martha Shelley, who formed the Gay Liberation Front (GLF) in New York within a month of the Stonewall riots. Nowhere was GLF's radical philosophy more sharply expressed than its attitude toward marriage: "We expose the institution of marriage as one of the most insidious and basic sustainers of the system. The family is the microcosm of oppression," said GLF's leaders in July 1969. "Homosexual marriages submitting to the guidelines of so-called conventional rites must be classed as reactionary."[17]

Gay-radicals viewed the formal equality sought by gay-liberals such as Baker and McConnell as reactionary. Formal access to oppressive institutions such as marriage would only strengthen them; gay liberation must seek to transform the status quo rather than join it. The National Coalition of Gay Organizations' list of demands for law reform reflected the radicals' ideal of transformative equality. Its last demand was "Repeal of all legislative provisions that restrict the sex or number of persons entering into a marriage unit and extension of legal benefits of marriage to all persons who cohabit regardless of sex or numbers."[18]

The United States firmly rejected this demand in the 1970s. There was no serious consideration of the proposal to recognize polyamorous relationships, and same-sex marriage claims fared little better. Every judge and state attorney general who addressed this issue agreed that states could exclude same-sex couples from civil marriage, and several states enacted laws making it clear that civil marriage was limited to one-man, one-woman couples.[19] This string of defeats ended the initial gay-liberal movement for same-sex marriage. Activists turned to other issues, including antigay violence, job discrimination, and the AIDS epidemic.[20]

In 1981, San Francisco gay rights attorney Matt Coles and his colleagues proposed a new and genuinely secular institution for state recognition of intimate relationships that they called "domestic partnership." Starting with Berkeley in 1984–85, municipalities in at least nineteen states have established registries where same-sex (and usually different-sex) couples can declare their domestic partnership. Such a declaration entitles the partners to fringe benefits from local governmental and (often) private employers and perhaps hospital visitation rights. Although Jack Baker rejected this as a small crumb, most gay-liberals supported domestic partnerships because they reduced the formal inequality of lesbian and gay couples; gay-radicals supported or acquiesced in them because they represented a novel, nonmarriage family form. Coles's hope was that the gay rights movement would focus on the achievable goal of domestic partnership recognition from cities with large LGBT populations; the next step would be to add more legal rights and benefits to such partnerships, probably through state laws.[21]

And then along came Denmark.

After Denmark: The Renewed Debate and the (Strategic) Triumph of the Gay-Liberals

By 1989, same-sex marriage seemed all but dead as a goal of the American LGBT rights movement. In May of that year, the Danish Parliament voted to enact the Registered Partnership Act, which accorded almost all the same rights and duties of marriage to registered same-sex partners (see chapter 2). American gay rights leaders started to rethink their priorities. In the autumn of 1989, the two top lawyers at Lambda Legal Defense and Education Fund, the leading LGBT litigation group, debated the issue in print. Tom Stoddard, Lambda's executive director, took the gay-liberal position that the desirability of formal equality required the gay rights movement to press for same-sex marriage. Paula Ettelbrick, Lambda's legal director, took the gay-radical position that same-sex marriage would associate gay rights with a patriarchal institution that most gay men and (especially) lesbians do not want to join. The Stoddard-Ettelbrick exchange revived the liberal-radical conversation about marriage from the 1970s, and updated it with new arguments.[22]

Pressing the point of view Baker and McConnell had propounded almost twenty years earlier, Stoddard credited the radical critique of marriage and offered a response appealing to the radical notion of transformational equality: "marriage may be unattractive and even oppressive as it is currently structured and practiced, but enlarging the concept to embrace same-sex couples would necessarily transform it into something new." As former ACLU attorney Nan Hunter would later argue in detail, same-sex marriage would remove the last gendered feature of marriage law and would also create a model in law for a more egalitarian kind of interpersonal relationship. (Same-sex marriage, in our view, would also automatically undermine the gendered roles associated with patriarchal marriage, where only the husband works outside the home. Even if one of the women in a lesbian marriage stayed at home to keep house and take care of the children, the traditional "woman's role," the female partner working outside the home would be following the traditional "man's role.") Hunter and Stoddard suggested that this lived experience, multiplied by thousands of couples, would contribute to the feminist project of undermining the sexist features of marriage.[23]

Ettelbrick, for her part, deepened the radical critique of formal equality. Not only was access to marriage not sufficient for the needs of most LGBT people but it would as a practical matter harm most sexual and gender minorities. Same-sex marriage, she argued, "would be perpetuating the elevation of married relationships and of 'couples' in general, and further eclipsing other relationships of choice." This critique suggested the coercive power of liberal reform. In the United States, marriage is the norm, and those not joining that norm are marginalized and denigrated. Ettelbrick's fear was that state recognition of same-sex marriages not only would reinforce the normalization of marriage, bad in itself, but also would be detrimental to the interests of LGBT people who do not want to marry. They would be further marginalized.[24]

While leaders debated, lesbian and gay couples voted with their feet, as they started a new march to the marriage license bureau. Craig Dean and Patrick Gill, a District of Columbia couple, wanted to get hitched after the Danish breakthrough, and they brought a test case in the District. Although Lambda Legal and the ACLU felt their effort was premature, the Gay and Lesbian Attorneys of Washington (GAYLAW) agreed to assist after they filed their lawsuit in December 1990. In May 1991, Ninia Baehr and Genora Dancel and two other couples filed a similar lawsuit in Hawaii, also without ACLU or Lambda support.[25]

Gay-liberals such as academic Cheshire Calhoun have responded to Ettelbrick that same-sex marriage would normalize homosexuality more than it would normalize marriage.[26] And this is the way the same-sex marriage issue played out in the 1990s. In *Baehr v. Lewin* (1993), the Hawaii Supreme Court ruled that state refusal to issue marriage licenses to same-sex couples is a suspicious sex discrimination that must be justified by a compelling state interest. The Court remanded the case to the trial court, so that the state could make out its case—but the country as a whole woke up to the possibility of *gay* marriage.[27]

And the country didn't like that one bit. Americans of various ethnicities, religions, and political orientations united in opposition to extending the valued institution of marriage to *homosexuals*. Between 1995 and 2005, forty-three states adopted statutes or constitutional amendments barring their judges from recognizing same-sex marriages in their jurisdictions.[28] States have a fair amount of discretion to refuse to recognize out-of-state marriages, but Congress enacted the Defense of Marriage Act (DOMA) in 1996 to make doubly certain the states would not have to recognize such marriages. Moreover, DOMA mandated that more than eleven hundred federal statutory and regulatory provisions using the terms "marriage" or "spouse" could never include same-sex couples married under state law. Heading off same-sex marriage and overriding the trial judge's injunction in *Baehr*, Hawaii in 1998 adopted a state constitutional amendment allowing the state to limit marriage to different-sex couples.[29]

Ironically, the backlash against gay marriage paved the way for the triumph of the gay-liberal position within the LGBT community. Virtually no one in the mass media or American public life assailed *Baehr* for reinforcing marriage as the norm in this country. Almost every public objection to *Baehr* condemned it for undermining marriage or normalizing homosexuality or condoning unnatural lifestyles. Once the public debate was framed as a referendum on homosexuality, gay-radicals were substantially silenced. Although theorists such as Ettelbrick still considered gay marriage a queer error, they were among the staunchest in support of Baehr and Dancel's ongoing claims of homo equality. The backlash has not permanently silenced gay-radicals, but it has imposed a united front upon LGBT leaders in support of the gay-liberal demand for formal equality.

The Evolving Opposition to Same-Sex Marriage

For most of the twentieth century, homosexuals were unmentionable, and homosexual marriage was inconceivable to most Americans. When Tracy Knight and Marjorie Jones asked for a marriage license in 1970, Jefferson County clerk James Hallahan was speechless. So he asked for guidance from

District Attorney J. Bruce Miller, who told him that the application should be denied, because it represented "the pure pursuit of hedonistic and sexual pleasure." Finding his voice, Hallahan later testified that their marriage would "lead to a breakdown in the sanctity of government," would jeopardize the country's morality, and "could spread all over the world."[30] Like the Jefferson County officials, many of the early responses to lesbian and gay couples seeking marriage recognition were thoughtlessly apocalyptic.

Once they thought about it, most Americans remained skeptical, on the ground that same-sex marriage was an oxymoron—wrong as a definitional matter. It was no more possible for a woman to marry a woman than for her to marry a cat. Through the 1970s, this argument and its corollaries were usually the only arguments advanced. With the revival of the same-sex marriage movement after 1989, the definitional argument was supplemented by the argument that same-sex marriage would place a state stamp of approval on homosexuality, which was by then fully out of the closet but still morally unacceptable to most Americans. If the state extended civil marriage to lesbian and gay couples, opponents contended, it would be encouraging a "homosexual lifestyle" that was not as healthy or good (the stamp-of-approval argument). In the mid-1990s, with openly lesbian and gay persons assuming prominent roles in public debate, opponents of same-sex marriage emphasized a third kind of argument: excluding same-sex couples is necessary to "defend" marriage, an institution in decline, and also to defend the rights of children to be raised in heterosexual households (the defense-of-marriage argument).

The evolution of arguments against same-sex marriage has been from definitional arguments appealing to linguistic or moral intuitions, toward the stamp-of-approval and defense-of-marriage arguments, which look to the consequences of marriage recognition. This is important, as moral definition-based arguments tend to be nonfalsifiable or otherwise hard to refute. Consequentialist arguments can be more neutrally tested. On the other hand, the evolution we will describe has also been *sedimented:* older definitional arguments are not abandoned in favor of newer consequentialist ones; instead, the newer arguments layer on top of the old ones, often reflecting their underlying moral vision. (As we shall show in chapter 6, the new arguments might also be considered updated versions of the old ones.)

Natural Law and Definitional Arguments against Same-Sex Marriage

In the 1970s, district attorneys defending the exclusion of same-sex couples from civil marriage relied primarily, often exclusively, on definitional arguments: marriage has got to be a man and a woman. Always has been.

Always will be. Judges uniformly agreed. In *Jones v. Hallahan* (1973), the Kentucky Supreme Court ruled that "marriage has always been considered as the union of a man and a woman and we have been presented with no authority to the contrary." Hence Knight and Jones were "prevented from marrying, not by the statutes of Kentucky or the refusal of the County Clerk of Jefferson County to issue them a license, but rather by their own incapability of entering into a marriage as that term is defined."[31]

The Minnesota Supreme Court was even less receptive to Baker and McConnell's claims. On September 21, 1971, the justices heard oral argument in *Baker v. Nelson.* As Mike Wetherbee addressed the court, Justice Fallon Kelly rotated his chair to face the wall, literally turning his back on Baker and McConnell's arguments for equal treatment. None of the seven justices asked a single question of Wetherbee or Assistant County Attorney David Mikkelson. Three weeks later, they dismissed the appeal. The Court began and pretty much ended its constitutional discussion with the premise that "the institution of marriage as a union of man and woman, uniquely involving the procreation and rearing of children, is as old as the book of Genesis." The probable reference is Genesis 2:21–25, describing the creation of Eve from Adam's rib. "Therefore a man leaves his father and his mother and cleaves to his wife, and they become one flesh."[32]

Dissent from this definitional axiom was dealt with swiftly and decisively. Not only did Hennepin County deny Baker and McConnell's right to marry but the University of Minnesota revoked McConnell's job offer in July 1970. The Board of Regents gave as its reason that McConnell's "personal conduct," namely, his public declaration of lifetime committed love to another man, "is not consistent with the best interest of the University." The university's librarian and some of the regents privately hoped that the courts would reinstate McConnell's offer, but a federal appeals court upheld the discrimination.[33] Ironically, the plucky couple ultimately did obtain a marriage license, on August 16, 1971, from the clerk of the court in Blue Earth County, because the application was ambiguous as to Baker's sex. Reverend Roger Lynn married the couple in a public ceremony on September 3. The county later claimed that the marriage was null and void, because the license was issued under "false circumstances," and Hennepin county attorney Scott tried to indict Reverend Lynn for his role. The Board of Law Examiners almost denied Baker the right to practice law because of this stunt, and Chief Justice Oscar Knutson of the Minnesota Supreme Court reportedly wanted to block Baker's admission to the bar for this reason. Even in liberal Minnesota, uppity homosexuals had to be disciplined.[34]

They fared little better in conservative Colorado. In May 1975, Boulder county clerk Cela Rorex issued marriage licenses to a handful of same-sex couples after district attorney William Wise told her that Colorado's gender-neutral marriage law did not clearly forbid same-sex marriages. "I don't profess to be knowledgeable about homosexuality or even understand it," said Rorex. "But it's not my business why people get married. No minority should be discriminated against." Rorex and Wise received bushels of hate mail, including death threats from outraged citizens.[35] The Colorado attorney general rebuked Rorex and issued a legal opinion that marriages performed under those licenses were null and void.[36]

A large majority of Americans in the 1970s would have agreed with the Colorado attorney general. Most had never heard of homosexual marriages and did not consider the matter worth further thought. Many Americans who gave the issue a second thought considered homosexuals to be sexual psychopaths or (at best) misfits for whom marriage would be a bad joke. In 1971, homosexual sodomy was a crime in all but two states (Illinois and Connecticut). As suggested by *Baker*'s reference to Genesis, many Americans dismissed homosexual marriage for religious reasons. In 1975, the Roman Catholic Church reaffirmed its traditional understanding that homosexual acts (sodomy) are "a serious depravity" and "intrinsically disordered." The Church's view was based on the natural law philosophy its early Fathers had drawn from Leviticus 20:13, which declares men "lying" with men an "abomination," and Romans 1:26–27, where Saint Paul condemns "unnatural relations" between women or between men. Under the natural law philosophy, it is a grave sin for a human being—the only life created in God's image—to deploy his or her body (especially its sexual organs) in an instrumental way. The only morally acceptable deployment is the union of a male and a female body through procreative intercourse within a faith-sanctioned marriage. Thus, oral and anal sex can never be anything but "disordered," and the homosexual Christian must remain chaste. Certainly, he or she cannot marry someone of the same sex. The Catholic Church's reasoning was embraced by Protestant fundamentalists during the 1970s.[37]

The Roman Catholic position was reflected in the leading federal case rejecting same-sex marriage. In *Adams v. Howerton* (1982), a federal judge ruled that a Colorado same-sex marriage, performed according to a license Rorex had issued, was not a valid basis for federal immigration rights accorded the legal spouses of American citizens. The judge's opinion rested upon a simple syllogism: "The definition of marriage [is] now governed by civil law," which took all its essential concepts from ecclesiastical (canon) law. "Canon law in both Judaism and Christianity could not possibly sanction any marriage between persons of the same sex because of the vehement condemnation in the scriptures of both religions of all homosexual relationships." Thus civil as well as canonical recognition of same-sex marriage is "unthinkable and, by definition, impossible."[38]

Oxford professor John Finnis, a leading natural law thinker, argued that the Judeo-Christian vision of one-man, one-woman marriage is universal—consistent with the vision of marriage held by Plato, Aristotle, Plutarch, and other leading philosophers who viewed marriage as natural and understood nonprocreative sexuality as antimarriage and unnatural. Finnis and other "new natural lawyers" maintain that this consensus bespeaks an underlying human truth that is independent of (even while consistent with) Roman Catholic and other religious doctrine: the intrinsic good of marriage is its one-flesh communion of persons consummated by procreative sexual intercourse, which alone unites the spouses biologically and interpersonally.[39]

The natural law philosophy suggested an interesting variation of the standard definitional argument. In January 1971, Minnesota representative Thomas Ticen debated Jack Baker on a radio talk show. Ticen deemed Baker and McConnell's relationship "foreign to the whole idea of marriage." Baker responded that if the purpose of *civil* marriage is to recognize life-committed partnerships, why shouldn't his commitment be honored by the state? Ticen responded: "It would open Pandora's box." If the state recognizes same-sex marriage, then what other limits can the state impose? Age of consent? Numerosity? Consanguinity? Wouldn't pedophiles, polygamists, and incestuosexuals have the same kind of civil rights claim Baker was pressing?[40]

The Pandora's box point reflects a familiar form of legal or policy argument, namely, the "slippery slope" argument. According to this argument, if you take step 1 (same-sex marriage), then the same reasoning will lead to step 2 (no age-of-consent rules), step 3 (polygamy), and so forth. At some point, everyone agrees the state has gone "too far." We can avoid slipping all the way down the slope by not taking step 1.

Baker could easily distinguish Ticen's parade of horribles, on the basis of his core principle that marriage represents a lifetime mutual commitment. Minors are not mature enough to consent, and polygamy is a terrible legal regime from women's point of view. But these reasoned distinctions have less bite when people's fear is mobilized, and nothing mobilizes anxiety like sexuality unleashed without clear limits. Pandora's story, for example, is a metaphor for sexual experimentation. Once you open the box, namely, lose your virginity, all sorts of unanticipated demons escape. The Minnesota legislature closed Pandora's Box in 1977, when it voted to clarify state law to provide for marriage only between one man and one woman. Slippery slope objections have become almost boilerplate in speeches or books that oppose same-sex marriage.[41]

Stamp-of-Approval Arguments against Same-Sex Marriage

The definitional and slippery slope arguments suggested by the natural law tradition triumphed so completely in the 1970s that even Baker and McConnell retired from the fray. There was no serious debate to be had until 1989, when the Danish registered partnership law helped reignite the same-sex marriage movement. Opponents revived the definitional and slippery slope arguments in the marriage lawsuits brought by Craig Dean and Patrick Gill in the District of Columbia and Ninia Baehr and Genora Dancel in Hawaii. In 1991, Superior Court Judge Shellie Bowers, a devout Baptist, asked the parties in the Dean and Gill litigation to brief the history of marriage issue—all the way back to "Adam and Eve," as the judge put it. (At counsel table, Dean whispered, "Adam and Steve.") Although legal counsel for the couple assembled a vast history of state- or culture-recognized same-sex marriages, including *berdache* marriages (Native American same-sex unions) recognized in the United States, the judge followed *Howerton* and rejected the claim. Quoting passages from Genesis, Deuteronomy, Matthew, and Ephesians, Judge Bowers ruled that "societal recognition that it takes a man and a woman to form a marital relationship is older than Christianity itself."[42]

Remarkably, the District's corporation counsel refused to defend this particular reasoning on appeal. By the 1990s, lawyers opposed to same-sex marriage worried that the definitional argument, standing alone, sounded sectarian. Quoting scripture, Judge Bowers seemed to be importing religious values into positive law, at odds with the Constitution's establishment clause. Also, the argument that marriage can only be different-sex took a hit when Denmark recognized a marriage-like institution in 1989, over such definitional objections, and even without opening Pandora's box. Finally, by 1991 it was firmly established that the purpose of the equal protection clause was to require the state to explain questionable discriminations, however long-established they were. (*Loving v. Virginia* [1967], for example, had overturned a bar to different-race marriages that had existed since Virginia's founding.) Natural law definitions and the risks of opening Pandora's box had been the last refuge of racists and sexists in earlier eras. Although the District's lawyers dutifully made a definitional argument, their main defense of the marriage exclusion was that the City Council had concluded in the 1970s that marriage should be limited to different-sex couples, and that such a judgment was reasonable.[43]

Why is such a judgment "reasonable" and not "discriminatory"? One answer was suggested by Judge Richard Posner, America's leading appellate judge and its most thoughtful legal pragmatist. In *Sex and Reason* (1992), he rejected natural law, religion, and old-fashioned morality as a proper basis for public policy regarding sexual activities in the United States. Posner advanced the notion that tolerance of sexual variation must be the basis for state policy. Hence *Sex and Reason* contains a scathing analysis of state laws making it a crime for consenting adults to engage in private anal or oral sex (sodomy). Explaining why he thought that sodomy law repeal is an easier issue than same-sex marriage, however, Posner cautioned that "permitting homosexual marriage would be widely interpreted as placing a stamp of approval on homosexuality." Because even tolerant Americans considered homosexual conduct disgusting and felt that homosexuality was not a good "lifestyle," the most that homosexuals could expect from the tolerant state is noninterference in their relationships—but not positive support and approval that equal marriage rights would signify.[44]

Jean Luscher understands how tolerant heterosexuals, like Posner, can reject same-sex marriage. Before she settled down with Diana Skovgaard, Jean had never told her mother about her sexual orientation. The couple's plan to register as partners required Jean to come out as a lesbian to her mother in Buffalo, New York. It was a difficult conversation. Luscher recalls: "It's weird, because my mother likes Diana, but she doesn't approve of the relationship. For example, I was back in the states visiting with Diana and her son, and I was introducing him as my stepson—and my mother drew me aside and told me that I shouldn't introduce him as my stepson, that it wasn't the case." Part of Mrs. Luscher's reaction was definitional; she could not integrate her daughter's relationship into her own concept of marriage and family. But part of it involved her view of what was best for her daughter. If she accepted Diana as Jean's spouse, she was placing her stamp of approval on the "homosexual lifestyle" that she apparently thought was *not* the best life path for Jean.[45]

Many parents who love their lesbian daughters and their gay sons oppose state recognition of same-sex unions for this stamp-of-approval reason. Opponents of domestic partnership legislation found the argument a perfect way to express moral concerns in a rhetoric of toleration, and without reference to religious morality. New York state senator John Kuhl put it this way: "Sexual orientation is their choice and I don't think it's our place to force people that might have a moral opposition to it to have to put up with it and condone it." U.S. senator Trent Lott cited the stamp-of-approval argument as his main justification for refusing to fund the District of Columbia's domestic partnership legislation in 1993.[46] The House Judiciary Committee presented DOMA this way: "Civil laws that permit only heterosexual marriage reflect and honor a collective moral judgment about human sexuality. This judgment entails both moral disapproval of homosexuality, and a moral conviction that heterosexuality better comports with traditional (especially Judeo-Christian) morality." Senator Dan Coates deployed Posner's argument as his reason to support DOMA in the Senate debate: "when we prefer traditional marriage and family in our law, it is not intolerance. Tolerance does not require us to say that all lifestyles are morally equal."[47]

Also during the DOMA debates, Florida representative Charles Canady said the key issue was "whether the law of this country should treat homosexual relationships as equivalent to heterosexual relationships," the stamp of approval point. He thought not: "Should the Congress tell the children of America that it is a matter of indifference whether they establish families with a partner of the opposite sex or cohabit with someone of the same sex?" He liked this language so much that he uttered exactly the same words on two successive days of debate. Canady personalized Posner's argument. Politically, the main audience for the stamp-of-approval objection is parents (or grandparents) who love their children and want what's best for them. Even if "gay is good," they think, straight is great. Parents, their churches, their communities, and, yes, even the state ought to express this moral and lifestyle preference, especially by refusing to recognize same-sex marriages. Don't we want our confused teenagers to go straight? They declared that DOMA will help send a message that the state does *not* approve of homosexual relationships. Presumably, this will help sexually confused teens "choose" (excellent) heterosexuality over (not-so-good) homosexuality.[48]

Canady's variation exposed some problems with the stamp-of-approval argument, however. There is no reputable scientific evidence demonstrating that sexual orientation is a matter for parental or state lobbying. Whatever the "cause" of one's sexual orientation, whether it be a gay gene or some arbitrary fixation from infancy, no reputable scientific theory suggests that young people choose a sexual orientation the way they choose clothing at The Gap. Ever since Romeo and Juliet, sensible parents have realized that they cannot impose their preferences about what or who is sexy on their children, and the notion that the state can influence adolescent sexual preferences is even more far-fetched. Conversely, there is a growing body of survey evidence that antigay cultural messages contribute to anguish and suicide among LGBT adolescents.[49]

Once respected scientists began criticizing state policies lobbying for heterosexual choices, the stamp-of-approval argument took on more sinister overtones. It appeared to be an example of symbolic politics, whose thrust was not a tolerant one. The roots of Canady's speech were not as much Posnerian pragmatism as a philosophy of "no promo homo" (no promotion of homosexuality). Not too far from Canady's Florida district was Dade County, the home of Anita Bryant's 1977 campaign to overturn a sexual orientation antidiscrimination ordinance. Bryant's campaign

operated under the banner "Save the Children"—from predatory homosexuals or from homosexual schoolteachers whom children might admire
as role models. The campaign triggered a wave of homophobia and antigay
violence that went on for years after 1977. There was a nasty edge to the
stamp-of-approval argument.[50]

Nonetheless, many intellectuals endorsed this argument. Harvard professor Harvey Mansfield, for example, asserted that homosexual relationships are an "open challenge to society's sense of shame, as the gays recognize
quite well. For if the practices of homosexuals are not shameful, what is?"
Amherst College professor Hadley Arkes opined that gay marriage "would
appear almost as a mocking burlesque" of marriage. Such public comments
echoed remarks that many Americans were making privately, little realiz-
ing the effect of such remarks on their friends and relatives who were themselves gay or lesbian. Many homosexuals were ashamed, but in large part
because society and the state told them they should be ashamed. Others,
such as Jean Luscher and Jack Baker, were not ashamed and believed that
their own happiness depended upon a stable, committed relationship to a
life partner. In the face of lesbian and gay relationships such as these, the
stamp-of-approval or no-promo-homo argument was potentially mean and
smacked of antigay prejudice and stereotypes.[51]

Children and Defense-of-Marriage Arguments against Same-Sex Marriage

Once they were fleshed out by zealous advocates, lawyers shied away from
no-promo-homo arguments. On May 20, 1996, soon after DOMA had been
introduced in Congress, the Supreme Court, in *Romer v. Evans,* ruled that
an antigay Colorado initiative violated the equal protection clause because
it was apparently inspired by "animus." The reach of *Romer* remained unclear, but its antianimus rationale raised red flags about the DOMA enterprise. Oklahoma representative Tom Coburn, for example, supported
DOMA because he and his constituents found "homosexuals" to be "immoral" and "promiscuous." The issue, he said, is not "diversity," it is "per-
versity." Senator Robert Byrd, the senior Democrat in the Senate, denounced
homosexuality as inconsistent with the Bible and spoke forcefully against
the "homosexual agenda."[52]

Responding to *Romer* and anticipating intemperate language that would
accompany the congressional debates, DOMA's sponsors relied on purely
consequentialist arguments. Chaired by Illinois representative Henry Hyde,
a distinguished Republican Party elder, the House Judiciary Committee
concluded that the federal government has "an interest in maintaining and

protecting the institution of heterosexual marriage because it has a deep and abiding interest in encouraging responsible procreation and child-rearing." (The premise is that children are best raised by two parents married to one another.) Heterosexual marriage is an imperiled institution already, and "homosexual marriage" threatens to knock it off entirely. The federal government can "defend" heterosexual marriage and help children by assuring that traditionalist states would not have to recognize Hawaii same-sex marriages and by excluding same-sex married couples from the benefits and obligations of spousehood under federal law.[53]

Critics of DOMA asked how the institution of marriage was threatened by adding new recruits, namely, eager lesbian and gay couples. (That DOMA had key support from the nation's three highest ranking adulterers—President William Clinton, Senate Majority Leader Robert Dole, and House Speaker Newt Gingrich—was a family values irony.) The closest any DOMA supporter came to answering that key question was its thrice-married House sponsor, Representative Robert Barr of Georgia. He proclaimed that the "flames of hedonism, the flames of narcissism, the flames of self-centered morality are licking at the very foundation of our society: the family unit."[54]

Although Barr used inflammatory rhetoric, he had a serious point: historically, the great virtue of marriage is the creation of an altruistic space, where adults sacrifice their own self-interest in service of mutual commitment to one another and to children they raise together. The reason marriage has declined in the twentieth century is that the populace, and their legislators and judges, have increasingly understood marriage as a hedonic (pleasure-centered) space. Marriage as an altruistic space serves important public functions, as it trains good citizens, rears superior children, and creates greater happiness in the long run. The state needs to preserve as much of this vision of marriage as possible. Traditionalists believe that legal recognition of same-sex marriage would devalue marriage as an altruistic space and thereby undermine its ability to advance the community values it has long promoted.[55]

This defense-of-marriage argument linked the *liberal, prochoice* feature of the case for same-sex marriage with the *liberal, prochoice* philosophy of hedonism that had been corroding marriage. That most Americans still associated homosexuality with narcissism and hedonism, as Barr did, made the defense-of-marriage argument more emotionally powerful. Defense of marriage was also analytically smart. Unlike the various definitional arguments, it was nonsectarian and noncircular. Unlike no-promo-homo arguments, it was not necessarily negative toward LGBT people.

Indeed, if you struck the right tone in making the defense-of-marriage argument, it re-positioned opponents of same-sex marriage: they were not like the bigots who opposed different-race marriage, and in fact they were not even opposed to civil rights for sexual minorities. The most vulnerable minority is the children, and if there is the slightest risk that homosexual marriage would hurt the children, then that should suffice. For these reasons, defense of marriage was the sort of consequentialist argument that would appeal to moderates and evangelical Christians who had sympathy or pity for gay people, yet it would also be persuasive to fundamentalist Christians, homophobes, and others who were opposed to gay marriage primarily for other reasons. It was the perfect umbrella argument.

After DOMA, the defense-of-marriage argument went on the road, and it was a hit. In 1998, traditionalists were able to place on the ballot in Hawaii and Alaska proposed amendments to the state constitutions that would allow the legislature to limit marriage to different-sex couples. In both states, the Church of Jesus Christ of the Latter-Day Saints and other religious donors funded a lavish media campaign in support of the amendments. Reflecting the sedimentary nature of the analytical evolution we have traced, the media campaign made all three arguments: (1) "Socially, we're taught from childhood it's for a man and a woman." (2) Don't promote homosexuality; tolerance does not require "special rights" for homosexuals. (3)"If you don't think homosexual marriage will affect you, how do you think it will affect your children?" The problem with modern society is its increasingly "hedonistic and selfish world view." Traditional marriage is the main cultural bulwark against the culture of narcissism that homosexuals (among others) represent. Yet it is in peril. If the courts hand over marriage to the homosexuals, the forces of narcissism will have won. Sixty-nine percent of the voters in liberal Democratic Hawaii agreed with these arguments, as did 68 percent of those in libertarian Republican Alaska.[56]

The defense-of-marriage argument has met resistance among some legislators and judges. In *Baker v. State* (1999), Vermont defended its exclusion of same-sex couples in largely symbolic terms. The limitation of marriage to different-sex couples reinforced the self-giving link among spousal love, procreation, and raising children. The attorney general's argument could scarcely have been more respectful to LGBT people. (Amicus briefs supporting the state made natural law and no-promo-homo arguments.) Yet the Vermont Supreme Court unanimously rejected the defense-of-marriage argument. The majority opinion, by Chief Justice Jeffrey Amestoy, ruled that the state has "a legitimate and longstanding interest in promoting a permanent commitment between couples for the security of their children." But this interest, the Court found, did not justify the particular discrimination. The state gave marriage licenses to straight couples who did not raise children, and so the discrimination was underinclusive. The discrimination was overinclusive, because many lesbian and gay couples (including two of the three plaintiff couples) bore and raised children within their unions.[57]

Amestoy did not directly respond to the claim that denying same-sex marriage was a state symbol of respect for traditional marriage and its illiberal (procommitment) features. But it is clear that the Vermont justices found the linkage between hedonism and homosexuality not only too speculative to credit but also contrary to that state's repeated recognition that lesbians and gay men are responsible citizens and parents. Moreover, the majority justices credited the similarities between *Loving* and the case before them. In both instances, the state was denying a fundamental right to consenting adults who wished to marry. In both, the state interest was largely symbolic and speculative. In both cases, the exclusion closely fit traditional prejudices harming a minority group. In both, justices relatively insulated from the political process protected minority access to civil marriage. The Massachusetts Supreme Judicial Court followed *Baker* in *Goodridge v. Department of Public Health* (2003), holding that the same-sex marriage bar violated the state constitution and essentially ignoring the defense-of-marriage argument. Unlike the Vermont court, however, the Massachusetts court required the state to issue marriage licenses to same-sex couples, starting on May 17, 2004, the fiftieth anniversary of the Supreme Court's opinion in *Brown v. Board of Education.*[58]

The Vermont and Massachusetts cases have hardly been death knells for the defense-of-marriage objection to same-sex marriage. The objection is too speculative or symbolic to be persuasive to many judges in gay-friendly states. But it remains persuasive to most Americans (many of whom also accept the definitional and stamp-of-approval arguments as well). Religious leaders such as Dr. James Dobson, head of Focus on the Family, have endorsed this argument as consistent with their faith concerns. President George W. Bush has made it the central argument for the proposed Federal Marriage Amendment (FMA). The version debated in 2004 would have added the following language to the Constitution:

> Marriage in the United States shall consist only of the union of a man and a woman. Neither this Constitution, nor the constitution of any State, shall be construed to require that marriage or the legal incidents thereof be conferred upon any union other than the union of a man and a woman.

Before examining the FMA in greater detail, we ask the reader to step back and consider the expanding context of the same-sex marriage debate.[59]

The Internationalization of the Same-Sex Marriage Debate

The same-sex marriage debate has been imperial, occupying increasing space in the gay rights agenda, as well as mainstream political discourse. It has also been imperial in a geographic sense. In the United States during the 1950s and 1960s, the same-sex marriage debate was confined to the small homosexual *subcultures* in a handful of America's largest cities. No one outside of these subcultures would have known that some homosexuals wanted to marry partners of the same sex. Few would have found such claims comprehensible.

After Stonewall, as couples such as Baker and McConnell asked court clerks for marriage licenses, the debate grew beyond the subculture and became *municipal or local,* of concern to cities and counties. Gerald Nelson of Hennepin County, James Hallahan of Jefferson County, and Cela Rorex of Boulder were just some of the public officials who had to respond to same-sex marriage petitions. The failure of the marriage movement in the 1970s gave way in the 1980s to the domestic partnership movement which was even more sharply focused on local politics. Mayors Diane Feinstein of San Francisco, Ed Koch of New York, and Tom Bradley of Los Angeles struggled with this issue skeptically in the early 1980s, followed by mayors who were more responsive in the 1990s. Today several dozen cities and counties either provide domestic partnership benefits to their employees or have domestic partnership registries, and more than forty of them have both.

In the 1970s, the same-sex marriage debate reached the level of *state* politics, because couples like Jones and Knight as well as Baker and McConnell brought lawsuits challenging their exclusion. Like Minnesota and California in 1977, some states amended their codes to make clear that civil marriage required one man and one woman. Given the minimal clout of LGBT citizens, no state seriously considered recognizing lesbian and gay unions. The *Baehr* decision in 1993 immediately placed same-sex marriage on the agenda of every state legislature, because both gay and traditionalist attorneys opined that the Constitution's full faith and credit clause would require other states to recognize Hawaii same-sex marriages. And lawsuits by lesbian and gay couples have pressed gay-friendly states like Vermont and Massachusetts to recognize same-sex unions or marriages. California, ironically, has done both: the 2000 Knight Initiative barred recognition of same-sex marriages, but the Domestic Partnership Act of 1999 (as amended through 2003) gives same-sex registered partners almost all the same rights and duties of marriage.[60]

The DOMA debate reflects *national* engagement with the issue after *Baehr.* Representing a Republican strategy of pressing a wedge issue upon a wily Democratic president, DOMA is the most ambitious national marriage-regulatory legislation in American history. Its provision mandating that federal statutory and regulatory duties and rights of spousehood can never be extended to same-sex married couples assures the Supreme Court a role in the debate sooner or later. Defeated in 2004, the FMA will remain on the national agenda, as traditionalists seek to reverse the imperial features of the debate. (If adopted, the FMA would be a partial national resolution, taking marriage off the table nationwide, but it might also encourage state and local experimentation with other regulatory forms.)

Finally, and inevitably, the same-sex marriage debate is now *international*, in a variety of ways. One is personal. Many Americans have found their soul mates abroad. In addition to Jean Lusher, another example is Eddie Moris. Born in 1957, he grew up in a southern Californian household dominated by fundamentalist religious values. Eddie became estranged from his parents after they learned that he was gay. One of his boyfriends was a Norwegian man he met in Los Angeles, and that relationship occasioned a trip to Scandinavia. Eddie planned to return in 1990 but learned that his lover had died of complications associated with AIDS. Devastated by the news, he flew to Scandinavia anyway and stayed with another friend in Copenhagen. Two weeks after arriving there, he met Jens Boesen, a police officer. After dating for several weeks, Moris moved in with Boesen, who warned him that his tourist visa would run out in a few months.[61]

Explaining to his astounded friend that Denmark had just recognized registered partnerships, Jens asked Eddie to marry him. Eddie said no. How could he make such a commitment to a man he barely knew, and live in a country that was way too cold? Eddie missed sunny California. But Jens won him over—and there was something liberating about living in a country where homosexuals were not public scapegoats. When Eddie and Jens got married, Jens's entire family came and celebrated. His sister and her husband fixed up their car with a "Just Married" sign and tin cans hanging from the back. The ceremony, still a novelty to many city officials in charge of conducting wedding ceremonies, was less than inspiring. "The official performing the ceremony kept making mistakes . . . he said, 'I now pronounce you man and wife'—then he blushed, and corrected himself." After the ceremony, Jens and Eddie drove to the household of Jens's parents, twenty miles outside the city. "At first I wasn't too much looking forward to meeting his parents," Eddie recalls. "I expected them to be as homophobic as mine were. But as soon as I got there, [Jens's mother] gave me this huge hug." Decoration with Danish flags is a common custom to celebrate festive occasions such as weddings in Denmark, and so the Boesens had decorated their driveway with American and Danish flags, flapping together. In Eddie's words, "The acceptance was just unbelievable."[62]

Jean Luscher and Diana Skovgaard became registered partners five years later. There are untold other American citizens who have become registered partners with persons of the same sex since 1989 in Denmark and the other Scandinavian countries. Persons of the same sex have been legally marrying one another in the Netherlands since 2001, in Belgium since 2002, in Canada since 2003, and in Spain since 2005. Because of its proximity, Canadian same-sex marriages are more likely to involve American couples, more than one thousand by the end of 2005. Other countries, mainly in Europe, have enacted various levels of recognition for their same-sex couples at the national level in recent years. And countries offering same-sex marriage or marriage-like partnerships are already recognizing the relationships of same-sex couples from other countries who now live in their country and have entered into similar legal unions. Such international recognition is certain to expand as more countries recognize same-sex marriages, registered partnerships, or civil unions.[63]

So the geography of our same-sex marriage debate has expanded to include international as well as national, state, local, subcultural, and private discussions about what should be done about same-sex couples. Set aside this personalized geopolitics, however, and consider how international experience has become increasingly prominent in the American same-sex marriage debate, culminating in the recent debates over the FMA.

International Experience and the Gay-Liberal Case for Same-Sex Marriage

Because Canada, Scandinavia, the Netherlands, Spain, and other European countries have recognized same-sex marriages and partnerships, the international experience has been important to American supporters of same-sex marriage. The international developments have been agenda-setting for the American gay rights movement, have provided analytical support for the gay-liberal case for same-sex marriage, and have given the movement cause for optimism that same-sex marriage is an idea whose time is coming. Denmark jump-started the current wave of gay marriage activism. Although the Danish Registered Partnership Act did not bestow exactly all the same legal rights on registered partners that married couples enjoy, it was the first modern recognition of same-sex unions that explicitly tied their benefits and duties to those associated with marriage. Although few straight Americans paid it much heed, the Danish law sparked the imaginations of

LGBT Americans, rekindling hopes that their relationships would be recognized in this country as well.

Nevertheless, Lambda and the ACLU proved to be right—that open demands for gay marriage would trigger a backlash. (They were wrong only in failing to predict how tremendous it turned out to be.) On the other hand, the overwhelming defeats represented by DOMA in 1996 and the Alaska and Hawaii referenda in 1998 did not extinguish the same-sex marriage movement the way less crushing defeats did in the 1970s. Ironically, just as the *Dean* and *Baehr* lawsuits were being squashed, exactly as they had predicted, Lambda and the ACLU were joining the same-sex marriage bandwagon. One reason the movement showed such resilience was that LGBT people could see success abroad that could be contrasted with (temporary) failure at home. At the same time that states were responding to *Baehr* with antirecognition statutes, Norway and Sweden were following Denmark to enact registered partnership laws. Soon after Congress enacted DOMA, France adopted legislation creating *pactes civils*, a "marriage-lite" institution for same-sex (as well as different-sex) couples. The Hawaii and Alaska antimarriage referenda in 1998 could be paired with the Netherlands' registered partnership law and signals that recognition of same-sex marriage would shortly follow (as it did in 2001).[64]

In July 1999, Professor Robert Wintemute of Kings College, London, convened the first major international legal conference on same-sex marriage. Lawyers and professors from the United States exchanged information and ideas with those from Europe, Canada, Australia, Africa, and Asia. The American lawyers and professors benefited from the advanced conceptualization and experience their sisters and brothers from other countries brought to the table. The conceptual hit of the conference was Professor Kees Waaldijk's "small change" argument. The architect of the soon-to-be-successful marriage campaign in the Netherlands, Waaldijk argued for a step-by-step approach. According to the argument, once a country has rid itself of consensual sodomy laws, it will soon be open to sexual orientation antidiscrimination legislation; once that legislation sinks in, the country will be willing to give limited recognition to same-sex partnerships (usually under its cohabitation law). Only after these preliminary "small changes" have been made would the country be ready for same-sex marriage.[65]

Waaldijk's theory helped explain not only why Alaska and even Hawaii were not ready to accept same-sex marriage in 1998 but also why Vermont and Massachusetts were. The latter two states had deregulated sodomy and adopted sweeping antidiscrimination and hate crime laws protecting LGBT people, but each had also adopted statewide domestic partnership regimes for state employees. More important, Waaldijk's theory argued for the *inevitability* of same-sex marriage. Once LGBT people could live their lives openly and in peace, they would be recognized as decent and responsible people. And public opinion would change, slowly among older citizens, but decisively among young people who would grow up knowing gays.

The London conference came right before the first genuine victories in the United States. The plaintiff couples were disappointed that the Vermont Supreme Court did not require same-sex marriage recognition in *Baker*, but no one thought the limited triumph in Vermont would be the end of the campaign, so long as the parallel campaigns in Ontario, Quebec, and British Columbia were ongoing. The Ontario Court of Appeal required same-sex marriage under the Canadian Charter in June 2003, just as the Massachusetts Supreme Court was deliberating *Goodridge*. The *Goodridge* justices had the benefit of two detailed amicus briefs, which laid out the international developments and suggested that same-sex marriage was an idea whose time had come.[66]

Moreover, supporters of same-sex marriage have invoked the international experience, starting with Denmark, to answer the objections traditionalists have advanced. The definitional objection has taken hits every time a new jurisdiction disagrees. It is harder to believe that the Western philosophy of marriage won't tolerate same-sex couples now that Canada and much of Europe recognize their unions.[67] Likewise, the slippery slope objection is beginning to look like a lavender herring. Denmark has been registering same-sex partners for more than fifteen years now—without any slippage toward child marriage, polygamy, or incestuous marriages. There is not even a public campaign we know of to expand marriage in these other ways. Pandora opened her box, and nothing else came out!

The international experience also provides a pragmatic way to deal with no-promo-homo anxieties. Gay-liberals had originally responded that same-sex marriage would not particularly "promote" homosexuality. The experience of countries that have recognized same-sex partnerships or marriage suggests that this response was too timid. At the London conference, Professor Ingrid Lund-Anderson reported that the Danish registered partnerships law had contributed to pro-gay feelings among the population at large. Some opponents of the law had made intemperate appeals to antigay stereotypes and prejudice. During the law's operation in the 1990s, straight Danes were impressed by the couples who took partnership vows. Several prominent Danes, including a former minister of health, Yvonne Herlov Andersen, have come out as lesbian or gay. Andersen was the sponsor of 1998 legislation allowing registered partners to adopt one another's children. There was virtually no opposition to this proposal, which had been too controversial in 1989.[68]

Finally, the international experience provided evidence that the defense-of-marriage argument was overstated. Apocalyptic claims that gay marriage would lead to immediate ruin have been routinely made, and routinely forgotten. As one of us (Spedale) first argued as early as 1998, the Danish experience calls into question the defense-of-marriage argument.[69] During the first eight years of partnership registration, Danes did not give up on marriage, as the critics predicted. Indeed, the marriage rate actually went up in that period. Provisional evidence, to be sure, but a striking departure from the predictions of naysayers.[70]

International Experience and the Traditionalist Case against Same-Sex Marriage

Initially, American critics of same-sex marriage ignored international experience or maintained that it is irrelevant. An aggressive version of this strategy is the one deployed by Justice Antonin Scalia's dissenting opinion in *Lawrence v. Texas* (2003), where the Supreme Court overturned consensual sodomy laws. The Court cited constitutional court decisions from Europe as evidence that sodomy laws violate the fundamental right of privacy the Court has long recognized. Scalia's dissent assailed the Court for "'impos[ing] foreign moods, fads, or fashions on Americans.'" A few pages later, he raised the stakes of the case (which involved a law that was almost never enforced). Citing the Ontario same-sex marriage case, Scalia warned that the logic of the Court's disposition required recognition of same-sex marriage in America as well. The implication was that same-sex marriage is the same kind of "foreign mood, fad, or fashion" that Americans should not have forced upon them by judges.[71]

Since 2004, however, social scientist Stanley Kurtz has been arguing that the experience in Scandinavia and the Netherlands supports the defense-of-marriage objection. Kurtz maintains that same-sex marriage or registered partnership has contributed to the decline of marriage and the rise of nonmarital children in Scandinavia and the Netherlands (his more recent focus). He dismisses the fact that recognition of same-sex partnerships has coincided with a decline in the divorce rate and an increase in the marriage rate in Denmark. Because marriage in Denmark was already, in his words, so "decimated" before 1989, the increase in marriage rates is easily explained as a random spike. Focusing on Norway and Sweden, Kurtz has argued that the overall family dissolution rate has gone up and, more important, that the number of out-of-wedlock births has increased significantly. Overall, he says, a growing number of children in Scandinavia are being raised in nonmarital or broken homes.[72]

Furthermore, Kurtz has claimed that children of broken homes are suffering *because of* state recognition of homosexual partnerships. That is, there is a direct causal link between the decline of marriage and marital families and the introduction of registered partnerships in Scandinavia: "once marriage (or a status close to marriage) has been redefined to include same-sex couples, the symbolic separation between marriage and parenthood is confirmed, locked-in, and reinforced." In addition, same-sex marriage is a cultural signal that "all family forms are equal" and that traditional family values are obsolete. The separation of marriage from parenthood, the validation of other family forms, and the decline of traditionalist philosophies are, according to Kurtz, interlinking ways that same-sex unions directly *cause* different-sex couples to abandon marriage as a focus for their relationship and family aspirations.[73]

Kurtz associates his causal assertions with the work of British demographer Kathleen Kiernan. Kiernan says family law in Europe has evolved in stages that have progressively undermined marriage. In stage 1, marriage is the norm, cohabitation a disapproved exception. Stage 2 sees cohabitation accepted as a probationary period, a trial marriage before the couple decides whether to tie the knot. When a country enters stage 3, cohabitation becomes culturally acceptable as an alternative to marriage, but is not considered as acceptable for raising children. After stage 3, cohabitation and marriage are indistinguishable, with children increasingly raised by cohabiting rather than married parents. In the twentieth century, industrial countries moved from stage 1 to higher stages. The United States, for example, went from stage 1 to stage 2 in the 1970s and is now probably at stage 3. From this model, Kurtz argues that registered partnerships are driving Denmark and the other Scandinavian countries beyond stage 3 to the "end of marriage" and will do precisely the same to the United States.[74]

Some eminent conservative thinkers have taken up this Scandinavian twist on the defense-of-marriage argument. Since May 2004, Judge Robert Bork has been arguing that Scandinavian registered partnerships have led to a cultural collapse, with marriage as its primary victim. Senator Rick Santorum argues that toleration of same-sex unions has not only undermined the altruistic ideals of marriage but also depopulated Europe, as straight couples abandon marriage and the family as aspirations for their lives. Grassroots family values activists treat Santorum's argument and Kurtz's evidence as gospel. "You know the family has disappeared in those Scandinavian countries," Maryland activist Evalena Gray told a reporter, as evidence that gay marriage would ruin marriage in this country.[75]

The Federal Marriage Amendment and the Scandinavian Twist
on the Defense-of-Marriage Argument

In the winter and spring of 2003, Judge Bork and others worked with members of Congress to draft an amendment to the Constitution that would block efforts by gay-liberals to procure same-sex marriage through constitutional litigation. *Baker* had already established the civil unions beachhead in Vermont, and it was widely believed that the *Goodridge* litigation in Massachusetts would yield same-sex marriage in that state. The proposed amendment, as introduced in Congress, read:

> Marriage in the United States shall consist only of the union of a man and a woman. Neither this Constitution or the constitution of any State, nor state or federal law, shall be construed to require that marital status or the legal incidents thereof be conferred upon unmarried couples or groups.

Texas senator John Cornyn's subcommittee (on constitutional amendments) of the Senate Judiciary Committee held a hearing on the FMA in September 2003. The theme of the FMA hearing was that same-sex marriage represented a serious threat to traditional marriage, an institution already in decline. Cornyn's witnesses never quite explained how *expanding eligibility* for marriage *undermined* the institution. Maggie Gallagher, the president of the Institute for Marriage and Public Policy, came closest to answering this question. "In endorsing same-sex marriage, law and government will thus be making a powerful statement: our government no longer believes children need mothers and fathers. Two mothers or two fathers are not only just as good as a mother and a father, they are just the same." Gallagher's assumption that children must have a mother and a father, and must not have two mothers, has little if any rigorous empirical support. Dozens of studies of lesbian households rearing children have found no significant disadvantages for those children, compared to mother-father households. Because they involve small and nonrandom samples, those studies are preliminary, but they undermine Gallagher's point.[76]

In 2003, the FMA supporters were without evidence to support their key defense-of-marriage argument. The Scandinavian version of the defense-of-marriage argument has saved them from this embarrassment, and FMA supporters have seized upon it like driftwood after a shipwreck. In July 2004, the Senate debated a slightly altered version of the original FMA. Consistent with the sedimented quality of oppositional discourse, the senators supporting the FMA made definitional, stamp-of-approval, and defense-of-marriage arguments. But they emphasized the last, and the only evidence cited by any senator was experience in Scandinavia and the Netherlands.[77]

Educated by the detailed testimony in his hearings on same-sex marriage, Senator Cornyn's was the most elaborate analysis. Invoking Kiernan's model, Cornyn worried that the decline of marriage meant that increasing numbers of children are being raised outside of that institution. He then relied on Kurtz's data to assert that fifteen years after Denmark recognized marriage-like unions for same-sex couples, a majority of Scandinavian children are born outside of marriage (50 percent in Norway, 55 percent in Sweden, and 60 percent in Denmark itself, he asserted, erroneously). If the United States followed Scandinavia, the same fate would befall American children, Cornyn argued. Most of the senators speaking in favor of the FMA agreed with his Scandinavian version of the defense-of-marriage argument.[78]

Few FMA opponents disputed Cornyn's analysis. Illinois senator Richard Durbin pointed out that lesbian and gay couples reared children and did so as competently as straight couples, according to the studies. If marriage contributed to the stability of those lesbian and gay relationships, why shouldn't it help those children, he wondered. New York senator Hillary Clinton went to the analytical heart of the defense-of-marriage argument. The main reason for the decline of marriage, she asserted, is the ease of divorce. So if you want to "defend" marriage, you should propose "an amendment to the Federal Constitution to make divorce really, really hard, to take it out of the States' hands and say that we will not liberalize divorce."[79]

The FMA supporters relied on Kurtz's theory of causation to answer arguments such as those made by Clinton, in particular. In the most sophisticated analysis, Senator Santorum agreed that the decline of marriage has many causes, including the ease of divorce. But same-sex marriage exacerbates the decline because it reinforces the notion that marriage is all about the pleasure and happiness of adults, and not about adult responsibility toward rearing children under the best possible circumstances. This is the reason, according to the senator, that the out-of-wedlock birth rate in Scandinavia is 60 percent (another figure that is not accurate). Other senators cited Kurtz's work for the proposition that even registered partnerships represent a strong state signal of a "cultural separation of marriage from parenthood."[80]

On July 14, the Senate voted 50 to 48 against the FMA, well short of the two-thirds majority required (in each chamber of Congress) to propose a constitutional amendment. Although the FMA had failed in the Senate, the Republican leadership called it up for a vote in the House on September 30. House majority leader Tom DeLay and other supporters relied critically on the Scandinavian (and Dutch) twist on the defense-of-marriage argument.

Representative Barney Frank questioned, indeed refuted, the argument in detailed memoranda inserted into the Congressional Record. The House voted for the amendment, 227 to 186, well short of the required two-thirds majority.[81] The FMA will probably be reintroduced in subsequent Congresses. (President Bush, for example, plugged it in his 2005 State of the Union Address.) More important, states are debating similar amendments to their state constitutions. In 2004, thirteen states amended their constitutions to bar judicial or legislative recognition of same-sex marriages created outside their states.[82]

The same-sex marriage debate that McConnell and Baker started in the United States is an important national debate that will not end anytime soon. The defense-of-marriage argument is the main traditionalist response to the gay-liberal case for same-sex marriage. So far, the only evidence traditionalists have raised in support of the defense-of-marriage argument is that suggested by the experience with registered partnerships in Scandinavia and same-sex marriage in the Netherlands. Baker and McConnell consider this evidence yet another excuse for homo-anxious Americans to postpone the day that this country will accord full formal equality to lesbian and gay couples. After years of lying low, with McConnell working on several successful projects for the Hennepin County Library System and Baker practicing law, the couple reemerged in 2003. Specifically, they put their tax refund where their mouth is. On May 18, 2004, Baker and McConnell filed suit in federal court, asking for an injunction requiring the Internal Revenue Service to allow them to file a joint tax return. According to another longtime Minnesota gay activist, "[their] idea was to wait for a generation that we helped educate and enlighten. When that generation moved into positions of power, it would be time to act again."[83]

So is the Baker and McConnell idea, relaunched a generation later, an idea whose time has finally come? Or does the internationally updated defense-of-marriage argument lay their idea to rest, for good? The remainder of this book will focus on that evidence from other countries, especially Denmark, Norway, and Sweden, where partnerships have been recognized for more than a decade. What does that experience teach us?

CHAPTER 2

The Same-Sex Marriage Debate
in Scandinavia and the Rest of Europe

Eigil and Axel Axgil,
January 1950.

On October 2, 1989, readers of the *New York Times* opened up the front
section of the newspaper to see an odd photo: two elderly, balding
gentlemen, sitting in a horse-drawn carriage traveling down a cobblestone
street. Both men appeared to be in their mid- to late seventies, each sport-
ing large, square-rimmed glasses that would have been in vogue around 1955.
One wore a beige suit with an orange tie, the other a blue suit with a blue

tie. While one appeared to be drinking—champagne? grape juice?—from a small flute, the other was looking directly into the camera with a gaptoothed smile that appeared simultaneously exhausted and triumphant. To the reader, the significance of this photo was not at all apparent. Until one read the headline next to the photo: "Rights for Gay Couples in Denmark," followed by a story about the extension of the legal rights of marriage to same-sex couples.

To the casual reader, it might seem odd that such an elderly couple was chosen for a photo of the new face of "gay marriage." If the media generally portrays love and weddings as the province of youth, why would the *Times* choose to profile two grandfatherly types in a front-page photo for this article, when many other younger couples married on this day? While Americans might have been puzzled by this question, Danes were not. Axel Axgil, seventy-four years old, and Eigil Axgil, age sixty-seven, the featured couple, were the patriarchs of the gay rights movement in Denmark. Without their involvement, there might not have been the legal possibility to exchange vows in 1989.

Love was young for the Axgils once, when they first started dating in 1949. They legally combined parts of their first names to obtain their surname in 1957. The men were among the founders of the Danish Society of 1948, one of the world's oldest gay and lesbian organizations still in existence. And it was over the course of their adult lifetimes—from the time they helped found the society, through their elderly years—that "gay marriage" gained a foothold in Denmark.[1]

This chapter examines the process by which the Axgils' dream of legal unions in Scandinavia (and later, in other countries) came to fruition, as well as the arguments for and against same-sex marriage that have shaped the debate among gays and lesbians, within Parliament, and in mainstream society. It also examines the cultural and religious elements that made it possible for Denmark to lead the way in enacting same-sex legal unions. Almost all of the arguments raised for and against same-sex marriage in Scandinavia are similar to, and often the same as, those currently being debated in the United States (as explored in chapter 1) and elsewhere. Yet the cultural and religious foundations of the Nordic countries, as explored in this chapter, made the political palatability of same-sex partnerships more quickly feasible here than elsewhere. Ultimately, those in favor of legal unions for same-sex couples prevailed—but not without a long and difficult struggle.[2]

Denmark and the Danish Registered Partnership Act of 1989

Like the United States and other European countries, Denmark saw the emergence of a visible subculture of "homosexuals" in the late nineteenth century. Although Denmark repealed its consensual sodomy law in 1933, homosexuality was not an accepted element of Danish society for the first two-thirds of the twentieth century. By the 1950s, gay men had become a visible target for police efforts to clean up society, and public expressions of homosexuality were penalized. Considering the social hostility toward gays and lesbians (particularly gay men) after World War II, much of the punishment for being openly gay was not legally sanctioned but was a social consequence of refusing to conform to existing moral standards.[3] Axel Axgil's life provides a dramatic example. He founded Forbundet af 1948 (the "Society of 1948," later Landsforeningen for Bøsser og Lesbiske, the National Organization for Gays and Lesbians, or LBL) in 1948 as Denmark's first gay and lesbian rights organization. Considering the isolation and lack of networks among homosexuals in that time period, it was meant to serve as an organization to help gays and lesbians find each other, and give them social and moral support. However, on the exact day that Axel Axgil's involvement in founding the Society of 1948 was reported in a Danish newspaper, he was fired from his job, evicted from his residence, and expelled from the political party to which he belonged.[4]

Social and then political attitudes softened in the 1960s, as progressive voices criticized existing political philosophy. A backlash against the moral rigidity that was being enforced began when the Copenhagen police used a homosexual prostitution law to stalk and entrap homosexuals when no illegality was taking place. The Danish press dubbed the measure the "Ugly Law," and Parliament repealed it in 1965.[5] In 1976, the age of consent for homosexual sex was lowered to fifteen, the same as for heterosexual intercourse.

The first serious discussions of gay marriage accompanied the social changes of the 1960s. Like student radicals in the United States, young Danes challenged traditional norms and institutions, including marriage. For example, Danish students in 1966 demanded that universities accord same-sex couples the same student housing opportunities they offered married couples. Some student leaders demanded a broader state recognition of cohabitating relationships among same-sex as well as different-sex couples, and the national media began covering stories on alternative family living arrangements, including gay and lesbian couples.[6] In conjunction with the student movement, gay and lesbian leaders worked to bring same-sex marriage to the attention of the political establishment. Martin Elmer, a gay activist and editor of the national gay publication "the *Friend,*" wrote about the lives of gay couples in Denmark, and the inheritance, support, and breakup problems they faced because the Danish marriage laws did not recognize their relationships.[7] Working with the Axgils and other members of the Society of 1948, Elmer began an information campaign to educate straight allies (students in particular) about gay and lesbian couples and their legal needs. For example, he related stories of partners in long relationships who lost their property and their livelihoods when their loved ones died, because their committed unions were not recognized by the state. Elmer also met with government representatives to explain the needs of gay and lesbian couples. He even attempted to submit a marriage application to Copenhagen's Town Hall, which was flatly rejected.[8]

Activists like Elmer put same-sex marriage on Denmark's public agenda a few years before post-Stonewall activists put it on America's agenda. The arguments for state recognition of same-sex marriage in Denmark reflected the ones later deployed in the United States. In both countries, the debate was similar in nature. What was most different was the forum. In the United States, the same-sex marriage debate played out primarily in courts through constitutional challenges to the same-sex marriage bar, while in Denmark the forums for debate were the legislature and a series of parliamentary study commissions.

Same-Sex Marriage and Parliamentary Study Commissions, 1968–88

The voices of students, gay and lesbian activists, and other progressive allies convinced some in the Danish Parliament that changes in family recognition were needed. In October 1968, the Socialist People's Party (SF) introduced a bill into Parliament to recognize alternative forms of cohabitation. One section of the bill would have recognized as married any couple, including gay and lesbian couples, who had lived together for three years or more. Parliament rejected the bill because of fears it would create a form of "forced marriage" (i.e., a marriage claimed by one party but protested by the other) but in 1969 created a special parliamentary "Marriage Committee." The Committee's assignment was to review all existing legislation related to marriage, to consider the proposal by SF for recognition of other forms of cohabitation, and to make recommendations for change in Danish marriage law.[9]

Since the late 1950s, the Danish Parliament has used temporary committees to investigate major legislative initiatives. By mixing together interest group representatives, academics with a specialty in the field, and "common people" (i.e., government bureaucrats), legislators expect a committee to involve a cross-section of Danish society and informed opinion. Their recommendations are usually adopted into law. All the Scandinavian countries follow this approach.

The seating of the Marriage Committee sparked a heated debate in Denmark's gay and lesbian community. What exactly, gays asked themselves, do we want? The Society of 1948 created panels of interested members to discuss this topic, and the panels suggested three alternatives to the Society for consideration in a future lobbying campaign for legal recognition of lesbian and gay partnerships: (1) full *equality* between homosexuals and heterosexuals, which would entail either full marriage rights for homosexuals or, as some wanted, the abolition of marriage-related benefits for heterosexuals and the establishment of equal legal rights for all cohabiting couples; (2) the creation of a *separate-but-equal* legal framework for cohabitating same-sex couples that would offer the same legal rights and benefits as married couples, but neither the name nor the religious ceremony; and (3) the extension to same-sex couples of certain *marital benefits* conferred by Denmark's family law to married couples.[10]

On April 8, 1973, members of the Society voted to pursue the second option, legal "partnerships" for same-sex couples carrying "in all areas the same legal rights as marriage." A partnership would be available for "two people regardless of gender, that both desire to live in a lasting relationship." In fact, the only difference between full marriage and the Society's "partnership" was that church weddings were not automatic. Instead, "the church shall only bless each relationship if the partners wish it."[11] The Society did not seek marriage rights, because "marriage" had negative connotations for some gay activists, especially feminists who considered it a bulwark of patriarchy. Pragmatists in the Society believed that the benefits of marriage would be easier to obtain if it had a name other than marriage; giving it a different name would diffuse a great deal of the expected criticism of the proposal.

In October 1973, the Marriage Committee issued its first report, which ignored the Society's partnership proposal and recommended that marriage not be extended to gays and lesbians. Its members reasoned that marriage was "between a man and a woman," and that gay marriage would be a "decisive break with the traditional understanding of marriage," which in their opinion was undesirable. Furthermore, the Committee expressed concerns that if gays were allowed to marry, it would have a detrimental effect on Denmark's relations with the rest of the world. Not only would gay marriages not be recognized in foreign countries, but by legalizing gay marriage "it must be feared that it would influence international estimation in an unfavorable way of the validity of marriages entered into here in the country." In other words, the validity of *all* marriages contracted in Denmark would become questionable in the eyes of other countries. The Committee majority stated that the problems of gays and lesbians could be solved through inclusion of gay couples in existing law, a project they promised to take up in the next portion of their work.[12]

In 1980, the Marriage Committee published its eighth report, "Cohabitation without Marriage I." After twelve years of study, the Committee flatly rejected the Society's call for legal partnerships for unmarried couples. Registering unmarried couples, either same-sex or opposite-sex, would lead to an undesirable form of "second-class marriage" that would be both burdensome and unnecessary, the Committee concluded. Straight couples could simply marry and thereby obtain all the benefits without any problem. For gay couples, the Committee suggested that certain laws should be changed to incorporate them piecemeal.[13]

The Society was disappointed by the Committee's reasoning. It felt a marriage-like structure was a necessity in order to ensure, among other things, that the partnership was entered into voluntarily by both parties. It could also help determine the conditions for a settlement between the two parties in case of divorce. Rejecting the Committee's recommendation, lawyers and others within the Society of 1948 began formulating a proposal for a bill to legalize partnerships carrying all the rights of marriage, which some were now calling *registered partnerships*. Their 1981 proposal thus became the focal point for discussion of registered partnership for gays and lesbians, both within the gay community and in the Danish Parliament.

Thinking that a committee focusing solely on gay and lesbian issues would likely be more sympathetic to their needs than the Marriage Committee, LBL (the Society of 1948 became LBL in 1982) successfully lobbied Parliament in 1984 to create a "Commission for the Enlightenment of the Situation of Homosexuals in Society," soon dubbed the "HomoCommission." Following the example of Sweden, which had created a similar committee in 1977, the Danish Parliament charged the HomoCommission with studying the problems faced by homosexuals and proposing "measures aimed at removing existing discrimination within all sectors of society and at improving the situation of homosexuals, including proposals making provision for permanent forms of cohabitation."[14] The HomoCommission began its work in January 1985.

Although the attention of gay activists was diverted into health-care issues by the AIDS epidemic hitting Scandinavia in the early to mid-1980s, AIDS ultimately (and ironically) had a positive effect on partnership proposals. Until the 1980s, homosexuality had been considered a private affair and relatively invisible in mainstream society. However, as the names and faces of AIDS patients began to appear in interviews and discussions on TV and in the newspapers, the Danish public (and many politicians) were, for the first time, becoming more acquainted with homosexuality in Denmark.[15] Published in February 1986, the HomoCommission's first report, on the inheritance tax, acknowledged the effect of AIDS and the hardships faced by gay couples during this crisis (i.e., the death of a partner). Historically, a surviving spouse fell in the lowest category of taxation, whereas a surviving gay or lesbian partner fell in the highest category, since they were not officially "related." Positions on inheritance tax reform for gay and lesbian couples were divided on the HomoCommission along gay/straight lines. The four gay members, in the minority, voted to recommend that the surviving partner in a gay couple should be taxed at the same level as married couples as long as he or she lived together with the other partner at the time of that partner's demise. This would be consistent with the taxation of married couples, who were eligible for the marriage-class taxation as soon as they married. The heterosexual majority, however, voted to recommend that gay and lesbian couples only fall into the marriage-class category after they had lived together for five years.[16] After four months of intense lobbying, LBL convinced Parliament that fairness required equal treatment of couples regarding taxation. Parliament voted to equalize the inheritance tax between gay and straight surviving "spouses," so long as the gay couple shared a residence upon the death of the one partner.

The Registered Partnership Law, 1989

Although the HomoCommission proposed antidiscrimination recommendations in 1987, which Parliament promptly adopted, lesbian and gay activists became frustrated with the Commission's slow pace and its skepticism toward same-sex partnership proposals. They felt that it was time for a direct appeal to Parliament. Prodded by LBL, three minority political parties announced on December 22, 1987, that they would introduce a registered partnership bill in Parliament. The bill would give gay and lesbian couples all the same rights and responsibilities as married couples, except in the areas of adoption and church weddings. The bill's sponsors justified the legislation as meeting the "need for equality between two equal forms of cohabitation," between heterosexual couples and homosexual couples. More important, they emphasized the desirability of state support for committed lesbian and gay unions. The bill would provide greater legal security for same-sex partners, encouraging them to live "in accordance with their own desires and own choices." State validation of same-sex unions would also send a positive and helpful signal to young lesbians, gay men, and bisexuals struggling with their sexuality, and would encourage young gays to form long-lasting relationships. Finally, the sponsors maintained that the legislation could have a positive effect on the containment of AIDS, for the encouragement of permanent relationships could reduce the number of casual sex partners gay men have. Although this was not a primary reason for the bill's passage, it would nonetheless be an "extra advantage." (The sponsors' introductory remarks to this bill are reprinted in their entirety as appendix 2.)

The fate of the registered partnership bill seemed uncertain. Early in 1988, the HomoCommission issued its final report, recommending (by a six-to-five vote) that the Parliament should *not* establish registered partnership for gays and lesbians and should, instead, amend several benefit laws to include their relationships. The majority doubted the need for a registered partnership law, because they believed few couples would take advantage of it. (And closeted gay couples, who the HomoCommission felt most needed the protections of such a law, would be least likely to claim them.) Furthermore, the majority found that gay and lesbian couples have different needs from heterosexual couples, as such couples are less likely to have children living with them and are also unlikely to have as great differences in economic status as are often found in heterosexual couples. For most of these couples, existing laws designed to protect unmarried cohabitants already provide sufficient protection. Finally, the majority feared that passage of a "gay marriage" law would elicit negative reactions within Denmark and from foreign countries.[17]

The minority (one feminist and four gay representatives) argued the necessity of registered partnership for gays and lesbians. Lesbian and gay couples ought to have the same benefits and obligations as accorded to straight couples, in accordance with the principles of equality and fairness. In promoting equality, registered partnership would be a key catalyst toward changing social attitudes about gay and lesbian couples. Furthermore, piecemeal changes to family law, to occasionally include same-sex couples for certain provisions, would be administratively burdensome, as the government would often have to readdress which benefits to extend to same-sex couples as additional legal issues arose in the future.[18]

In addition to the HomoCommission's bombshell, another obstacle to the registered partnership proposal loomed on the horizon, in the form of strong political opposition. The Christian People's Party (CPP), in particular, adamantly opposed it. The CPP, whose political philosophy is based on fundamentalist Christian principles, is an advocate of morals-based legislation. Its chairman stated that the party would "go against [the bill] with all the power we can put together" because of the party's view that "marriage is the truest and best form of living together. It is undermined by this bill."[19] More important, the governing party was also opposed to the proposal.

When the bill was first introduced into Parliament on March 16, 1988, the minister of justice announced his support for the recommendation of the HomoCommission's majority in concluding that the registered partnership bill did not "cover a real need" and that it posed terrible risks for Denmark in the international community. Danish recognition of "marriage between homosexuals" would make other countries "suspicious" of Danish family law, and could effect how other countries viewed the validity of Danish marriages. He then recommended that the other Nordic countries be consulted for their views before passing this legislation, which would have the effect of stalling the bill.[20]

After the minister was finished, several members of parliament (MPs) stood up to attack the legislation and urge its rejection. Some followed the minister of justice in focusing on practical problems and administrative issues with the proposal: Was there an urgent need for a whole new institution? Why broaden the concept of marriage for what was likely only a small number of same-sex couples? Couldn't heterosexuals manipulate this legislation for fraudulent registrations? Why should the government adopt what one member of Parliament claimed was "a widened concept of marriage—in fact widened to such an extent that neither the Danish people nor the world around us in all reality could understand or accept?" Wasn't there a risk of adverse international reaction? Couldn't equitable treatment for same-sex couples be accomplished by simply amending specific benefits laws? Other MPs objected on the more fundamental grounds of religion and morality. Members of the CPP and the Conservative People's Party called gay couples "unnatural" and described the bill as "a danger to us all," "against everything we stand for," and "a bomb under [the institution of] marriage." These legislators to some extent used biblical arguments to support their point, and made clear that, in their view, marriage was only natural between a man and a woman.[21]

Several MPs then took the floor to defend the legislation, most of them stating that the bill would simply recognize a living situation that already existed. They spoke of the dedication that gay couples shared for one another, and their need to be protected if something should happen. Supporters emphasized themes of equality: lesbian and gay couples had just as much a right to legal recognition of their relationship as did straight couples. They also attacked the critics' arguments. There were an ample number of lesbian and gay couples who wanted and needed this legislation, the supporters declared. Furthermore, the number of people who registered was unimportant, as it was the principle of equality that mattered. As regards potential abuse of the law, supporters pointed out that people could also have pro forma heterosexual marriages in abuse of the system, and there was no reason to suspect that this abuse would be any greater with same-sex partnerships. And instead of envisioning the international condemnation suggested by the opponents, one legislator concluded that "Denmark's first step here will rub off on other lands."[22] In other words, Denmark might become the first country to give gay couples the same legal rights as married couples, but would not be the last.

This initial debate was inconclusive, for a political crisis dissolved the government and required new elections. The bill was reintroduced in November 1988; by this time, polls suggested that public support for recognition of same-sex legal unions was growing.[23] On December 15, the parliamentary debate resumed, with new arguments on the table.[24] Some supporters argued that the encouragement of legal relationships between same-sex partners would discourage promiscuity and thereby reduce the rate of HIV infection among gay and bisexual men. One of the bill's opponents, on the other hand, remarked that she thought the bill's passage would bring HIV-infected men from other lands to come live in Denmark with a Danish registered partner.[25] Thus AIDS remained a divisive feature of the struggle for gay rights. Opponents also argued that the legislation would impose hardship on "closeted" gay couples, who would be forced to publicly register to receive the same benefits as married couples. Proponents responded that nobody would be forced to register, just as unmarried heterosexual couples were not forced to marry.

Even most of those who expressed sharp opposition to the bill still suggested there was room for compromise. Conservatives were willing to change some laws in order to accommodate the needs of gay and lesbian couples, if the bill was dropped. Yet proponents of the bill demonstrated no willingness to make such a compromise. Other MPs (on both sides of the issue) suggested that the political parties should not take an official position on the bill if it should come to a vote, and let their members vote their own consciences. In the words of one MP, "it is unreasonable to make this a question of party politics."[26]

After the first hearing in the newly elected Parliament, the bill was referred to its Legal Committee, which posed a series of questions to the minister of justice regarding the effects such a law would have. Although opposed to the bill, the new minister, H. P. Clausen, responded thoroughly to the questions, which included a broad range of issues, ranging from the required minimum age for those wishing to register to the effect the bill would have in Greenland and the Faroe Islands, both part of the Danish Kingdom. His staff, with the aid of each government ministry, combed the Danish legal code to identify all the laws specifically relating to marriage and married couples that would be affected by the legislation.

The Legal Committee sought and received input from private groups, including LBL. Its representatives met with the Committee and argued that the law was necessary to create a security net for gay couples. Changes in individual laws could not do this, they said, since the number of laws that would have to be changed and the number of situations that would have to be addressed were almost innumerable. Furthermore, changing only certain laws would create a burdensome new system of legal paperwork for gay and lesbian couples, separate from that of married couples. The passage of a partnership law, LBL also argued, was important symbolically. Passage of the law would demonstrate that the government was truly interested in giving equality to its gay and lesbian citizens. Referring to the mandate laid out for the earlier HomoCommission, LBL told the Committee that "the passage of partnership is the Parliament's way of living up to the obligation that was laid before the general public, specifically not to discriminate against gays and lesbians on the grounds of their identity and lifestyle."[27]

The Committee also concerned itself with collateral issues important to many Danes who favored some legal recognition of lesbian and gay unions, especially adoption law. There was almost no parliamentary support at the time for allowing gay and lesbian couples to adopt children from other countries, but LBL argued that registered partners ought to be able to at least adopt stepchildren (the biological children of their partners). Such adoption would secure the right of children to live with their stepparents, should their natural parents die. Most other groups urged the Committee to reject all forms of adoption for gay and lesbian couples. The stated fear was that such children would be ridiculed and taunted for having gay parents, which could cause them severe trauma in their adolescence. Although members of the Committee were skeptical of this argument on the merits, it voted to prohibit all types of adoption. Their reasoning was that this would make it easier to pass the bill through Parliament, and the issue of adoption could be readdressed separately after the partnership law passed.

Parallel to the Committee's deliberations, the entire country debated the partnership bill in other venues; gay marriage became one of the hot topics of social and political discussion. The issue was particularly important for fundamentalist Christians. Although small compared to the community in the United States, Denmark's fundamentalist Christian community was capable of swift mobilization, as had occurred in earlier years when Parliament debated legalizing abortion and legalizing pornography. Small local newspapers all over Denmark were suddenly filled with letters to the editor, berating Parliament for even entertaining the partnership bill and warning of the dire consequences to Danish society if such a bill should be passed. Opponents called homosexuality "a sin," "an abomination," and "against the word of God."[28] The Committee examined many articles sent from critics of the legislation, such as one entitled "A Law's Consequences," which had been published in the *Christian Daily News*. It argued that the law would "open the door for the entrance [into Denmark] of sexual deviants from the whole world, for example from San Francisco's milieu" and make it easier for Danish pedophiles to bring children into their homes as part of the households.[29] Fundamentalist Christian preachers and lay leaders urged their followers to express their disapproval of the partnership bill to their representatives. Soon thereafter, both the Legal Committee and members of Parliament were inundated with constituent letters opposing the bill, a rare occurrence in Denmark. A petition from 122 Danish priests urged the Committee to kill the bill. "The State may not make laws against God's command," the petition stated. The priests feared that the bill would "privilege abnormality." Furthermore, should the state order the Church to marry gay couples, this would, according to the petition, cause priests to "lead people astray."[30]

Yet for all the effort made to reject the bill on natural law arguments, the percentage of Danes who subscribed to these fundamentalist viewpoints was actually very small. This is in part because Denmark does not have a tradition of using religious arguments in any way that could be construed as suppressing or discriminating against minorities. In fact, tolerance of differing viewpoints is an integral part of the teachings of the Danish Lutheran Church.[31]

After consideration of all the arguments, including the natural law arguments made by opponents, the Committee reported the partnership bill favorably back to Parliament, with only minor amendments. On May 23, 1989, Parliament once again debated the bill.[32] The debate began mundanely, centering on technical issues such as how same-sex couples were to be treated in regards to international treaties on married couples and similarly detailed provisions. However, the pragmatic focus of the discussion disappeared when a CPP member, in a harsh tone, indicted the partnership bill as "a catastrophe" that would set Denmark "against the whole world." She argued: "It is so fundamentally against that which this Christian society is built upon, that we must turn against it and absolutely not have anything to do with this law."[33]

Member of Parliament Margrete Auken, a priest, took the floor and responded:

> Under the discussion of this bill it has been quite unusually unpleasant to experience not just the Christian People's Party, but also [other] groups, that inflate themselves up not only to represent themselves but also Christianity, like it was a primitive fertility religion. Christianity is not that. Christianity deals with [the fact that] our sexuality is also about the ability to love. That is what most of us heterosexuals have been easily able to manage, with all the troubles that [love] otherwise gives us, and with the protections of the law that are found in marriage. That is what the Christian People's Party doesn't want to

give homosexuals. That has nothing to do with Christianity—it is petty and narrow-minded and a little bit primitive, housed in a different religious tradition than that we, as the church and Christianity, ought to be representatives of.[34]

Rarely had the Danish Parliament experienced a debate as fundamental as this one, in which MPs openly examined, and disagreed about, the role of religion in political decision-making. Yet that was now what was happening, and the next several speakers ventured up to the podium to weigh in on the subject, with no holds barred. Several fundamentalist MPs responded to MP Auken: "God created humans as man and woman" whose sexual relations with each other were necessary for the continuation of life. In no other country, said one, could gay and lesbian couples be interpreted by Christians to be included in this definition. "There are a lot of [Christians] in this country," he stated, "who are crying" as Parliament debated the bill.[35] Others rejected this view of Christianity. Member of Parliament Peter Duetoft had this to say:

> The reason I am so fond of the Danish Church is that it is built upon charity . . . the charity and the tolerance which lies in the Christianity that I believe in is based upon [the fact that] I will have respect for other people who have chosen to live life in a different way than I could ever dream of living. It is exactly for that reason that I believe that I will be in favor of [the bill], to give them a practical guideline in order to live the life they have chosen. When all of us in some years, hopefully in many years, sit on our small clouds with our small trumpets and small wings on our back, then we can see who among us did the Christian thing, and who among us didn't.[36]

It was clear that the partnership bill had hit a nerve among members of Parliament, and when the bill came to its third and final reading on May 26,[37] passions remained heated. As opponents recognized this as their final opportunity to defeat the bill, many took the floor to express their concerns. These MPs, as well as the minister of justice, argued that the Committee's amendments were insufficient to solve the unanswered questions remaining in the bill, in particular the effect that same-sex unions would have on laws in Denmark affecting marriage. Arguing that same-sex partnerships were an untested concept, they declared that more research was needed to see what its effect on marriage law would be. Five MPs announced that although they supported the bill in principle, due to this particular concern they would vote neither for nor against the bill. In addition, a CPP spokeswoman appealed to children's welfare, suggesting that the bill's passage would be harmful to

Danish youth, who "could get tied up in a relationship they don't want." She stated that the partnership bill could create a situation in which youth unsure of their sexuality may get "stuck" in a gay relationship, and may stay in it even after they have decided that they're not gay. "We have received examples of lesbians who later find their man and live happily that way," she said.[38] And finally, the CPP threatened, if the bill should pass, the CPP would force a public referendum on the subject as Parliament was pressing this issue way beyond what the country would tolerate.[39]

The bill's sponsors responded that enough work had already been done on the bill. Those still uncertain, they argued, had already had a year and a half since the bill's first introduction to gather all the information they needed. (The issue had also been before Parliament for twenty years at that point.) Now was the time to act. The sponsors declared that this would be a day in which a form of discrimination against gays and lesbians would be removed from the law books. One of the sponsors even prophesied that those benefits that the bill withheld from gays and lesbians—adoption and a church wedding—would eventually come to them as well. "When it will be seen that society hasn't fallen down on the grounds of [the partnership law]," she said, "then I think it will be possible to take up the few issues of equality that still exist."[40]

All political parties had declared no official party position on the bill and therefore permitted their members to vote according to their consciences. According to one MP, this was done "in acknowledgement of [the fact that] this is a subject that has political workings and aspects, but is first and foremost a question of moral and personal beliefs, perhaps even, if one will raise it a little higher, a question of human rights and human nature."[41] And so the arguments came to a close. The time for a vote had arrived. Although indicators pointed in favor of the bill's passage, nobody could be absolutely sure what to expect as the MPs each pressed a green or red button in front of them to tally their vote. Parliament's public gallery, packed with gay rights advocates, was silent, as observers held their breath.

The final tally then appeared on the screen that hung over the parliamentary chamber: seventy-one in favor, forty-seven against, five not voting. The public gallery exploded in cheers. In the center, Axel and Eigil Axgil, the fathers of the modern Danish gay movement, smiled in triumph. As word spread over the next several hours, gay and lesbian establishments in Copenhagen overflowed with jubilant supporters of the law. At its offices LBL hosted a huge party, attended by supportive MPs, leaders of the Norwegian and Swedish gay organizations, Danish gay activists, couples soon to be legally partnered, and others from around the country. Toasts were offered to the fine work that had been done in securing the law's passage, such as the one offered by MP Pia Gjellerup: "Congratulations with this great step forward!"[42] Activists cheered the result, while at the same time publicly pledging to continue work to remove those few differences that remained between registered partnership and marriage.

The Registered Partnership Law went into effect on Sunday, October 1, 1989. On that day, town halls all around Denmark opened specially for this celebration. Copenhagen, the Danish capital, was the natural focus. Mayor Tom Ahlberg opened the celebration with a speech and then officiated at the ceremony for the first two same-sex partners to be joined—Axel Axgil and Eigil Axgil. "Do you, Axel Axgil, take Eigil Axgil to be your partner?" the mayor asked. Eleven couples were joined in partnership in Copenhagen that day, most of them tuxedo-clad gay men. All of those legally joined together on this first day of the law's validity were well known in the gay community and had been active in the movement toward registered partnership. By the end of 1989, over 270 gay men and seventy lesbians had registered their partnerships with the state. This number has risen steadily every year since then.

The language of the new law (which, along with its amendments, is reproduced as appendix 1) is simple. "Two people of the same sex may have their partnership registered." The law then states that, wherever the word "marriage" appears in Danish law, it will now be construed to include registered partnership, and wherever the word "spouse" appears, it will also be construed to include registered partners.[43] Thus, upon registering their partnerships, gay and lesbian couples become subject to the hundreds of laws that refer to married couples.[44]

Among other things, registering in Denmark means that all of the belongings that the partners have brought into the partnership, and all of the assets they accumulate during the partnership, are legally shared by both of them. There is also an obligation of mutual support; both partners are required to contribute to the maintenance of their family, either through financial contribution, work in the home, or other means. Social programs, inheritance rights, and other marital benefits also became automatically available to registered partners. But there were a couple of exceptions to the equal treatment norm. Under the 1989 law, registered partners could not adopt children or even share joint custody over children either partner brought to their union. Also unlike married couples, registered partners did not have access to state-provided artificial insemination services. In 1999, Denmark's Parliament amended the original statute to allow registered partners to adopt and have joint custody of children; there are still limits on adoptions from other countries. (Chapters 3 and 4 take up these topics in greater detail.)

Why Was Denmark the First?

The same-sex marriage debate in Denmark from the 1960s to 1989 was in most respects very similar to, and often mirrored, that in the United States. Gay-liberals argued for full marriage rights for reasons of formal equality and functional advantages that the benefits and obligations of marriage would confer upon lesbian and gay couples. On their left, gay-radicals and many feminists argued that marriage should be replaced by a civil institution untethered to patriarchy. They understood equality as transformational and not just formal or functional. On their right, traditionalists argued that marriage should not be changed at all. As in the United States, most traditionalists understood equality from a natural law perspective: it was no discrimination to exclude from marriage couples who did not biologically or morally fit within that institution's essential nature or function. Many of the traditionalists' public arguments focused on the pragmatic, however: recognition of same-sex marriage would have bad consequences for the country, for marriage, and for children.

Yet Denmark's Parliament substantially rejected the traditionalist arguments, and accepted the gay-liberal ones in 1989, while American state legislatures and Congress have overwhelmingly followed the traditionalist arguments after 1993, when the Hawaii Supreme Court put same-sex marriage on America's national agenda. Why such different reactions? The riddle becomes even more mysterious when one observes that Denmark's lesbian and gay community is not as visible or politically mobilized as that in the United States. Yet Denmark was willing to accommodate this newly salient minority much more rapidly than the rights-loving United States or other European nations. Indeed, Denmark moved before Sweden, its Nordic neighbor, which had been the first country to recognize the legal rights of lesbian and gay cohabiting couples by statute (1987). Why was Denmark the first?[45]

To understand why Denmark took the lead in legalizing same-sex unions, one must understand the relationship between Danish religion and national identity. Outsiders often say that the Scandinavian countries, with a seemingly loose moral code, are almost devoid of religion. Same-sex marriage, according to this view, has stemmed from the breakdown of religious beliefs and moral principles. Yet those who understand Scandinavian, and particularly Danish, religious tradition understand that actually the opposite is true: Denmark's religious history is one of the most important reasons that its Parliament was able to recognize same-sex legal unions.

Denmark's modern interpretation of Christianity, and its reputation as country of tolerance and openness, did not first develop in the second half of the twentieth century, as some believe, but rather began in the mid-

1800s. Its modern religious and social philosophies are to a great extent dependent on the teachings of one individual—N.F.S. Grundtvig, a priest, educator, and prolific writer. He wielded great influence in Denmark through his writings, teachings, and development of new educational institutions.[46]

Grundtvig's philosophy centered around the Danish concept of *frisind* (pronounced "free-sihnd"), which can be roughly translated to mean "open-mindedness" or "tolerance." *Frisind* over the past 150 years has become a cornerstone of Danish political and cultural philosophy. Departing from the viewpoints of other Christian theologians, Grundtvig saw the basis for Christianity not just in the written words of the Bible but in the members of the Church itself, in the congregations of people who called themselves Christians. In Grundtvig's view, the Christian community existed long before the Bible itself did. It was the faith one was baptized into, and not just the Bible, that bound the congregation together from the very beginning. In his words: "Our Lord had not founded a reading club but a congregation." Because Christianity was to be found in the people who made up the members of the Church, "the interpretations and constructions of theologians were of less importance than the living community, and that this assumed freedom and emancipation from a rigid and authoritarian system." In other words, it was up to Christians themselves to decide how to live in accordance with their Christian beliefs. They were not obliged to adopt the religious interpretations of any particular theologian.[47]

Thus, while other denominations such as Catholicism required strict interpretations of the Bible and expected church members to comply with church dogma under the threat of eternal punishment for noncompliance, Grundtvig's interpretation of Danish Lutheranism only demanded tolerance within the Church for differing opinions. He believed in the greatest possible freedom of worship for individual congregations, and believed that people should be free to formulate and express their own religious views in accordance with their own personal feelings and beliefs. "First a human being, and then a Christian," in his words.[48]

However, *frisind* was not to be the responsibility of the Church alone, and was not limited to religion. Grundtvig's teachings made it clear that it was the responsibility of each individual to respect and value the opinions of others in regard to secular issues as well. One did not necessarily have to accept the expressed opinions of others as correct, but one was at least required to value the fact that others are entitled to their own opinion, and that this opinion may be just as valid as one's own. Rather than condemning the opinions of others, Grundtvig taught, one should accept them as an alternative way of viewing a situation.[49]

The spread of Grundtvig's views on Christianity occurred in conjunction with his involvement in transforming the educational system in Denmark. Himself a recipient of a formal education, Grundtvig found traditional education undesirable, calling it "alien to everything in a higher sense natural and alive, and devoid of everything that ennobles, but full of everything that can degrade, dull and corrupt a person." He particularly disliked how formal education created a divide between itself and humanism, for it involved a multiyear study of a narrow subject matter that, he felt, in no way prepared students for life. Lectures might be effective in imparting facts and figures, but could not, in his opinion, "nourish" students to achieve their full potential as human beings. Furthermore, advanced formal education in Denmark, as elsewhere, was limited to a small group of bourgeois Danes and not available to the people as a whole. In response, Grundtvig founded the "folk high school" system in Denmark in 1844, meant to be a school system for the general population, not just an educated elite. Entered into after a basic education, their purpose is to advance student's intellectual curiosity without the pressures of traditional education (thus, no exams). These schools, which remain an important educational force in Denmark even today, operate on the principle that students must be gripped by enthusiasm for a subject before they will truly learn it. They focus on the subjects of life that affect their students directly—including, among other things, the subjects of religion and national identity.[50]

Through the widespread influence of the folk high schools, which by the late nineteenth century had become the center of Danish culture, Grundtvig's views of religion, tolerance, and *frisind* were discussed and eventually absorbed into the Danish identity. By the mid–twentieth century, the concept of *frisind* could no longer be separated from what it meant to be Danish. This held true not only in urban areas, which were likely to be more tolerant of differences to start with, but also in the rural parts of Denmark, where Grundtvig had focused on establishing folk high schools in order to provide a broader education for those least likely to have access to formal education.

Perhaps the minister of justice in the late 1960s, Knud Thestrup, best summed up the influence of *frisind* in his remarks to the 1969 legislation that would make Denmark the first country in the world to legalize pornography:

> Even though liberalization [of the law] will, we hope, reduce interest in these pictures, we must of course accept that there will still be some people interested in buying them. It is a question, however, of whether this is a sufficient argument against liberalization. In my view, by leaving the matter [of purchasing pornography] to indi-

vidual decision, you will strengthen the development . . . towards greater freedom for the individual citizen to plan his own life, and towards the greater personal responsibility which follows.[51]

While the government had no interest in promoting pornography, neither did it want to impose its own decisions on its citizens as to whether viewing pornography was morally unacceptable. Rather, Danes should make such decisions for themselves.

Thus, the tradition of tolerance and acceptance of differing opinions in Denmark, steeped in a long history of religious and cultural tradition, is why the CPP's opposition to the partnership law had so little impact. In Denmark, it is simply not considered acceptable to declare that one's interpretation of God's intentions is the only acceptable one. Indeed, after the speech of MP and pastor Margrethe Auken during the second reading of the partnership bill on the role of religion, in which she argued that Christianity was broad enough to accept love between two adults in more than one form, the chief MP of the CPP conceded that just as the CPP was entitled to its own opinion regarding the registered partnership law, so were others entitled to their own Christian perspectives.[52]

The difference between Denmark and the United States, therefore, is *not* that religion plays a role in public discourse only in the latter but rather that the conservative religious and natural law arguments against same-sex marriage have been more persuasive to more people in the United States than in Denmark. The Danish audience was less receptive to conservative natural law arguments. Due to their understanding of religion and their belief in *frisind*, many Danes were open to a nontraditionalist understanding of marriage, and many who accepted the traditional understanding did not feel intensely invested in that norm.

The Vikings Collaborate: The Spread of Registered Partnership Rights throughout Scandinavia

For the most part, the stories of the other Nordic nations (Norway, Sweden, Finland, and Iceland)[53] are similar to those of Denmark. This is not coincidental. The Scandinavian countries share a common ancestry, history, and even language base (for Denmark, Norway, and Sweden). These cultural connections have, after a long history of strife, evolved into significant political and legal cooperation. One of the areas in which these countries cooperate most closely is family law. There is, for the most part, a common system for marriages, divorces, and inheritance. All the Scandinavian countries removed

fault requirements from their divorce laws in the early 1970s and then extended some benefits and duties of marriage to cohabiting couples. Planned
changes in family law are often discussed between Nordic governments in
order to ensure that those changes operate smoothly. During Denmark's
registered partnership debate, opponents maintained that Denmark should
be reluctant to create a new institution without consulting and working in
conjunction with its Nordic partners. However, once Denmark acted in 1989,
the tradition of Scandinavian cooperation put the issue on the political
agenda of the other countries and provided a powerful reason for them to
follow.[54]

In addition, Denmark's pattern of urbanization, economic opportunities
for women outside the home, and state support for child-rearing is by and
large replicated in the other countries. The countries have also seen similar
changes in family formation. The marriage rate in Scandinavia steadily eroded
after 1950, and the divorce rate increased. In the last generation (and probably before), the percentage of live births outside of marriage has steadily
increased. In all of these countries, gay people remained closeted until the 1960s
and have been modest presences in public culture since then. All the countries have had state churches (Sweden's separated from the state in 2001) and
relatively low levels of religious fundamentalism, hence also lessened commitment to a traditional concept of marriage.[55]

Within a decade, each of the Nordic countries passed a law virtually identical to the one passed in Denmark, giving gay and lesbian couples all the rights
and responsibilities of marriage other than a church wedding or adoption
rights. The Nordic countries also initiated the international movement for
cross-border recognition of same-sex partnerships, by legally recognizing the
relationships of same-sex couples coming from countries having "equivalent
legislation"—mainly couples from the other Scandinavian countries. The
order in which Denmark's Nordic neighbors followed its innovation to
marriagelike partnerships would not have been predictable, illustrating how
local politics affects patterns of legal change.

Norway, 1993

Because it is less urbanized and relatively isolated, Norway is more culturally conservative than either Denmark or Sweden. Like American Baptists,
fundamentalist members of the Norwegian Lutheran Church are more likely
to involve themselves in politics than their counterparts in Denmark and
Sweden. An example of their influence was the survival of Norway's sodomy law. Whereas Denmark legalized consensual homosexual relations
between men in 1933, and Sweden did so in 1944, it wasn't until 1972 that

Norway decriminalized male-male sex. Even then, many legislators announced their intention to change the law not because it was unfair to gays but rather because it was a sexist law that discriminated against men because lesbians were not subject to punishment! However, once Norway finally did decriminalize homosexual sodomy, it made the legal age for gay sex the same as that for heterosexual sex, sixteen, thus being the first Nordic country to have an equal age of consent.[56]

Notwithstanding Norway's more conservative culture, Norwegian gays and lesbians have been able to lead relatively free lives. Even in the post–World War II period, there was relatively little state witch-hunting of homosexuals, as there was in the United States and even Denmark. The Norwegian gay organization, Det Norske Forbund af 1948 (the Norwegian Society of 1948, or DNF, and later Landsforeningen for Lesbisk og Homofil Frigjøring, the National Organization for Lesbian and Homophile Liberation, or LLH), has been working to improve gay and lesbian living conditions for over fifty years. After Parliament decriminalized sodomy in 1972, DNF turned its attention to gay marriage. In their 1973 general assembly, after debating the pros and cons of various types of legal recognition for gay couples (including the option to press for the elimination of all benefits associated with marriage), DNF resolved: "An individual's worth is not dependent on their ability, desire, or possibility of living with another person. DNF-48 cannot accept any form of discrimination of single people—economic or socially. The Society will support every policy that has as its goal to remove this discrimination wherever it may exist. DNF-48 will, at the same time, work to [create a safety net for] other forms of cohabitation than that of traditional marriage."[57]

The resolution masked big disagreements within Norway's lesbian and gay community, however. Radicals in DNF and Fellesrådet for Homofile Organisasjoner I Norge (the Joint Council for Homophile Organizations in Norway, or FHO), a more left-wing gay organization, opposed marriage as an aspiration for the gay rights movement, and that issue languished during the 1970s. But DNF and FHO worked together to persuade Parliament, in 1981, to enact the world's first nationwide statute barring discrimination based on sexual orientation. The law prohibited the denial of goods or services in or from any business establishment on the basis of "homosexual disposition, lifestyle or orientation."[58] Emboldened by this success, DNF turned its attention to same-sex marriage rights. "The Norwegian Society of 1948 accepts that a legal regulation of homophile cohabitation should take place through voluntary registration."[59]

The progress of the Danish registered partnership bill in the late 1980s stimulated more aggressive political action in Norway. In 1988, DNF and

FHO created their own "partnership committee" to make recommendations and produce draft legislation. This proposal, in turn, alarmed Norway's fundamentalist Christian community, represented in Parliament by the Christian People's Party (CPP), a much more powerful force than its counterpart in Denmark. For example, the CPP was a coalition member in the Norwegian government seated in 1989, which foreclosed any possibility that DNF's bill would be government-sponsored. In November 1989, DNF decided to press for partnership through a "private bill." (In contrast to the normal route for legislation, in which the bill in question is introduced, examined, and passed by the government in power, a private bill is introduced by individual MPs and is usually passed mostly with the votes of members of minority parties. This unusual route is almost never successful in Norway.) DNF wanted its legislation to be "as parallel as possible with the Danish bill." Because of the Nordic tradition of "common legislation in, among other things, family law, we therefore believed that it would be an argument for the law in itself that a corresponding law had been passed in Denmark."[60]

After the introduction of the private bill, DNF and FHO discovered that many of their parliamentary allies had decided they were uncomfortable with passing such major legislation without research and input from the coalition government. Thus, they changed the proposal to direct the government to address the issue. The conservative government dutifully sent the bill to various ministries and other interested parties for their factual and normative input. Facing an uncomfortable battle over gay and lesbian rights, the government in December 1991 offered DNF a compromise: in exchange for dropping their demand for a comprehensive partnership law, the government would support some basic (and less controversial) legislation to establish legal security for gay and lesbian couples. While there were concerns that sticking to their principles could come at the cost of *any* legislative reforms, the leaders of DNF ultimately felt that the government was bluffing and the country was ready for equality; they voted unanimously to reject the offered compromise and accept nothing less than a comprehensive law that paralleled Norwegian marriage law.[61]

In addition, DNF's Partnership Group, with the help of the national gay organizations and local gay activists, used the mainstream media to their advantage. From 1990 onward, gay leaders and activists gave numerous interviews to garner public sympathy. Gay and lesbian couples, they explained, have little legal protection under the law, even if they have lived together for many years. Only through passage of a partnership law could gay and lesbian couples be secure if anything should happen to one of the partners. These straightforward, and often personal, accounts worked to sway public opinion in DNF's favor. The Partnership Group also contacted Members of Parliament to lobby in personal or telephone conversations. According to the Partnership Group, several key MPs, who had little or no interest in helping to pass a partnership law, became advocates of the law after personal meetings with the lobbyists that they found informative and compelling.[62]

At the same time, the Norwegian CPP and fundamentalist Christians mobilized against the partnership proposal. Part of their strategy was to use an American-style grassroots campaign, inundating MPs with constituent letters, phone calls, and newspaper editorials. Despite better organization and a larger constituency than their Danish counterparts, Christian organizations in Norway suffered from a series of unexpected (some have even described as comical) events. First, as the CPP began discussing strategy on how to defeat the law in 1990, a leader of DNF got a call from a key member of the party. This CPP member was in favor of a partnership law but explained to the DNF leader that it would be impossible for him to express such a view publicly. Thus, the CPP member became a spy for DNF on the partnership issue. This Norwegian "Deep Throat" kept DNF updated on CPP's discussions and planned strategies regarding the registered partnership law, giving DNF advance warning on how to defend the partnership bill against attacks from CPP. The DNF was thus always up to date on CPP's political strategy.[63]

Second, the CPP was dealt another blow in its efforts to defeat the partnership bill from another member of its own party. Anders Gåslund, the leader of the CPP's youth organization, "came out" as gay in early 1992, and at the same time announced his support for the partnership bill. The media response was tremendous. Gåsland's homosexuality was the top story in Norway on most media outlets for a period, and the story of his internal struggle garnered public sympathies. Some CPP leaders denounced the young man as an immoral traitor, tactics that did not have a positive effect on public opinion. Gåslund's coming out may have been a knockout blow to the CPP's efforts to defeat the partnership law. According to the Partnership Group, "that he came out at the point in time that he did contributed to our ability to park CPP in on a side track."[64]

Third, and according to many gay activists the most damaging development for opponents of registered partnership, was the founding of "The People's Movement against the Partnership Law" by a group of Christian fundamentalists. The leader of this grassroots movement, Ivar Belch-Olsen, was well known for his previous fights to criminalize abortion in Norway. Borrowing techniques used by America's Christian Coalition, the People's Movement organized postcard mailings to politicians and encouraged concerned Christians to contact their MPs, arranged public demonstrations and other made-for-media events, and published an antipartnership petition signed by eighty-two of Norway's best known personalities in the fields of sport, politics, and religion. However, these tactics were not well received by ordinary Norwegians. Because some People's Movement speakers were inexperienced in dealing with the media and even speaking in public, they made blunt, opinionated statements about gay people and their relationships that seemed to reflect antigay prejudice. In public debates with supporters of partnership rights, who could relate clearly why same-sex unions were important, members of the People's Movement were often unable to articulate neutral reasons why the state should *not* be encouraging lesbian and gay unions. The print and electronic media portrayed opponents negatively due to their perceived extremism, but they did not do much better when the media let them speak for themselves.[65]

Most surprising, the People's Movement antagonized conservative MPs who were otherwise reluctant to support such a major change in Norway's family law. For example, one government minister, targeted for a postcard campaign, was annoyed with the People's Movement when thousands of identical postcards appeared on his desk. Other legislators were not particularly receptive to a "prayer vigil" in which religious opponents gathered in front of the Parliament and prayed for MPs in order to give them the guidance not to pass the law. They felt that such tactics demeaned religion and were unresponsive to the genuine issues of public justice posed by the partnership law.[66]

Faced with growing public support for (and diminishing public opposition to) the partnership law, the government announced its support for the partnership demands of Norwegian gays and lesbians. In July 1992, the Ministry of Children and Family Affairs recommended that the Norwegian Parliament pass a registered partnership bill for gay and lesbian couples that was virtually identical to the Danish bill. Speaking for the government, the Ministry recognized that "regardless of attitudes on the origin of marriage and its central importance, it should be emphasized that marriage is *also* a legal contract that regulates the financial situation of two people who live in a close union and become dependent on each other,"[67] and thus "the reciprocal economic and legal needs of two people of the same sex who live together in a committed relationship will be virtually the same as those of a married couple."[68] In a remarkable statement from a conservative government, the Ministry argued that a partnership law "will mean a public acceptance of homosexual relationships. The Act will therefore encourage more gays and lesbians to come out, and thus reduce the problems created by their need to hide their own nature and live in isolation."[69]

Indeed, the Ministry's report argued that the partnership law would contribute to stability in gay and lesbian relationships: "Homosexuals have the same need for security and growth within a lifelong relationship as do heterosexuals, and should therefore be given the same support in establishing permanent, committed relationships."[70] Furthermore, "whereas the attitudes of the community help to prevent heterosexual relationships from breaking up, such attitudes may encourage the opposite among homosexuals."[71] Thus, "a formally established partnership will in itself represent a commitment. It is a sign to others that the couple wishes to form a lasting relationship. This commitment may mean that greater efforts are made to avoid a breakup if the relationship undergoes a crisis."[72] For all its positive words about homosexual couples, the Ministry's report also recommended that areas of marriage law concerning children be omitted from the partnership law, which was in line with the existing Danish law. "Little is known about the effects of growing up in a family setting of two adults of the same sex. The question of adoption must be considered independently of the right to a registered partnership."[73]

Unlike those of its Nordic neighbors, Norway's Parliament has a bicameral legislature. Thus, the partnership bill would have to pass not one but two chambers to become law. The legislative debate was similar to that of the Danish Parliament four years earlier. Those against the bill made three kinds of arguments. Their main argument was that state recognition of homosexual relationships is contrary to the Bible and therefore morally wrong. Second, the CPP argued that registered partnerships would needlessly undermine the institution of marriage. Third, such a drastic change in state family law was administratively burdensome and unnecessary, since the problems of gay couples could be solved with some changes in existing legislation. Finally, some MPs maintained that the proposal would besmirch Norway's international reputation. In the upper chamber, an MP who was a retired military officer linked the bill to the 1993 winter Olympics, which Norway would be hosting. "During the Olympics, we will try to sell Norwegian culture and tradition," he said. "If anyone believes that this law would be a good commodity to sell, they ought to think twice."[74]

Those in favor pointed to the partnership bill as the best way to secure the full range of legal rights for gay and lesbian couples. They also argued that the bill was needed to eliminate existing discrimination against such couples, whose relationships were no less worthy than heterosexual relationships. Supporters also cautioned that, if a separate legal structure was created for gay and lesbian couples that contained only limited rights in comparison to married couples, a number of heterosexual couples might decide that they wanted a similar "no-frills" legal structure for their own relationships. If that happened, then the institution of marriage would indeed have been weakened.

On March 29, 1993, the partnership law passed Norway's lower chamber by a comfortable margin of fifty-eight to forty. On April 1, it squeaked through the upper chamber by a vote of eighteen to sixteen. As a testament to its efforts, the Norwegian Parliament in a later vote pronounced DNF "the best lobbyists of Parliament in Norway."[75] In contrast, the People's Movement might have won a vote as one of the worst. A number of Norwegian MPs who had previously been undecided as to how to vote on the partnership bill became supporters of the bill simply to distance themselves in the public arena from the unsavory arguments of the antipartnership activists. After the vote, gay and lesbian activists sent their thanks to the People's Movement for their help in getting the law passed.[76] Norway's Registered Partnership Law was virtually the same as the Danish law, except that the Norwegian law specified that the couple must be homosexual. On August 6, 1993, the first gay and lesbian couples to be joined in Norway registered as part of a grand ceremony in Oslo.[77]

Sweden, 1995

Sweden epitomizes the welfare state more than any of its Nordic neighbors. Its governments have redistributed social benefits to a greater extent than in the other Nordic nations, and there is a large safety net in existence to take care of the needs of all Swedish citizens. Furthermore, the Swedish government has had a greater hand in shaping and directing social policy than in any other Nordic country, following the theory that more government can be a good thing, if such power is not abused. An example is the Swedish government's response to AIDS. While other governments worked with gay organizations to distribute condoms and AIDS-educational information in gay bars, saunas, and sex clubs, Sweden in 1987 went further and closed all places where sexual contact between people could occur. This of course applied to heterosexual sex establishments as well. While the other Nordic countries established anonymous AIDS testing sites in order to encourage people to check their HIV status, Sweden kept files on all those who tested HIV-positive, in order to monitor cases of HIV and AIDS in Sweden and to use such information to prevent its spread.[78]

Swedish women have more economic opportunities outside the home than those in any other country, because the welfare state provides liberal child care and other support. For this and other reasons, the family-formation trends noted for Denmark were even more pronounced for Sweden. Since 1950, the marriage rate has fallen, the divorce rate has soared, and increasing numbers of families have formed outside of marriage. Sweden not only adopted no-fault divorce in 1973 but in 1987 created the world's first cohabitees laws, giving cohabiting couples (both different-sex and same-sex) many of the legal benefits of marriage.[79] Soon after these family law liberalizations, Sweden undertook a series of reforms to protect lesbian and gay citizens against discrimination. Given a vigorous history of state regulatory activism, it is surprising that Sweden was the last of the "big three" Scandinavian countries to adopt a comprehensive registered partnership law.

The movement for gay marriage in Sweden began as early as 1953, when the national Swedish gay and lesbian organization, Riksförbundet för Sexuellt Likaberättigande (the National Organization for Sexual Equality, or RFSL) sent a letter to the Swedish government asking for enactment of legislation to allow gay couples to get married.[80] The government never even bothered to reply to the 1953 letter, but proved more responsive to student demands in the 1960s. In 1967, Sweden's University of Uppsala treated gay and lesbian couples the same as married couples for purposes of student housing.[81] Two years later, Sweden's Social Democratic government put together a committee to look into legal regulation of persons who lived together without being married (similar to Denmark's Marriage Committee). As a result of this committee's work, Parliament in 1973 declared that "cohabitation between two partners of the same sex is, in society's opinion, a fully acceptable lifeform." This is probably the earliest modern government endorsement of same-sex relationships.[82]

During the next few years, RFSL and its parliamentary allies introduced a series of legislative proposals to improve the legal situation of gays and lesbians in Sweden, addressing antigay discrimination in housing, the labor market, and insurance options for couples. Recognizing that its members were largely ignorant of the situation of lesbians and gay men in their country, Parliament in 1977 created a Committee on Homosexuality to make a comprehensive analysis of the legal and social situation of homosexuals living in Sweden. The Committee conducted written and oral interviews with thirty-three hundred Swedes. It met with a large number of organizations with opinions on homosexuality, including religious organizations, left-wing interest groups, political institutions, specialists in specific subject areas, and academics and professors. In 1984, the Committee promulgated its 568-page report, whose twenty-six chapters covered a wide range of subjects that concerned homosexuals, from health to immigration, culture to the labor market, military service to religion.[83]

And cohabitating lesbian and gay couples. Of the thirteen hundred gay and lesbian Swedes interviewed by the Committee, 51 percent reported that they were currently living in a relationship, with an additional 41 percent stating that they would like to be living in such a relationship. Of the two thousand heterosexuals interviewed, 54 percent opined that two people of the same sex should not be permitted to get married with one another, while only 21 percent were in favor. The report demonstrated that part of the problem was the use of the terminology of "marriage." Many interviewed heterosexuals objected to the marriage of homosexual couples, but were willing to extend some legal benefits of marriage to such couples. For example, 46 percent agreed that same-sex couples should qualify for mortgages normally reserved for married couples.[84]

With this research in mind, the Committee on Homosexuality evaluated three legal options for gay and lesbian couples. It rejected the first option, *same-sex marriage*, largely because "present-day value judgments with regard to marriage are so firmly rooted that it is hardly possible to speak of marriage between two individuals of the same sex, without defining marriage in a different way from that practiced today." Recognition of same-sex marriage "would run completely against the overwhelmingly dominant opinion in society" as to what constitutes a marriage. Furthermore, the Committee worried about the international consequences of Swedish recognition of gay marriage, and felt that other countries might come to question the validity of Swedish marriage law. The Committee also rejected the second option, *registered partnerships*. It concluded that creation of a new and separate institution was not necessary, nor would it reduce discrimination against homosexuals, as it would single them out as a separate group rather than integrate them into the same legal rules that covered heterosexuals. The Committee endorsed the third option, to extend legal *cohabitation* to gay and lesbian couples. This option would not disturb people's beliefs about the nature of marriage yet would offer legal protections needed by gay and lesbian cohabitating couples.[85]

The Committee on Homosexuality also addressed the question of children in gay and lesbian relationships. It found no reason to believe that gays and lesbians make better or worse parents than heterosexuals; "homosexuality in itself may never be seen negatively in matters relating to custody, where the prime consideration is the well-being of the child." Furthermore, "there are no impediments to a right of joint adoption by two persons of the same sex." Yet the Committee rejected the idea of permitting gay and lesbian couples to jointly adopt children. Their concern was that children raised in homosexual households would suffer social disadvantages. "The situation is probably such that homosexual cohabitation is today not considered to be equally natural to that of heterosexuals, and we cannot disregard the fact that there may be a risk that adoptive children can come to regard themselves as deviant if they grow up in a homosexual family environment. The homosexual family must first be accepted as a natural part of society before two persons of the same sex should be allowed to adopt jointly."[86]

On the basis of this report, and with some pressure from RFSL, the Swedish government introduced a number of legal reforms regarding gays and lesbians, including the Homosexual Cohabitees Act, which Parliament adopted in 1987. This legislation extended legal protections to gay and lesbian couples living together in such circumstances as "divorce" (which governed the separation of property upon breakup of the relationship), death of a partner (granting inheritance rights), and taxation (treating such couples similarly to married couples under certain circumstances).[87] The Homosexual Cohabitees Act is a chief reason Sweden took longer than Denmark and Norway to provide the full range of marriage benefits for gay and lesbian couples. Having just granted a package of legal rights to such couples in 1987, Sweden did not feel much urgency after Denmark passed its registered partnership law.

Nevertheless, Denmark's 1989 law started the ball rolling again in Sweden. The RFSL convinced its contacts in the National Board of Health and Welfare to submit draft legislation on registered partnership to the government. Like the Norwegian legislation, the Swedish legislation was almost identical to the Danish model. In March 1991, the government created the Partnership Committee, to review the 1987 Homosexual Cohabitees Act and make recommendations about registered partnership. Released in November 1993, the Partnership Committee's report found a significant shift in social opinion as regards gay and lesbian couples.[88] In contrast to the earlier report, the Committee found that legal equality, and legal security for the couples, had become the predominant concerns.

> We do not feel it to be incumbent on society to have viewpoints concerning the way in which people choose to live together. Society's tasks ought instead to be that of enabling people to live in accordance with their own preferences and personalities, not preventing them from doing so, so long as this does not cause harm to others.

Furthermore,

> We wish to accommodate the desire of homosexual couples for a valuable setting for their relations, as a way of manifesting their love. . . . We also wish to accommodate the need of homosexual couples for economic and legal security in their relations. We wish to create

greater awareness of, understanding for and openness concerning homosexuality and homosexual relations. One important way of achieving this, in our belief, is by establishing, as far as possible, legal parity between homosexual and heterosexual cohabitation.[89]

Drawing from the foregoing factual material, the Partnership Committee presented its reasons in favor of a Danish-style registered partnership law. To begin with, legal unions that correlate with the rights of marriage would give gay and lesbian couples a greater amount of "emotional security." A formalized partnership would demonstrate, both to the outside world and to the partners themselves, "how profound and important their relationship is and that it must be taken seriously." Moreover, the Committee acknowledged that married heterosexual couples and homosexual couples generally have the same need for legal and economic protections in regard to their life together, and recognized that "an equivalent of the system of marital property rights probably cannot be achieved by written agreement" or, for that matter, by changes in specific laws. The Committee concluded that "partnership legislation is the only possible way of fully accommodating the need of homosexual couples for economic and legal security."[90]

Implementation of a partnership law, according to the Committee, would also have a "conditioning effect on attitudes." Permitting gay couples to enter into a partnership, openly and officially, "would make other people more aware of homosexuality and would contribute towards a more open attitude." The partnership law would speed up acceptance of homosexuals and homosexuality among the general public, which would have the reciprocal effect of making it easier for gays and lesbians to come out and to accept their own homosexuality. Finally, the Committee concluded that enactment of partnership legislation would lead to "equality, freedom, and justice." Equality in the sense that "our proposals imply equating homosexual love with heterosexual love, homosexuals with heterosexuals, and, last but not least, the minority with the majority." Freedom in that "homosexuals would get greater liberty, equaling that of heterosexuals, in choosing their form of cohabitation." And justice in that, just as any two people of the opposite sex can go to city hall and thereafter be covered by marriage legislation, so now could any two people of the same sex.[91]

Addressing objections to the law, the Partnership Committee acknowledged that many feel homosexuality to be against God's order and that the Bible includes passages suggesting that homosexual conduct is a sin. On the other hand, "the Christian message implies love and tolerance towards one's fellow beings." Furthermore, "the Bible is interpreted by other Christians in such a way that no condemnation of homosexuals can be read into it. In these circles, the gospel of love and the idea of universal human equality before God leads to an acceptance of homosexuality and, sometimes, to action in favor of partnership." The Partnership Committee then dodged injecting itself into this theological debate, concluding: "This is mainly a question of individual belief. Nor do we feel that religious aspects should determine our standpoint. This view is of course influenced by the fact that neither the Church nor other religious denominations will incur any ceremonial obligations in connection with entry into partnership." Like the Danish law, the Swedish proposal was not to include a church wedding for gay and lesbian couples who register.[92]

The Partnership Committee found "no justification" for allegations that a partnership law would undermine the institution of marriage or lead to a moral collapse. These kinds of fears, it stated, are simply "an expression of the moral panic which can occur in times of upheaval and change."[93] Like the earlier Committee on Homosexuality, the Partnership Committee rejected the possibility of allowing gay and lesbian couples to adopt children or have access to artificial insemination. On the one hand, "there is nothing to suggest that homosexuals make worse parents than heterosexuals," and "there is a great deal of research to suggest that children growing up in homosexual families do not differ from children growing up in heterosexual families." On the other hand, the Committee expressed concern that the existing research remained preliminary, at best. "In our view, failing a reasonable degree of consensus among researchers on the possible consequences to a child of growing up in a homosexual family, it is not appropriate for homosexual couples to be enabled to adopt or to be given access to various forms of artificial fertilization. For the same reason we feel that it should not be possible for homosexual couples to be made joint custodians of children." However, the Committee also made it clear that they did not want to dismiss the possibilities of adoption and insemination for gay and lesbian couples, and recommended that the government investigate this issue separately.[94]

Although the Partnership Committee gave Parliament the green light for enactment of registered partnership legislation, political conditions had changed in 1991 with a new, more conservative government, which included Sweden's religion-based Christian Democratic Party (CDP) as a coalition partner. As in Norway, this Swedish party precluded a government-sponsored bill, so gay activists (RFSL) proposed a private bill, which would be sponsored by individual members of Parliament rather than by the government. Although no private bill had been enacted without government support since

1866,[95] Parliament passed the Registered Partnership Act by a vote of 171 to 141. The new legislation, virtually identical to that of both Denmark and Norway, granted all of the same rights as marriage except for adoption and a church wedding. Previous laws on artificial insemination and other forms of assisted reproduction, which required that a woman be part of a heterosexual couple in order to apply for such services at public hospitals, were not affected by the new law.[96]

Iceland, 1996, and Finland, 2002

Isolated in the middle of the North Atlantic, Iceland was long considered the least gay-friendly of the Nordic countries. Even in the 1980s, it was difficult to be openly gay in Iceland, where gays and lesbians experienced discrimination in employment and housing, and often found it difficult to find romantic partners.[97] The first gay and lesbian organization in the country, Samtökin '78, was only established in 1978. Yet Iceland's 1996 registered partnership law became the most progressive one of its time, being the first of the Nordic laws to recognize joint custody of children growing up in same-sex households of registered partners. How did this small country of about three hundred thousand inhabitants move toward such broad legislative acceptance of gay and lesbian couples in such a short time?

The answer, in part, lies in the nature of the tightly knit Icelandic community. The small population means that Reykjavik (the capital) and other Icelandic communities are more like large villages rather than cosmopolitan cities. Icelandic gays and lesbians are therefore likely to be integrated into mainstream culture and to have many heterosexual friends. Thus, the average Icelander is more likely to know and work with someone who is gay or lesbian than in many other countries, which was significant as more and more gays and lesbians came out of their closets in the 1980s and 1990s. These "extended family values" among Icelanders made acceptance of their neighbors, and thereafter the legislation, easier for the public.[98] In addition, there is no strong fundamentalist religious party in Iceland. The lack of an organized center of opposition made it easier for the government to support a liberal registered partnership law.[99] While over 90 percent of all Icelanders belong to a Lutheran church, this state-sponsored Church is one of the most tolerant Protestant churches in the world. Another factor was the enactment of registered partnership legislation in Denmark, Norway, and Sweden. These laws put considerable peer pressure on Iceland to do the same. According to Lana Eddudottir, the former chair of

Samtokin '78, the Icelandic legislators "did not want to be seen as making a fool of themselves, because we like to think of ourselves as very educated people here in Iceland."[100] Thus, if the legislation had been good enough for the other Nordic countries, it was presumptively good enough for Iceland. In the end, only one member of Parliament voted against the partnership law.

Samtökin '78 paved the way for these developments by developing a network of gays and lesbians throughout Iceland. Lesbian and gay engagement with the media, through interviews and speeches, gave a face to homosexuality for the Icelandic population. Icelanders came to understand the lives and issues of their gay and lesbian colleagues, and acceptance of gays and lesbians came relatively quickly to the country. Pressed by gay lobbyists, Iceland's Parliament seated its own "HomoCommittee" in 1993, with an emphasis on addressing the question of registered partnership. When the Committee recommended registered partnership in October 1994, the government ordered the Ministry of Justice to draft the legislation. The lawyer drafting the legislation had herself sat on the HomoCommittee, and as the bill was drafted, it was decided to include the provision on joint custody of children growing up in gay and lesbian registered partnership households.[101] After a brief debate dominated by supporters of the legislation, Iceland's Parliament enacted the Registered Partnership Law in June 1996.[102] The reception for the first registered couples was attended by none other than the president of Iceland herself, as one of the guests of honor.

More religiously and culturally conservative than its Nordic neighbors, Finland was the last to join the ranks in establishing a comprehensive registered partnership law. The Finnish penal code listed homosexual conduct as a crime for both men and women until 1971, decades after such a crime was taken off the books in Denmark, Sweden, and Iceland. Unlike Norway, Finland vigorously enforced its law as late as the 1960s; it was the only Nordic country to prosecute lesbians as well as gay men. Even when Finland repealed its sodomy law, it adopted a new law prohibiting "encouragement of homosexual activity," meaning that no person or organization could speak out about homosexuality in any way that could be construed as being positive, or in practice even neutral, about homosexuality. This law was used as a tool to censure radio and television programs that touched on the subject of homosexuality.[103]

The Finnish gay and lesbian community was slow to organize in this harsh environment. The first national gay rights organization, Seksuaalinen Tasavertaisuus (Sexual Equality, or SETA), was founded in 1974. Although the issue of legal security for gay and lesbian couples was occasionally discussed within SETA, Finnish interest in a partnership bill was first sparked by news of the Danish statute in 1989. Before the Danish bill was passed, SETA and other gay activists in Finland had not given the idea of gay marriage much serious thought, in part because they had not conceived that the passage of such a bill could be possible in the Finnish Parliament.[104] In 1990, the Finnish Ministry of Justice seated a "Family Committee" to review a number of general issues regarding family law in Finland. On the subject of registered partnership, the Committee's 1992 report stated that "same-sex couples should have, if they desire, the possibility to register their partnership."[105] Nevertheless, a private bill introduced by allies of SETA in the Finnish Parliament in 1993 only managed to attract eleven signatures in a Parliament of two hundred, demonstrating the more conservative nature of the Finnish culture and politics.[106]

Enactment of partnership legislation in Norway and Sweden put pressure on Finland to follow. In August 1995, Finland passed legislation prohibiting discrimination on the basis of sexual orientation, and by early 1996 fifteen of the eighteen government ministers were in favor of partnership legislation. Unfortunately for SETA, one of the three against partnership was the minister of justice, whose department was in charge of such legislation. A new private bill introduced in May 1996 attracted fifty-eight signatures from MPs. The bill was referred to the Parliament's Committee of Law, which held hearings and received comments regarding the legislation. In September 1997, the Committee reported the legislation, with a favorable recommendation. Parliament then appointed a separate "Partnership Committee" to examine the details of what a Finnish partnership law should look like.[107]

In June 1999, this Committee recommended a registered partnership law in line with those existing in the other Nordic countries, with all the rights and responsibilities of marriage outside of adoption and a church ceremony. There was a division within the Committee over lesbian and gay adoption. Emboldened by Iceland's inclusion of joint custody for registered partners, SETA's representative on the Committee argued in favor of permitting adoption for same-sex couples. On the basis of the recommendations of the Partnership Committee, the government drafted Finland's own registered partnership bill. While the original version of the bill contained a ban on the ability of lesbian couples to use nongovernmental artificial insemination services in Finland, this provision proved controversial and was dropped. Without as much fanfare as had accompanied the Danish and Norwegian laws, Finland's Parliament passed the registered partnership law on September 28, 2001, and the law went into effect on March 1, 2002.[108]

Following the Nordic Lead: State Recognition of Lesbian and Gay Unions in Europe and Canada

With Denmark leading the way, the Nordic countries were a foundation for comprehensive state recognition of lesbian and gay relationships in the modern West. Ironically, only one country (the Netherlands) followed Scandinavia in establishing *registered partnerships*, but the Scandinavian approach of creating a new institution-not-called-marriage has been widely influential. And, as this book goes to press in late 2005, three European countries (the Netherlands, Belgium, Spain) and Canada have taken the next step and enacted statutes recognizing same-sex marriages. There will probably be more to come, including Sweden and other Scandinavian states. But what does all this activity abroad mean for same-sex marriage or civil unions in the United States?

New Family Institutions in Europe

The Danish registered partnership law inspired lesbian and gay activism around the marriage issue in Europe, North America, and even parts of Africa and Asia. In the next seventeen years, the West saw not only the first modern recognition of same-sex marriages in four countries but also a multiplication of new legal institutions providing partial state recognition. Only the Netherlands followed the Nordic terminology, *registered partnerships* (in a statute adopted in 1997). Elsewhere, new institutions flowered like azaleas in April—Hungarian *common-law marriages* (1996 statute), Belgian *statutory cohabitation* (1998), French *pactes civils* (1999), Canadian *common-law partnerships* (2000), German *life partnerships* (2001), Portuguese *de facto unions* (2001), and British *civil partnerships* (2004). Other authors have laid out the details of those statutory regimes, and the political debates surrounding them. We want to use these laws to make three general points about how these new laws expand upon the Scandinavian model.[109]

Process: role of courts as well as parliaments. Judges had almost no role to play in the campaign by gay rights organizations for same-sex marriage in Scandinavia—a striking contrast to their predominant role in the United States (chapter 1). Other countries have shown a different pattern from both America and Scandinavia. In 1995, for example, the Hungarian Constitutional Court ruled that it was unconstitutional for its common-law marriage law to exclude same-sex couples, but constitutional for the state to exclude such couples from civil marriage. Common-law marriage, established by a case-by-case factual showing of a common life together, entitles couples to most of the rights and obligations of civil marriage in Hungary, including mutual support duties, social security and pension rights, inheritance and other property rights, testimonial immunity, and so forth. Parliament codified the Court's ruling in the Common Law Marriage Act of 1996, which added same-sex couples to that institution. The Hungarian two-step anticipated a similar two-step in Vermont, where the judiciary struck down legal discriminations against same-sex couples and the legislature responded with the civil unions law (see chapter 1).[110]

Although there was no vigorous gay rights group pressing for the Hungarian Court's intervention, this has been the pattern elsewhere. Courts in Israel, South Africa, and Canada have found that state discriminations against same-sex couples violate the constitutional norms of those countries. Responding to Canada's well-organized and active gay rights organizations, the Canadian Supreme Court suggested in *M. v. H.* (1999) that all government discriminations against same-sex couples were suspect under the Canadian Charter's equality guarantees. Parliament's Modernization of Benefits and Obligations Act (2000) responded to this decision by extending most of the legal benefits and duties of marriage to "common-law partners." The provinces of Ontario, Quebec, and British Columbia created their own novel institutions to provide a greater measure of equality as well. Judges in neither Canada nor the other countries presume that their judgments are the final word; indeed, parliaments have the authority (rarely exercised) to override constitutional judgments under some circumstances in Canada. Instead, the point of constitutional, or sometimes statutory, judgments in these countries has been to *reverse the burden of inertia*—to insert the rights of same-sex couples onto the legislative agenda, and impose a presumption that equalization will follow.[111]

Courts are not inevitable allies for marriage rights petitioners. Lesbian and gay couples in France sued for the benefits of *concubinage*, statutory rights of cohabiting couples. In 1997, the French Cour de Cassation ruled that the surviving person whose partner had died of complications associated with AIDS could not succeed to the partner's lease, a right he would have had if they had been a cohabiting different-sex couple. The Cour ruled that "concubinage can only result from a stable and continuous relationship having the appearance of marriage, therefore between a man and a woman." In 1993, Gemany's Federal Constitutional Court also upheld the exclusion of same-sex couples from civil marriage. Even though the German Constitution guarantees a "freedom to marry," the Court ruled that such a right was limited to different-sex couples. Even in the Netherlands, perhaps the most gay-friendly country in Europe, the Supreme Court ruled in 1990 that Parliament could exclude lesbian and gay couples from civil marriage. The exclusion was not discriminatory, the judges reasoned, because Dutch law contemplated the possibility of procreation flowing from marital unions.[112]

New institutions are sometimes open to different-sex couples. With courts unwilling to recognize same-sex relationships, gay rights groups in both the Netherlands and France redoubled their efforts in the parliaments of both countries, with surprising results. Within weeks of the Dutch Supreme Court's decision rejecting same-sex marriage claims, a majority in Parliament requested that the government Advisory Committee for Legislation study the issue. A number of local authorities began registering same-sex partnerships, although such registrations held only symbolic, rather than legal, significance. Furthermore, the Danish Registered Partnership Act emboldened activists in the Association for the Integration of Homosexuality (COC) to seek full marriage rights; they suggested to the Advisory Committee that anything less than the Danish law would be a step backward.

In 1992, the Advisory Committee recommended a registered partnership law like that of Denmark, and the government introduced such a bill in 1994. Only after significant discussion in Parliament, along with amendments to the legislation, was it finally passed in 1997. The Netherlands became the fifth country to have a registered partnership law for same-sex couples, beginning on January 1, 1998. Unlike the Nordic laws, which transferred the body of marriage law onto same-sex couples by stating that "registered partnership" and "registered partner" would be synonymous with "marriage" and "spouse" for the purposes of reading family law, the Dutch legislation was much more complex, achieving its goal by amending over one hundred existing statutes relating to marriage to include registered partners. In addition, unlike the Nordic laws, the Dutch registered partnership law included different-sex couples, an expansion added during the round of compromises in 1997. Surprisingly, more than half of the couples entering into registered partnership in the Netherlands are different-sex. According to a Ministry of Justice study, straight couples choosing registered partnership rather than marriage did so because of an "aversion to marriage as a traditional institution" and their impression that "registered partnership is less binding than marriage" and can be exited more cheaply.[113]

As in the Netherlands, French AIDS and gay rights groups pressed Parliament in the early 1990s to enact a law patterned on the Danish statute, but packaged with a French flair. Gay groups pushed for creation of *contrats d'union civile* in 1992 and *contrats d'union sociale* in 1997; the latter were open to different-sex as well as same-sex couples. In the wake of the Cour de Cassation decision, the parties of the left campaigned in the election of 1998 on a platform that promised legal recognition of same-sex relationships and won a smashing electoral victory. In May 1998, the victorious parties introduced a bill proposing to create *pactes civils de solidarité* (PACS), which would allow different-sex as well as same-sex couples to assume mutual responsibilities for one another. On October 13, 1999, the National Assembly passed the PACS law in a party-line vote, 315 to 249.[114]

New "marriage lite" compromises. The biggest departure from the Nordic model was the creation of new lines of compromise, as countries struggled with clashing identity politics claims entailed by the same-sex marriage debate. Whereas the registered partnership models vested all but a few of the legal rights and duties of marriage and spousehood in a new institutional form, a separate-but-not-quite-equal regime for lesbian and gay couples, most of the new national statutes provided only some of the rights and duties of marriage. The main reason for this partial investment of rights and duties was the strong opposition roused by proposals that looked like same-sex marriage. Generally speaking, the stronger the religion-based opposition to same-sex marriage, the more likely a country was to do nothing or to adopt a *marriage-lite* institution rather than either same-sex marriage or registered partnerships.

Return to France, whose PACS is the classic example of marriage-lite. Proposals, even those advanced by gay activists, took account of the strong religion-based opposition to state recognition of homosexual relationships. The response to the Socialists' 1998 proposal was even stronger than its supporters expected. Thousands of letters poured into Prime Minister Jospin's office, protesting "the unspeakable and repugnant proposal for homosexual marriage." The Conference of Catholic Bishops denounced the proposal as "dangerous," and the Association of Catholic Families and the Families of France conducted an intense campaign against the proposal. Traditionalists in Parliament publicly compared homosexuals to "zoophiles" and argued that the bill would be "a return to barbarism." On January 31, 1999, Deputy Christine Boutin led a demonstration of almost one hundred thousand people against the bill, perhaps the largest such protest march in European history. The marchers carried signs reading "The homosexuals of today are the pedophiles of tomorrow," "No nephews for the big aunties," and "Jospin take care of your rear end!" Throughout the march, people reportedly shouted "Burn the fags at the stake!" Although this fierce opposition delayed but did not kill the bill, it served notice that its compromise features could not easily be expanded.[115]

A PACS is "a contract concluded between two adult individuals, of different sexes or of the same sex, to organize their life in common [*vie commune*]." Entering into a PACS is like entering into a contract: you and your partner fill out a PACS form, submit it to the town clerk, and you are "PACSed," as the French say. Partners joined by a PACS undertake to help one another "mutually and materially," and they are jointly liable to third parties for debts contracted by either of them "for the necessities of their daily life and for expenses relating to their common residence." Property purchased by the partners is presumptively jointly owned, and (after three years) their income is subject to joint taxation rules. Partners benefit from health insurance coverage, employment benefits (such as bereavement leave), and some social security rights. For straight, lesbian, and gay couples opting for PACS, the new law provides many of the legal benefits of married couples, but without most of the obligations and the difficulty of divorce. The law says nothing about sexual fidelity, inheritance rights, adoption, or obligations and rights toward children of either partner.[116]

The PACS law is marriage-lite in several respects. One is ease of divorce. Exiting a PACS is as easy as filling out a form, in contrast to the long and expensive marital divorce process in France. (This feature helps explain the popularity of PACS among different-sex couples.) Another "lite" feature is the law's silence on the matter of sexual fidelity. Although the law contemplates a joint life in common, and a sexual relationship between the partners, it does not impose the fidelity rules of marriage. These two features treat lesbian and gay relationships either like completely voluntary unions or less serious unions, depending upon one's normative perspective. A third feature, the omission of adoption or joint parenting rights, treats these relationships as unlike traditional parent-child families.

Other countries with strong traditionalist-religion political presences have either not acted or have adopted similar marriage-lite compromises. In Germany, for example, Roman Catholic opposition diluted the legislation creating a *life partnership* (*nichteheliche Lebensgemeinschaft*) for lesbian and gay couples. Registered couples are entitled to many of the benefits of marriage, including hospital visitation, immigration and naturalization (for registered partners of a German national), some coparenting rights, joint tenancy, inheritance rights, and pension and health insurance, as well as the main obligations, that is, mutual support and a formal process for dissolution of the life partnership, with the possibility of a judge-imposed directive for continuing financial support. The law excluded adoption rights, and traditionalists in the upper chamber of Parliament blocked that part of the law that would have given registered partners more of the state-supported financial benefits of marriage, namely, those governed by the labor, tax, and welfare codes. A similarly cautious process of compromise produced legislation recognizing de facto unions in Portugal.[117]

In November 2004, the United Kingdom's Queen Elizabeth II signed the Civil Partnerships Act into law. Opposition within the Church of England

and elsewhere motivated the cautiously progressive Labor government to avoid any statutory link to marriage rights and procedures. Since December 2005, same-sex couples have been able to register as civil partners, with a court procedure for termination. For these partners, the new law sets forth a duty to provide reasonable maintenance for civil partners and children of the family; assessment, in the same way as spouses, for child support; employment and pension benefits; inheritance rights; compensation for fatal accidents; and recognition for immigration and nationality purposes. Although carefully delinked from the marriage provisions of British law, the partnership statute does grant key obligations as well as benefits of marriage to registered couples.[118]

In June 2005, Switzerland became the first country to enact partnership legislation by a national referendum. On June 5, the Swiss population voted to approve of the Federal Registered Partnerships Act, which gives same-sex couples the same rights as married couples in a number of areas, including inheritance, pensions, and welfare benefits. The law is expected to come into effect in 2007.[119]

While Europe has taken the lead in providing same-sex couples with access to new institutions granting some or most of the benefits of marriage, other parts of the world are slowly following suit. In 2004, New Zealand passed the Civil Union Act, which opens up most of the benefits of marriage for either same-sex or different-sex couples. In a number of other countries, same-sex relationships are recognized in various forms at the state or regional level, including regions of Australia, Brazil, and Argentina, among others.[120]

Same-Sex Marriage in the Netherlands, Belgium, Spain, and Canada

While the Dutch registered partnership law (1997) generally followed the Danish model, there were some differences. Like the Danish statute, the Dutch law did not permit joint custody of children to registered partners. Thus, a registered partner in the Netherlands would not have legal rights (or obligations) over the children of his or her partner. (The Dutch Supreme Court confirmed this understanding in a judgment delivered a few months after the partnership law was enacted.) Unlike the Nordic model, a foreign partner of a Dutch citizen or permanent resident could not enter into a registered partnership, unless he or she had already acquired entitlement to residency in the Netherlands on other grounds. Finally, pension funds in the Netherlands were not required to treat surviving partners of pensioners in the same manner that they were required to treat surviving spouses. While surviving registered partners were entitled to a pension, it could be much smaller than those provided to spouses, as pension funds were permitted to calculate pensions to surviving registered partners based on only those premiums paid after 1997.[121]

Under pressure from lesbian and gay activists, the Dutch government addressed the inequalities between registered partnership and marriage, especially those related to rights over children reared in partnered households. Like the Nordic nations, the Netherlands created an expert commission, the Kortmann Committee, to examine the pros and cons of joint parental rights for registered partners. The Committee unanimously recommended in October 1997 that Dutch law should permit joint adoption of Dutch children by lesbian and gay partners, and the adoption of the child of one partner by the other. The government introduced such a bill in Parliament in July 1999, with this explanation: "A child being cared for and brought up in a lasting relationship of two women or two men, has a right to protection in that relationship, including legal protection." With little public opposition, Parliament enacted this law in December 2000. Also enacted in 2000 were other statutory amendments allowing foreigners without entitlement to residence in the Netherlands to enter into a registered partnership with either a Dutch citizen or a legal resident of the Netherlands, and equalizing the position of registered partners and spouses in relation to pensions.[122]

As Professor Kees Waaldijk, the chief architect of the Dutch movement toward equal treatment of lesbian and gay families, has explained, the passage of registered partnership in the Netherlands

> did not silence the call for the opening up of marriage. On the contrary, the social and political pressure increased. In retrospect, it seems that the whole legislative process leading to the introduction of registered partnership and joint custody, served to highlight the remaining discrimination caused by the exclusion of same-sex couples from marriage: the awkward exceptions [to marriage], and the *separate and unequal social status* of registered partnership as compared to marriage. With the introduction of the very marriage-like institution of registered partnership (alongside joint authority and joint custody, and individual adoption), the number of legal reasons *not* to open up marriage to same-sex couples was of course also approaching zero.[123]

It was only a matter of time.

Unlike the Scandinavian parliaments, which needed a breather from the issue of same-sex marriage after the registered partnership battles, the Dutch Parliament was receptive to gay marriage claims, in part because public opinion was strongly in favor of equal marriage rights, in part because faith-based opposition was not so forceful as in France or Germany or even Norway, and in part for local political reasons. As to the last point, the Christian Democratic Party (similar to the Nordic Christianity-based political parties) was not a government partner after 1994. Although the government itself still moved cautiously, the Lower House of the Dutch Parliament passed a resolution in 1996 calling for the opening up of marriage and adoption to same-sex couples. In response, the government created the Kortmann Committee, whose 1997 report on joint parenting by same-sex couples also recommended that marriage be opened up to those couples. The government initially supported just the joint-parenting recommendations, on the ground that marriage rights for same-sex couples were unnecessary after the passage of comprehensive partnership legislation. In April 1998, the Lower House of Parliament passed a new resolution demanding legislation that included same-sex marriage. After elections in that year, a new parliamentary coalition in August 1998 promised to introduce legislation to this effect. After a final issue regarding legal rights of same-sex parents was resolved, the Act on the Opening Up of Marriage was signed into law on December 21, 2000, taking effect April 1, 2001. At midnight on March 31, the first same-sex couples converted their registered partnerships into marriages.[124]

In 2002, Belgium followed the Netherlands in recognizing same-sex marriages, after introducing the interim step of "cohabitation legale" in 2000.[125] Pressed by court decisions enforcing the Canadian Charter of Rights, three Canadian provinces—Ontario, Quebec, and British Columbia—recognized same-sex marriages and started issuing licenses in 2003. Five other provinces subsequently followed suit. The Liberal Party government chose not to appeal those judgments to the Canadian Supreme Court and instead proposed legislation recognizing same-sex marriages everywhere in Canada. After three thousand same-sex couples (including 1000 from the United States) had already gotten married, the House of Commons voted 158 to 133 for such legislation in June 2005. Chief Justice Beverley McLachlin signed the Civil Marriage Act into law on July 20, 2005. Stephen Harper, leader of the Conservative Party, vowed to repeal the law if he were elected prime minister.[126]

Perhaps the most dramatic campaign for same-sex marriage came in Spain, the site of a notorious fifteenth-century religious inquisition. Led by José Luis Rodriguez Zapatero, the Socialist Party proposed same-sex marriage legislation in early 2005. The Roman Church fervently opposed the legislation. Its Bishops' Conference claimed gay marriage would "impose a virus on society" and would entail "a backward step on the path of civilisation." As many as half a million people, including bishops, priests, and nuns, staged a demonstration in Madrid in mid-June 2005 to protest the new law, although almost as many attended a rally that the gay community billed as a counter-protest. Rejecting the Catholic position, Prime Minister Zapatero told Parliament:

> We are not the first to adopt such a law but I am sure we will not be the last, many other countries will come after, pushed by two unstoppable forces, liberty and equality. . . . We are not legislating for people remote or unknown, we are increasing the chances of happiness for our neighbors, our friends, our work colleagues, the members of our family. It is true that [homosexuals] are only a minority but their triumph is a triumph for everybody, their victory makes us all better, makes our society better.[127]

On June 30, Parliament voted 187 to 147 in favor of the legislation, and King Juan Carlos II signed it shortly thereafter. On July 11, Carlos Baturin and Emilio Menendez, partners for more than thirty years, became the first same-sex couple to be joined legally in marriage. Thousands more have followed, but the debate has not ended. "The legal relationship between homosexuals must be different from conventional marriage," Mayor Mario Amilivia (of Leon) said in a statement explaining his decision to refuse to marry gays. "This type of thing only generates friction in society, in a gratuitous way."[128]

The International Marriage Debate and the American Experience

The foregoing discussion helps place the American same-sex marriage debate in a larger framework. Throughout the postindustrial world, lesbians and gay men are joining in committed partnerships, many of them rearing children. Once demonized by the state, this openly gay population now demands dignified and even equal treatment. Almost all postindustrial countries have repealed or nullified their laws making homosexual intercourse a crime, and most have eliminated other state discriminations. Unequal treatment of lesbian and gay couples has become increasingly questionable, especially in countries that offer legal benefits and duties to different-sex cohabiting couples. The main arguments against state recognition of lesbian and gay unions—the definitional, stamp-of-approval, and defense-of-marriage arguments—gained traction because same-sex marriage was such a novelty. Legislatures all over the world were able to dodge the issue, until Denmark enacted its registered partnership law in 1989. Since then, same-sex unions or marriages have been on the political agenda of every state with a large openly gay population. (States whose lesbian and gay citizens have remained hidden from view, securely in the closet, have generally not been under pressure to consider this matter.)

In the many years since Denmark acted, the response has been diverse. Some governments, such as those in Scandinavia and Vermont, have followed Denmark to create new institutions carrying all or almost all the legal entitlements of marriage but not the name. Others, such as France and California, have created new institutions with many but not all the entitlements of marriage. The Netherlands, Belgium, Canada, Spain, and Massachusetts have gone all the way to same-sex marriage. Table 2.1 provides a snapshot view of the different benefits and obligations accorded same-sex couples under various legal regimes discussed in this and the previous chapter.

The jurisdictions that have recognized same-sex marriages, partnerships, and civil unions share several common features. Most important, equality-seeking lesbian and gay political groups have been active for many years in all the recognition-conferring jurisdictions except Hungary. Marriage or partnership recognition did not come out of the blue but after decades of political and community activism in the Nordic and other European nations discussed in this chapter. Such activism proceeds in a roughly predictable pattern. The initial task is usually to persuade legislators to repeal consensual sodomy laws, so that homosexuals are not per se criminals, to be harassed at will by the police. As more lesbian and gay citizens are open about their sexual orientation, it becomes both important and possible to obtain legislation protecting gays against hate crimes and private as well as public discrimination. Such laws make it possible for lesbian and gay culture to integrate with mainstream society; if that happens, gays will seek some legal protections for lesbian and gay couples. Municipal and regional governments may act first; if the sky does not fall, national governments may follow. It takes years of "equality practice"—experience with progay legislation and openly gay citizens—for mainstream citizens to become receptive to the concept of gay people as citizens presumptively entitled to full legal equality. (More on this theme in chapter 6.)[129]

So the first feature of a jurisdiction recognizing same-sex marriage or marriage-lite institutions is a legislative track record of progay reforms, including antidiscrimination laws. A second feature is suggested by the empirical work of Professor Lee Badgett. She reasons that there ought to be social variables that help explain why it is that certain countries are willing to adopt progay legal reforms, including recognition of same-sex partnerships. She identifies three potentially significant ones, which we think are interrelated: (1) broad (even if not universal) acceptance of sexual minorities, (2) low salience of fundamentalist religious views in public debates, and (3) relatively high rates of cohabitation among straight couples.[130] All of these social variables point to an underlying social phenomenon that is friendly to gay rights generally and same-sex unions in particular: most citizens

Table 2.1

A European Menu of Partnership Recognition Options

	Cohabitation (Hungary); De Facto Unions (Portugal)	Pactes Civils (France)	Life Partnership (Germany); Civil Partnership (United Kingdom)	Registered Partnerships (Scandinavia)	Marriage (Netherlands; Canada; Spain)
Employee Health etc. Benefits	✓	✓	✓	✓	✓
Joint Property; Lease Sharing	✓	✓	✓	✓	✓
Family and Bereavement Leave	✓	✓	✓	✓	✓
Wrongful Death Claims	✓	✓	✓	✓	✓
Mutual Support	✓	✓	✓	✓	✓
Various State Safety-Net Benefits	✓	✓	✓	✓	✓
Surrogate Decisionmaking Capacity	✓	✓	✓	✓	✓
Income Taxation		✓	(✓)*	✓	✓
Joint Parental Rights over Partner's Kids			✓	✓	✓
Inheritance			✓	✓	✓
Joint Adoption			(✓)*	(✓)**	✓
Dissolution thru Formal Proceeding			✓	✓	✓
Fidelity Requirement				✓	✓
Cultural Association with Traditional "Marriage"					✓

*Not available in Germany

**Stepchild adoption in all countries; adoption of unrelated children only in Sweden.

accept a norm of tolerable sexual variation, and relatively few are personally invested in the traditional definition of marriage. We are not suggesting that religion itself is unimportant in jurisdictions recognizing same-sex marriages or partnerships. Danes have a strong foundation in religion, but their religion emphasizes the inclusive and tolerance messages of the Gospel and less attention to the Old Testament and Pauline rules of sexual conduct.

Thus, countries most likely to recognize same-sex marriages or partnerships are those that have decriminalized sodomy and enacted antidiscrimination laws, that see relatively high cohabitation rates and tolerance among the heterosexual mainstream, and that have experienced little involvement of fundamentalist religion in politics. The Scandinavian and Benelux countries rank high on these scales, and so it is no surprise that they were pioneers. (Nor is it surprising that Iceland and Finland were the last of the Nordic nations to act, as they had not developed track records of progay legislation, and in Finland's case included many traditionalists.) Contrariwise, countries least likely to recognize same-sex marriages or partnerships are those that have little history of progay legislation, low cohabitation rates, and a more important role for traditional religious views, including anti-homosexual views, in politics. Thus, the new nations of eastern Europe and the Roman Catholic bastions in southern Europe and Ireland have done nothing or adopted more modest state recognition regimes.[131]

The third feature suggested by the European experience is that local politics remains highly relevant, and determinative in the short term. Under the aforementioned progay reforms and social conditions approaches, Sweden would seem to have been the odds-on favorite to recognize same-sex marriage first. (Sweden had a long track record of progay legislation, and its 1987 Homosexual Cohabitees Law was the first of its kind. Sweden ranks first in cohabitation rates, and traditionalist viewpoints play relatively little role in its politics.) Yet Sweden was not the first to recognize same-sex marriage, or even the first (or second) to recognize marriage-like registered partnerships. Politics are hard to predict, and local political shifts have determined the fate of marriage or partnership proposals. The socialist tilt of the Nordic and Benelux nations assured an audience for experimentation with institutional forms for state family recognition. Contrariwise, conservative governments, with participation by Christian democrat types of parties, precluded partnership recognition in countries such as France, Germany, the United Kingdom, and Spain—until those governments were replaced by socialist or labor ones.

An irony of history: President George W. Bush, a critic of gay marriage in the United States, helped bring it to Spain. The "Coalition of the Willing" that Bush assembled to invade Iraq in 2003 included Spain, a move that was highly unpopular with Spanish voters. After terrorists bombed a train station in Madrid days before the 2004 elections, presumably to retaliate against Spanish cooperation, voters turned the conservative government out and gave the Socialists a big parliamentary majority. (The government contributed to its own demise by erroneously blaming the bombings on Basque dissidents.) And in July 2005, the Socialists delivered on their campaign promise to recognize same-sex marriages. Even though Spain does not have a long track record of progay legislation and has relatively low cohabitation rates and a moderately powerful Roman Catholic presence in politics, local politics created circumstances ripe for same-sex marriage. It remains to be seen whether a return of the prior government (the Popular Party) to power would result in repeal or significant modification of the new marriage law.

Return to Denmark, where it all began. In downtown Copenhagen in 2005, LBL held a celebration for Axel Axgil's ninetieth birthday. While Eigil had passed away in 1995, after forty-six years together with his beloved partner, the story of the Axgils, slowly morphing into legend, remains a powerful one among gays and lesbians in Denmark. While not directly involved in the later years of the political fight for same-sex partnerships, their relationship continued to be held up during the struggle for same-sex legal unions as an example to all gays and lesbians—that it is possible to find one's life partner, and that there can be a "happily ever after" for same-sex couples. As the Axgils aged and physically became more frail, their relationship also served as a reminder of why the issue of same-sex marriage, and the need for the legal possibility to secure one's partner, was so important.

Despite the early years of legal and social persecution experienced by Axel and Eigil in Denmark as they tried to establish a safe environment for gays and lesbians, the Axgils both lived long enough to find themselves exchanging vows in Copenhagen's city hall, and becoming the main love story on a chilly October day for news outlets around the world. While their carriage ride through the cobblestoned streets of old Copenhagen may have been seen by some as little more than quaint symbolism, the Axgils themselves knew that theirs was but the first same-sex wedding of thousands, if not millions, more to come around the world in the decades ahead. As history is likely to remember, their life spent together is a true demonstration of the old cliché: true love conquers all.

CHAPTER 3

A New Look for Legal Unions
Sixteen Years of Scandinavian Partnerships and the Changing Conception of Family

Peer Toft and Peter Mols at home.

Many traditionalists believe that marriage, as a definitional matter, is comprised of one man and one woman. But meet the new face of marriage in Scandinavia: Peer Toft and Peter Mols.

Tall, blue-eyed, with a chiseled jaw and full lips, Peer is classically handsome in the Scandinavian tradition. His partner, Peter, has virtually the same light brown hair, eye, and skin color; he could almost be Peer's twin. Sitting down for an interview, the two are giddy, and giggle like schoolchildren. There is an air of playfulness between them, reminiscent of a young couple in their earliest stages of romance. One almost expects them to begin pillow-fighting.[1]

Yet these two men are no longer adolescents. At the time of our first interview, in 1997, Peer, a thirty-nine-year-old policeman, and Peter, a thirty-five-year-old naval engineer, had been together for fifteen years. They met in one of Copenhagen's gay discos, where they caught each other's eye. Peer invited Peter home to his house that night, even though he was only twenty and living with his mother at the time. "The next morning," according to Peter, "Peer went downstairs to wish his mother goodbye before she went to work. I was in the bedroom, and I heard her ask him: 'Did you bring someone home last night?' Peer said yes, and then she asked, 'Is it a boy or a girl?' Peer replied that it was a boy. There was a pause, and then his mother said, 'Hmmm.' Then she left for work. I met her three days later, when I came back to the house as a guest for dinner."[2]

Despite the initial awkward episode with Peer's mother (whom Peter soon won over), the two found themselves quickly falling in love. Before long, they were virtually inseparable, and the relationship grew deeper and stronger as the years passed. In 1992, after ten years together, Peer and Peter tied the knot and entered into a registered partnership. They describe themselves as a "normal couple." Indeed, as forty-something, well-educated male professionals living in Copenhagen, Peer and Peter are, demographically, the *typical* couple under Denmark's Registered Partnership Act. But why are same-sex couples in legal unions more likely to demonstrate certain demographic characteristics over others?

The first part of this chapter will explore the typical features of registered partnerships in Denmark, Norway, and Sweden, and why we see such patterns. The underlying reasons shed light on the larger normative debate, especially the definitional objections to same-sex marriage. By their very existence, Scandinavian registered partnerships (and certainly Dutch, Belgian, Spanish, and Canadian same-sex marriages) cast new light on the definitional claim that "marriage" has never been understood as anything but a different-sex union. The stories of registered couples like Jean Luscher and Diana Skovgaard (from our introduction) or Peer Toft and Peter Mols (and others) undermine the related claim that the unitive purposes of marriage can only be served when the couple is male-female. These lesbian and gay couples are committed to one another in a way that is hard to distinguish from the commitment of one-man, one-woman marriages. Has registered partnership started Denmark (and the other Nordic nations) down a slippery slope toward polygamy, incest, and child marriage? There is not the slightest evidence of this. If you ask Danes this question, they think you are joking.

Just as the definition of *marriage* has been opened up by the Scandinavian experience, so has the definition of *family*. The second part of this chapter explores a type of partnership not originally contemplated by the Scandinavian partnership laws—lesbian and gay couples raising children within the relationship. An increasing number of lesbian couples, and some gay male couples as well, are bearing and raising children within their partnerships, and doing so successfully. Their life experiences are changing the way Scandinavians conceive of family. (Peter Mols, for example, has attempted to have a child with a lesbian couple through artificial insemination.) Commissions of experts have recommended changing registered partnership laws to reflect this new conception. As of 2006, Denmark, Norway, and Sweden have adopted either some or all of such changes, and Iceland and Finland are likely to follow.

Changing too is the way Scandinavians understand their religious faith. This chapter's third and concluding part examines the dynamic relationship between the new legal unions and religion. Originally, the partnership laws in Denmark and all the other Scandinavian countries provided that the state Lutheran churches would have no role in celebrating or recognizing lesbian and gay unions. Some Danes, such as Peer and Peter, have become alienated from the Church because of this unwelcoming attitude, but other Danes are working within the Church to produce more welcoming attitudes. Slowly, but increasingly, the Church has been reaching out to its members who live in same-sex unions. Thus the future of the Christian tradition, as practiced in Scandinavia, offers hope for couples like Peter Mols and Peer Toft.

The Demography of Registered Partnerships in Scandinavia

How Many Couples Are Taking Advantage
of the Registered Partnership Laws?

When Denmark was debating its partnership law, opponents warned that granting same-sex couples the rights of marriage would lead to an unimaginable volume of same-sex couples from around the world descending on Denmark. Their country, they cautioned, would become an international gay Las Vegas. Danes feared this would arouse the ire of foreign governments, whose lesbian and gay citizens would return brandishing a marriage certificate from Denmark and demanding home-country recognition. Parliament dealt with these international concerns by restricting partnership eligibility to Danes and their foreign partners (later expanded to include long-term noncitizen residents and citizens of countries that have comprehensive same-sex partnership or marriage legislation that corresponds to the Danish legislation). So Americans like Jean Luscher, whose partner is Danish, can marry, while their colleagues who are not tied to a Dane are left out. But dual-citizenship couples aside, proponents and opponents alike believed that there would be many thousands of Danish couples like Peer Toft and Peter Mols who would take advantage of the law.

Such fears—or hopes—have not been realized. The numbers of same-sex couples who have entered a legal union have been, at best, modest. For Denmark, a total of 5,953 persons were classified as being in a registered partnership in 2005.[3] In comparison, 2,155,743 persons were listed as being in a marriage.[4] In Norway, 1,293 partnerships were contracted between 1993 and 2001, compared with 190,000 marriages, for a ratio of seven partnerships per one thousand marriages. And in Sweden, 1,526 registered as partners between 1995 and 2002, while 280,000 persons married in this period, for a ratio of 5:1,000. Relative to the total population of their respective countries, the number of couples who have entered into a registered partnership is very small. With 5.4 million people, registered partners in Denmark account for less than 0.1 percent of the population. The same is true for Norway (population 4.6 million) and Sweden (population 9.0 million), where less than one of every thousand residents is in a registered partnership.[5]

The percentage of the gay and lesbian population of these countries who have entered into partnerships is relatively small. Under a conservative assumption that 1 percent of the entire population of these countries is homosexual (about fifty-four thousand gays and lesbians in Denmark, forty-six thousand in Norway, and ninety thousand in Sweden), no Scandinavian country sees even 10 percent of its gay and lesbian population in a registered partnership. Using a more liberal estimate, that gays and lesbians constitute 5 percent of the population, less than 1 percent of the gay and lesbian population of Sweden or Denmark, has taken advantage of the legislation.[6]

Nevertheless, these numbers are rising. As figure 3.1 shows, the aggregate number of registered partnerships in Denmark (netting out partnerships that have dissolved) has grown significantly each year—tripling in the first four years of the law, and doubling again in the last ten years. There is not yet a stable plateau, because some couples are still making up their minds, and the first generation of Danes to have grown up with the partnership law is only now coming of marrying age. Peer Toft and Peter Mols, for example, did not rush to the altar. They waited three years to register, and then did so only after a trip to the United States revealed to them how politically important the Danish approach was to the rights of gay people everywhere in the world. Nonetheless, even as they grow, the numbers re-

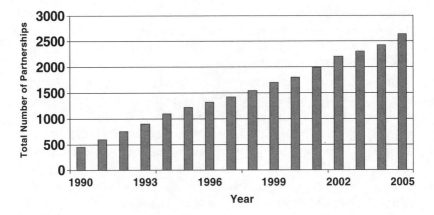

Figure 3.1
Total number of registered partnerships (netting out dissolved partnerships) in Denmark, 1990–2004. Source: Statistics Denmark.

main modest. Why so few registered partners? To supplement the stories we heard from Danes who actually did register, we also conducted a survey of 812 gay and lesbian Danes in 2005, which tested various explanations for the low rate of registration.[7] Consider some of the theories.

Separate and unequal: registered partnership as second-class marriage? Perhaps the most obvious reason more have not registered is that registered partnership is a separate-but-unequal institution that does not satisfy same-sex couples who want to "marry." Some of the couples we met raised this concern, but it does not appear to be the primary reason for low registration rates, as most gay and lesbian Danes do not claim to draw a deep distinction between "registered partnership" and "marriage." More than three-quarters of the 812 Danish respondents to our on-line survey said they considered registered partnership "about the same thing" as marriage. Like Peer Toft, almost four-fifths said they used words like "marriage" and "spouse" to describe their relationship.[8]

Of those surveyed who had not previously been in a registered partnership, about three-quarters stated that they would enter into a registered partnership if they found "the right person." One-quarter said they would not or were unsure. We asked that last one-quarter whether they would reconsider if the law were changed to give full and equal marriage rights to same-sex couples. Just over one-sixth said they would, a third said they would not, and almost half were uncertain.[9]

These results suggest that the distinction between registered partnership and marriage has not had a great effect on the choice of Danish gays and lesbians to legalize their unions. Only twenty-four of the respondents said they would not consider registered partnership, but would consider marriage if that were available as a legal option. While many couples in registered partnerships would like to see the name of their union changed to "marriage," some of our interviewed couples preferred registered partnership over marriage because of the negative connotations they associated with marriage. In contrast to his partner, who usually refers to their relationship as a marriage, Peter Mols put it this way: "No, we don't like to call ourselves 'married'—if someone asks us if we're married, we say, 'No, we're not, we're registered.' We like to be different in that way. A registration is not a marriage because a marriage thing is a church thing. Why should we pretend to submit ourselves to an institution that is so conservative?"[10]

Some Danish same-sex couples associate marriage with boredom. "It implies living in the suburbs, seeing your parents-in-law every Sunday, and only making love every Sunday night after the evening news," says Anne-Vibeke Fleischer, who has been with her registered partner, Elisabeth Bjerre Knudsen, since 1985.[11] Uffe Størner, who was previously married with children before meeting his partner, Kaj Kristensen, in 1983, has a similar opinion on marriage: "An ordinary heterosexual married couple lives together, and they stay home a lot, maybe playing cards with their friends and some trips to the beach or the woods. That's not us—we do some of that, but we go out more, and we have a lot of fun and crazy friends."[12]

Registered partnership laws have been unfriendly to couples raising children. Another suggested reason for the low numbers of registered partnerships is the fact that certain rights given to heterosexual married couples are unavailable to registered partners. As we explain in the next section, registered partners originally did not have the right to adopt their partners' children, and children born within the partnership were treated as children of single parents. These features of the law have been mentioned as a factor that might discourage registration by female couples especially.

Take the case of Birgitte Haase and Kirsten Jepsen, who live in southern Jutland with their young daughter, Maia. The couple met in 1985, and by the early 1990s decided to have a child. While Kirsten had adult children from a previous marriage, she and Birgitte decided that they wanted a child of their own relationship. With the help of an anonymous donor, Birgitte became pregnant after several attempts over a two-and-a-half-year period. Maia was born in 1993. Her birth was a joyful event, but Kirsten found herself in a frustrating position. If they registered, Kirsten would have mutual support obligations for both Birgitte and Maia, as the mutual support provisions of marriage law apply equally to registered partners, but she would have no parental rights as regards Maia. That is, in the eyes of the law, there was no legal relationship between Kirsten and her nonbiological but beloved daughter.[13]

Kirsten and Birgitte nevertheless *did* register in 1994, notwithstanding their objections to this ongoing discrimination. And the available data suggest that such discrimination was not a significant reason for the low registration figures. In 1999, Denmark changed its law to allow stepparent adoption. But that legal change did not result in any significant uptick in the number of couples entering into registered partnership after 1999. Sweden in early 2003 lifted the restrictions on all forms of adoption by registered partners, without any discernible effect on registration, yet. The evidence, thus far, does not support the hypothesis that stepchild restrictions have kept people away from registered partnership.[14]

Marriage and registered partnership as patriarchal institutions? Some feminists (mainly lesbians, but also some gay men) want nothing to do with any institution that even resembles marriage. Traditionally, Scandinavian marriage, like its American counterpart, entailed rigid gender roles backed up by legal rules and sanctions. The formal rules imposing such a *patriarchy* are long gone in Scandinavia (as in America), but marriage still carries associations with that philosophy. Under marriage laws of the Nordic countries, women are sometimes presumed to be the weaker, more dependent partners, as demonstrated by a number of old Danish gender-specific laws that offer legal protections to the wife alone (e.g., the right to a widow's pension). It has been suggested that registered partnership is seen as no less of a patriarchal institution than marriage. Such sentiments could be responsible for a limited interest among same-sex couples. Together with restrictions on joint parental rights to children, this might help explain why female couples have been less likely to register than male couples in all the countries except Iceland.[15]

But the very nature of the partnership laws undercuts this argument. Anne-Vibeke Fleischer, a self-proclaimed "longtime political lesbian," recalls how her thinking on registered partnership has changed. The editor of Denmark's largest gay and lesbian magazine called her up to set up an interview in 1989 regarding the new registered partnership law. "When the law passed the Parliament, she knew I was very much against it. At the time, I felt it was very politically incorrect to marry. It was a conservative, heterosexual model. So we set up the interview, but then I began thinking about it—and the longer I discussed it with others, the more I thought, 'what's wrong with it?' It's a very practical piece of legislation," she reflected. For example, Anne-Vibeke and her partner Elisabeth "could secure each other economically. She could have my property and I could have hers if something happened to either of us. So in the end, I changed my mind, decided I was for it, and couldn't do the interview after all."[16]

Indeed, the gender neutrality of the partnership legislation creates a formal challenge to the Danish presumptions of dependence for female spouses and authority for male spouses. The assumed model of the breadwinning male and homemaker female cannot apply to all-male or all-female couples. It may nevertheless be granted that, simply because registered partnership by its very nature may not support a patriarchical model, this does not necessarily translate into the absence of a perception that marriage and registered partnership are equal in this regard, and therefore this may have some minor effect on the number of couples who register.[17]

Cultural conditioning discourages gay marriage. A more plausible factor pressing some couples not to marry is cultural conditioning. How does one react when marriage or partnership, which has never been considered as a serious option in one's life, suddenly becomes a valid option? Many gays and lesbians, for whom this option only first became available during their adult lives, were already "culturally conditioned" to envision marriage as unavailable to them as a way of understanding or structuring their family life. Even for those who envisioned eventually settling down with a significant other, the "opening up" of marriage may have struck many as a bit odd or foreign in concept. And do not forget that in the 1970s and 1980s, straight Danes were running away from marriage, a point we shall develop in chapter 5.

Peer Toft and Peter Mols are good examples. Each realized from an early age (as early as age six for Toft, sixteen for Mols) that they were attracted to other boys, and not to girls. As young Danes, each assumed that he would never get married; in tolerant Denmark, there was less social pressure to enter into a phony marriage than there historically has been in the United States. But neither had any model for a long-term homosexual relationship. Even gay-friendly movies, television, and novels depicted homosexual relationships as fun but fleeting; other cultural signals depicted them as sad and tragic. Like other couples of that era, Peer and Peter stumbled into a long-term relationship and found that it worked for them. The Registered Partnership Act provided a model for their relationship, but neither man thought much about registering until 1992, three years after its passage. Surely, other gay and lesbian partners chose not to tie the knot because they had worked out their relationships on their own terms and, like straight couples before them, found state-sanctioned marriage or partnership an idea whose time had passed.[18]

Closeted couples would be outed by public registration. Even in the tolerant Scandinavian countries, there is some anxiety about homosexuality, and many gay and lesbian people are at least partially closeted. When Peter Mols first got a job as a policeman, he kept his sexual orientation (and his homosexual relationship) a secret at work, as did Peer Toft when he began working as a naval engineer. They even maintained separate addresses. "We wanted to show that we were just as good as anyone else—we didn't want to be judged by our sexuality. So we kept a low profile. We wanted them to know us as people first rather than gay. We were young then too, and not so confident."[19] Even today, more than a decade after they registered as partners, neither man is completely out of the closet in his work environment.

The regime of the closet is particularly severe outside Copenhagen, Oslo, and Stockholm. Couples living in small towns or rural areas outside these urban security zones may have fears as well as discomfort in registering their partnerships at city hall. While some of this homophobia may be falsely perceived by such couples, many of them may choose not to register their partnerships rather than risk a miniature scandal in their small towns. Consider the story of Claus Rasmussen and Niels Andersen, a blue-collar couple living in Kaas, a little town in northern Jutland. Niels, who is about twenty years older than his partner Claus, has a teenage son from a previous marriage. After several years together, Claus and Niels decided that they wanted to register in order to secure inheritance rights for each other, should something happen to either one of them. At first, they went to the local city hall of their small town in 1996, with the plan to apply for a partnership license. According to Niels, "the town hall clerk told us, 'you're the first couple here in town to try this, and we don't want to do this here because people will talk. And we know that Niels has a son and [this could harm him].' So we decided to do it in [the larger city of] Aalborg so people wouldn't talk about us. We didn't want to create a sensation here."[20]

Like Mols and Toft, Rasmussen and Andersen ultimately decided to go through with the registration. But how many other same-sex couples did not? We do not know how many, but we are certain that the remnants of the closet remain an important reason militating against *public* registration, especially for couples living outside the more progressive city centers like Copenhagen.

Only a small pool of committed same-sex couples exists. One final explanation is that there are not so many same-sex couples living in committed relationships in the Nordic countries. It is possible, but unlikely, that there are relatively few lesbians and gay men in the Nordic nations. More plausible is the possibility that lesbian and gay Scandinavians are less likely to be in committed long-term relationships than their straight counterparts. There are several reasons this might be the case. During the 1970s and 1980s, when most of these gay people were coming of age, there were no cultural models of committed same-sex partnerships readily available, as we explained earlier. Moreover, gay men in particular are less likely to have children within their relationships, and lesbians (today) may be somewhat less likely to have children than straight women and men. Children tend to cement relationships, in part by creating a shared project involving both partners. Perhaps most important, lesbians and gay men are financially independent, relatively speaking. Financial dependence of one spouse on another is an economic motivation for partners to commit to one another, especially if they intend to raise children within the partnership.[21]

A factor we should neither emphasize nor rule out is the supposed lack of monogamous commitment attributed to gay men by many well-meaning as well as prejudiced observers. The average gay man in most Western countries has more sexual partners than the average straight man, straight woman, or lesbian. That phenomenon may have purely social roots, or deeper biological reasons, but whatever the cause it probably contributes to some reluctance among at least some, and perhaps many, gay men to marry. Yet, just as complete sexual fidelity is not essential to many heterosexual relationships in Scandinavia (or the United States), so it is not to same-sex partnerships. Moreover, registered partnerships have led to changes in sexual behavior, either eliminating sex outside the relationship or giving rise to changes in extramarital sexual practices to protect the health and well-being of one's partner (a point we explore in the next chapter).[22]

Registered Partnerships Have Been More Popular among Gay Men than Lesbians

Lesbian couples, in Scandinavia as well as the United States, are more likely to rear children and to be sexually monogamous than gay male couples are. One might think, therefore, that more lesbian couples would register as partners. Probably for these reasons, in the United States, lesbian couples have joined in Vermont civil unions (between 2000 and 2003) at much higher rates than gay men have.[23] Are we Americans copying the Scandinavians? Not at all.

Overall, the total number of men in registered partnerships is significantly greater than the number of women. In Denmark, there were approximately 1,617 male couples and 1,359 female couples registered in 2005. In Norway, 979 male partnerships (61 percent of the total) and 637 female partnerships (39 percent) have been registered between 1993 and 2003. In Sweden, 1,794 male partnerships (61 percent) and 1,149 female partnerships (39 percent) have been registered between 1995 and 2002. Figure 3.2 graphically illustrates the yearly pattern in Sweden, which is typical for all the countries except Iceland. Espe-

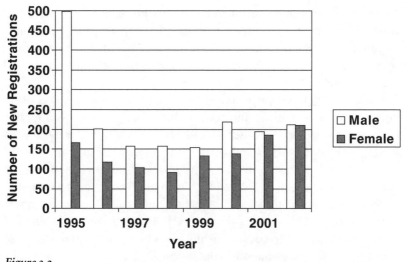

Figure 3.2
Male versus female registrations in Sweden, 1995–2002. Source: Statistics Sweden.

cially in the first few years of registered partnership in each of these countries, the number of men entering into partnerships was several times higher
than that of the number of women, reaching up to almost five times higher
in the first year.[24]

Looking back at the history of registered partnership, this pattern seems
almost predictable. Female couples were especially prone to skepticism toward registered partnership because the original laws discouraged family formation and, for some feminists, were indistinguishable from the patriarchical
institution of marriage. In contrast, gay men had a stronger incentive. When
the AIDS epidemic descended upon Denmark in the mid-1980s, the same
horrific survivorship struggles played out in Denmark as in the United
States—stories of surviving long-term partners with no legal rights in their
relationship, who could only sit by helplessly as the family of the deceased
partner claimed legal right to all of the decedent's estate. Once the partnership law was passed in 1989, a number of these couples wanted to secure the
partner's legal rights of survivorship. Thus the early years of registered partnership likely found those same-sex partners who felt most vulnerable—that
is, gay men—the most motivated to register their partnerships.[25]

Moreover, gay and bisexual men have greater incentives for registering
on the basis of their higher levels of income and material wealth. Even in
Scandinavia, with more equal job opportunities for women, men still have
a higher level of income then women, on average. In Denmark, for example,

the typical woman in the private sector earns approximately 86 percent of what a man would earn.[26] Men, therefore, have had a greater economic incentive to register in order to provide financial security for their partners without inheritance complications or high taxes in case something should happen to them.

Legal union among men has also been higher due to the greater likelihood of gay men entering into relationships with partners from foreign countries. The percentage of female couples with one non-European partner is 3 percent in Norway and 9 percent in Sweden. In contrast, the percentage of male couples with one non-European partner is 19 percent in Norway and 21 percent in Sweden.[27] (We do not have data for Denmark.) These patterns reflect the social fact that men are still more mobile, as well as richer, in Western societies than women. And they reflect the legal fact that marriage or registered partnership solves many of the practical problems presented by transnational relationships.

Take the case of William Waite, a thirty-three-year-old musician from Indiana, and Ken Nielsen, a twenty-one-year-old student of theater design in Copenhagen. They met in Lithuania, where the American was teaching music and the Dane was taking an English course. The two immediately fell for each other, and a relationship ensued. However, Ken's English course was of a limited duration, and he soon found himself preparing to return to Denmark. William was willing to move to Denmark to be with Ken, but had no legal means for staying in the country. Thus, they decided that if their relationship were to continue, registered partnership would be their only option. "I had a hard time deciding to get registered so quickly," Ken related. "It was a very big commitment to go into at my age—so I had to work on it with myself until I was convinced that it was the right decision for the time. But it was either we got married or he had to go home."[28]

Another reason for the disparity between male and female registered partnerships is that there are probably more self-identified gay men than lesbians in Scandinavia. Samples from the United States and Europe suggest that, in today's modern societies, a significantly higher percentage of men than women self-identify as homosexual. This may reflect an underlying biological disparity that persists over time or, more likely, social phenomena affecting men and women differently. Recall Jean Luscher, the Fulbright scholar. Unlike Toft and Mols, who knew they were gay during their early teenage years, Luscher gave the matter of her sexual orientation little thought until she was propositioned by a fellow Bryn Mawr student. It is not uncommon for men to have firm views about their sexual orientation, often at a very young age. Openly gay men tend to be more firmly set in their sexual orientation, while women remain less dogmatic. For many women: "Well, it just depends on the person!"[29]

On average, gay men are also more visible than lesbians. This owes something to the more dogmatic feelings gay men have about their sexual orientations, but perhaps even more to the fact that men have long been more publicly visible than women in Western societies. Whatever its reason, this may have contributed to the fact that male couples dominated the registered partnership rolls in the early years. There may be no better way for gay men to broadcast pride in their homosexuality to the world than to send out their same-sex wedding announcements. To the extent that women are more discreet as well as ambivalent about their orientation, they would be less likely to make it a matter of public record.

Ironically, the gendered pattern has changed over the past few years. The numbers have equalized somewhat, with gay men entering into registered partnerships at about the same rates as, or even somewhat less than, lesbians. In 1998, for the first time, the number of women entering into registered partnerships in Denmark was higher than the number of men. Sweden saw female couples reach rough parity with male couples in 2001 and 2002. In Norway, the number of registering female couples has not yet surpassed the number of male couples, but they were almost equal in 2000. Since its law took effect, Iceland has seen a few more female than male couples register. The recent gender equalization may owe something to the fact that Denmark, Sweden, and Norway have eliminated the stepchild adoption restrictions of their original registered partnership legislation (and Sweden has gone further). Some lesbian couples who first rejected the idea of registering their partnership due to the adoption restrictions, as well as those who disliked the patriarchal setup of the institution of marriage, have given up their objections and have entered into registered partnership as an acceptable institution.[30]

Age of Registered Partners: A Wide Variation,
but a Focus on the Middle-Aged

While registered partners range in age from eighteen to their nineties, it appears that same-sex couples wait longer to enter into a legal union than their heterosexual counterparts. While the mean age of heterosexual couples entering into their first marriage was about thirty (32.2 in Denmark in 2003, up from 28.6 in 1989), the mean age of gays and lesbians entering into registered partnership was in their late thirties, approaching forty. In Sweden, half of the male partnerships have been contracted by couples where the mean age of the couple was over forty. Compare this to heterosexual couples in Sweden, where only 14 percent of new marriages have a mean age of over forty.[31]

The age of entry into registered partnership has been relatively constant since 1989. Even in the Danish law's first few years, it was gays in their thirties, then their forties, who dominated the demographics. Peer Toft and Peter Mols, our demographically average couple, illustrate a common pattern of thinking about, and postponing, state registration. Although they had been together since their early twenties, they chose not to enter registered partnership until November 1992. According to Mols, "we could have gotten registered much earlier, but we really didn't see a reason to do it when we first talked about it. We didn't think that much about mutual support if one of us became disabled or died—we were young, and we could both do fine on each of our own salaries." It was only after they saw friends becoming ill, and became more aware of their own mortality, that the idea of legal union sounded more compelling to them.[32]

Same-sex couples, furthermore, tend to approach legal union with more pragmatism than their heterosexual counterparts. Modern cultural conditioning presses straight people toward weddings early in their relationships, but has not exerted similar pressure on gays. For this reason, one should expect gay couples to marry at an older age. This also helps account for the more casual way many same-sex couples approach their wedding day, as recounted by many interviewed couples in regard to their wedding ceremony. When Toft and Mols set a date at City Hall, for example, they decided to keep it low-key. "We didn't tell anyone. . . . It wasn't a big deal for us. We'd already been together ten and a half years. To our wedding we wore jeans and our regular jackets. And we were late. And our mothers, who were the only people we invited, said, 'Why are you late?'" To which Toft jokingly responded, "We couldn't decide which one of us was going to wear the white dress."[33]

These age-of-registration patterns for same-sex couples may not persist, of course. Because legal union has only been an option for less than two decades even in Denmark, the average age of contracting a partnership will be skewed by the fact that many older couples have taken advantage of an option that was not available before. On the other hand, older gay men and lesbians are less likely to be open about their sexuality, hence also less likely to take advantage of this law than their younger counterparts, who are more comfortable with the idea of gay marriage. These two factors suggest that the average age of same-sex partners at the time of their legal union may decrease in the future.

In addition to a higher mean age, registered partners differ from their heterosexual married counterparts in that there is a greater likelihood of a greater age spread between the two individuals in a partnership. Although Toft and Mols are only four years apart in age, Eddie Moris and Jens Boesen are separated by nine years, Diana Skovgaard and Jean Luscher by fifteen years, and Claus Rasmussen and Niels Andersen by nineteen years. Overall, more than one-third of the male couples have an age spread of at least ten years in Norway and Sweden; this number is much lower for female couples. In comparison, about 9 percent of heterosexual couples have such an age spread in Sweden.[34] We do not know why gay male partners, in particular, exemplify such striking age differentials, beyond the banal observation that male partnerships, as a social matter, involve such differentials. Throughout Western history, middle-aged and older men have formed sexual relationships with younger men. Traditionally, these relationships have been more pedagogical and economic than romantic, but the romantic features have certainly blossomed in the last century. There remains something sexy, for many gay men, about "May-October" romances.[35]

Registered Partners Are Mainly City-Dwellers

Most of the registered couples live in urban areas. Toft and Mols live and work in the Danish capital of Copenhagen, which in 2005 was home to 904 registered partners, or 34 percent of the Danish total. The greater Copenhagen area, which includes its suburbs, is home to one-quarter of the Danish population and more than one-half its registered partners. In Norway, about 62 percent of all male couples and 45 percent of all female couples reside in the greater Oslo area (which is home to 11 percent of the Norwegian population), while in Sweden 47 percent of all male couples and 36 percent of all female couples reside in the greater Stockholm area (approximately 21 percent of the total population).[36]

It is no surprise that most registered partners are located in urban areas. As in other countries, the large majority of gay people feel more comfortable in urban areas, and often move there after discovering their sexuality. Farm and small town communities expect their young people to marry persons of the opposite sex, exactly as Diana Skovgaard (now Jean Luscher's partner) did at age twenty-one, right after she finished college. (Her first son was born nine months and fifty minutes after the wedding ceremony.) Like Diana, many lesbians and gay men still living in less developed areas remain closeted and therefore unattached to a same-sex partner. Even when partnered, they are less comfortable with the idea of making a public statement of their sexuality by getting registered in the local city hall. As Claus Rasmussen and Niels Andersen discovered, small town city halls tend to be less comfortable with same-sex couples. In many less populated areas, homosexuality is still frowned upon—or at least not something to flaunt through a public ceremony. It was from the rural parts of each of the Nordic nations that the greatest opposition to the registered partnership law came. In such areas many gay and lesbian couples may choose not to draw local attention to themselves through registration of a partnership.

Many Registered Partners Have Previously Been Married

A high percentage of lesbian and gay registered partners have previously been in a heterosexual marriage, many of them with children. Diana Skovgaard, for example, had been married to a man for thirteen years. In Norway, 15 percent of all male registered partnerships and 26 percent of all female registered partnerships have at least one member who has previously been in a heterosexual marriage. In Sweden, this number is 20 percent of male registered partnerships and 27 percent of female registered partnerships. About the same percentage of heterosexual spouses have a history of a previous marriage.[37]

These data suggest a significant amount of switching from heterosexual relationships to homosexual ones, though not from a homosexual orientation to a heterosexual one. This also suggests the following hypothesis. Lesbians and gay men with more conservative values—including a traditional sense of family—will on average be the most attracted to the institution of marriage. Those with a conservative upbringing and/or more traditional values may be more prone to rejecting their feelings of same-sex attraction until a later age; hence they may not come out as homosexual (to themselves or others) until later in their lives. Meanwhile, bowing to social expectations, they may have already entered into a heterosexual marriage. Even after they acknowledge their homosexuality, their conservative values and traditional sense of family make them more likely than others to envision marriage as a model family structure. More progressive gays and lesbians, on the other hand, who may be more comfortable with their sexual orientation from an earlier age (and therefore less likely to have a heterosexual marriage), may feel less tied to traditional notions of family, and therefore less interested in marriage or partnership to validate their relationship.

Registered Partners Are Relatively Well Educated

Lesbian and gay couples who have registered their partnerships have a significantly higher level of education than the general population. Approximately 83 percent of the Danish population (aged twenty to sixty-six) finished their schooling after completing the basic education, roughly through the end of high school. Only 12 percent have achieved the equivalent of a bachelor's degree or higher. In contrast, 65 percent of all Danish registered partners stopped at the minimum level of education, and 27 percent of those partners had achieved the equivalent of a bachelor's degree or higher.[38]

Norway and Sweden reveal the same pattern. An empirical study conducted by Gunnar Andersson and his colleagues found that the percentage of same-sex registered partners in Norway and Sweden where at least one of the two partners had a tertiary education at the time of entering into a partnership was between 56 and 67 percent, compared to 44 percent for all new heterosexual marriages.[39] As the Andersson group suggests, if one considers that younger people are more likely to have higher levels of education and that registered partners are on average ten years older than their heterosexual married counterparts, the actual educational divide is likely to be greater if age were taken into account.[40]

Andersson's study also analyzed the educational *orientation* of registered partners in Norway, compared to those of married spouses. It found the greatest differences for married versus partnered women in the areas of liberal arts education (as compared to a technical education), which was much higher for partnered than married women, and in administrative work, which was higher for married women than for partnered women. For men, the greatest differences were also in liberal arts education, which was higher for partnered men, in technical education, which was much higher for married men, and in health care, which was higher for partnered men.[41]

Registered Partners Tend to Hold Professional Jobs

Registered partners are worker bees. In almost every household we interviewed, both partners worked outside the home. They hold professional jobs that run the gamut of industries, such as vaccine supply (Diana Skovgaard), interpreter (Jean Luscher), lithography (Eddie Moris), and creative designer (Kirsten Jepsen), as well as the more traditional occupations of schoolteacher (Birgitte Haase), policeman (Jens Boesen and Peter Mols), and engineer (Peer Toft).

Moreover, these registered partners tend to hold relatively high-level positions within their industries. In Denmark, approximately 14 percent of registered partners working within a company or organization hold an executive position, compared to only 8 percent of all workers in the general population. Eighteen percent of registered partners hold managerial positions in such entities, while 13 percent of the population hold similar positions. There are a smaller number of registered partners in lower level positions. Twenty percent of Danish registered partners are nonmanagerial staff in white collar work, as compared to 22 percent of the general population. And when it comes to blue-collar work, the differences are much greater: 4 percent of the registered partners are skilled laborers, compared with 8 percent of the general population. Only 7 percent of all registered partners are unskilled workers, while 16 percent of all Danes are. There are nevertheless some occupational similarities: 6 percent of the registered partners are self-employed, and 10 percent are unemployed, compared with 7 and 9 percent in the general population, respectively.[42] (See figures 3.3 and 3.4.)

One explanation for the occupational differences is the higher level of education achieved by individuals in registered partnerships. Another partial explanation may be related to the fact that many same-sex couples register primarily for economic benefits, such as the smooth transfer of property from one to another in the case of death of one of the partners. This suggests that the higher their occupational position (and therefore the greater their earnings), the greater the incentive gay and lesbian couples

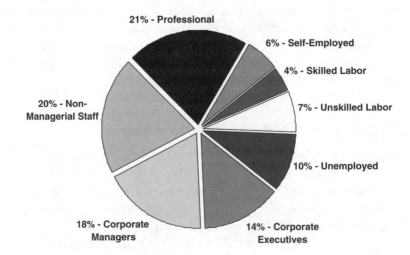

Figure 3.3
Job categories for Danish registered partners. Source: Church Report on Blessings.

Figure 3.4
Job categories for the Danish general population. Source: Church Report on Blessings.

have to register their partnership. Furthermore, those gay men who are blue-collar workers may also be living in more conservative blue-collar communities (i.e., smaller towns) and may therefore be more reluctant to publicly register their relationship.

Registered Partnerships Sometimes End in Divorce

Unlike most of our demographic variables, which are measured at the time of entry into a marriage or registered partnership, divorce statistics can only be measured at the termination of such relationships. Therefore, we approach an analysis of divorce statistics with caution, because of the short history of registered partnerships. Only after registered partnerships (or same-sex marriages) have been in existence in Scandinavia for a generation or more will we be able to draw more definite conclusions on the patterns of divorce for same-sex couples. Nonetheless, with three of the Scandinavian countries having had registered partnership for at least a decade, it might be useful to make some tentative observations about the patterns of divorce among same-sex couples.

Because the institution is new, divorce rates among same-sex couples have changed in the years since registered partnership was introduced. In the early years of the laws, divorce rates among same-sex partners were low.

For example, Norway registered 758 male and 471 female partnerships between 1993 and 2001, but entered only sixty-two (male couple) and fifty-six (female couple) divorces during the same period. The ratios between registering and divorcing couples were 1:13 (male) and 1:9 (female). Similar patterns exist for the other Scandinavian countries.[43]

Although interesting, such data are not terribly meaningful. The numerator (number of divorces) ought to be much higher for heterosexual married couples because the pool of potential divorces, and the time frame from marriage to divorce, is much larger, even relatively speaking. Scandinavians have been getting married throughout the twentieth century, and so the pool of marriage breakups is much higher than the pool for partnership breakups (whose pool has been constructed for little more than a decade). These raw data also do not take into account a number of demographic variables. For example, this absolute number does not take into account the effects that such demographics as age, education, nationality, and children—and other demographics that differ between spouses and partners—have on the rate of divorce.

Gunnar Andersson and his colleagues did a sophisticated comparison between Norwegian and Swedish partners who registered and those who married during a relatively similar time period. They not only compared the raw number of breakups for each group but also considered whether different breakup rates could be explained by other variables such as age and income. According to their study, same-sex male couples had a somewhat higher risk of divorce than their heterosexual counterparts, and female couples had a significantly higher risk of divorce than gay men. (These higher rates persisted even when the authors considered other divorce-inducing variables.) The authors suggest that the higher divorce rate for gay and lesbian partnerships owes something to the fact that traditional social norms and the exclusions in the Scandinavian registered partnership acts (for adoption and joint custody) created hurdles for lesbian and gay couples to engage in the family-building and joint parenthood that holds many couples together. The trend in divorce rates is one worth following, as it will reveal much about the dynamics of the new institution.[44]

As one would expect from the experience of straight people, divorce risks are greater for those who marry or enter a registered partnership at a younger age; this risk decreases as the registering couple's age increases. Likewise, the greater the age spread between the individuals in a marriage or registered partnership, the greater the risk of divorce. (This holds true for all groups surveyed except Norwegian female couples.) Divorce risks are about the same for couples living in urban areas (Oslo and Stockholm) but are greater for partnerships and marriages with a foreign partner or spouse, with even greater effect if the partner/spouse is non-European. The risks are also higher for couples with lower educational achievement. Other variables had different effects for different groups. For example, while the existence of a previous heterosexual marriage for at least one of the partners in a marriage had a strongly negative effect on heterosexual married couples surveyed (increasing the risk of divorce by 77 percent), such previous marriages had a much lower effect on the risk of divorce for registered partners who had previously been married.[45]

For those registered partnerships where at least one of the partners has children existing from a period before entrance into a registered partnership, the patterns are different for males and females. For male couples, previous parenthood somewhat increases the risk of divorce, whereas for female couples it cuts the risk, slightly. Heterosexual couples seem to be at increased risk where at least one of the partners has a previous child. However, this conclusion can only be tentative, because the Andersson study did not differentiate between children belonging to both members of the couple, and children that were born to one member of the couple and another parent. Furthermore, the study did not include information on whether such children were being raised within the partnership or by the other parents.[46]

Same-Sex Couples with Children: Redefining Family in Scandinavia

Of the differences between registered partnership and marriage, none has been more contentious than children's issues. While the Danish parliamentary supporters of registered partnership were able to sidestep the issue of children in 1989 by creating a blanket exception on the ability of registered partners to adopt, this proved to be a temporary solution. The original partnership laws in Denmark, Norway, and Sweden prohibited any type of adoption within registered partnerships. This bar included three types of adoption: (1) "stepparent" adoptions, where one becomes the legal second parent to the child of his or her spouse/registered partner; (2) joint adoption by a couple of children within the country (i.e., Scandinavian children), or (3) adoption of children from abroad. The first kind of prohibition reflected ignorance (and possibly, residual homophobia) among lawmakers, but the second and third prohibitions have social and political roots.

In Scandinavia (as well as many other countries such as the United States), adoption policy has revolved around the concept of "what is best for the child."[47] As understood in Scandinavia, this has historically meant rearing by a committed male-female couple, since it has traditionally been believed that a child grows up best where there are a mother and father present. The complete exclusion of gay and lesbian couples from adoption policies meant that same-sex couples could not have joint custody of children they were raising together in a household.[48] Thus, the government has encouraged adoption (and artificial insemination) only in such cases where the child would be raised by different-sex parents, namely, a man and a woman.

This reasoning has been fatal to the adoption hopes of same-sex couples, because there are few children available for adoption in the Nordic countries. Sex education and the availability of birth control have enabled those countries to enjoy very low rates of unwanted pregnancy—but as a result, few children are given up for adoption. For example, only about twenty-five Danish children are available for adoption each year. In 2004 this number was fifteen.[49] There have always been more male/female couples desiring to adopt Danish children than there have been such children available, and therefore in practice these children are not available for same-sex couples. Because of the dearth of Nordic children, over 90 percent of children adopted in Denmark and its neighbors come from foreign countries. These children, too, have been unavailable to same-sex couples. Adoption organizations and the government have long feared that permitting gays and lesbians to adopt children would cause foreign officials to cut off the supply of babies to Denmark, in order to ensure that they would not be adopted by gay parents. Thus, as a matter of adoption policy, registered partners have been prohibited from adopting children from foreign lands.[50]

In the last fifteen years, these policies have come under fire in all the Scandinavian countries. The process by which their parliaments have responded has been gradual as well as cumulative, each country learning from what its Nordic sister states have accomplished. And it has been social and cultural, driven by the fact that lesbian and gay registered partners are already raising children within their relationships, and they are doing it well.

Children in Lesbian and Gay Households

Even in 1989, when Denmark enacted its partnership law, children were growing up in lesbian and gay households. As figures 3.5 and 3.6 demonstrate, the number of partnerships with children has exploded since 1990. Today, almost one-sixth of all partnerships in Denmark are raising children. The absolute as well as relative figures will surely continue to rise. Approximately two-thirds of the young (under age thirty) lesbians and gay men in Denmark who responded to our survey reported that they want to raise children, most of them within committed relationships.[51]

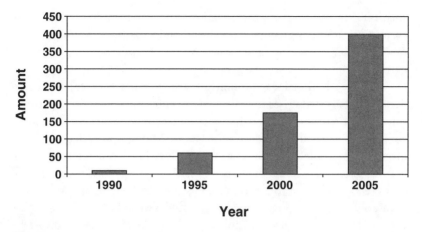

Figure 3.5
Number of Danish registered partnerships raising minor children, 1990–2005. Source: Statistics Denmark.

Some couples had children before they became registered partners. Recall Birgitte Haase, Kirsten Jepsen, and their daughter Maia. Birgitte and Kirsten knew that they wanted to start a family together, regardless of the lack of legal security for their family. Under the 1989 statute, Maia, born in 1993, had only one legal parent, her birth mother Birgitte, even after the couple registered in 1994. Notwithstanding the legal wrinkle, Maia deep-

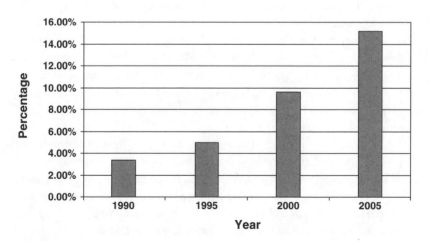

Figure 3.6
Percentage of Danish registered partnerships raising children. Source: Statistics Denmark.

ened Birgitte and Kirsten's own relationship, as they bonded over family events. "We love to go camping together," said Kirsten. "We also go swimming together all the time, and we take Maia to horseback riding and gymnastics lessons."[52]

With the additional responsibility of raising a child, Birgitte and Kirsten decided in 1994 that it was time for them to enter into a registered partnership. "The first time we thought about getting married, in 1990, we were going to get married to publicly show that we belonged to each other," says Birgitte. "We wanted to show how much we loved each other. It would have been a big step for us, emotionally speaking. But by the second time, we knew we were a couple, and so it was more to secure each other, and Maia, economically. Without being married, you would have to fill out a lot of paperwork and even then you would not be legally covered in most situations the way married couples were. So we decided that the only solution was to get registered." The ceremony itself was marked by gaffes on the part of the official administering it, as there had never been a registered partnership before in their little town of Haderslev. But the couple's friends, neighbors, coworkers, and parents cheered their decision and showered them with gifts.[53]

If they had chosen to wait in 1990, why go through with it four years later? On the one hand, they knew in 1994 that if Birgitte were to die or become incapacitated, Kirsten would not automatically have any parental rights over Maia. This could lead to the problematic situation where the nonbiological parent, raising a child as his or her own, could find himself or herself suddenly in a complicated legal battle to continue raising his or her own child should something happen to the biological parent. Ironically, Kirsten retained financial responsibility for Maia (due to being in a registered partnership) while simultaneously being denied the legal rights of a parent. On the other hand, "we wanted Maia to have married parents like other couples," said Birgitte. "And we also wanted to make sure Maia was secured economically." Thus they were willing to overlook the deficiencies of registered partnership and focus on the benefits they thought that legal union would bring to their family.[54]

In contrast to Kirsten Jepsen and Birgitte Haase, other couples started thinking about children only after they became registered partners. Our "typical" couple, Peer Toft and Peter Mols, is one example. As Peter stated, "We've been talking about having children. I tried for three years to have children with a lesbian couple—but we didn't succeed. We even tried going to a clinic. And once the woman had a miscarriage. But we never actually had a baby. . . . The child would have lived with them but we would have been involved as parents." This disappointment has not completely extinguished their interest in raising children. They are not interested in adopting an infant but would consider adopting "an older Danish boy or girl who had problems with their own parents."[55]

Peer and Peter's experience, as well as those of others (and including our survey findings) suggest that Denmark's creation of a new institution for recognizing and formalizing lesbian and gay relationships has triggered increased interest in *family* as well as *marriage* among Scandinavian homosexuals—especially gay men. Although gay men are increasingly interested in family formation, it is much harder for them to accomplish than for lesbians. Unless one of them has a child from a previous relationship with a woman, the men must make arrangements with a female acquaintance or (more likely) a lesbian or lesbian couple who want some kind of joint parenting arrangement. But Denmark's original partnership law did not allow gay men to adopt, nor did it allow the nonbiological father any rights over the child.[56]

The Law Slowly Relents—Joint Custody and Adoption Rights

Couples like Toft and Mols, as well as Haase and Jepsen, have well-formed views and criticisms of the child-based discrimination in Danish partnership law. Toft put it this way: "Politicians are focusing on the concept that gay men would adopt little boys and they would abuse them. That's how some of them think. I don't think they are afraid lesbians would do this to their daughters, but some are afraid that gay men would do this to their sons." It's not clear that many legislators actually had this argument in mind, but the argument itself is nonsense. Studies have shown that openly gay men are less likely to abuse children than men married to women. Mols added, "If they are worried about third world countries' opinions, why don't they just put some kind of choice in the law that countries can opt out of having gay couples adopt children from their country?" (This screening process has since been adopted; see the discussion of Sweden later.) Birgitte Haase has a broader explanation. "So many things in Denmark are changing," she says. "It's becoming a multicultural society, and many people feel that Denmark is falling apart and we are losing our culture." Homosexual adoption, she explains, fuels conservative fears that the idea of what a normal family is supposed to be, is being threatened.[57]

As the number of registered partnerships with children continued to soar, and critical voices such as these grew increasingly vocal in the 1990s, LBL, the Danish national gay and lesbian organization, brought those stories and concerns to the attention of the Danish Parliament. Similar to the stories it related about men dying from AIDS in the 1980s and the lack of legal recourse for their surviving partners, LBL pointed out the legal injustices that were being created by the blanket restrictions on adoption in Denmark. Other gay and lesbian groups have pressed their respective parliaments in Sweden and Norway. Recognizing that there is a problem, legislators are now moving to bring the legal rights of same-sex registered partners into line with those of heterosexual married couples. The process by which this is occurring is slow but sure.

Generally, younger politicians are more likely to take the lead in this issue, because they are more comfortable with homosexual unions and the concept of same-sex couples raising children. Thirty-five-year-old Frank Jensen, the Danish minister of justice, was the sponsor of legislation to relax the existing adoption restrictions on registered partnership. In 1999, a parliamentary committee proposed to add the following language to the Registered Partnership Act: "A registered partner can adopt the other partner's child, unless the child was adopted from a foreign country." Legislative debate on this amendment in May 1999 made clear that members of Parliament had become less afraid of the idea of same-sex parenting over the past decade. Of the seven members who spoke out on the bill as representatives of their parties, only two (the Christian People's Party and the Danish People's Party) spoke against the bill.[58]

Those in favor of permitting registered partners to have access to stepchild adoption focused their arguments not on the rights of gay and lesbian couples, but rather on what is best for the child. As Yvonne Herlov Andersen of the Central Democrats (the party sponsoring the bill) put it, "this is a question about the child's legal equality. We can keep away from the debate about gay rights in general, which is very difficult to discuss in this parliament. This is moreso concerned with the question about the rights of the child; that is, the child's right to have two legal parents."[59] Member of Parliament Dorte Bennedsen added, "This is not a place to decide on whether or not we believe that a child is best off with both a father and a mother; we should make a decision based on the facts and on that obvious truth that today there are children that live with a parent who is in a registered partnership."[60] Proponents of stepchild adoption further argued that, at present, many children living with a parent in a registered partnership were worse off than other children, who had the legal protections of a second parent should the first one die. Furthermore, children living with a parent in a registered partnership would be at a disadvantage for inheritance purposes and for a number of other laws as well.[61]

Opponents of the legislation expressed concern that allowing gay and lesbian couples to adopt stepchildren was the beginning of a slippery slope that would ultimately lead to a right to adopt foreign children, and could therefore threaten the flow of adoptable children into Denmark. Notwith-standing this argument, the legislation passed in 1999, giving registered partners the option to adopt their partners' children as their own (just as married stepparents are able to do). In addition, if one of the partners has adopted a Danish child as his or her own, the other partner may also adopt the child. The 1999 legal reforms still do not allow stepparent adoption, however, if the child was adopted by the one partner from a foreign coun-try. In a bow to the traditionalists in Parliament, the government accepted the argument that permitting adoption by the other partner could stem the flow of children available for adoption from other countries. But the change is an important step in resolving a number of problematic situa-tions that have existed since the passage of the partnership law. Long Maia's caregiver and devoted parent, Kirsten Jepsen can finally be her legal mother as well.

Recall how the Scandinavian countries tend to move in similar patterns when one of them adopts a new legal policy. In 2002, Norway adopted simi-lar stepchild legislation but took it a slight step further than Denmark. The Norwegian legislation allows for adoption not only of a registered partner's biological child but also of a registered partner's child who was adopted by the first partner, either domestically or internationally. If the child was an international adoption, the adoption can only occur if the country of ori-gin allows for stepchild adoption.[62]

Also responding to the call to recognize the growing number of same-sex couples raising children, the Swedish Parliament in 1999 appointed the Commission on the Situation of Children in Homosexual Families. The Commission included eleven political appointees from each of the parties in Parliament as well as twelve specialists and experts in the field. Its charge was to investigate and analyze the existing conditions for children in homo-sexual families. Analyzing more than forty international studies on children in same-sex families, as well as additional studies conducted by the Com-mission within Sweden, the goal was to determine whether or not the existing restrictions on same-sex couples in relation to children were justi-fied, and if not, what changes should be made. As always, "the reference point for the Commission's considerations should be the best interest of the child." The Commission issued its report in 2001.[63]

After a thorough analysis of the existing studies and their own additional studies, the Commission concluded:

> The combined research shows that children with homosexual parents have developed psychologically and socially in a similar way to the children with whom they were compared. Nor did any differences

emerge as regards the children's sexual development. For some children, conflicts may arise at certain stages of growing up that are
related to their parent's sexual preferences. These mainly relate to
the fact that in the early teens they may experience their parent's
homosexual preference as a problem in relation to peer groups and
children of the same age. Research shows that children's ability to
handle such conflicts depends on how [their relationship] is to their
parents. Children growing up in a loving environment where the child
is the focus of its parents' love and care are well equipped to handle
crises and conflicts of this kind. Nor have any differences emerged from
the research between homosexual and heterosexual parents as regards
their ability to offer children good nurturing and care.[64]

Therefore, "in the light of what has emerged in the research in the field, the
Commission considers that the legal differences that exist today regarding
homosexual and heterosexual couples' abilities to adopt are no longer
objectively justified."[65]

In its discussion of insemination for lesbian couples, the Commission
also addressed the often-argued point that it is in the best interest of the
child is to have a mother and a father.

A basic value in Swedish legal rules relating to children and parenthood is that a child has the right to two parents. Traditionally the
attitude has been that it is best for the child to have parents of different sexes. But the studies that the Commission have examined or
commissioned show that a child's developmental potential is just as
good in a homosexual family formation as in a heterosexual family
formation. If a child is to develop well, it makes no difference if
the parents are of different sexes or of the same sex. There is therefore—on the basis of the principle that the child should grow up
in favourable conditions—no reason to exclude a couple from the
chance of obtaining assisted insemination solely on the grounds
that they are of the same sex.[66]

Because younger people are more positively disposed toward the concept of
gay parenting than older people, the Commission opined that same-sex
families would continue to be less stigmatized in the future. "The attitude to
allowing homosexuals to adopt is to a great extent a generational question.
The younger generation is considerably more positive towards or neutral to
homosexuals being allowed to adopt children than the older generation. There
is therefore reason to assume that the small children growing up today in a

homosexual family are in a different situation in relation to the attitude of those around them than the children who are now grown up."[67]

Finally, to address the expressed concerns that Third World countries would stop making their children available for adoption in Sweden if same-sex couples were allowed to adopt children together, the Commission asked two questions of the twenty-five countries that contributed the most children to adoption in Sweden in 1999. One question was whether such countries would consider allowing same-sex couples in Sweden to adopt children from their country, and the second question was whether such a policy would adversely affect the possibilities for heterosexual couples in Sweden to adopt children from such countries. Every one of the seventeen countries that responded to the first question stated that only heterosexual couples would be considered as adoptive parents. In respect to those that answered the second question, seven countries stated it would not adversely affect heterosexual couples' chances for adoption; one (Ethiopia) stated that it probably wouldn't affect heterosexual couples' chances but could affect the chances of single persons wishing to adopt; and one (Guatemala) stated that it would have no legal effects but that it was impossible to give an opinion on the indirect effects. Only one (Latvia) stated that there was a risk that heterosexual couples could be adversely affected.[68]

On the basis of its findings, the Commission in 2001 submitted its report to the minister of justice, recommending that all restrictions on adoption and artificial insemination be removed from same-sex couples. In 2002, the Swedish Parliament voted to allow same-sex couples all rights of adoption. Thus, as of February 1, 2003, Sweden became the first of the Nordic countries to fully remove the restrictions on adoption for same-sex couples.[69] The Commission's learned report has created a stir throughout Scandinavia and has triggered further consideration of the remaining restrictions on adoptions in the other Nordic countries.

New Rules Allowing Artificial Insemination

As demonstrated by the Swedish report on homosexual families, the concept of what is best for the child in Scandinavia is evolving. This evolution is also driving a reconsideration of artificial insemination rights for lesbian couples. Oddly, this road has been an unusually bumpy one, especially in Denmark. Until 1997, no legislation existed regulating artificial insemination in Denmark, but it was not widely available to lesbians. The gynecological departments of the Danish state hospitals have traditionally tied their criteria for insemination close to that of the criteria for adoption. Thus, with a few exceptions, each county limited state-supported artificial insemination to married heterosexual couples or male-female couples in a "marriage-like" relationship. Both lesbian couples and single women have generally been rejected for such services.[70]

A number of hospitals have given other reasons as to why they were unwilling to inseminate lesbian couples. Some pointed to the fact that hospital facilities were only to be used for those who were "physically compromised," such as a partner/husband with a poor sperm quality. Lesbians, these doctors argued, were not physically compromised, and therefore could not qualify to use hospital facilities. Others have claimed that their financial resources were limited, and that certain procedures (i.e., insemination) had to be prioritized so only those who were "most qualified" received it. Some doctors stated that lesbian insemination was an ethical problem, as the hospital did not want to impose the procedure on doctors who felt it was morally wrong. And others relied on the traditional notion of what was "best for the child"—that insemination should be offered only when the child would have a mother and a father present. Nevertheless, insemination was sometimes offered "quietly" to lesbian couples. Because the restrictions only applied to the free services of public hospitals, lesbian couples could go to private clinics for insemination services. A number of lesbian couples have availed themselves of this option, and on average have paid about 3,000 Danish Crowns (approximately $500) for the service.

In 1997, a parliamentary committee formulated a bill regarding reproductive services in Denmark. The resulting bill was a disappointment for lesbian couples. No mention of artificial insemination for lesbians was made, which meant that the de facto prohibition of using public hospitals would continue. It also prohibited lesbian couples from using the other most-used reproductive service, egg fertilization, where a woman's eggs are removed from her body, fertilized with male sperm, and then replaced in her body. During parliamentary debate, an amendment was added to the bill that would further restrict the rights of lesbian couples by prohibiting them from using private clinics as well. The bill passed, with this amendment. Starting October 1, 1997, it has been illegal for lesbians to receive insemination services at either public or private facilities. Insemination arrangements that take place outside of a medical setting are still legal.[71]

How did this happen? Birgitte Haase has a sensible and well-informed theory. "Something like lesbian insemination only adds to the fears of these conservatives that the idea of what a normal family is supposed to be is being threatened. And indeed, right now many Danes feel threatened by the changes in society—the passage of the anti-insemination legislation, it seems to me, was a response to this."[72] Was Denmark having second thoughts about the new family law it was creating?

The LBL adamantly protested the 1997 law, which raised more than a few eyebrows in this nation of tolerance and socialized medicine. More important, some private clinics balked at the idea that they should be forced to deny services to lesbians. In response to the new law, these clinics objected that they would not play a police role for the state, and thus would not check to see if an applicant for insemination was telling the truth about her living status. Thus, if a lesbian came in and told the clinic that she was indeed in a "marriage-like" relationship with a man, they would take her word for it and provide her with insemination services. Some doctors even stated that they would not ask the woman about her status. Gay and lesbian groups around Denmark have created private networks for lesbian women desiring artificial insemination.[73]

In Denmark, there is some hope on the horizon for lesbian couples desiring to utilize public insemination services. A bill introduced in the summer of 1998 to repeal the ban on lesbian insemination failed by a vote of seventy to fifty-seven, much closer than the original vote on the comprehensive reproduction legislation that included the original restrictions on lesbian couples (which had passed 119 to 26).[74] There have been other attempts in Parliament to remove this restriction, most recently in 2005.[75] Furthermore, some politicians have expressed a willingness to change their votes if certain modifications are made. Former member of Parliament Margrete Auken, for example, a strong supporter of the partnership legislation, voted for the insemination restriction. She would support insemination rights if the child could later find out who the donor father was.[76] The short-term prospects for repeal are dim, because the current government is right of center. In the longer term, the law will probably be repealed or narrowed— especially if the Nordic neighbors move in this direction.

And in Sweden, movement in this direction is exactly what has happened. Since July 1, 2005, Swedish lesbian couples have been entitled to the same insemination and assisted reproduction services as married couples. In its 2001 report, the Commission on Children in Homosexual Families found that there was no reason to treat lesbian couples desiring insemination differently from heterosexual couples in the same situation, as both types of families would be equally capable of raising children. These recommendations were implemented in Sweden's Parliament on June 3, 2005, when it passed legislation giving lesbian couples the same rights to state-funded insemination and procreation services that are offered to heterosexual couples.[77]

While Denmark may have been the first to have a marriage-like relationship for same-sex couples, it is Sweden that has taken the lead on eliminating the restrictions placed on same-sex couples who are raising, or desire to raise, children. Yet the conclusions espoused in the Swedish Commission's report on Children in Homosexual Families are slowly gaining converts throughout Scandinavia: Not only are same-sex couples raising children but according to the experts they raise children just as well as do their heterosexual counterparts. Therefore, the concept of "what is best for the child" is now transitioning from a rigid concept of mother and father to "two loving parents," regardless of gender. And as more and more same-sex couples construct for themselves a more traditional family relationship (i.e., one that includes children), the prejudices against such families and their stigmatization will continue to decrease.

Registered Partnership and the Church

The role of religion in the context of legal unions for same-sex couples has long remained a controversial topic in Scandinavia, both inside and outside church walls. Members of Parliament, not wishing to impose their views on the clergy, have left it to the state churches to establish policy regarding same-sex blessings. As MP Margrete Auken, a priest and one of the greatest supporters of gays and lesbians in Parliament, said to *Pan* magazine: "Church weddings or blessings are not a parliamentary matter—that would constitute an abuse of power, pure and simple—but a church matter."[78]

Some lesbian and gay couples have not necessarily felt the need for a church wedding. When we asked Peer Toft and Peter Mols whether they would have liked a church wedding, they were not enthusiastic, even though both were born into the Lutheran Church. "No, it's too much of a straight institution," Toft responded. "It depends," said Mols. "If I had decided to go, it would have been to be in the navy's old and beautiful church. But it wasn't a big deal for me."[79]

For other same-sex couples, the idea of a marriage without God's blessing has been simply unacceptable. Jan Lorenzen and Lars Henriksen exemplify the conflict that the church faces when it addresses the subject of same-sex weddings. The two met in Copenhagen in 1990, when Lars was nineteen, Jan twenty-three. The inseparable couple soon decided that they wanted more open space than the city would allow. Within a couple of years, they made the transition to the countryside, where they bought a farm together and raised cattle, sheep, and horses. While they knew they wanted to marry because of their love for one another, the actual registration ceremony was done on a last-minute basis, when they found out in December they could have some tax benefits if they registered before the end of the year. Said Lars, "The farm was in Jens's name and we had a tax deficit on the farm, so this deficit could be transferred to my name if we were registered, and I could pay less in taxes."[80]

But the actual registration was not a wedding, in Lars's mind. "I had said previously that, if I ever got married, I wanted to be married in the church, which is the proper place for it." Both men were disappointed that the Registered Partnership Act excluded gay and lesbian couples from having a church ceremony. "After we registered, we came to the decision that marriage was not only a bond between two people, but also a bond between two people as witnessed by those who are important in their lives. It is also an opportunity for our friends and family to commit to supporting us as a couple, as we go through our lives. And so we decided to have a separate ceremony involving a promise to each other and to God, to take place in front of our friends and family." The issue, Lars recalls, was that

> the priest in the town we were in was very conservative and I didn't think he would be comfortable with it. . . . But we knew a female priest. I told her what we were looking for, and I explained to her that it didn't have to take place in a church—you see, it wasn't the Church's blessing we wanted, but God's blessing. She wrote back to us that she would be happy to have a ceremony for us, and that we were entitled to a blessing just as any other couple. So we visited her and she had written a ritual for us.
>
> The ceremony took place on our farm, in a field of a grove of trees. We built a small altar for the ceremony, and, with the sky as our cathedral, we had the ceremony. This was our "real" marriage, and it was a truly spiritual experience. We felt that all of our friends there were truly supporting us and wanted to help us through our lives, and were there to witness our promises to each other and our blessing from God. We had about fifty-five people there. We were singing and chanting, our friends and our dogs were there, and our priest made a personal speech. She decided to give her sermon on the book of Genesis, chapter 32, Jacob wrestling with the angel for a blessing. It was the story of Jacob holding on to the angel, and telling him "I won't let go of you until I get God's blessing." And in the end God gave in and gave his blessing. And so the priest explained how everyone has the right to God's blessing. It is something we can go out and fight for. It is something that cannot be denied.[81]

It is stories like that of Jan and Lars, a couple that had to circumvent the restrictions on church participation in order to have their relationship blessed, that have wrought conflict within the Danish Lutheran Church. The conflict pits those who feel that same-sex couples are as worthy of God's blessing on their relationship as any other couple against those who believe that blessings of same-sex couples go against the word of God. The desire of many same-sex couples to have God's blessing on their relationship is compelling for many priests. But, for others, to give such blessings would contradict their own beliefs about God's position on same-sex couples.

This conflict has not been lost on couples like Niels Andersen and Claus Rasmussen, who often see the problem not so much with the church itself as with its administration. Niels remarks: "I believe very strongly in God. I would have liked to have a church wedding if I could. I think God's word is good for people. I would like to go to church more often than I do, but I don't go because the church is too conservative—it's being led by old men. But inside, I feel like I would like to hear more of God's word, and I would like to have God's blessing on my relationship, but our priests don't see it this way."[82]

The reason that the issue of church blessings of same-sex relationships plays a greater role in Scandinavia than it has in other countries debating same-sex marriage is that in these countries, with the exception of Sweden, the Church has a role in the government. The Danish Lutheran Church is a state-supported church; about 85 percent of the overall population, including two-thirds of all registered partners, are members of the church and pay taxes in support of church activities.[83] Priests and other church officials are also employees of the government. The Danish government even has a Ministry of Ecclesiastical Affairs to administrate the relationship between the church and the state. As a government institution, the church administers a number of activities that have civil as well as religious implications. In contrast to the United States, for example, where only the civil marriage is of legal importance, a church wedding in Denmark fulfills both a couple's civil and religious obligations, as priests also take care of the paperwork for civil authorities. Thus the denial of a church ceremony for registered partners means that gay and lesbian couples are being denied equal access to a government-sponsored (and tax-supported) institution. This is one reason why church participation has, since the enactment of the partnership bill, become an important goal of gay and lesbian activists. Without it, there is not formal state equality for lesbian and gay couples.[84]

Governed by twelve bishops who together form the College of Bishops for Denmark, the Danish Lutheran Church has been slow to address the matter. Only after considerable prodding by LBL did the bishops decide to seat a committee in 1994, similar to the Parliament's previous "HomoCommission," to examine the role of church blessings for regis-

tered partners. Unlike the HomoCommission, however, the church committee was comprised solely of church officials, and there were no openly
gay and lesbian representatives.

During the church's internal debate regarding the blessing of gay and
lesbian couples, newspaper editorials passionately argued on both sides of
the issue. Fundamentalist Christians in Denmark opposed to church weddings for gay and lesbian couples wrote letters interpreting the Bible as dis-
approving of homosexuality or gay marriage or both. Similar to those who
earlier argued against passage of the registered partnership law itself, opponents of church blessings pointed to biblical passages supporting the
notion of marriage as one man, one woman (e.g., Genesis 2:24) or specifically condemning homosexual activity (e.g., Leviticus 13:20 and Romans
1:26–27). How could the church even consider church blessings for gay
couples, they argued, when such unions were by their very nature a sin?[85]
As MP Inger Stilling Petersen, of the Christian People's Party, put it: "Some
believe it should be just as natural to be married to someone of the same
sex as it is to [someone of] the opposite sex, but that will never be, because
it is simply against the [biblical] order of nature."[86]

Another line of criticism focused on the effect that same-sex marriages
would have on the Church. Many devout Lutherans feared that recognition of homosexual relationships with a church blessing would devalue
the church in the eyes of others. The Danish Church would be criticized
and lose the respect of other religious denominations (including other
Lutheran churches). This, they feared, could be the beginning of a "slippery slope" in which the Danish Church would then fall under pressure to
bless such groups as pedophiles and polygamists. This would ultimately
devalue not only the church but also the institution of marriage.

In response to such arguments, proponents of same-sex weddings observed that Christians in Scandinavia neither read the Bible literally nor
followed all its apparent commands. For example, Leviticus 13:20 states that
it is an "abomination" to the Lord if a man "lies" with a man as with a
woman, but Leviticus 19:19 also declares it an abomination to wear "a gar-
ment of cloth made of two kinds of stuff." What Christian, some have asked,
has not violated the word of God by wearing a blend of fabrics? There are
dozens of odd purity rules in Leviticus that no Christian obeys, and few even
know about. While Saint Paul condemned "unnatural relations" (without
defining the term) in Romans 1:26–32, he also admonished slaves to obey
their masters in First Timothy 6:1–2. If the Bible must be taken literally and
is understood as announcing universal moral principles, there is a lot more
to be said for slavery (and polygamy, repeatedly endorsed in the Old Testament) than modern Christians will allow. How can the Christian selectively

choose which passages should apply (e.g., homosexual conduct) and which should not (e.g., bans on wearing cotton-polyester blends)?[87]

Furthermore, gay-friendly Christians argued, the Bible has nothing to say against homosexual *love*. While there are isolated passages that condemn particular acts, nothing in the Bible condemns a loving, stable, monogamous relationship between two men, and lesbian love or sex is not explicitly mentioned. The Old Testament presents exemplars of same-sex commitment and, in the eyes of some readers, intimacy—Jonathan and David (1 Samuel 1:26), as well as Naomi and Ruth (Ruth 1:14–18). In the New Testament, Jesus never disapproved of same-sex intimacy. Not only are His principles inclusive but Jesus Himself showed special favor to Mary Magdalene, a fallen woman viewed with the same scorn by Jews of his era that some fundamentalists now show to homosexuals. Some Danish supporters of church marriage for gay couples argued that the Church "owed" something to homosexuals after condemning and persecuting them for such a long period of history. Others pointed out the hypocrisy of condemning homosexuals for being too promiscuous, and then denying them the opportunity to receive a blessing for their committed relationships.

A final argument in favor of same-sex church weddings was that of equality. As the Danish Church is a state institution, and gay and lesbian members pay taxes to the church, so are they entitled to be treated just the same as other taxpaying members of the church, and this includes the receiving of church blessings for their unions. Some priests sense that there is a danger of alienating their gay and lesbian parishioners, who may feel like they are being treated less than equally. Anne-Vibeke Fleisher and her registered partner Elisabeth Bjerre Knudsen, for example, left the church for this reason. Says Anne-Vibeke: "if it was a different church, I would be a member. But it's a church where I can't get be married . . . I am a religious person, but I don't want to belong to the Danish Church. If they had passed legislation that would include lesbians in the church, where we could have a ceremony, then I would become a member of the church again."[88]

In May 1997, the College of Bishops released its report, entitled "Registered Partnership, Cohabitation, and [Church] Blessings," which supported a stronger relationship between same-sex couples and the Danish Lutheran Church. "Registered partnership and gay couples are not, in the opinion of the committee, in opposition to Christian teachings and morals," the report stated. "The [Bishops'] committee has not found the traditional ethical arguments that have been presented against homosexual practice to be valid."[89] The committee acknowledged that the Bible condemned sex between men, but felt that it was unclear as to how this condemnation should be interpreted. The condemnation of particular acts should be read in the context of the time the Bible was written, when homosexuality "was not known in the form that registered partnership is built on: a stable, mutually responsible relationship, built on a faithful love."[90] Thus, the committee decided that this condemnation was in need of interpretation and could not be accepted directly. "The biblical assertion against practiced homosexuality is reckoned by the committee to be [part of the] culturally qualified historical assertions in the Bible, which do not have a normative character," the report stated.[91]

After expressing a gay-friendly understanding of Scripture, the committee offered three suggestions for church blessings of registered partnerships. The first suggested ritual would give registered partners the same blessing that heterosexual couples receive in a church wedding. Only a few words would be changed, to recognize that it is two people of the same sex receiving the blessing. The adoption of this option would place the emphasis on equality between homosexual and heterosexual partnership. The second ritual is based on an old tradition of church blessings in Denmark. It would direct this form of blessing toward registered partners, in which the pair would perhaps kneel before the priest and then receive the priest's blessing. However, under this option, there would be no exchange of vows by the couple as part of the blessing (i.e., the opportunity to say "I do"). The third possibility would be a special blessing created for registered partners. This option, while creating an entirely new blessing for gay and lesbian couples, would also include an exchange of vows by the couple in the church. Thus, while the third option has the wedding ritual as its model, most of the blessing would be formulated to address the special nature of a same-sex partnership.[92]

To address the concerns by conservatives that some priests could be forced to perform blessings for gay couples against their will, the report suggested that priests be allowed to refuse to bless a couple if it is against their personal beliefs. "The creation of a ritual to bless registered partnership will be a break with tradition. For many, it's something foreign and objectionable, and it will be understood to be for some incompatible with their conscience. It must therefore be decided that no priest can be forced to take part in blessing registered partnerships."[93]

Ultimately, the bishops decided not to embrace any of the three possible options. To the disappointment of LBL, the bishops announced that they were not yet ready to create an official church blessing to be used by gay and lesbian couples. Such a decision, they stated in an official release, was one that the church would only make after further deliberation on the subject. But, recognizing that some priests wished to give their blessing to same-sex couples, the College of Bishops lifted the complete ban on church blessings for gay and lesbian couples and agreed to let a ceremony be performed for same-sex registered partners. Under this compromise, if a gay or lesbian couple want to have a church ceremony to celebrate their registered partnership, they would first sit down with the priest who they want to perform the service and together they should work out their desired arrangements for the service. Once the desired ceremony has been worked out, the priest will then bring the proposal to the local bishop, who will give final approval for the ceremony as set out by the partners and priest. However, the bishop has the power to modify the plans for the ceremony if he or she so desires.

The issue of church weddings for registered partners remains far from settled. Some traditionalists within the church remain opposed to the allowance of such weddings at the discretion of local priests. Gay activists and their church allies are still asking for complete parity, for the aforementioned reasons. Most interesting, however, is that some gay activists and supportive clergy call for a different type of blessing for same-sex couples from that given to heterosexual couples, but not because they fear that parity will be construed as church endorsement of homosexual lifestyles. Instead, they feel that same-sex couples are by their very nature different from opposite-sex couples, and that same-sex couples would be better served by a blessing that is tailored to their needs and isn't simply a carbon copy of the blessing given to opposite-sex couples. In any case, it is clear that the Danish Church cannot simply ignore the issue; the Church of Sweden in October 2005 voted to authorize a special ceremony for registered partnerships, which is likely to place additional pressure on the Danish Church to take some form of action.

Yet the debate within the Danish Lutheran Church poses several interesting questions. Are equality and sameness the same thing? If the Church were to provide religious weddings for same-sex couples, would the equality principle call for a blessing crafted to directly address same-sex couples, rather than the blessing developed over the decades for different-sex couples? The biggest question is this: Are lesbian and gay couples equal parishioners in the eyes of the state-supported Church?

With these questions—of church weddings, adoption rights, and insemination opportunities for gay and lesbian couples—in mind, we reflect upon how the personification of "homosexuals" in the public eye has changed dramatically since the partnership laws were first being seriously considered. For most of the latter half of the twentieth century, media portrayal of gays and lesbians focused on the flamboyant, or even the extreme. Television coverage of gay and lesbian pride parades would inevitably air the images of men in leather, women on Harley motorcycles, and drag queens with three-foot hair. Footage of middle-aged NAMBLA members holding the hands of their youthful interests was not uncommon.

Yet over time, as gays and lesbians have become integrated into the mainstream, average citizens have become aware that gay people are just as variegated a group as any other, and most gay people are rather normal in most respects. Moreover, imagery and public controversy associated with the word "gay" or "lesbian" have shifted away from such topics as promiscuity and fetishism, and toward matters of same-sex marriage, church acceptance, and raising children. As the members of mainstream society recognize that the gays and lesbians in their midst are often living the same kinds of family lives they lead—going to work, spending the day in the office, returning to their spouses (and perhaps, children) in the evenings, and waking up in the morning and doing it all over again—its members are changing their attitudes. This is what has been happening in Scandinavia.

We interviewed Peter Mols and Peer Toft again in 2005, shortly before this book went to press. "We've been together now for twenty-two years, and we both have more gray hair," says Peter. But they are still together, still in the same jobs, and still very good-looking men for their age. Their views on registered partnership, the Church, and adoption and insemination rights have not changed, but they believe that the government is close to eliminating the remaining differences between registered partnership and marriage in Denmark.

"Of course, like any couple, we've changed as we've gotten older," says Peter, "and we're not the same people we were when we first met as young men. We still love each other very much, but we've been though our share of crises, the same crises that other married couples have dealt with during their marriages."[94] How couples in registered partnerships such as Peer and Peter have dealt with such crises along the course of their relationships is part of the subject of the next chapter. But each time, these two men have worked through the issues, and their relationship has become stronger because of it. And their experiences together, it appears, have kept them youthful; despite their protests of growing older, it is hard for an outside observer to tell any physical difference when watching the two hold hands together. They still display the same mischievous smiles, and carry the same gleam in their eyes, that they did several years earlier. It might still be best to hide the pillows.

CHAPTER 4

The Benefits of Same-Sex Marriage
Lessons from Scandinavia

Otto Bygsø and Palle Heilesen, receiving a salute from Bygsø's fellow police officers as they emerge from their wedding in Copenhagen City Hall.

To step inside the apartment of Lars and Johnnie Fledelius is like stepping into a Disney Store. After walking across the Mickey Mouse rug, you may be offered a seat on the sofa covered with a blanket that has an image of King Stephen's castle from *Cinderella*, a Disney animated classic. While admiring a lamp in the image of Ariel, from *The Little Mermaid*, and other pieces of Disney furniture around the apartment, perhaps you will be offered a cup of tea—in a Disney mug, of course. And don't miss the wall stacked with Disney videos—in both English and Danish. "We collect every one as soon as it comes out, in both languages," says Johnnie. "There's a lot of magic in Disney."[1]

Johnnie and Lars's relationship is a Disney romance, with a modern twist. They met during a weekend seminar for Stop-AIDS youth volunteers in 1992 that Johnnie was running. Although the attraction was instantaneous, Johnnie jokes that getting together was hard work: "I started working on him Friday night, but nothing happened—he was clueless. But Saturday night, when he got drunk . . . wham! That's when I got him." After a flirtatious seminar, the two agreed to meet in Copenhagen, and by January 1993 Lars had packed his bags and moved to the capital city. Although he was nominally living on his own for a time, he was in truth spending all his time at Johnnie's place. Johnnie proposed to Lars in February 1993, and they had a ceremony at City Hall shortly thereafter; like most other registered partners, they consider themselves "married."[2]

American as well as some Nordic traditionalists would not be amused by the appropriation of marriage by these Danish Disneyphiles. Some Americans say Johnnie and Lars's relationship is a "mocking burlesque" of marital vows.[3] The state, in their opinion, should not be promoting homosexual relationships such as this one, and certainly not equating them to marriage. From their point of view, same-sex partnership or marriage is a state stamp of approval for homosexuality, which most traditionalists consider deeply immoral.

Is this a fair objection? On the one hand, the objection suffers from logical problems. By recognizing Johnnie and Lars Fledelius in a legal union, Denmark is not placing a state stamp of approval on homosexuality any more than a state marriage license issued to a criminal constitutes a stamp of approval for criminal conduct. Instead, what the state is approving and promoting is committed relationships. Same-sex partnership or marriage signals that gay and lesbian couples, like Johnnie and Lars, who want to make a life commitment to one another ought to have the same state-assured benefits and responsibilities that straight couples have when they choose to marry. On the other hand, registered partnership or same-sex marriage laws do "promote" homosexual couples in a sense. Before the laws, such couples were second-class citizens, their "disapproved" relationships considered unworthy of state recognition and regulation. After the laws, such couples are (almost?) first-class citizens, their relationships treated (almost?) the same as those of their straight counterparts.

So the stamp-of-approval objection to same-sex marriage may have some bite. How persuasive it is depends upon one's normative baseline. If for religious reasons one believes that the only moral consummation for marriage can be procreative sex between a husband and a wife *and* that civil marriage ought to track religious morality, the answer is yes, this is a persuasive objection. Most Americans reject at least one of these premises, and American law regulating civil marriage is mainly premised upon a social policy favoring interpersonal commitment. The state promotes committed romantic relationships because it believes they are good for its citizens, good for the children they are bearing and rearing, and good for the community. Do these policy goals have application to lesbian and gay couples who want to marry (or its equivalent)?[4]

This chapter will explore the reasons Scandinavian couples like Lars and Johnnie have registered as partners, and the effects that legal union has had on their relationships. It will also examine the effects of these same-sex unions on the children many couples are raising within their households, on their extended families, and on their friends and coworkers. For Lars Fledelius, the primary reason to get married was "to show our love for one another." While this was certainly an important motivation for Johnnie, he had another as well. "My primary reason was based on the fact that I was HIV-positive. I felt that, if I were to die, I didn't want Lars to be left with nothing. If I were to leave the planet, I would want him to have everything."[5] The possibility of a partner's death from AIDS was indeed one of the early motivators for passing a comprehensive marriage-like law in Denmark. As in the United States, the 1980s in Scandinavia saw many cases of gay men who were left with nothing after the death of their partner. In the absence of a will or other legal documentation, many blood families seized the remaining belongings of their dead relative from the residence that the deceased shared with his same-sex partner, leaving the surviving partner with nothing but his memories.

There is no single overriding reason that all same-sex couples give for wanting legal recognition of their partnerships. Each couple who has tied the knot has their own story, and there are as many reasons for entering into a legal union as there are stories to be told. Yet there are recurring themes that relate the couples' reasons for legal union. Many of these themes point to the benefits of same-sex marriage for the couples themselves, especially a sense of legal security for the couples and a feeling that the legal recognition deepens the relationship, encourages monogamy or safe behavior, and prevents breakups. Legal recognition also provides security, comfort, and legitimization for same-sex couples raising children. These are quite similar to the policy reasons supporting state recognition of marriages for straight couples.

But the legal and financial benefits of same-sex marriage are only a part of its overall impact. An analysis of the Scandinavian experience with registered partnership demonstrates that the potential benefits for society from extending such benefits to same-sex couples are much broader than simply the tangible benefits that accrue to the couples themselves. Same-sex marriage positively impacts those who in some way are part of the couple's lives—their family, friends, neighbors, community, and compatriots. Using the stories of registered partners to demonstrate these points, we embark here on an analysis of the beneficial role that same-sex marriage can, and does, play in societies where it has had the opportunity to become integrated into mainstream culture.

Legal Benefits of Marriage: Making Life Easier and More Secure

In an on-line survey we conducted of 812 Danish gays and lesbians, 49 percent of the respondents reported that the main reason to enter into a registered partnership would be "to secure the legal rights of marriage for myself and my partner."[6] These findings are consistent with the personal accounts we gathered from talking with registered couples. This was certainly one reason Jean Luscher and Diana Skovgaard (from our Introduction) registered as partners in 1995. Like the United States, Denmark does not allow noncitizens (here, non–European Union citizens) to remain within its borders indefinitely, with some exceptions. The main exception is for spouses or registered partners of citizens. If Jean wanted to live in Denmark with Diana, they needed to register, and so they did. (Diana would not have been entitled to similar treatment if the partners had settled in the United States.) This benefit has become even more important over the course of their marriage. Jean is now a simultaneous translator for the European Union in Brussels and spends much of her time on the road. As the "spouse" of a Danish citizen, now with a Danish passport, she can travel everywhere in Europe with no hassle.[7]

Immigration and naturalization rights are only the tip of the iceberg for married or registered couples in Scandinavia. There are more than a hundred legal rights and benefits of marriage and registered partnership. Most of these rights and benefits presume that spouses as well as registered partners constitute an integrated economic and social union, where each partner is the surrogate decision-maker for or beneficiary of the other. Some of the legal rights are matters of convenience, but others are important for the security of the partners, in particular inheritance rights, tax treatment, and health and employee benefits. Our interviews informed us that, for many same-sex couples, the intangible rights and security were just as important as the tangible rights and benefits.

Tangible Rights and Benefits: Inheritance and Taxation

Niels Andersen and Claus Rasmussen are blue-collar workers who live together in a small town in rural Jutland, far away from the cosmopolitan life of Copenhagen. Both work in a car sales shop, and together they own a modest house. While Niels was aware of his interest in men from a younger age, he nonetheless did his best to conceal such inclinations. He married when he was twenty-eight and had a son, now in his teens. Claus, on the other hand, knew he was gay from age thirteen, though he hid this fact from his family. The two met on a gay chat line. After a number of phone conversations, Niels and Claus met in person, and the relationship began. Their affair took place for several years while Niels was still married, until he divorced his wife. Claus moved in soon thereafter, and they were registered three years later.[8]

As described in chapter 3, Claus and Niels did not feel welcome registering their partnership at the local Town Hall. In fact, they were discouraged from doing so by the Town Hall clerk, out of concern that "people would talk." The town they lived in was particularly religious and not as open-minded as people were in larger cities. Considering the hostility, or at least discomfort, that some locals felt toward gay couples, why bother with registering? According to Claus, "we registered because we have a house together, and we own a car—if anything happened to Niels, I would have legal problems because his son would inherit all his things, and I would be left with nothing. We could of course make a will, but the taxes on the inheritance would be very high without a legal relationship. So we wanted to secure each other legally."[9] Consistent with Claus's fears, Danish inheritance law is more rigid than that in the United States. Inheritance rights of children and spouses are determined by law and cannot be entirely negated by a will.[10]

When considering the legal rights of marriage, the specific rights contemplated by couples vary, depending on the age and situation of the partners. Like Claus and Niels, most long-term couples see registered partnership as a vehicle for securing inheritance rights for the partner in case of death or incapacitation. While inheritance issues may be more important for older couples, or where one of the partners is ill, interviews suggest that even young, healthy couples have considered the inheritance issue as part of their interest in entering into registered partnership. Peer Toft had the following thoughts on why he and Peter Mols (introduced in chapter 3) entered into registered partnership. "Some older friends of ours started to die around us. And we thought about that. And then we went to the United States, to Orlando. And we encountered people who were having unsafe sex, like AIDS had ceased to exist. And when we came back to Denmark, we were uncomfortable about that, and we began thinking about our own mortality. We talked about what might happen to one of us, like if I got shot in my job as a policeman, or if Peter drowned in the Navy. So we said, why don't we get registered, so we can inherit from each other if something happens."[11]

One of the important inheritance rights of marriage or registered partnership is lower inheritance taxes. In fact, spouses and registered partners enjoy a number of tax benefits. In Diana Skovgaard and Jean Luscher's household, for example, because Jean was still a student with no steady income in the early years of their partnership, money was tight in their household. Under Danish law, spouses (and after 1989 registered partners) such as Diana could take a number of tax deductions during the period that Jean remained a student. Thus, while registered partners remain liable for mutual support obligations, they are nonetheless entitled to certain tax benefits that make such a burden easier in a number of situations. As Jean jokingly puts it, "it works out for us because I spend as much of her money as she saves [from the deductions]!"[12]

The tax benefits of marriage also support younger couples, who may be struggling financially. As part of their decision to start a new life together, Lars Henriksen and Jan Lorenzen also decided to purchase a farm together and begin a career in raising livestock. However, for two young men in their twenties with limited financial resources, making a farm profitable would be a risky undertaking. Their decision to register was partially predicated on discovering that they would be entitled to additional tax benefits from losses incurred in the early years of starting up the farm, which would help the two of them out financially. "The additional income from the tax benefits as registered partners were quite helpful to the two of us," says Lars. (For other couples, there may be financial disadvantages to being married or partnered under Danish tax law.)[13]

Tangible Benefits: Health and Employee Benefits

In the United States, health insurance is usually the most prized benefit for domestic partnership programs offered by employers. Considering the high costs of self-insurance, health benefits in the United States often trump all other rationales for registering a domestic partner with one's employer. In the Scandinavian welfare states, where universal health coverage is offered to all citizens and legal residents, health benefits are usually not as much of a priority for those desiring to enter into registered partnership. But where one of the partners is a foreigner who is otherwise not entitled to legal residency, the health benefits attached to legal union can be of great importance. About

20 percent of all male registered partnerships include one non-European partner; this pattern is also not uncommon among female partnerships.[14] In the case of Jean and Diana, for example, Jean's chronic asthma meant that she needed the security of the state health-care coverage. "Once we got registered, I didn't have to worry that I could have health-care problems that would not be covered," she says. "It was an added sense of security that I could stay with Diana in Denmark and my health care would not be an issue."[15]

For several of the other couples we interviewed, the main health-care benefit of registered partnership was the security of knowing that one's life partner was empowered to make decisions in the event of a personal calamity. Danish law, like that in other Scandinavian countries and the United States, provides that if a person is incapacitated, his or her spouse (or registered partner) has the legal right to make health-care decisions.[16] In the event of death, the spouse or partner presumptively decides what the funeral arrangements shall be, and how the estate is to be managed. (One can designate someone else to make these decisions, and cohabiting couples in all of these countries can designate their cohabiting partners. But these are matters where ordinary healthy adults do not go to the trouble and expense of making such designations.) These rules are sensible. One's soul mate not only wants to do what is best for an incapacitated person but knows his or her preferences, probably better than his or her blood family. This provides some peace of mind and, more important, creates clear and sensible rules of decision in matters of life and death.

The source of tangible marital benefits is not limited to the government; employers often have their own spousal/partner benefit programs. A number of the interviewed couples cited employer benefits for their partners as important for providing additional assistance to their family. An example is the right to a survivor's pension. Enactment of the registered partnership law in Denmark automatically entitled the partners of government employees to pension rights in 1989, but private pension funds had to change their own rules to extend a survivor's pension to same-sex partners. This was completed by 1991, and registered partners now have the security that they will be entitled to their deceased partner's pension, as are heterosexual spouses.[17]

In addition, particular employers offer spousal benefits related to their business, such as product discounts, free merchandise, and transportation deals. Recall Per Kjær and Barry Winter, a Danish/British couple who live in the town of Aalborg in the northern part of Jutland. Per works for the Danish State Railways system as a driver of train engines. As his registered partner, Barry is entitled to the same employee benefits as heterosexual spouses. "Because I work for the railway, Barry gets spousal discounts. He can travel twenty-four times a year with free train travel. There is also an international recognition of spouses among the state train systems, but other countries haven't fully recognized same-sex couples yet—but when they do, I imagine he will be able to travel internationally by train also, with the same spousal discounts."[18]

Finally, some employers offer additional benefits to employees above and beyond what is required by the government, and same-sex registered partners are given the same entitlement to these benefits as are different-sex spouses. Some employees, for example, have taken time off from work to care for sick partners; others have taken a leave of absence to spend time with their newborn children. The interaction between the employer and the employee may even have the effect of affirming the company's recognition of its same-sex employees, as Anne-Vibeke Fleischer discovered: "I had to call the administration at my office, to speak to them about my sick mother-in-law whom I wanted to spend some time with. I knew that you got certain benefits for family at my office if you were married. I asked the office administration for the benefit of a day off, as I told her I was in a registered partnership. She called me back and said, we've never dealt with this before, but we would treat your relationship as any other marriage, so you should take the day off."[19]

The list of legal benefits presented here is in no way exhaustive. With over one hundred laws, and countless regulations, regarding marriage and spouses now applicable to registered partnerships and registered partners, there have been many tangible legal benefits that same-sex couples may now take advantage of, in the same way that many heterosexual spouses have been enjoying these benefits for years. For many same-sex couples, these legal and financial benefits have the effect of making their lives, and their relationships, a little bit easier.

Intangible Legal Benefits of Marriage

The extension of the tangible benefits of marriage to same-sex couples has significantly helped some couples care for each other, both legally and financially. But these tangible rights often have intangible payoffs experienced by couples over the course of their partnerships. Most important of these intangibles is the sense of personal and family security that the tangible benefits bring to many couples. The legal benefits of registered partnership mean that same-sex couples who register are relieved of the burden of worrying about unforeseen contingencies, and are given an additional sense of comfort. After Jean Luscher made her career shift, with her primary job now located in

Brussels, she "realized that registered partnership was adding stability to our relationship. We haven't been in the same country, but registered partnership has allowed me to move back and forth for my job and my wife. When you consider the other issues [such as health care, financial incentives, and immigration issues], we couldn't have legally and financially managed without marriage. It clears away a lot of daily stresses—all of the daily life issues."[20]

Gunna Højgaard, who lives with her registered partner Eva Fog in Copenhagen, recalls a number of troubling legal experiences of her unmarried friends, both heterosexual and homosexual, and how registered partnership has made her feel more secure: "My older sister's male partner died at a time that they weren't married, and it was horrible to see what happened thereafter. His relatives came in, and his friends, and they wanted all kinds of things, and my sister had no rights to the property at all. She had previously offered him marriage, but he hadn't wanted to. She offered him marriage on his deathbed, but he said, 'I'm not that far gone, am I?' And of course she didn't want to disagree. So they were never married, and she suffered because of that." Gunna also knew "another lesbian couple where one died and the one left behind had no rights, and couldn't even come to the funeral. She had no say in what was going on. It made me think, that when I got older, if anything should happen to me or my partner, I would like to know what my legal options were, so that there were no surprises. So registered partnership has given us that security."[21]

Interpersonal Relationships: Strengthening the Bonds of Committed Partners

Even before passage of the Danish Registered Partnership Act, its parliamentary supporters envisioned that legal unions would have a greater effect than simply the extension of benefits to same-sex couples. In their comments introducing the legislation, the sponsors of the Act stated that "a formal acknowledgement through explicit legislation will improve the opportunities for long-lasting and permanent relationships between two people of the same sex, since the existence or just the feeling of a negative reaction from society's side is known to work against the durability of a long-term relationship in a negative way." In other words, public recognition of a same-sex partnership will have the effect of supporting and strengthening the relationship, thereby promoting interpersonal commitment and the security of the partnership and the partners.[22]

It is too early to draw final conclusions on whether this aspiration will be fully realized, but our interviews with Danish registered partners, and other evidence, suggest that state recognition of lesbian and gay unions does have pronounced positive effects upon the nature of those relationships. We hypothesize that, for a significant number of couples, state recognition creates a focal point for people's relationship aspirations and discussions, enhances the commitment features of their relationships, and encourages health-conscious behaviors.

Partnership/Marriage as a Focal Point for Aspiration and Discussion

State- or culturally sanctioned institutions serve as focal points for young people's aspirations and discussions regarding their romantic relationships. From an early age, boys and girls learn that marriage is a special institution—pleasing to God, approved by parents and the state, and esteemed by their peers as something that everyone should seek as the highest expression of romantic love and the creation of a family with children. In the last generation, marriage has lost much of its cachet along these lines in the United States and, especially, Europe, as other options now compete. (In France, for example, straight couples now have the options of cohabiting, entering a *pacte civil*, or marrying.) Still, marriage remains special because of its overlapping endorsement by the state, religious tradition, and social culture. More important, even as marriage has lost its monopoly, it has remained a focal point for *discussion*.

For heterosexual couples, the existence of marriage as a possible end goal encourages dialogue about the direction in which the relationship is heading. If the young man hesitates on the marriage question, that is a signal as to his level of commitment, and the young woman can respond accordingly. If the young Frenchman says that he is not ready for marriage, but would like to enter a *pacte civil* (which is much easier to exit than marriage), the young woman might reasonably deduce that he is not as committed to the relationship as she might be. Or she might readily agree with the young man, for both might like a trial period before they make the firmer commitment. Our point is this: so long as civil marriage carries with it the greatest range of legal benefits *and* the strongest set of obligations and difficulty of exit, it will be the ultimate referent for discussion. Lesbian and gay couples have, traditionally, lacked such a referent for their discussions. The mere existence of same-sex marriage or registered partnership, therefore, acts as a catalyst for couples to reflect on the status of their relationship.

Thus, the simple existence of a state-sanctioned legal union will stimulate a dialogue among long-term same-sex partners. What stage is our relationship in? What is our long-term goal? Do I think that my partner is "the one"? At what point should we consider marriage? Why should we consider marriage? Without same-sex marriage or an equivalent form of legal union, couples may not feel pressure to consider the nature of their relationship and the direction in which it is heading—which may have the effect of discouraging (or at least not encouraging) communication between the partners, thereby missing opportunities to strengthen the bonds that hold them together.

One American-Danish male couple we interviewed (William Waite and Ken Nielsen, discussed in chapter 3) raised this point explicitly. They met while both were living in Lithuania. While falling in love was easy, the fact that they were only temporarily in Lithuania meant that they would have to think about the possibility of legal union if they wanted their relationship to continue. Because Denmark offered them the possibility of a state-sanctioned partnership, this provided a structure for the discussion as the two men considered the nature of their relationship. As one of them told us, "Registered partnership does make you take the relationship more seriously, even if you are sometimes not aware of it. Because it's a decision you have to make—you decide whether this is 'it' or not. Contemplating marriage makes you think about your relationship in a way that you might not have done otherwise. It hasn't changed my feelings, but it has changed my way of thinking about my relationship with [my partner]." After careful consideration, they decided that their relationship was strong enough, and deep enough, to warrant a legal union to secure their relationship.[23]

Same-sex marriage (or registered partnership) can serve an important purpose in the opposite manner as well—to screen out relationships that don't rise to the level of seriousness that would be destined for a legal union. Deborah Kaplan, who has been registered with her partner, Anne Jespersen, since 1997, had another long-term relationship with a Danish woman in the early 1990s. When asked why she hadn't pursued registered partnership with her previous partner, Deborah replied: "Registered partnership was never really a serious topic of discussion between us. I think that, subconsciously, the two of us knew that there were problems with our relationship—so we never really talked about getting married."[24] A couple's interest in discussing the possibility of marriage or partnership, therefore, can act as an indicator of the seriousness of the relationship.

Public Commitment and Longer Lasting Unions?

Registration as partners in Scandinavia is a public act. Unlike dating or even cohabitation, partnership is a matter of public record in the same manner as a heterosexual marriage. There is a public ceremony, sometimes only a simple one in the local town hall, more often a wedding reception where family and friends are invited. Such a public declaration of one's feelings in the form of a same-sex marriage/partnership adds an additional layer of commitment onto many relationships. Formalizing their partnership through a legal union serves as an announcement to friends, family, co-workers, the government, and all others that both members of the couple are committing themselves to each other. And, as everyone knows, partnership, like marriage, entails legal duties of mutual support and maintenance. Exit from these duties, through divorce, entails expense and bother and is not casually initiated.

If the benefits of marriage reflect the legal side of the commitment, then the public declaration element of marriage reflects the emotional side of the commitment. And indeed, gay men and lesbians value the emotional side of registered partnership to about the same extent that they value the tangible benefits of registration. In our survey of 812 gay and lesbian Danes, the second most often cited answer to "What would be your *primary* reason for entering a registered partnership?" was "To demonstrate my commitment to my partner." Almost 40 percent of the respondents identified this reason.[25]

While few interviewed couples claimed that the emotional benefits of registering were their *only* rationale, many cited the emotional side as the *primary* reason, above and beyond the legal benefits. Eva Fog, the registered partner of Gunna Højgaard, recalled her thoughts on legal union before tying the knot:

> I felt very clearly that our relationship was right, and I wanted to show it to the world. There is a feeling of emotional security, both for yourself and for your partner. It was a way of saying, "You know I am here and you can count on me." It's a clear demonstration of your intention to stay together, and that feels good. It's quite powerful, and I had never felt like making such a promise before, even though I had quite long-term relationships, but now I think I am ready to publicly vouch for my feelings for Gunna.[26]

Eva recognizes that her public declaration of commitment to Gunna may curtail the openness of relationships that she had once had, but now at a different point in her life, she is willing to make that compromise. "We grew up in the sixties and seventies, where you changed partners every two years—it was quite decadent. I used to think—'Well, I have had my share of fun, and I have had a nice life with lots of friends.' But I wasn't expecting that [marriage] would ever be possible. But now I find it wonderful that I can permanently share my life with someone and make a public statement about it. Getting registered was the right thing to do. Of course there is a price to pay, because my friends see me less now—but having this woman in my life is wonderful."[27]

In the absence of any legal regulation of their relationships, many same-sex couples feel little compulsion to work through rocky periods in their romances. Without the burden of divorce proceedings, breaking up could be as simple as packing one's belongings and finding a new home. Lack of legal, financial, and other consequences for breaking up may make dissolution of a relationship a more appealing option for unmarried same-sex couples than their married heterosexual counterparts. For these reasons, same-sex marriage or partnership may serve another important purpose— to compel same-sex couples who are contemplating a breakup to spend more time considering opportunities to solve problems in the relationship than those who might not be in a legal union. In other words, contemplating the process of divorce will have the effect of encouraging many couples to focus on the existing conflicts in the relationship, and consider whether there might be solutions that could prevent the relationship from breaking up.

Anne-Vibeke Fleischer and Elisabeth Bjerre Knudsen live together in a cozy cottage within the city limits of Copenhagen. Now in their late fifties, the two women have a wizened look about them—the look of experience, exemplified by their matching set of smile lines around their eyes. While they may come across as young, sweet grandmotherly types today, their stories reveal a rich history of loves and romances that have come and gone. Both have both had their share of previous relationships. Anne-Vibeke, in particular, has had a string of previous female lovers. As she reflects upon her previous relationships through the sixties, seventies, and eighties, she observes: "Every time I fell in love, my lover and I had a good time together. But then at some point, the daily feelings of love would slow down. Conflicts came in, and when the conflicts came in, I said to myself, 'it's time for me to leave.' And then I would start from scratch with a new woman, and the same thing would happen all over again." Anne-Vibeke followed this pattern many times with many lovers. But when her relationship began with Elisabeth, something was different. The emotions seemed stronger than before. Slowly she became confident that Elisabeth was to be her true life partner. They had met in 1985, while helping some mutual friends move furniture out of their apartment. A year later, after an intense courtship, Elisabeth moved her furniture into Anne-Vibeke's house. In 1989, they became one of the first female couples to enter into a registered partnership.[28]

But even in this country of fairy tales, relationships don't necessarily end happily ever after. Several years later, Anne-Vibeke began feeling that the same "relationship cycle" that had defined her earlier relationships was starting again. She began an affair with a woman she had met while on a skiing holiday with Elisabeth. The affair, when discovered, was devastating to Elisabeth. She moved out of the house, and the two of them lived separately for two years. While the two of them remained friends and met regularly, they eventually decided that they should get a divorce. But for Anne-Vibeke, it wasn't going to be as easy to break up as it had been with her past relationships. Now that their relationship was governed by the legal rules of marriage, breaking up would require undergoing mediation before having a divorce. They scheduled the mediation with a government official, which would take place a couple of months later.

But as they discussed their divorce together, they began discussing the role of their marriage and their relationship: "When we had the discussion about getting divorced, and we had to plan for the legal process of divorce, this meant something to us." According to the two women, it made them think about their relationship, and their feelings for one another. "And you couldn't just leave and say goodbye, because of the legal status of our relationship," says Anne-Vibeke. This open dialogue about their relationship, sparked by the divorce process, made each of them realize how important the other was to their lives. Soon thereafter, "we became close friends again [and] after two years, we both started to be lovers again. It was very difficult at first, Elisabeth being both my new and my old lover." But then Elisabeth moved back into the house, and things started to fall back in place. Ultimately, the two decided not to divorce but to work on strengthening their lives together. "I'm quite sure that the registered partnership affected our staying together," says Anne-Vibeke. "If we didn't have the partnership law, we wouldn't have gotten back together again. We couldn't simply part ways, as I had done before with other lovers. It really meant something."[29]

Johnnie and Lars Fledelius encountered a similar hurdle several years ago, when the two had to deal with the pain of a sexual encounter outside the relationship: "The one-night stand tore up our relationship for some time," says Lars. "Getting married is a serious commitment, and to betray the relationship in that way also betrays the trust that is part of the relationship. It made me realize how important trust is to a relationship. And so the encounter made things very difficult for a while, and I had even thought about breaking up. But now that we're married, we have to sit down and talk about these things more. We couldn't just break up—we have legal obligations to one another. And this brought us more commitment to working things out in our relationship." Eventually, Johnnie and Lars were able to communicate about what had happened, and work through the issue, deciding that their relationship was strong enough to overcome what had happened.[30]

Not all couples will come to the same conclusions about their relationship as did Anne-Vibeke and Elisabeth or Johnnie and Lars. And there may be couples whose relationships were simply not built on a foundation stable enough to last. But the public features of same-sex marriage or registered partnership complement the goals of these couples, which is to form a *committed* union that is *long-lasting*. Some critics of marriage suggest that lasting commitments are overrated, but the stories of these two couples (similar to the others we interviewed) suggest that their happiness and their delight in the relationship were enriched by the mutual commitment. Anne-Vibeke and Elisabeth, as well as Johnnie and Lars, felt a sense of mutual accomplishment and even deeper love because they had negotiated breaches in their relationships successfully.

Monogamy and Safer Sex

As gays and lesbians in industrialized countries began lobbying for legal rights in the latter third of the twentieth century, those opposed to legal reforms to accommodate homosexuals focused a great deal on their moral unfitness for legal protections. One of the most prevalent arguments was that homosexuals, particularly gay men, were promiscuous and therefore not morally admirable citizens deserving of legal rights.[31] It is ironic that the same cultural conservatives who once denounced homosexuals for their promiscuity now denounce homosexuals for seeking the legal recognition of their committed, long-term partnerships. Some have gone so far as to suggest that one of the reasons that same-sex legal unions in the United States would make a mockery of marriage is that, rather than marriage having a domesticating effect on the sexual practices of gay and lesbian couples, it would be gay male promiscuity that would have an effect on the institution of marriage, further undermining the already eroded monogamy norm and making it more acceptable for *all* married couples (gay or straight) to have extramarital sex. In other words, gay men would be unlikely to change their practices once inside a legal union, and the traditional understanding of the institution of marriage would suffer as a result.

It is true that men who have sex mainly with other men have a larger number of sexual partners, and higher incidences of sexually transmitted diseases, than men who have sex mainly with women, women who have sex mainly with men, and women who have sex mainly with women (the group least at risk of disease). This kind of argument, however, is largely inapplicable to lesbians and not clearly applicable to gay or bisexual men who would choose to marry. Judge Richard Posner and others have suggested that same-sex marriage would probably reinforce norms of sexual moderation or monogamy among gay men. The logic is that the more committed a relationship is, the less utility either partner will derive from sex outside the relationship. If there is sex outside the relationship, the partner will be somewhat more careful. If he or she contracts a sexually transmitted disease, it will not only expose the cheating (or become a burning reminder of an already admitted tryst) but also will put the beloved spouse also at risk. Although marriage has never eradicated promiscuity and cheating among heterosexuals, most experts do think it has had a dampening effect.[32]

To be sure, there are certain factors whereby same-sex marriage would increase rather than diminish the riskiness of sexual encounters. For example, partners within a same-sex marriage are much more likely to engage in unsafe sex with one another, which greatly increases the risks if one partner is cheating. Yet our hypothesis is that, on the whole, same-sex marriage and partnership will reduce nonmonogamous and, especially, unsafe behaviors. Our interviews with same-sex partners found strong support for the notion that marriage has had an impact on their feelings about sexual fidelity. It has affected them in one of two ways.

For most couples interviewed, monogamy became an important element of their relationship. Take the example of Uffe Størner, who entered into a registered partnership with Kaj Kristensen in 1993. In the earlier years of their relationship, when the relationship was more casual, Uffe was not monogamous, but that changed as the status of the relationship changed: "Kaj has been monogamous since I met him. I used to play around a little, but now I've stopped. So getting married had a little effect on me. I said to myself, 'Get yourself together—now you're living together, and you have what you want with Kaj—so don't spoil it.' But of course we can still talk to each other about other guys, and say who is cute and who isn't."[33]

Even for some who originally weren't interested in monogamy as part of the relationship, the emotional effect of marriage may change attitudes. Jean Luscher found herself surprised by her own transformation:

> I feel very strongly about monogamy now. Previously, I had accepted the view that monogamy was a bourgeois invention—and that if you were really liberated, you didn't need it. But ever since I've been with Diana I've been monogamous. And just before I got married, I realized that I wasn't being monogamous for lack of opportunity, but rather for emotional reasons. I spoke with my therapist about monogamy, and eventually I came to the understanding of my earlier resistance to monogamy and fear of commitment—this was in preparation for actually entering into marriage. But since I've been married, I've been so into being married that I can't even imagine sleeping with other women. I can joke about it if we see an attrac-

tive woman, but I've never thought to actually act on anything. And we're not jealous, we can talk to other attractive girls, but we don't think much of it.[34]

Of course, not all couples in relationships choose to practice monogamy. Several of the partnered gay men we spoke with were not monogamous. They were open about this with their partners, which is something of an advance over the twentieth-century marital norm of repeated, but secret, cheating (traditionally by the husband on the unsuspecting wife). Yet legal union has had an effect on the sexual practices of all the nonmonogamous couples we interviewed. For those gay men who chose not to remain exclusively monogamous, the fact that they were in a legally binding, stable partnership has encouraged them to think about the welfare of their partners (as well as themselves) and therefore practice only safe sex outside of the relationship. One couple put it this way: "One of our reasons for getting married was to show each other that we were going to be responsible for one another— responsible in the sense that, if we go and fuck around somewhere, we know that we have to be responsible for what we're doing sexually, because we know that our partner is depending on us. It's a way of telling your partner, 'I'm serious about our relationship and I don't want to jeopardize anything, including your health.'"[35]

These and other accounts we have gathered suggest that same-sex marriage, or registered partnership, gives the couples reason to feel more secure about the fidelity, or at least the sexual practices, of their partner. While registered partnership has the effect of increasing monogamy among some gay and lesbian couples, it also has a positive effect on safer sex practices among those couples who are not monogamous. A recent National Bureau of European Research study provides preliminary empirical support for these propositions. Comparing rates of syphilis and gonorrhea in twelve European countries that have recognized same-sex marriage, registered partnership, or another form of legal union (the five Scandinavian countries, plus seven others, together described as the "recognition" countries), with those of other European countries, Professor Thomas Dee found a correlation between the new institutions and lower rates for these sexually transmitted diseases. Syphilis rates started off higher in the "recognition" countries (Denmark and others) but converged after Denmark adopted its registered partnership law in 1989. In the 1990s, rates soared in the nonrecognition countries, while they continued to decline in the recognition countries. The lower rates for syphilis were statistically significant, meaning that it is highly unlikely to have been the result of a random variation. Gonorrhea rates were declining in the recognition countries even before they adopted their new laws, and continued their sharp decline afterward, so it is hard to identify the precise connection with same-sex marriage or partnership, though the data are certainly consistent with our hypothesis.[36]

Interpersonal Relationships: Children Raised in Lesbian and Gay Families

The number of same-sex couples in Scandinavia raising children is growing rapidly.[37] While only 3 percent of Danish registered partners in 1990 had households with children, for example, over 15 percent of such households are raising children today. Yet for some Scandinavians, and even more Americans, the increasing numbers of children raised in state-sanctioned lesbian and gay households is cause for concern. What is the impact on such children when their parents are allowed to enter into legal unions?

The Report from Sweden's Commission on Children in Homosexual Families concluded that legal recognition of same-sex parents has a positive effect on children growing up in such relationships. "Legally acknowledging the homosexual family therefore gives an important signal, not least to the child. It shows that the child's family is just as accepted as other families in society," states the report.[38] When the state rejects legal recognition of same-sex couples, it is sending the opposite message to the children of same-sex couples: society does not view your parents' relationship to be as legitimate as the relationships of the parents of other children. Most critics of same-sex marriage agree with this descriptive analysis but view the consequences as lamentable. The state stamp of approval, in their opinion, encourages unsuitable (i.e., same-sex) couples to undertake the difficult task of rearing children. But even the staunchest opponent, especially those motivated by religious reasoning, ought to concede that those children who are being raised by lesbians and gay men in any event would be better off if their parents' union were more secure and more socially accepted. Same-sex couples (with children) whom we interviewed certainly agreed with this assessment. Birgitte Haase and Kirsten Jepsen, for example, discussed how it was helpful for their young daughter, Maia, to have marriage as a reference point for her parents' relationship, in the same way that many of her friends have married parents.[39]

The Swedish Commission also concluded: "Children have poorer legal protection in a family where only one parent is the guardian, both during the time the parents live together and in the event that they separate or one of them dies."[40] Thus, if government policy denies same-sex parents the opportunity to share legal responsibility and guardianship of their children, the government is putting the child at risk in the event of unforeseen circumstances. Same-sex marriage or partnership in which both members of the couple are recognized as the legal parents of the children in question will thus better secure the child both legally and financially. The child will be better off legally because there will be someone who is responsible for the child's welfare, should anything happen to the child's biological parent. The child will also be better off financially, since the mutual maintenance obligations of family law would require the nonbiological partner to financially support the child if the biological parent were incapable of doing so. Without same-sex marriage or partnership (and thus no legal responsibility for the child by the biological parent's partner), the nonbiological parent would have neither authority over nor responsibilities toward the child, should anything happen to the biological parent, which could lead to undesirable consequences that are ultimately not "in the best interests of the child."

Interpersonal Relationships: Family, Friends, and Coworkers

Also affected by Scandinavian registered partnerships are relationships between the same-sex partners and their greater community, including family, friends, coworkers, even neighbors. While the decision to enter into a registered partnership has its initial effect on the couple itself, its effects ripple through the entire community of which these couples are a part. That effect will vary from couple to couple, and of course will occasionally be negative. For example, the traditionalist neighbor might find it inappropriate that the lesbians next door are not only raising a couple of children but are "flaunting" their marriage license as well. In Denmark, however, the effects seem to have been overall quite positive. On the basis of media reports and our conversations with Danes from all walks of life and different perspectives, we have found that registered partnership rarely has negative effects on others in the community and sometimes has very positive effects. In many cases, it helps to strengthen relationships with family members and colleagues, foster communication, promote understanding, and thereby increase acceptance of alternative family structures. It has helped to reduce discrimination based on prejudice and promote equal treatment of individuals regardless of sexual orientation.

Family Members

For centuries, marriage ceremonies have been occasions to bring couples and those closest to them together, particularly family members, in order to help celebrate the new bonds being made by the groom and bride. As such, marriage (as well as major anniversaries) is an opportunity for those close to the couple to celebrate the love and commitment between two people as they travel the road of life together. The advent of registered partnership, with ceremonial features and process parallel to those of marriage, has afforded Scandinavian same-sex couples the same opportunity to celebrate their relationship with others. Nevertheless, because some family members may be uncomfortable with the concept of a same-sex partnership or marriage, it may take some extra effort, both on the part of the couple and the uncomfortable family members, to adjust to the new relationship being forged by the couple, as well as the concept of same-sex marriage in general.

Because of longstanding family bonds, it appears that most family members of Scandinavian registered partners have been willing to work at overcoming their negative opinions and at least meeting gay marriage halfway. With the help of the family member living in a registered partnership, many have put forth extra effort to integrate the same-sex couple into the family structure. And this extra effort from both parties has had the dual effect of strengthening family bonds between the registered partners and their families and normalizing same-sex couples as part of the greater family organization. Sometimes, of course, parents have refused to accept that they have a son or daughter who is gay or lesbian, choosing to reject their child rather than accept homosexuality into their home. Several registered partners reported rejection by their parents upon the disclosure of their homosexuality. When he was a teenager living at home, Per Kjær recalls that his boyfriend "sent me a letter. My father accidentally opened the letter and read it. When I got home from school, my parents confronted me with it. My father told me that I had to make a choice—either give up the relationship, or leave the family. So three months later I moved out of the house to be with my boyfriend."[41] Lars Fledelius had a similar experience at the age of nineteen: "I told my parents once I was sure of who I was. My father then told me, 'You have a half hour to pack and get out.' We didn't speak for a while after that."[42]

Such reactions are now rare in Scandinavia. Rather than rejecting their child because of his or her sexual orientation, parents today having a negative reaction to their child's homosexuality are more likely to be confused or upset and unsure of how to deal with the situation. For Jens Boesen, who had previously been married to a woman, there was a struggle in the family to accept the information. "At first my parents didn't understand. They thought that to be gay, you had to be effeminate, like the ones they saw on the street. They didn't think that masculine men like me were gay. But they made a real effort to understand me—they had a family meeting about it with my brother, and my brother went to the library to read about homosexuality. So they worked with their own feelings to become more comfortable with it."[43]

Many Scandinavian parents tacitly accept, but would rather not discuss, their children's homosexuality. Such a silent treatment may be psychologically harmful to the gay son or daughter, and certainly impedes the development of a mature adult relationship between parent and offspring. The silent treatment is not easily maintained, however, once the gay son or daughter marries someone of the same sex. Just as entertaining the idea of marriage or partnership serves to spark a discussion within a couple about the nature of their relationship, entering into a formal legal union also encourages (or forces) family members to discuss their child's (or sibling's) relationship. For many such families, same-sex marriage encourages family members to recognize the seriousness of such relationships, to think about the emotional bonds between the two partners, and to accept and acknowledge the importance of the emotional bond between their relative and his or her partner.

For some couples, the formal process of entering a registered partnership became an opportunity to share the importance of one's relationship with one's family. After years of struggle to accept Jens for who he was, the Boesen family made an extra effort to make Jens and Eddie feel comfortable when they married. Because Jens and Eddie registered their partnership within months of meeting, so that Eddie (an American citizen) could remain in Denmark, Jens's parents had never met Eddie before the couple's partnership ceremony. Jens recalls: "We drove to their house for the first time together just after getting married, and my mother had decorated the driveway with Danish and American flags. As soon as my mother saw Eddie, she gave him a huge hug—and my mother has pretty big boobs, so Eddie almost disappeared in there—he was shocked at how welcoming she was. And then my parents arranged a big celebratory dinner for us and invited my whole family there. It was wonderful. My sister and her husband fixed our car with a 'Just Married' sign, with paper and cans hanging from the back of it. We drove twenty kilometers in our car like that—it was pretty funny." Eddie adds: "At first I wasn't particularly looking forward to meeting his parents—I didn't expect them to be very welcoming. But as soon as I got there and she gave me this huge hug, it was amazing—the acceptance was just unbelievable to me."[44]

For Uffe Størner and Kaj Kristensen, family acceptance was a great deal more subtle, but just as important. While Uffe's parents knew he was gay, it was rarely discussed within his family. He had some limited conversations with his mother about it, but he and his father never spoke of it. But when Kaj became part of Uffe's life, his parents made an extra effort to make Kaj feel part of the family. "The first time I took Kaj out to meet my parents, he was extremely nervous. But when we arrived, my mother took Kaj by the hand, and told him—'Welcome to our cottage here—you will be a good member of the family. Welcome.'" Kaj adds: "Then she said, 'I never thought that I'd be welcoming a son-in-law.' It was very emotional, and also very funny."[45]

Uffe's experience with his parents also points out another benefit of legalized unions. For many parents and other relatives, government sanction of same-sex relationships makes it easier for them to accept the legitimacy of such relationships, and also makes it easier for them to describe the nature of the relationship to others. Uffe explains: "My mother thought it was a good thing to do, that we got registered. In her mind, that's the proper way to do it if you're living your life together with someone. So she's traditional, but that also means that she thinks two people who love each other should get married."[46]

In other cases, it is not the immediate act of getting married that forces family members to confront their own feelings regarding homosexuality— but rather, a mental absorption of the nature of the relationship over time. Just as some parents have an instantaneous negative reaction to learning of their child's homosexuality but come to accept it over an extended period, so do other parents need time to adjust to the idea of their child being in a same-sex marriage before they come to accept the relationship within their family. Jean Luscher, married since 1995 to Diana Skovgaard, has experienced an evolving relationship with her mother in regard to her legal union. In our original interview, Jean expressed some disappointment at her mother's unwillingness to accept her marriage to Diana: "It's weird, because my mother likes Diana, but she doesn't approve of the relationship. For example, I was back in the states visiting with Diana and her son, and I was introducing him as my stepson—and my mother drew me aside and told me that I shouldn't introduce him as my stepson, that it wasn't the case. But I always travel with my marriage license, for clarity if there are any questions—I keep it with me in a plastic case. And I said to her, 'I have my marriage license with me, mother, do you want to see it?' And of course she said no."[47]

In a follow-up interview in 2005, Jean had the following information to add. "My mother's attitudes have evolved regarding our marriage. I went home to the town we lived in for a visit, and now she has a picture of the two of us together, just like she has pictures of my brothers' weddings. I couldn't have imagined that earlier, but she has become much better about the situation." And it's not just her mother whose attitudes have evolved:

"My family has become much more interested in the issue of gay marriage. I'm the only liberal person in a Republican family—but when we talk about gay marriage, I notice that my brothers and sisters-in-law, people who don't normally think along those lines, don't think gay marriage is the end of the world as we know it. And I don't think they would have thought so if I hadn't been in a gay marriage."[48]

Jean's partnership with Diana has also encouraged her siblings to raise their own children with an understanding of, and respect for, their lesbian marriage. "My brother's children are being raised to think of Diana and [me] as normal—they have been very up front about our relationship. [The children] are six and eight years old—and they will ask us questions, me and Aunt Diana. They understand I can't get married in the U.S., which is why I live in Denmark. My nephew once asked: 'Why did you go all the way to Denmark to marry Aunt Diana when you could have married a boy here?' And my sister-in-law replied: 'That's because Jean loves Diana very much.' And he was satisfied with that answer."[49]

The experiences of different gays and lesbians in registered partnerships suggest that same-sex marriage has varying effects on families, depending on the family's baseline comfort level with homosexuality and same-sex relationships. For families who have already become comfortable with their family member's sexual orientation, gay marriage serves as a catalyst for initiating dialogue among family members about same-sex relationships within their family. For families who remain uncomfortable with the issue of sexual orientation, the same-sex legal union still serves to bond families closer together, but acceptance may be demonstrated by these family members in a more passive manner.

Friends and Acquaintances

While the romantic feelings unmarried or unregistered partners have for one another may be strong, the seriousness of the relationship (and how it should be treated) remains open to question from the perspective of outside parties. In the absence of a legally recognized union, it can never be completely clear to friends exactly what the nature of the relationship is. Questions may arise, such as these: Are they just dating? How serious are they? Is it appropriate to invite them out separately, or should I only invite them out as a couple? Can I take the liberty of asking one of them out on a date? Traditionally, gays and lesbians have had no way available to indicate the permanent nature of their same-sex relationship. Living together gave some indications of relationship stability, but even then the message sent out by this situation was less than clear.

The ability to enter a legal union, therefore, sends a clearer message to friends and acquaintances: our relationship is long-term and we are deeply committed to one another. It also indicates to others that the couple should be treated like any other married couple in terms of social interactions with their friends, such as invitations to dinners, parties, and weddings. Consider the experience of Deborah Kaplan and her partner, Anne Jespersen. "In a marriage, other people have taken our relationship more seriously. If they know I'm married, nobody is going to try to hit on me, and nobody is going to invite me to a party without the other half—but if you're just a couple, people don't know where your relationship is at, and they might invite one person out without the other." According to Deborah, this respect for her partnership wasn't limited to Denmark; she had similar experiences in her home country, the United States. "Even though we don't have gay marriage in the U.S., my family respects marriage, and they respect the institution of marriage—so they started respecting my relationship in a more mature way once I got married here." We heard the same kind of stories from other registered partners, male and female alike.[50]

Same-sex marriage may also be effective at counteracting certain stereotypes about the permanency of same-sex relationships. Jean Luscher believes that her partnership served to contradict a pervasive sentiment of cynicism and stereotyping. "We have some friends who are very pessimistic, who assumed that our gay relationship, like other gay relationships they knew, would eventually fail, and that we would grow apart. Those people who didn't know us intimately—well, they were surprised. They realized that our relationship was more serious than they thought, and that they were wrong that we would eventually break up."[51] Anne Jespersen felt a similar experience, particularly considering her heterosexual history. "Because I had been married to a man for so long, and now I have a woman in my life, many of my friends were thinking, 'Oh, she's just going through a phase.' But then, when they hear that I've gotten married, I can see that it makes an impression on them, and they see our relationship as more serious."[52]

Finally, the enthusiasm of many same-sex couples toward the concept of marriage may be having a beneficial effect on heterosexual couples' approach to the institution of marriage. The positive feelings with which many same-sex couples have approached their legal unions may rub off on their heterosexual friends and acquaintances in their own thoughts about marriage. Some interviewed couples reported that their own strong interest in tying the knot increased the interest of their heterosexual friends in marriage. We discuss this in greater detail in chapter 5.

Employers and Coworkers

While the impact of same-sex marriage on friends and family affects their interpersonal relationships with the partners, it has a different type of effect on coworkers and business associates who are not as emotionally connected to the couple. For them, revelations relating to same-sex marriage may have less of an effect on the person's bond with the registered partner and more of an effect on the person's opinions on same-sex marriage and homosexuality. Same-sex marriage has the potential effect of promoting understanding and tolerance in relation to both homosexuality and same-sex marriage, with the consequences of reducing prejudice and thereby discrimination against gays and lesbians and same-sex couples.

Entering into a same-sex marriage or partnership is often the catalyst for coming out to coworkers and business associates. Many lesbians and gay men who are out of the closet to their families and friends are not out to coworkers or business associates simply because they have never been asked about their sexual orientation. While direct questions regarding one's sexual orientation are indeed rare among coworkers and casual acquaintances, discussion of one's family life is more common. One is much less likely to encounter the question "Are you gay?" than the question "Are you married?" If a gay employee wears a wedding ring or another emblem of marriage, she or he is certain to field questions about the spouse and hence come out to coworkers, supervisors, and even the most casual business associate. In addition, being able to say "I am married," rather than "I am living with someone," enables lesbian and gay spouses to speak about their relationships with more confidence. The legal nature of the relationship both validates the strength of the relationship and makes it easier to discuss by giving a name to the relationship.

Often, the introduction of one's same-sex partner or spouse into a conversation is a less confrontational way of coming out to those who may be unfamiliar or uncomfortable with homosexuality in general. While a specific declaration of one's sexual orientation to an acquaintance ("I am gay") is more likely to elicit a moral response, a discussion of one's partner may be seen as having less of a need for moral judgment. In other words, the acquaintance has the opportunity to deal with homosexuality in an indirect manner—that is, through discussion of the colleague's same-sex partner—rather than needing to directly discuss homosexuality in general. Through this more subtle approach, gays and lesbians may find an easier path to acceptance of their sexual orientation, and may encourage their colleagues to open up to a discussion of homosexuality, rather than have them shut down through more direct confrontation. If the partners are raising children, the social situation is rendered even easier for most homo-anxious but essentially tolerant adults. They feel comfortable gabbing on and on about what delightful or cute kids the couple are blessed with—and offering friendly (and hopefully useful) child-rearing tips.

Recall another Danish-American couple, Jens Boesen and Eddie Moris. After registering as Jens's partner, Eddie took a job with the Danish postal service. According to Eddie, many of his colleagues were macho types who were not particularly familiar with homosexuality. He recalls how his experiences at the office changed after his coming out through the partnership registration. "There was this big macho guy at work who had heard that I was married, and he asked me whether I speak English or Danish with my wife at home. I paused—after all, this was a really big tough guy—but then I said, 'My *husband* and I usually speak English at home.'" Eddie smiles as he recalls what happened next. "That response really shocked him—he became visibly angry, turned to me, and said in a harsh tone, 'You and your husband should be speaking Danish! How else do you expect to learn the language?'" Through a discussion of his marriage, Eddie was able to break down the invisible barrier regarding his sexual orientation with a number of his postal colleagues. And in response, his colleagues made their own efforts to demonstrate their acceptance of Eddie. He recalls: "There is a calendar on the wall at work that has partially clothed female and male models on it. Normally the guys at the office had the calendar flipped open so that only the female models were visible. But now, when I am working in the room, they flip the calendar open so that the male models show too. I guess they think that I should also have something to look at." While perhaps not as direct as a discussion of Eddie's homosexuality, such small actions are sometimes just as revealing.[53]

Palle Heilesen, a high-level official in one of Denmark's ministries, began government service in the late 1970s. While not closeted, he has always been cautious at work. "I had a rule when working with people—don't tell people you're gay right at the beginning. Give them a while to get to know you first, so they remember your name before they think of you as a gay person." Nevertheless, his relationship with his partner led to an early coming out to his department. "When I started my first day at the Ministry, my chief introduced me to everyone…and later he asked me if I was living with someone. I said yes, then he asked, 'What's her name?' And I said, 'His name is . . . ' There was a short pause. And then my chief said, 'His name doesn't sound Danish, where does he come from?' So there was no issue there. And then of course the rumors spread at work, and a few people approached me to ask how other people had reacted. And I said, nobody's reacted. And so after that, a year later, there were five open gays in my department, where there were none before."[54]

Palle's account of the abilities of openly gay people to work productively with straights of all attitudes and beliefs is not unusual. What happened to Palle next would have been pretty rare a generation ago but is now more common in Europe and the United States. "In all my career, there hasn't been any bad reaction. In fact, I was approached by a minister at one time, asking me if I wanted to take the job as her private assistant. She was a female minister—and I asked her if she knew I was gay. And she said, yes, I've known since I came here as minister, and that's one of the reasons that I want you in the position—because your way of thinking is different than others, you're able to think independently. So I discussed it with Otto, and at first I said no, because it's a twenty-four-hour job. But she insisted because she really wanted me in the position. And so I eventually took it."[55]

In those cases where registered partners are already comfortably out at work, same-sex marriage gives their colleagues the opportunity to help celebrate their marriage. This not only offers an opportunity to help normalize the idea of same-sex marriages by treating them as heterosexual marriage would be treated but also affords an opportunity to help the registered partner bond more closely with his or her work colleagues. A number of interviewed partners reported that their coworkers had thrown parties for them, given them gifts, and offered their congratulations on the special event. Palle Heilesen and Otto Bygsø, in particular, were surprised and honored when they emerged after their wedding ceremony from Copenhagen's Town Hall: at the door's entrance were twelve policemen, heterosexual colleagues of Bygsø, in full ceremonial uniform, officer's caps lifted high, creating a line of honor for the two men to walk through in celebration of their new marriage.

The effect of same-sex marriage, and its ability to change attitudes, is not limited to the workplace. To the extent that partners are willing to share their experiences with others in their community who may be unfamiliar with gay and lesbian couples, they have the opportunity to change attitudes and to normalize the concept of same-sex relationships among members of their community. Those living in smaller towns and more rural areas, in particular, where homosexuality has less visibility, may be able to increase understanding of and support for same-sex relationships by sharing their partnership with others.

When Lars Henriksen and Jan Lorenzen made the decision to purchase a farm and move out of Copenhagen, they were aware of the fact that attitudes toward same-sex couples in their newly adopted country town of Holstebro would not be as open and accepting as such attitudes were in Copenhagen. Nevertheless, they decided that they wanted to be an active part of their new community—and as part of their involvement in the community, they would live their lives openly and honestly, and work to incorporate their community members into their lives just as much as they would become part of the lives of others. "When we first moved to this town, many of our neighbors avoided us because of our relationship together," explains Lars. "But once people actually started to know us, things began to change. For example, I joined a horseback riding school here because I have always been interested in horseback riding. And there were lots of teenagers in the school who weren't comfortable with the idea of homosexuality. But as they got to know me, they became more comfortable with it. Then they started asking a lot of questions about my relationship with Jan. I have to explain to them that my life isn't much different than their lives—just that I love someone of the same sex."[56]

When the time came for their wedding, Lars and Jan invited many members of their town to celebrate with them. "I invited a lot of teens from my riding school as well," says Lars. "When I told them I was getting married, they asked, 'Who would wear the white dress?' But then I explain to them that, since we are two men, neither of us will wear a white dress. And they think about it, and then they understand that. So many of these kids came to our wedding too, and I could see that it had an impact on them. And many of them changed their minds on the idea of same-sex relationships."[57]

Of course, there is no country free from antihomosexual prejudice or just homo-anxious attitudes, and the Nordic nations are no exception. Some couples, particularly some of those in smaller towns, indicated that they were not completely open about their homosexuality to coworkers and the greater communities in which they lived. Recall the story in chapter 3 of Claus Rasmussen and Niels Andersen, who chose not to register in their local township in order to avoid public attention. And even Peer Toft and Peter Mols, who have been together since 1981 and consider themselves very comfortable with their sexuality, are not completely "out" at work. According to Peter, "We don't talk about it at work. But rumors spread very quickly in the navy, and I'm sure most people know. I've never been in a situation where I needed to say it to someone. I did get a couple of questions after we got married and I had a ring on my finger. But I think a lot of people still feel uncomfortable asking 'How's your boyfriend?' We don't bring each other to our work parties. We invite some of our work colleagues to our own parties, though. But for those events at work like Christmas dinner or lunch, where people bring their partners, we don't bring each other. But of course, if they ask me about my wedding ring, I answer them honestly."[58]

In regard to such stories, it is unclear whether disclosure of one's partnership status (and thereby one's homosexuality) would have led to a negative reaction from coworkers and community or whether the main problem was the *fear* of a negative reaction. As the situation with Jan and Lars demonstrates, it could be argued that the extent to which same-sex marriage works to reduce prejudice and encourage acceptance is in part based on the extent to which same-sex couples are willing to share their relationship with the communities they live and work in. Nevertheless, it is clear that to the extent that discussion of one's family life arises in casual conversation among colleagues, same-sex marriage has the potential to break down barriers, tie same-sex couples more closely to their communities, and encourage those unfamiliar with homosexuality to reexamine their own feelings and prejudices about same-sex couples.

Greater Social Benefits of Same-Sex Marriage

While the parliamentary supporters of registered partnership were primarily focused on benefits accruing to the couples themselves (and, to a lesser extent, their communities), the Scandinavian experience demonstrates that same-sex marriage offers potential benefits for the larger national and even international community. These benefits are both economic and social in nature, and suggest that governments considering same-sex marriage should take a broad view when considering the possibility of enacting same-sex marriage or partnership in their own countries. We do not have the data, at present, to quantify the social benefits that ought to accrue, but our analysis below suggests that they ought to be substantial.

State Financial Obligations: Marriage and Partnership as Privatized Social Welfare

The Scandinavian countries have relatively generous welfare and other financial support programs to assist their citizens in times of need. Financial aid is calculated on an individual basis, based on the relative need of the individual. However, the amount of state aid that a resident qualifies for is likely to be higher for an unmarried person with no financial resources who is seeking state benefits than for a married or registered person seeking such benefits. This is due to the mutual maintenance obligations for married couples, under which one's eligibility for state aid and the level of aid is determined not by the financial resources of the individual alone but by the overall resources of the married couple. Thus, a same-sex couple living in a registered partnership, where one party is unemployed or financially distressed, is likely to be offered less financial support from the state than if the individual applying for aid was applying on his or her own and not in a partnership.[59] Likewise, a single parent raising children on her own will receive more financial support from the state than two married or partnered parents raising children.[60]

Thus, especially in a quasi-socialist country where the state assumes responsibility for social welfare, marriage for same-sex as well as different-sex couples stands to save the state a significant amount of its financial resources. To be sure, some money the state saves on social welfare programs will be offset by the spousal benefits, particularly tax benefits, that same-sex couples are now able to take advantage of in a registered partnership. (But the marital tax benefits available to some couples are partially offset by tax losses suffered by wealthier married couples.) Exactly how much money the state would save if everyone were married or partnered cannot be easily calculated, but it would appear to be substantial.

In any event, there is a broader policy point to be made as well. As in the United States (though less of a welfare state), Scandinavian marriage is a form of privatized social welfare, and the mixture of private and public welfare networks is superior to either system standing alone. The social safety net exists to provide citizens with security in the face of misfortune. Misfortunes include temporary or permanent illness, injurious accidents, disability, unemployment, and old age with its infirmities, disabilities, and illnesses. In Scandinavia and the United States, the government and (especially in the United States) employers insure most of us against such misfortunes. This is a potentially costly system. That many Scandinavian and American adults are married or partnered makes the system much less costly than it otherwise would be. Our spouses or partners, rather than expensive doctors, take care of us when we encounter routine injuries and ordinary scrapes. Our families often care for us, and we for them, if we suffer from debilitating illness, disability, or old age. Privatizing so much of the cost of misfortune not only saves government and employers a lot of money but it produces personalized, loving caregiving that is quite superior to that which institutions can provide.

Integration of Minority Groups into Mainstream Society

A number of studies have demonstrated that people who know and work with openly gay men and lesbians are likely to have lower levels of prejudice and hostility toward this group than those who are not personally acquainted with such persons. As discussed previously in this chapter, same-sex marriage is often the catalyst for coming out to work colleagues and other acquaintances, particularly as family life is generally considered a valid subject of conversation among casual acquaintances (whereas sexual orientation is not). Same-sex marriage, therefore, may work to encourage dialogue about homosexuality—not only directly between gays and lesbians and their colleagues but also between the colleagues and their friends. (E.g., "Did you know that our work colleague Lars is married to another man?") In both instances, this dialogue may foster a greater familiarity with gays and lesbians, and ultimately a greater sense of comfort with the issue of homosexuality. Furthermore, same-sex marriage offers a number of opportunities for gay and lesbian couples to integrate members of their community into their lives—through the wedding ceremony, anniversaries, and other occasions.

State sanction of same-sex relationships also signals that antigay conduct is unacceptable. For example, in the absence of same-sex marriage, the notion of two men or two women showing affection openly in public (e.g., holding hands, kissing) may serve as an invitation for antigay conduct—hurling epithets or throwing fists. Yet in a country that has given legal recognition to these relationships, it becomes less acceptable to publicly demonstrate hostility toward such couples and their public show of affection toward one another. Same-sex marriage or partnerships also promote a country's commitment to equality for all its citizens. Particularly in the more progressive nations of northern Europe, equality regardless of sexual orientation is seen as an important social goal. Legal unions for same-sex couples sends a strong message—not only to a government's own population but to outside observers as well—that it is committed to equality for all its citizens.

In the case of Denmark, we can see that its pioneer efforts in enacting a marriage-like law for same-sex couples led government officials in other countries to take action advancing their own equality goals. Over the course of the 1990s, government officials from countries as far away as Australia and Brazil visited the Nordic countries and/or requested information from their governments to learn more about the Scandinavian partnership laws, as part of their own efforts to enact legislation recognizing same-sex couples.[61] And in the United States, one of the first Danish couples to register in 1989 was given the honorary position of grand marshals of New York City's 1990 Gay Pride Parade, which served as an inspiration in the United States for those fighting for equal rights under the law.[62]

Attraction and Retention of Highly Educated Workers

In the United States, one of the reasons employers most often cite in support of the extension of same-sex domestic partnership benefits is to attract and retain highly skilled employees. The underlying theory is that, if a de-sirable gay or lesbian candidate for employment is choosing between rela-tively similar companies, one of his or her considerations may be the company's receptiveness toward gays and lesbians and their partners, as demonstrated by the existence of domestic partnership benefits. Compa-nies that don't offer such benefits, it is contended, may lose a competitive advantage in attracting some of the most highly desirable candidates in the workforce. A related point is the local community's receptiveness to gay people. A community that has a history of antigay violence and harassment will certainly scare away most such employees. Conversely, a community that respects lesbian and gay relationships will attract such employees. In-deed, many gay and lesbian employees will choose a lower paying job in a supportive community over a higher paying job in a highly prejudiced part of the United States.

How does this relate to same-sex marriage? Consider two sets of facts regarding registered partners in Scandinavia. First, registered partners are much more likely than the average person to have an advanced level of edu-cation. Second, many registered partners have a partner from another coun-try. From the statistics available from Norway and Sweden, we see that approximately 20 percent of male registered partnerships involve a partner from a non-European country.[63] What these statistics suggest is that there are a number of couples that would be unable to live together in Scandinavia in the absence of the immigration benefits of same-sex marriage. If the Scandi-navian partner were not able to bring his or her partner into the country, a substantial percentage of these couples might choose to live elsewhere, thus depriving the country of the potential benefits of additional skilled workers.

Andre Oriveira, from Brazil, and his Danish partner Jan Nørmark are a case in point. Andre, a chemical engineer with an advanced degree, met Jan, an educator of mentally retarded adults, in Berlin during a leave of absence from his company in Brazil. Although Jan was only in Germany for a short period for a volleyball tournament, the two fell for each other quickly. "At the time we met, what was going through my head was that he was the man of my life," recalls Andre. "We were thinking with our hearts, and we wanted to be close. So we took a vacation together in Miami, and soon thereafter I knew that we would have to be together. We knew that we would have to get married to have that possibility, and that I would have to move to Den-mark to be with Jan."[64]

In the absence of a registered partnership law in Denmark, couples such as Andre and Jan might have decided to move to another country that rec-ognized their union. For example, as a citizen of the European Union, Jan may have chosen instead to move to the Netherlands, which itself recognizes same-sex couples, and Jan could have joined him there. Thus would Denmark have been deprived of the skilled labor that Jan and Andre could offer. Same-sex marriage or partnership legislation, on the other hand, encourages the retention within the country of these partners and the skills that they bring with them to the labor force. In today's increasingly globalized economy, with its increasingly mobile workforce, signals of tolerance and support for gay and lesbian couples (such as same-sex marriage or partnership) can only strengthen a nation's competitive advantage in attracting and retaining highly skilled workers.

Sexually Transmitted Diseases and State Anti-AIDS Campaigns

In the late 1980s, before the advent of drug regimens that substantially prolonged the life of HIV-infected individuals, the subject of AIDS weighed heavily on the minds of policy-makers. Introducing the Danish registered partnership legislation, parliamentary sponsors said:

> Although the bill does not originate from the dangerous situation regarding the sickness AIDS, it has increased interest in its passage. ... The illness has given occasion for focusing on the collective life situation of gays, such as doctor Henrik Zoffmann [a Danish HIV specialist] on several occasions has given expression to: that a better life situation, changed opinions and less pressure on permanent relationships between two people of the same sex could reduce the number of casual relationships between gay men and thereby contribute to the fight against the disease's spread.[65]

Thus the authors of the partnership law argued that passage of the law would encourage committed, long-term relationships between gay men. The encouragement of these types of relationships, the argument continues, would work to encourage monogamy and reduce the amount of promiscuous sex engaged in by gay men in Denmark. Even if these gay men chose not to remain exclusively monogamous, it was thought, the fact that they were in a legally binding, stable partnership would encourage them to think about the welfare of their partners and therefore practice only safe sex outside of the relationship. As we demonstrated earlier, our interviews with partners who have registered under the law reveal that attitudes and conduct did change for some lesbian and gay Danes.

The recent study by the National Bureau of European Research found that, for the twelve European countries recognizing same-sex unions in 2004, gonorrhea and, especially, syphilis rates had plummeted to levels well below those of nonrecognition countries in Europe. After controlling for other variables, the study found that same-sex marriage accounted for a 26 to 53 percent reduction in a country's syphilis rate. This is an amazing statistic, and would reflect an enormous social benefit if replicated in the United States. HIV infection rates were higher in the recognition countries between 1985 and 1995, but converged in the period 1995–2005, averaging between three and four persons per one hundred thousand people. The HIV trend was not statistically significant, however, so this study leaves some doubt about the causal link between same-sex marriage and HIV infection. One reason for the less-than-significant correlation may have been that the study included Germany, France, and other countries that give marriage-lite institutions with many fewer benefits and, most important, fewer obligations to same-sex partners. Scandinavian HIV statistics, on the other hand, provide stronger evidence that same-sex marriage is an important part of a country's anti-AIDS campaign.[66]

There has been a significant reduction in the rate of HIV infection among men who have sex with men (MSM) in Denmark, Norway, and Sweden in the years since the enactment of their respective partnership laws. Denmark began recording statistics on new HIV cases in 1990, the year after enactment of the partnership law. In that year, an estimated 190 gay and bisexual men were newly infected with HIV, almost four persons per one hundred thousand people, which would have placed Denmark on the high end of HIV infection in Europe.[67] These new infections fell significantly after 1990, at a time when HIV infections in Europe as a whole were fairly stable. In 1991, 1992, and 1993, the number of new reported HIV infections fell to 152, 143, and 130, respectively; from 1994 to the end of 2004, there have been an average of 103 annual HIV infections of men having sex with men in Denmark (relatively stable except for a spike to 149 in 2004), not only a 46 percent decrease in the number of HIV infections from 1990 but a rate of about two per one hundred thousand people that places Denmark well below average for Europe during that period.

The data are similar for Norway, where mandatory annual tallies of HIV infection have been kept since 1986. An average of 50.5 annual infections were reported among homosexual men from 1986 to 1993, when the partnership law was introduced. From 1994 to 2004, there were an average of 40.1 annual infections among this risk group, or an approximate 20 percent decrease in the number of HIV infections annually after the partnership legislation went into effect.[68]

Sweden has recorded infection rates since 1985, about a decade before its registered partnership law was passed. From 1988 until the introduction of partnership, the annual reported HIV infection rate in Sweden among MSM was 120 new infections annually, a relatively low figure, reflecting infections in about 1.5 persons per one hundred thousand people.[69] From 1995 until the end of 2004, this rate was just under 75 new infections annually, not only a 38 percent decrease in the HIV infection rate, but also a rate of less than one person per one hundred thousand that was the lowest in Europe. Although the Swedish HIV infection rate showed some decline before 1995, surely owing to that country's astute AIDS-education program, the decline was much stronger after 1995. The only relevant variable that changed in that period, so far as we know, was the registration of same-sex partners starting in 1995.[70]

These data remain preliminary soundings on this important issue, but they support the notion that registered partnership in Scandinavia has contributed to the success those countries have had in reducing their HIV infection rates. As Bent Hansen, former chair of LBL, has stated, "Even if the partnership law has prevented just one person from becoming infected with HIV, it has done us a great service."[71] From society's perspective, a drop in the number of HIV infections equates to a reduction in medical costs. Considering that health services in Scandinavia are funded by tax dollars, a reduction in HIV infection leads to a reduction in government spending on health care and pharmaceutical products for those with HIV. Considering that current drug regimens for HIV-infected individuals may run in the tens of thousands of dollars annually, such savings per patient may be quite significant.

Taking a Broader Perspective on the Net Benefits of Same-Sex Marriage

There have been a number of variations on the traditionalist argument that same-sex marriage constitutes a demonstration by the government of its approval of gay and lesbian relationships. A more recent (and more tolerant-sounding) version of this argument in the United States is that recognition of same-sex marriage would "force" taxpaying Americans who disagree with the concept of same-sex marriage to spend their tax dollars on what traditionalists claim would be a controversial, and expensive, proposition for the state. Such conservatives claim that the government expenses associated with gay marriage should in themselves be enough of a reason to withhold the extension of marriage from same-sex couples. For example, during Senate hearings on the Defense of Marriage Act, Senator Robert Byrd pointed to a potential increase in Medicare and Medicaid spending as a problem that would result from the legalization of gay unions.[72] In the United States, this argument has particular bite in a time when government spending is a topic of concern.

Gay-liberals and their allies in the United States, on the other hand, point out that same-sex couples are presently subsidizing government benefits for heterosexual married couples with their own tax dollars, without receiving anything in return. The Government Accountability Office (formerly the General Accounting Office, the audit, evaluation, and investigative arm of Congress) in January 2004 outlined a total of 1,138 federal rights and responsibilities associated with marriage that are not available to same-sex couples, including areas such as social security, tax benefits, and benefits for spouses of federal employees.[73] The National Gay and Lesbian Task Force reports that a same-sex couple's combined federal and state tax liability could be 13–25 percent higher than that of married couples making the same income (varying by state and income levels). Furthermore, their social security retirement benefits are reduced by approximately one-quarter to one-third, and a surviving partner receives no Social Security survivor benefit – solely by virtue of not being able to marry.[74] Thus, from a fairness perspective, proponents of marriage equality argue that same-sex couples should be entitled to equal government benefits in relation to married couples in consideration of their equal (or perhaps greater) tax contributions toward such benefits.

More important to the taxpayer-funding variation on the stamp-of-approval objection, other studies, including those from the federal government, have suggested that the government would actually benefit financially from the extension of marriage rights to same-sex couples. A recent report by the Congressional Budget Office found that allowing same-sex couples to marry in all fifty states would save the federal government nearly $1 billion a year.[75] A joint research study by the Williams Project of UCLA and the Institute for Gay and Lesbian Strategic Studies at University of Massachusetts (Amherst) found that allowing same-sex couples to marry in the state of Connecticut would increase state revenues between $3.1 million and $13 million per year for each of the first three years of the law;[76] other reports showed similar benefits for allowing same-sex marriage in Vermont (net state benefit between $18.1 to $22.8 million)[77] and marriage-like partnerships in California ($8.1 to $10.6 million).[78] These studies, and others, suggest that the financial variation on the stamp-of-approval objection is likely misplaced.

However, looking past disagreements between supporters and opponents of gay marriage on the financial bottom line of such unions, one of the main purposes of this chapter is to demonstrate that calculating the benefits of same-sex marriage is much more than just a numbers game—or, conversely, more than just a moral debate. The focus of some traditionalists and some supporters of same-sex marriage on a single, and often narrow, aspect of same-sex marriage has the consequence of losing sight of the much bigger picture.

Based on the Scandinavian experience, we suggest that politicians and advocates on both sides of the issue step back and look at the much broader, and richer, array of benefits that same-sex marriage (or its functional equivalent) can bring to society. Such benefits not only support the well-being of the couples themselves, but also bring a diverse set of benefits to their families, their friends, their communities, and even on a national scale. Often, these benefits simply cannot be calculated in terms of a dollar value, but their impact is nevertheless visible, and often strongly felt.

We think that persons of all political persuasions—traditionalist, liberal, moderate, and others—will find benefits they find appealing in the extension of the rights and responsibilities of marriage to same-sex couples. Whether one's main interest in the subject is based in a traditionalist perspective of supporting commitment and family cohesiveness, or in a progressive perspective of promoting equality and tolerance, it appears that same-sex unions have benefits of interest for people on all sides of the political spectrum.

CHAPTER 5

Modern Scandinavian Families and the Defense-of-Marriage Argument

Per Kjær and Barry Winter, our "bear" couple.

Experience with Scandinavian registered partnerships casts new light on the stamp-of-approval and definitional objections to same-sex marriage, as we have seen in the previous two chapters. Nordic registered partnership laws have, as traditionalists claim, expressed a more positive state attitude toward lesbian and gay relationships. But their main effect, and one fully intended, has been to approve and encourage lesbians and gay men to enter into public commitments. More recently, the laws have been amended to approve and encourage same-sex couples to raise children within those relationships. These partnership laws and the same-sex marriage laws of the Netherlands, Canada, Belgium and Spain stand against the notion that marriage can *only* be comprehended as one man, one woman. They also undermine the Pandora's box argument—that opening the door to same-sex marriage will open the way to legalized incest, polygamy, and bestial marriages.

How does international experience bear on the primary argument against same-sex marriage, namely, the defense-of-marriage objection? Because the Dutch authorities and the Canadian provincial governments have only been awarding marriage licenses to same-sex couples for a few years, it is too early to draw many conclusions from their experience. But Denmark, Norway, and Sweden have been registering same-sex partnerships for more than sixteen, twelve, and ten years (respectively). Have legal unions for lesbian and gay couples undermined the institution of marriage?

Barry Winter and Per Kjær think not. They are a middle-aged, transnational couple. Barry grew up in a blue-collar town near Cambridge, England; Per's parents worked in a shipyard and telephone company in Aalborg, Denmark. Both had enjoyed long-term relationships with men when they met in 1987 while on holiday in the Grand Cayman Islands. Their mutual attraction was immediate, and soon thereafter Barry was visiting Per in Denmark. In 1988, Barry moved to Aalborg to be with Per (who had moved back to his hometown to help take care of his aging parents). They are self-proclaimed "bears," and have even given their house (and their website) the name *Bamsebo,* which is Danish for "bear's cave" or "bear's den." As Barry put it, "We consider ourselves bears—we have the belly and the bum to be bears, and we have a good life like that! More like teddy bears, though."[1]

Married on October 28, 1989, they were the first partners to register in Aalborg. The Christian People's Party (CPP) legislators who had opposed the Registered Partnership Act warned that couples like Barry and Per foreshadowed the end of marriage. But the Aalborg official who married Per and Barry did not see it that way. He told the couple "it was a great pleasure for him to be able to marry the first couple in Aalborg. He said it was his attitude for years that it should be possible." (The town also gave the couple a wedding present—wineglasses with the crescent of the town.) Per was touched that the local officials actively supported "this rich community of diversity in our society." In his view, "the partnership law helps our gay community come forward and be more a part of the community of society. Well, that's Denmark for you." Barry agreed. Growing up gay in a homo-anxious country (England) meant that he hadn't imagined himself in a legally recognized relationship, much less marriage. To have found the love of his life, and community acceptance, in Denmark was overwhelming for him.[2]

We asked the couple how their partnership has affected those around them, and found that it has stimulated a lot of friendly inquiry and conversation, sometimes from complete strangers. Barry also reported that "it has affected our straight friends, [especially] a straight couple with two children. When they saw us getting married, they decided it was time for them to do the same. [The husband] was frightened of the idea of getting married, but when they heard we were going to do it, he became more comfortable with the idea." Many Americans might be surprised by such an observation, for they seem committed to the idea that same-sex marriage (or its Danish equivalent, registered partnership) would actually scare straight couples away from, or otherwise undermine, the institution.[3]

Is this Case of the Converted Straight Couple an isolated event? Or is it overwhelmed by the number of straight couples who behave as though the registered partnership statute were the official death knell of marriage? Some American opponents of same-sex marriage remain certain that registered partnerships have somehow "ended" (or hastened the end of) marriage as an institution in Scandinavia. Among the most prominent proponents of the Scandinavian twist on the defense-of-marriage objection are Rick Santorum, the Republican Senate whip; empirical researcher Stanley Kurtz; and former Yale law professor, solicitor general, and judge Robert Bork. Other prominent political leaders, empiricists, and law professors have spoken and written in favor of the Scandinavian twist, but these are the leading advocates from different segments of American public life (politics, social science, and law). In a nutshell, their claim is that same-sex marriage or marriage-like partnership materially bolsters the liberal trends already afoot in those countries, including the delinking of procreation and parenting from marriage and the reconceptualization of marriage as an institution focused on selfish pleasure rather than altruistic service and commitment. These thinkers argue that any individualistic, choice-providing change in family law reinforces other *liberalizing* trends and therefore accelerates the demise of marriage. The empirical basis of this argument, primarily developed by Kurtz but echoed by the others, is the following: right after Scandinavian countries recognized same-sex partnerships, these advocates claim, more heterosexual Scandinavians decided not to marry in these countries, and unprecedented numbers of children were born out of wedlock.[4]

There are some preliminary problems with the Scandinavian twist on the defense-of-marriage argument. Well before Barry Winter emigrated to Denmark, the long-term trend in Scandinavia had been declining marriage rates, rising divorce rates, and soaring rates of nonmarital births. This has been a trend lasting two generations—long predating Scandinavian registered partnership laws. Pertinent to the defense-of-marriage objection to same-sex marriage is the following query. Have registered partnerships *accelerated* the pace of change in marriage that had been going on for most of the twentieth century, and that had been dramatic since 1970? If state-recognized same-sex partnerships "contributed" to the decline of marriage, as the critics maintain, we would expect to see *something more than* falling marriage rates, rising divorce rates, and soaring nonmarital birth rates in Denmark after 1989, Norway after 1993, and Sweden after 1995. Rather, we should expect to see marriage rates falling faster, divorce rates accelerating upward, and a surge in nonmarital birth rates. The data reveal no such trend. Not only do the registered partnership laws in Denmark, Norway, and Sweden not correlate to supernormal plunges in marriage rates and superelevated divorce rates but some of the trends move in the other direction. The 1990s do not even remotely indicate the approach of the "end of marriage"—rather, the institution shows renewed signs of life in the new millennium.

Even if marriage rates fell more dramatically and nonmarital birth rates rose more dramatically after registered partnerships, such a sequence would not establish that the latter *caused* the former. Santorum, Kurtz, and Bork make the classic *post hoc, propter hoc* ("after that, therefore because of that") mistake. It is common but usually not logical to think that because one phenomenon follows another in time it was "caused" by the former. Richard Nixon won the 1968 presidential election, and the New York Mets won the World Series the next year—but that sequence of events is no reason to think that Nixon's election "caused" the Mets to win. Likewise, the Supreme Court's invalidation of state bars to different-race marriage in 1967 came right before dramatic declines in American marriage rates and increases in divorce rates—but that is not evidence that the Court's activism "caused" changes in marriage patterns.

More important, a key assumption of the objection is wrong. Same-sex partnerships and marriages are not the triumph of a purely individualistic hedonism, nor do they represent a simple liberalization of family law. By choosing to register under the new Scandinavian laws, the partners are giving up choices by promising mutual commitment, and an increasing number of them are sacrificing their liberties to commit to families with children. Indeed, the Scandinavian data are more consistent with our account than with the traditionalist account. In fact, the trends in Scandinavian child-rearing are almost the opposite of the caricature painted by Santorum, Kurtz, and Bork. Rather than a country (like the United States!) where children are increasingly being raised by single parents, the countries for which we have gathered data (Denmark, Norway, Sweden) have seen more children raised by their biological parents after adopting their registered partnership laws. In short, the data suggest that Barry Winter and Per Kjær's experience can be, tentatively, generalized.

Marriage and Divorce Rates after Registered Partnership Laws

The long-term trend in Scandinavia has been lower marriage rates, higher divorce rates, and higher rates of nonmarital births—trends long predating registered partnership laws enacted in 1989 and thereafter. Experts point to demographic, social, and cultural reasons for these changes in family patterns. To the extent that law has made a difference, one would expect the liberalization of alternatives to marriage (cohabitation) and exit options (no-fault divorce) to be the primary legal developments contributing to these changes in marriage and divorce rates. In Denmark, Norway, and Sweden, these legal changes occurred between 1969 and 1980, and the data reveal a close correlation between these particular legal changes and lower marriage rates and higher divorce rates. According to social scientists, less dramatic legal changes, such as state support for working women with children, have also contributed to increasing numbers of nonmarital children.[5]

If the defense-of-marriage argument is correct, that according lesbian and gay couples the same rights and duties of marriage will independently cause a decline in marriage, one would expect registered partnerships to *accelerate*—either temporarily or long-term—the pace of change in marriage that had been going on for most of the twentieth century, and that had been dramatic since 1970. If state-recognized same-sex partnerships contributed to the decline of marriage and the rise of illegitimacy, even if indirectly by reinforcing an expanded-choice norm, we would expect to see *something more than* falling marriage rates, rising divorce rates, and rising nonmarital birth rates in the Scandinavian countries after enactment of their registered partnership laws. Rather, we should expect to see marriage rates falling faster, divorce rates accelerating upward, and a surge in nonmarital birth rates. Yet this has not happened. As we shall document, not only do the registered partnership laws in Denmark, Norway, and Sweden not correlate to supernormal plunges in marriage rates and superelevated divorce rates but some of the trends move in the other direction. We find the same phenomena in rates of nonmarital births, which we examine in the concluding section of this chapter. The 1990s see no stake through the heart of marriage. The data instead drive a stake through the heart of the Scandinavian twist on the defense-of-marriage argument. (Most of the data discussed here can be found in appendices 4–6.)

The evidence is particularly dramatic in Denmark. Consider the aggregate trends, set forth in figure 5.1 (next page). The average annual marriage rate in Denmark between 1985 and 1989 (before the Registered Partnership Law took effect) was 602 per one hundred thousand people, well below the

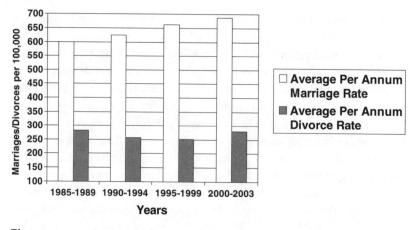

Figure 5.1
Denmark marriage and divorce trends, 1985–2003. Source: Statistics Denmark.

rate earlier in the century; the average annual divorce rate was 286 per one hundred thousand people, a historic high point. Although the declining marriage rate and rising divorce rate were not continuous (they did not show the same trend every year), the overall trend was in that direction since 1950. So it is of no particular significance if, after 1989, the marriage rate continues to decline and the divorce rate continues to rise.[6]

If the defense-of-marriage argument is correct, that same-sex partnerships have *independently* contributed to the "end of marriage" through some "mutually reinforcing" process, then we should expect to see a significant downward slump for marriage rates and upward bounce for divorce rates after 1989. Yet after 1989, the marriage rate *went up*. By 2000, the rate had soared to 720 per one hundred thousand people, the highest rate Denmark had seen since 1970. Even after a brief post-2000 decline, the average annual number of marriages for 2000–04 is almost 14 percent higher than the average annual number of marriages for 1985–89, the period right before registered partnerships were adopted. During the 1990s, Denmark's average divorce rate *went down*, to the lowest levels that country has seen since it adopted the no-fault divorce law. After 1997, the divorce rate inched upward. In 2000–04, the average rate was 283, slightly lower than in the period right before the partnership law (1985–89).[7]

The overall data deal a double whammy to the defense-of-marriage hypothesis—both because the numbers show marriage going "up" rather than "down" (toward its "end") and because even if they showed lower marriage rates and higher divorce rates, they would be indistinguishable from what had been going on before registered partnership. Is there a plausible explanation for why the "end of marriage" in Denmark produced annual marriage rates that dwarf rates in the pre-partnerships period? One might think that registered partnerships drove the higher marriage and lower divorce rates and, in effect, staved off the "end of marriage." Barry Winter's example suggests that this may be part of the story, but a more important factor contributing to the elevated marriage rate was that more Danes were entering adulthood and partnering in the 1990s than in the 1980s.

Statistics Denmark (the statistical branch of the country's bureaucracy) does not report the number of Danes who formally entered into consensual unions or cohabitation arrangements each year, but does report the aggregate number of cohabiting or unioned couples. Those numbers also increased in the 1990s, indeed, faster than marriages did. Have registered partnerships encouraged straight people to cohabit rather than marry? It's doubtful. Denmark's general trend toward cohabitation was certainly not accelerated by its Registered Partnership Law. If anything, the trend slowed down. Between 1980 and 1988, the period before the law, the rate of increase for cohabitation or consensual union in Denmark was on average 4.8 percent per year. Between 1989 and 2004, the rate averaged 1.4 percent per year. Similarly, the number of cohabiting couples with children rose 70 percent from 1980 to 1989, but less than 29 percent from 1989 to 2000 (including consensual unions), and just 0.4 percent from 2000 to 2004.[8] The rate of increase in unmarried cohabitations or consensual unions has dropped dramatically since enactment of the Registered Partnership Act in 1989. So there do appear to be other couples like the one Winter described: that is, straight couples otherwise inclined to remain unmarried but who changed their mind after 1989.

Unlike Denmark, Norway enjoyed high marriage rates and low divorce rates in the 1960s. In the next decade, marriage rates declined and divorce rates rose, both dramatically. Between 1973 and 1993, Norway's marriage rate declined by almost 40 percent; its divorce rate more than doubled, an astounding development for this traditionalist country. By 1993, Norway's marriage rate was almost one-third lower than Denmark's, and its divorce rate was about the same. (These data suggest that depictions of Norway as a culturally conservative version of Denmark are potentially misleading.) According to the Scandinavian twist on the defense-of-marriage argument, one would expect to see the declining marriage rates accelerate and the rising divorce rates soar after Norway adopted its Registered Partnership Act in 1993. The predicted phenomena did not occur. As figure 5.2 (next page) illustrates, the marriage rate soared in the years after the partnership legislation, while the divorce rate was on the whole stable (declining in the late 1990s and rising after that, but to a level still lower than in 1993).[9]

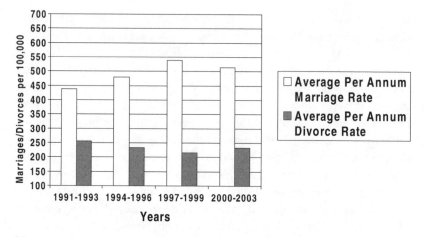

Figure 5.2
Norway marriage and divorce trends, 1993–2003. Source: Statistics Norway.

As with Denmark, we do not think that registered partnerships "saved" the institution of marriage, and may not have halted its decline relative to cohabitation. Stanley Kurtz claims that, as a result of the registered partnership law, marriage has started to vanish in rural and small-town Norway as well as Oslo. Even if it were true (Kurtz offers no survey evidence), this assertion cannot be generalized. The data suggest that cohabitation's popularity with Norwegians started in the 1980s, not after 1993. Statistics Norway does not report rates of cohabitation, but it has reported aggregate numbers for marital households (with or without children) since 1974 and cohabiting households (with children) since 1989. Through the 1980s, the number of marital households with children plummeted, falling more than 18 percent (83,474 households) between 1989 and 1993. The number of cohabiting households with children soared 70 percent (24,343 new households) in the same period. After the registered partnership law went into effect, the number of cohabiting households with children continued to rise, but at lower rates. Between 1993 and 1997, the number of cohabiting households increased by 35 percent (21,138 households); between 1997 and 2001, the increase was only 15 percent (11,993 households).[10] Overall, the data suggest a continuous increase in cohabiting couples (with children), both absolutely and compared to married couples, since the 1980s. Yet Norway's Registered Partnership Act of 1993 did not accelerate this trend; if anything, the trend slowed down a little bit after 1993.[11]

We see much the same pattern in Sweden. The marriage rate in Sweden has fluctuated between 400 and 550 annually per one hundred thousand people for the last generation—a pattern disrupted by the 108,919 Swedes who married in 1989, most of them taking advantage of a new pension law. From that 1989 peak, the marriage rate fell almost every year for the next decade, to below 360 in 1998.[12] This swooning marriage rate was a fallout from the 1989 boomlet, as the pool of marriageable Swedes emptied out in 1989, leaving a smaller pool for the 1990s. The declining marriage rate could be read in a contentious manner to support the defense-of-marriage hypothesis, for some of the decline occurred after 1995, when Sweden's registered partnership law went into effect. But any fair-minded observer would have to concede that the decline started before 1995, particularly when considering that the decline between 1995 and 1998 was minor compared to earlier declines. Indeed, the big decline in Sweden's marriage rate came between 1960 and 1973, plummeting by almost two hundred per one hundred thousand.[13]

Figure 5.3 reveals several family formation trends in Sweden after enacting its registered partnership law. First, the marriage rate not only rebounded in 2000–3, but it rebounded to a higher level than that of the four years prior to the registered partnership law's taking effect (1991–94). The rebound of marriage came at precisely the same time that an increasing number of Swedish same-sex couples were registering their partnerships. Second, the modestly resurgent marriage rate came in a period when Sweden was removing the adoption and joint custody restrictions, thereby making registered partnerships even more like marriages. That change in the law has, thus far, done nothing to scare heterosexuals away from marriage. Note, finally and most dramatically, the trend in divorce rates. The number of divorcing couples significantly and steadily declined after the registered partnership law took

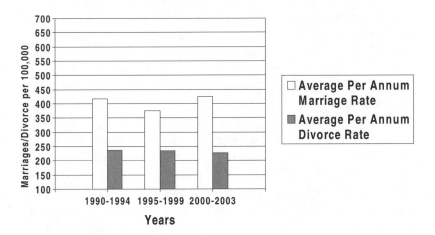

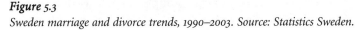

Figure 5.3
Sweden marriage and divorce trends, 1990–2003. Source: Statistics Sweden.

effect. This decline is all the more remarkable in light of the fact that a huge bubble of couples got married in 1989. So from a larger pool of married couples, a declining number of them got divorced after 1995.

The foregoing data for Denmark, Norway, and Sweden tentatively falsify the defense-of-marriage hypothesis. Even if defenders can come up with some dubious argument to "explain" the data, they are left with a hypothesis that itself lacks support. Moreover, the data set forth in figures 5.1 through 5.3 suggest an alternate hypothesis, that state recognition of same-sex partnerships contributes, marginally, to a fresh look at marriage as an alternative for straight people as well as gay people. There are straight couples in Sweden like the straight Danish couple described by Barry Winter.

Another point must be made. When the law does logically affect Swedish families, in the way that we have explained in the previous section, the data dramatically support its effect, in the short term dominating the myriad other variables that always come into play in a complex society. For social and cultural reasons, the marriage rate was falling and the divorce rate was rising in Sweden before 1970. In 1973, Sweden eliminated the "for cause" requirement in its divorce law. The divorce rate increased by two-thirds in a single year, before falling back to a relatively stable level that was double the rate of the 1960s and almost 50 percent higher than the rate in 1970. The marriage rate actually increased for a few years after 1973, before falling dramatically between 1976 and 1985. Legal change had its big impact on marriage rates in 1989, when Parliament granted pension windfalls for married Swedes, an event that fueled the largest marriage binge in that nation's history.[14]

The pattern is almost as dramatic for Denmark, which was the first Scandinavian country to remove the fault requirement from its divorce law, in 1969. The divorce rate responded immediately, soaring 40 percent in one year (1970–71) and remaining at historically high levels for the remainder of the century. At about the same time, Danish courts were enforcing agreements by nonmarried partners to cohabit and started vesting different-sex cohabiting relationships with some of the rights and duties of marriage, decisions ratified by the Danish Supreme Court in 1980. Statistics Denmark reports that there were more than 160,000 cohabiting couples by 1980. At the same time, the marriage rate was eroding. For every year of the 1980s, Denmark saw a significant increase in the total number of cohabiting couples and a small decline in the number of married couples. Interestingly, the 1990s, when Denmark was registering lesbian and gay partners, saw marriage rates rebound. The total number of married couples went up every year between 1995 and 2003, before dipping slightly in 2003 (then inching up a little in 2004). The number of cohabiting couples leveled off in that period and declined slightly in 2002–04.[15]

So the defense-of-marriage critics may be right to think the law can affect the structure of family life in a society, at least in the short term. They are certainly wrong, however, in their choice of legal change supposedly illustrating that effect. If the state vests legal benefits and obligations for different-sex couples in a new institution, some of those couples will opt out of marriage. And so they did in Scandinavia. If the state makes it easier to divorce, more couples will divorce. And so they did in Scandinavia. If the state allows lesbian and gay couples to express their mutual commitment by joining in an institution with the rights and duties of marriage, why should straight couples change their minds about marriage? They did not in Scandinavia, except possibly to think better of it, the point made by Barry Winter.

The Argument That Registered Partnerships Undermine Marriage by Delinking Marriage from Traditional Roots, Values, and Taboos

Professor Kathleen Kiernan of the London School of Economics demonstrates that cohabitation has replaced marriage as the partnership model of choice for an increasing number of families all over Europe. In the 1950s and 1960s, marriage was the norm. "Cohabitation . . . came to the fore in the 1970s and has escalated during the 1980s and 1990s, whereby young people live together as a prelude to, or as an alternative to marriage." Kiernan's data support the suggestion we made in chapter 2, that social and legal acceptance of cohabitation contributed to Scandinavian willingness to recognize same-sex unions as well. By the mid-1990s, young couples in Sweden, Norway, Denmark, and even Finland were much more likely to cohabit or cohabit-then-marry rather than marry without cohabitation.[16] All but one of the European countries that recognized same-sex partnerships in the last 20 years showed a similar pattern of cohabitation, according to Kiernan's data.[17]

Also invoking Kiernan, Texas senator John Cornyn, researcher Stanley Kurtz, and others make the converse claim—that the increasing popularity of cohabitation compared to marriage is a *direct result* of state recognition of same-sex partnerships in the Scandinavian and other countries. Kiernan argues that Western countries have been undergoing a transition in the last generation, away from marriage-only (her stage 1), toward acceptance of cohabitation-before-marriage (stage 2), then cohabitation-as-an-alternative-to-marriage (stage 3), and finally cohabitation-without-marriage as the norm (the last stage). She also suggests that once a country has moved from one stage to the next, it cannot return to the earlier stage. From this model, Cornyn and the others argue that the Scandinavian countries have moved from stage 3 to the last stage *because* they enacted registered partnership laws. By analogy, they warn that the United States, now a stage 3 country, will move irrevocably to the last stage (the end of marriage) if it recognizes same-sex marriages or marriage-like partnerships.[18]

This is an astounding claim. Kiernan's data and our statistics for Scandinavia demonstrate that the displacement of marriage by cohabitation has been a gradual but continuous trend since the 1970s in the Nordic societies—well before any of them recognized lesbian and gay partnerships. Indeed, our data for Denmark, Norway, and Sweden demonstrate that the trend toward cohabitation and away from marriage *slowed down* rather than speeded up after enactment of those countries' registered partnership statutes. Traditionalists invoking Scandinavian evidence for their defense-of-marriage objection have no systematic evidence to the contrary; the only evidence anyone has adduced is Kurtz's anecdotal accounts of cohabiting couples in rural and small-town Norway, from which he argues that "gay marriage" tipped traditionalist Norway toward cohabitation. These anecdotes can be met with counter-anecdotes that we report in chapter 4 and by the systematic evidence reported in this chapter showing that the triumph of cohabitation came in Norway between 1981 and 1993, *before* (not after) the country recognized same-sex partnerships.

Although the traditionalists' foregoing causal theory has no systematic evidentiary support, and is inconsistent with the data we and Kiernan have assembled, the rationales they have advanced in support of the theory pose some interesting issues of the relationship between family law and family formation. Consider three different rationales traditionalist defenders have floated for this ambitious theory. Same-sex marriages or marriage-like partnerships for same-sex couples undermine marriage by (1) separating marriage from procreation and parenting; (2) reinforcing previous family law liberalizations and thereby discrediting the altruistic core of marriage; or (3) "tipping" a country away from traditionalist and toward liberal family values. All three rationales are beset with problems, but problems that illuminate the debate.

Do Same-Sex Partnerships Delink Marriage from Procreation and Parenthood?

Family law theorist Maggie Gallagher argues that same-sex marriage interrupts the communicative, channeling, and signaling function of marriage law—to instruct young lovers and remind the wider society of two key ideas:

(1) children need mothers and fathers, and (2) societies need babies to survive and prosper. Decouple marriage law from its basic grounding—the people who make the baby are supposed to care for the baby and each other too—and you have gutted its major purpose and usefulness. Stanley Kurtz tied Gallagher's point to the Scandinavian experience in 2004, when he testified to a United States Congressional subcommittee that same-sex partnerships had undermined marriage in Scandinavia:

> The increasing cultural separation between the ideas of marriage and parenthood makes same-sex marriage more conceivable. Once marriage is separated from the idea of parenthood, there seems little reason to deny marriage, or marriage-like partnerships, to same-sex couples. By the same token, *once marriage (or a status close to marriage) has been redefined to include same-sex couples, the symbolic separation between marriage and parenthood is confirmed, locked-in, and reinforced.*

The first prong of his argument, that the decline of marriage in Scandinavia (weakly) facilitated state recognition of same-sex unions, is probably true. In chapter 2, we suggested that the lower numbers of citizens whose identities were wedded to different-sex marriage meant less intense opposition to same-sex partnerships or marriage.[19]

The second (italicized) prong of the argument, Gallagher's original point, is not so cogent. How does same-sex marriage, "or a status close to marriage," lock in "the symbolic separation between marriage and parenthood"? In the United States and Scandinavia, marriage has never required that spouses become parents. Does the law's willingness to recognize marriage between a man and a postmenopausal woman (who is biologically incapable of bearing children) lock in a separation between marriage and parenthood? If it sends such a signal, it is a weak one at best. Marriage between two young women is even less of a signal, and we think no signal at all, because there is a good chance they will have children. As we saw in chapters 3 and 4, many Scandinavian registered partners, especially female partners, are raising children. So it is just as possible that state recognition of their relationships will reinforce rather than negate some connection between marriage and parenting.

Recall Bodil Stavad and Britt Pedersen, the nurses who registered as partners in 1993 in the town of Rødovre, Denmark. Not too long after getting married, Bodil started to bring up the discussion of having a child. "I've always wanted to be a mother," she told us, but it did not seem possible until she got married. At first, Britt was against the idea. "Having a child means a lot of responsibility. It means having to give up some of your freedom."

But then, after a period of discussion and reflection on their life together, Britt "finally softened." Bodil became pregnant through artificial insemination from Steen, a gay man who had already had a couple of children with some lesbian friends. In March 1997, Bodil gave birth to Christine, whom she and Britt have been raising within a mom-mom-child family. For Bodil, Britt, and even Steen, registered partnerships are all about *family*, including children. They disagree with the notion that the Danish law has, even symbolically, severed the tie between marriage and procreation.[20]

There is another problem with applying the Gallagher logic to Scandinavia, as Kurtz does. Except for Iceland's statute, all the Scandinavian laws originally barred registered partners from adopting children or even sharing joint custody of children reared within the relationship. Initially, therefore, these laws entailed legal differences that signaled precisely the sectarian distinction that Gallagher emphasizes: marriage assumes procreation and children raised in the household; registered partnership does not. Like Kirsten Haase and Birgitte Jepsen, discussed in chapter 3, Bodil Stavad and Britt Pedersen were outraged at the distinction made in the 1989 Danish statute. "It's ridiculous," says Britt. "The government thinks it's better that Christine should have one parent instead of two parents? It doesn't make any sense." And it isn't fair to Christine.[21]

Responding to the social fact that lesbian and gay couples are bearing and raising children, Denmark (1999), Norway (2002), and Sweden (2003) have amended their laws to allow registered partners to adopt and to have joint custody of children. Sweden has in fact recently eliminated all differences between registered partnership and different-sex marriage in relation to children, and now allows insemination and assisted reproduction for lesbian couples. Under Gallagher's and Kurtz's logic, whatever "bad" effect the original Danish partnership law had on marriage, the 1999 amendment ought to have had a much worse effect. Yet the Danish marriage rate went up in 2000. And the ratio of cohabiting/married couples declined between 1999 and 2004. On the whole, we doubt the 1999 amendment had any significant effect on straight couples, married or not, but the statistics tentatively undermine claims for the essential relationship between marriage and parenting.

Does Same-Sex Partnership or Marriage Discredit the Altruistic Goal of Marriage?

Senator Santorum makes a somewhat different argument from the linkage between marriage and child-rearing. When he says that marriage is all about procreation and child-rearing, he is thinking about the altruism of traditional marriage, the way it calls us to sacrifice our selfish short-term plea-sure for the other-regarding good of bearing and rearing children. The fun-damental goal of marriage, in his words, "is in providing a stable environment for the raising of children. That's why we give marriage a spe-cial status, not because people like to hang out together and have fun." In his view, same-sex marriage not only fails to match up with this goal but teaches the next generation that "marriage is a self-centered endeavor pri-marily about adult satisfaction, not children's well-being." Gallagher puts it this way: "The family as a system is grounded not in equality and au-tonomy, but in dependence and obligation."[22]

This is a thoughtful argument, but evaluation of it demands more social context. Upon what basis do these marriage defenders assume that lesbian and gay couples view their relationships as nothing but a "self-centered endeavor primarily about adult satisfaction"? Speaking for themselves, American lesbian and gay couples report the same kind of self-giving altruism toward their partners that some straight married spouses have traditionally enjoyed. Jack Baker and Mike McConnell, the first gay couple to challenge the state's exclusion of lesbian and gay couples from civil mar-riage (chapter 1), have never viewed their relationship as such an endeavor. Like married straight couples, their initial attraction was rooted in sexual electricity, but their almost forty-year partnership has been rooted in de-votion to one another's well-being, and the well-being of the larger com-munity. Thousands of other selfless lesbian and gay couples have publicly celebrated their unions through sincere promises of mutual support and love, promises that have inspired service to their extended families and larger communities.[23]

Per Kjær explained that, for him and his partner, gay marriage is an effort to align themselves with an institution rich in connections with Danish (or American) history and ongoing community. "The partnership law," he continued, "helps our gay community come forward and be more a part of the community of society."[24] We posed this question to Gunna Højgaard, a sixty-year-old massage therapist, and Eva Fog, a sixty-year-old architect, who registered as partners in 1993. Why did they register, and not just cohabit? we asked. Gunna responded,

> It was a way of saying, "You know I am here and you can count on me." It's a clear demonstration of your intention to stay together, and that feels good. It's quite powerful, and I had never felt like making such a promise before, even though I have had quite long-term relationships, but now I think I am ready to publicly vouch for my feelings for Gunna.[25]

A substantial, and increasing, number of American as well as Scandinavian couples are raising children. Recall, from chapter 3, that about one-sixth of the Danish registered partners are now rearing children under the age of eighteen in their households. According to studies drawing from data reported in the 2000 census, a quarter or more of partnered same-sex couples are raising children in the United States. Similarly, the American Community Survey in 2002 found that children are being raised in 27 percent of the households headed by a same-sex couple in the United States. Gary Gates, formerly of the Urban Institute, estimates that one in five male couples are raising children under age eighteen, compared with one in three female couples.[26]

One such couple is Steve Lofton and Roger Croteau, who committed to one another more than twenty years ago in Miami, Florida, and now live with their five children in Portland, Oregon. Both dads are pediatric nurses, who adopted all of their kids when they were HIV-positive babies; all are being raised in a loving environment where their dads make happy sacrifices every day for their well-being. (At their children's urging, Lofton and Croteau applied for marriage licenses and were legally married, until the Oregon Supreme Court invalidated the licenses in 2005.) Every human being who has met Lofton and Croteau comes away thinking these are America's most selfless fathers. There are thousands of other mutually committed couples raising children like Lofton and Croteau. The center of their marriage is exactly what Rick Santorum extols, "providing a stable environment for the raising of children." How can Lofton and Croteau's marriage be anything but an inspiration to a traditionalist who values marital altruism? Shouldn't America be rewarding this couple, rather than disrespecting them?[27]

Consider Gallagher's and Santorum's normative inquiry from another angle. What kind of a legal regime links marriage to parenting, procreation, community, and traditional (Judeo-Christian) religious faith? The answer is the legal regime that the United States followed in 1900. That regime had the following characteristics.

Feature 1, marriage monopoly: marriage as the exclusive relationship for sex and parenting. The most important thing the law can do to link marriage with parenting and procreation is to give it a monopoly. And this was the American tradition. Everywhere in the United States circa 1900, it was a crime to have procreative sex or to sexually cohabit outside of marriage. Municipal police vigorously enforced those fornication, adultery, and lewd cohabitation laws. The state also penalized the nonmarital child, who was subject to a host of legal discriminations.[28]

Feature 2, sex for procreation: sex within marriage must be procreative. The link between marriage and procreation is stronger if the state also requires that sex within marriage must be procreative. As a formal matter, the United States did so in 1900. Federal law prohibited interstate mailing and trade in contraceptive materials, and most states made the sale or use of contraceptives a crime. Abortion was a crime. Sodomy, a form of nonprocreative sex, was a crime everywhere and was, by all authorities, a crime for married couples.[29]

Feature 3, lifetime obligations: strong and automatic parental obligations of spouses. The link between marriage and parenting is stronger if the married spouses have firm obligations to support and care for children born within the marriage. Many American states in 1900 conclusively presumed that any child born within a marriage was the progeny of the spouses. Although single people could adopt children, the states strongly preferred adoption by married couples. It was routine for a spouse to adopt his or her stepchild. Divorce was not common in 1900 and could only be had "for cause." Upon divorce, the court typically provided strong obligations for each spouse toward the children. Although the common law had given the father first claim on the children, by 1900 most states followed the "tender years" doctrine, whereby the mother typically received custody and the father was saddled with significant support obligations.[30]

Marriage monopoly is the most important element of a legal network supporting "traditional marriage," but all three features worked together to create a regime that was securely grounded in the Judeo-Christian tradition, strongly linked marriage to both parenting and procreation, and respected traditional taboos of sexuality and strongly differentiated gender roles. The Scandinavian countries had a similar legal regime in 1900: marriage was the only romantic relationship authorized or recognized by the state; marital sex was supposed to be procreative; and divorce was very difficult.[31] During the twentieth century, the United States and Scandinavia have relentlessly liberalized family law—opting to expand the choices available to adults involved in sexual relationships. Contrary to Scandinavia-bashers, the United States has been outdone only slightly by Sweden, and perhaps not at all by and Norway and Denmark, in its liberalized family law. By the end of the 1980s, all these countries had expanded the choices available to adults who are romantically involved. These new choices represented three different kinds of family law liberalization. Each is linked to a feature of the old regime noted above.

Liberalization 1, no marriage monopoly: marriage is no longer the exclusive relationship for sex and parenting. Since the 1970s, the United States and Scandinavia have allowed unmarried adults to engage in consensual sexual activities and have recognized parental rights and responsibilities for adults to their out-of-wedlock children. In America, the states are constitutionally prohibited from criminalizing most consensual sexual activities and from penalizing nonmarital children. Sweden has gone further than Denmark, Norway, and the United States in recognizing other institutions for sexual cohabitation and the rearing of children. In all four countries, marriage has lost its monopoly as the only situs for sex and parenting. Like other institutions deprived of their legal monopolies, marriage has seen its market share fall dramatically, especially after 1970.[32]

Liberalization 2, sex for fun: sex within marriage no longer has to be procreative. All these countries allow pretty much any kind of consensual sex within marriage, and all permit spouses to use contraceptives to prevent pregnancies and abortions to terminate them. Feature 2 has all but vanished, and its vanishing act occurred a generation ago.[33]

Liberalization 3, fewer lifetime obligations: marriage is easy to exit, and spouses have weaker spousal and parental obligations. Most of the Scandinavian countries have retained the old presumption that children born within a marriage are the progeny of the spouses, but many American states have abandoned that rule. Even more than in Scandinavia, American states routinely allow single adults and unmarried couples to adopt. All have retained strong obligations of married couples to their children, in theory, but the ease of divorce has diluted those obligations in practice. Especially in the United States, the ease of divorce and the tepid alimony and support obligations, and their substantial non-enforcement, have left father-husbands with fewer enforceable obligations toward their children. In Sweden, Norway, and Denmark, the state has assumed some of the obligations (for child care especially) once assumed by spouses.[34]

All of these liberal changes in Scandinavian and American family law came well before Denmark enacted its registered partnership law in 1989. At the same time that American and Scandinavian family law was liberalizing, so was social practice. Generally, social practice changed first, followed by liberalization of legal rules, which may have accelerated social change (at least in the short term). Once families demanded access to birth control and freedom to plan their families, the law allowed citizens to obtain contraceptives and allowed abortions more freely (a retreat from feature 2), which in turn contributed to the sexual revolution in these countries. Fornication and adultery laws, vigorously enforced in 1900, were effectively nullified by universal disobedience in midcentury; most were repealed in the last quarter of the century, a big retreat from feature 1. Once sexual cohabitation became widespread and socially tolerable, by the 1970s, the law not only ceased to criminalize these relationships but started regulating them, another retreat from feature 1. The lifetime marital obligations of feature 3 declined throughout the twentieth century, as the divorce rate steadily increased in all these countries. Once the state granted divorces without a showing of fault, as all did by the 1970s, the divorce rate soared. With husbands and wives separated, often by long distances and bitter divorces, parental obligations have become harder to enforce.

By 1989, marriage had "declined" along all three dimensions in Sweden, Denmark, Norway, and the United States. And those states' *liberalization* of family law—state creation of more choices available to adult marital partners—arguably contributed to each kind of decline.[35] We are using the term *liberalization* in precisely the same way Senator Santorum does, to connote a change in social norms or law that gives spouses more leeway to make choices that serve their own pleasure, at the expense of the altruistic goals of procreation and child-rearing. In contrast to Santorum and other traditionalists who see gay marriage as a threat to the institution, however, we distinguish

> (1) the *liberalization of alternatives to marriage*, through which the state provides adults with more choices around which they can structure their romantic relationships; this contributes to the decline of entry into parenting and marriage (feature 1)

> and

> (2) the *liberalization of state regulation of marital sex*, through which the state provides adults with more choices as to how they conduct their marital sex life; this contributes to the decline of procreation within marriage (feature 2)

> and

> (3) the *liberalization of exit from marriage*, through which the state provides married adults with an easier choice to leave the institution

through divorce; this contributes to the decline of marriage-for-life (feature 3)

from

the *expansion of eligibility* for the institution of marriage; this contributes to none of the aforementioned declines.

That is to say, the decline of marriage rates and the rise of divorce rates are, arguably, results of the three state liberalizations, but not of the state's expansion of eligibility. This distinction helps us to understand why yesterday's conservatives were entirely wrong to claim that allowing different-race marriage would undermine the institution of marriage for southerners. And why today's conservatives are wrong to claim that requiring same-sex marriage would undermine the institution for all Americans.

The Domino Theory of Gay Marriage as a Tipping Point

Judge Bork suggests another way of understanding the claims of same-sex marriage opponents. He argues that same-sex marriage is not only a "cultural debacle" but a disaster of "nuclear" proportions. "With same-sex marriage a line is being crossed, and no other line to separate moral and immoral consensual sex will hold." Opposition is "mandatory" for any sane American. Legal "liberalizations" undermine traditional institutions such as the rule of law and marriage, and it is essential for society to draw the line, lest any sense of limitation is lost. However bad legal cohabitation, the repeal of fornication and adultery laws, and the rise of nonmarital children have been for marriage, the institution has a chance to survive—*unless* the state adds one last liberalization, same-sex marriage. If that happens, all is lost, because the various liberalizations will be mutually reinforcing, and family will be reduced to a consumer good.[36]

As we suggested earlier, wedding straight cohabitation and gay marriage as equivalent liberalizations is arbitrary. We are not just playing a word game in distinguishing between *liberalization* and *expanded eligibility*. The liberalizations listed here all involve trading away some of the responsibilities of marriage so that adults can have more choices. No-fault divorce has diminished husbands' responsibilities to their children as well as their wives, so that they can choose to escape unhappy (or even semihappy) marriages when they like. Expanding eligibility for marriage, in contrast, does not trade off marital responsibility for free choice. Instead, it offers same-sex couples a choice to take on the responsibilities of marriage as an affirmation and a reinforcement of their mutual commitment.

The foregoing distinction helps us understand the flaw in the mutual re-inforcement argument. Cohabitation and no-fault divorce rules might be mutually reinforcing, because they are both liberalizations that allow people to have the legal advantages of marriage *without* all the burdens and costs. But same-sex marriage is different. Extending the marriage option to lesbian and gay couples is *not* simply another choice. As Eva Fog put it to us, "there is a price to pay" for commitment, for it represents a restriction of choice in many respects. Two people agree to restrict their choices in order to obtain the unitive advantages of marriage. Unlike a single person, a married person has support and fidelity obligations to his or her spouse, and has extra obli-gations to the state and third parties as well. For a simple example, if you are a public official, conflict-of-interest laws or rules restrict your ability to make decisions that affect your own financial and other personal interests. If you are married, your spouse's financial holdings and some personal interests count toward conflict. Fog suggested an even more mundane example: "There are friends of mine that feel like they see me less now, because you have some-thing going on every day." Moreover, the restricted choice of marriage is costly to escape. Divorcing is more costly in the United States (and to a lesser ex-tent in Scandinavia) than breaking up with a nonmarried lover.[37]

There is another kind of problem with a domino (mutual reinforce-ment) theory. After decades of catering to straight people's desires to have the advantages of marriage without its costs, through cohabitation regimes and no-fault divorce, it is unfair to draw the line with gay and lesbian couples, the group whose choices have been least honored by the state. If you really want to combat the expanded choice norm, it would be much more powerful to revoke no-fault divorce or cohabitation regimes and reintroduce features 1 (marriage monopoly) and 3 (lifetime obligations) into the law. Astoundingly, these are the two reforms most social conser-vatives are not pressing. As Stanley Kurtz puts it, the fate of marriage de-pends on stopping same-sex unions, and "repealing no-fault divorce, or even eliminating premarital cohabitation, are not what's at issue."[38] Under this logic, American society should swallow the liberalizations we have already adopted to accommodate the choices straight people want to have, even though this prochoice regime significantly undermines mar-riage and facilitates divorce—and should rescue marriage from decline by denying gay people eligibility for it, even though it is highly speculative that such denial would have any effect on the institution. This direct dis-crimination verges on hypocrisy.

Children Born outside of Marriage: The Dangers
of Overselling a Narrow View of Marriage and Family

The "end of marriage" forecasts by some social conservatives are overstated and probably flat wrong. But even if they were right that same-sex partnerships sped marriage to its demise, the question remains whether that phenomenon is a lamentable development. After all, "traditional marriage" is an institution that was dead as a doornail by the end of the 1970s, when no-fault divorce, legalized adultery, and state cohabitation regimes became the legal status quo in this country and elsewhere. Numerous family law scholars around the world have questioned the virtue of marriage and have argued that other institutional forms would better serve the needs of families. Maggie Gallagher and other traditional family values advocates have a powerful response to these scholars. Even in its diluted form, they argue, marriage benefits children. An impressive, even if not definitive, array of studies have found that children thrive in two-parent households and suffer if their parents break up. Other studies have found that cohabiting couples are much more willing to split up than married couples. If marriage declines as the preferred relationship for child-raising and is replaced by cohabiting households, the logic is that children will suffer, so long as there are not offsetting benefits.[39]

According to Stanley Kurtz, this is what has happened in Scandinavia, and the culprit is that all-purpose bogeyman, registered partnerships. Young Danes, Norwegians, and Swedes are cohabiting and no longer marrying. Out-of-wedlock births, he says, have soared in these countries, during the same period when they were creating registered partnership regimes. "Gay marriage," he stated, "is both an effect and an enduring cause of the separation of marriage and parenthood," for the reasons we have just criticized. As a result of the substitution of cohabitation for marriage, the children of this generation will suffer—victims, Kurtz would maintain, of "gay marriage."[40] This is a serious but ultimately hopeless argument against state recognition of same-sex unions, partnerships, or marriages. Let's start with the data and then consider the deeper normative problems with this form of argument.

Nonmarital Children in Scandinavia, 1970 to the Present

As we suggested earlier, Kurtz has a tendency to claim that gay marriage caused phenomena that were longstanding trends in Scandinavian society. The same point can be made, even more dramatically, with regard to what traditionalists consider his best argument. In Denmark, Norway, and Sweden, out-of-wedlock births had been on the rise for decades before those countries recognized same-sex unions in their registered partnership laws. The big jump in births outside of marriage occurred during the 1970s in Denmark and the 1980s in Norway; we have insufficient data for Sweden to say for sure, but experts say that its nonmarital birth rate soared in those decades and probably started to increase in the 1960s. If Kurtz is right to say that registered partnerships hastened the end of marriage, or even were a mutually reinforcing factor, we should expect to see the rates of nonmarital births increase at a *faster* pace after 1989 in Denmark, after 1993 in Norway, and after 1994 in Sweden. In none of these countries do we observe the predicted pattern. In one country, the registered partnerships regime coincided with a reversal, not an exacerbation, of the pattern. In the other two countries, the new regime coincided with a slowing down, not an exacerbation, of the pattern.[41]

Our data are most complete for Denmark. Between 1970 and 1980, the percentage of nonmarital births *tripled* (moving from 11 percent to 33 percent of total births). Between 1980 and 1989, the percentage went up from 33 to 46 percent of total births. Given Kurtz's theory, one would expect that nonmarital births would zoom up after 1989, perhaps to 100 percent of all births (consistent with the "end of marriage" tag line) or at least 70 or 80 percent. Yet this did not occur. Rather the opposite did. After twenty years of steady and significant increase, the nonmarital birth rate in Denmark started a modest decline in 1994, from a high point of 47 percent. In 1997, it fell to 45 percent, and since 1998 (with the exception of 2004) the percentage of nonmarital births has hovered between 44 and 45 percent. Figure 5.4

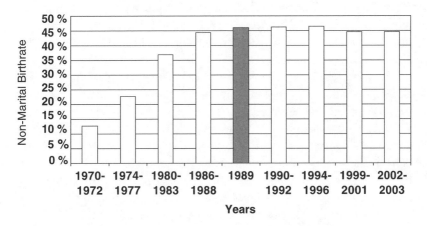

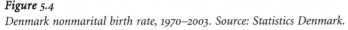

Figure 5.4
Denmark nonmarital birth rate, 1970–2003. Source: Statistics Denmark.

illustrates the pattern in Denmark's nonmarital birth rate—before and after Denmark recognized lesbian and gay partnerships.[42]

Statistics Denmark also reports data on the makeup of households raising children in Denmark, starting in 1980. Between 1980 and 1989, the number of married households raising children fell 21 percent, a decline that probably followed a similar decline in the 1970s (for which we do not have data). Between 1989 and 1999, when registered partnerships were recognized, the number of married households raising children continued to decline, but by 11 percent, a much slower pace. And between 1999 and 2004, when registered partners were able (for the first time) to adopt and enjoy joint custody over children, the number of marital households with children *increased* by 2 percent. The number of couples cohabiting or living in a consensual union increased by about 70 percent between 1980 and 1989 and increased by another 28 percent between 1989 and 1999. Since 1999, the number of cohabiting or unioned couples with children has been flat, and so the ratio of married to cohabiting couples has increased for the first time since 1980. These are not the numbers Kurtz's theory would predict if marriage were in its death throes. The Danish data do not demonstrate that registered partnerships rescued the institution of marriage, but they certainly falsify Kurtz's hypothesis that partnerships hastened its demise.[43]

Kurtz ignores the Danish experience, even though Denmark adopted the first registered partnership law and provides the longest and richest set of data. Instead, Kurtz says that Norway's 1993 registered partnership law demoralized traditionalists and drove the nonmarital birth percentage up to over 50 percent for the first time in Norway's history. Again, let's examine the data, illustrated by figure 5.5. The ratio of nonmarital to marital births increased from 11 percent in 1976 to 21 percent in 1984, almost double. The rate more than doubled between 1984 and 1993, rising to 44 percent. Between 1993 and 2000, the ratio increased from 44 to 50 percent. It has remained at about 50 percent since 2000.[44]

As before, the long-term pattern is clear. Young couples started having children outside of marriage in big numbers during the 1970s and 1980s, well before Norway established registered partnerships. The data after 1993 reveal no upward spike in the portion of children born outside of marriage and, to the contrary, reveal a new counter-trend. For the first time since Norway started reporting nonmarital births, they declined in absolute terms between 1996 and 1997. Since 1997, the ratio has been fairly stable (about 49 to 50 percent) for the first time as well. The aggregate number of married and cohabiting households with children has continued to show an increasing portion of cohabiting families, but that has simply been a continuation of the trends set in the 1980s.

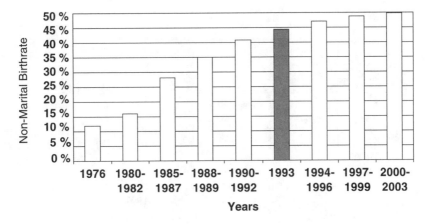

Figure 5.5
Norway nonmarital birth rate, 1976–2003. Source: Statistics Norway.

Pointing to anecdotal accounts from several towns and cities, Kurtz's last stand is the argument that cohabiting Norwegians are so demoralized by registered partnerships that they are no longer marrying after the birth of their first child. Again, the data undermine his claim. Economist Lee Badgett reports that in 1985, 10 percent of second children were born to unmarried parents in Norway; following the other trends we reported for Norway, that portion almost tripled, to 31 percent, by 1993, when Norway adopted its partnership law. Since then, the increase has slowed down, stabilizing at 41 percent by 2003. Just as the number of nonmarital births stabilized around the turn of the millennium, so has the number of second and third births outside of marriage. From this evidence, Badgett concludes that the sky is not falling on Norwegian families.[45]

For Sweden, the decades-long pattern saw higher levels of nonmarital births than that of Denmark or Norway. Indeed, in 1993 the number of nonmarital births exceeded the number of marital births, for the first time in Swedish history. The registered partnership law was passed the next year, when only 48 percent of Swedish births were to married couples. Under Kurtz's theory, we should expect the ratio of marital to nonmarital births to plummet. Again, that did not happen. Between the beginning of 1990 and the end of 1994 (five years), the percentage of marital births declined from 53 to 48 percent, a fall-off of five percent. When he discusses Norway, Kurtz laments that once the nonmarital birth rate exceeds 50 percent, marriage is sunk, with catastrophic results. That has not happened in Norway, nor did it occur in Sweden after 1994. Between the end of 1994 and the end of 2002 (eight years), the percentage dropped to 44 percent, a fall of just 4 percent

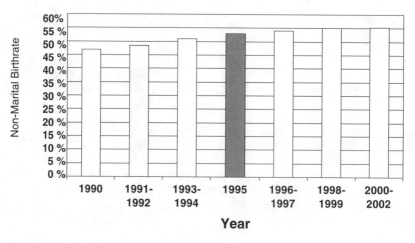

Figure 5.6
Sweden nonmarital birth rate, 1990–2002. Source: Statistics Sweden.

in almost twice the time. The number of marital births was relatively stable from 1996 to 2002, while the number of nonmarital births went up slightly.[46] Figure 5.6 maps these numbers graphically.

The Experience of the Netherlands and Other Countries in Europe

The foregoing analysis casts doubt on the argument that registered partnerships in Scandinavia have caused or even encouraged straight couples to have children outside of marriage. The trend was in that direction long before any of the Scandinavian countries adopted registered partnership laws. Contrary to end-of-marriage hypotheses, not only have the post-partnership trends not spiked with unexpectedly high numbers of nonmarital births but the once-soaring nonmarital birth rate has actually stabilized. Theoretically, it is possible that state recognition of committed lesbian and gay unions has actually encouraged Danes, Norwegians, and Swedes to have children within marriage. This is an unfolding story, but one that provides no basis for invoking children's welfare as a reason to dismiss same-sex marriage.

There is other evidence that we consider equivocal at this time but may ripen into something more decisive. For example, the Netherlands provides a new laboratory for exploring the effect of same-sex marriage upon the welfare of children. We caution, however, that the Dutch reforms are too recent. Because the Netherlands adopted same-sex marriage in December 2000 (and did not implement the law until 2001), there are not enough years of data to draw firm conclusions from the Dutch experience. It is, however, interesting to note that many Dutch couples cohabited in the 1970s, but few had children outside of marriage. In 1980, only 4 percent of Dutch births were nonmarital. That portion tripled to 12 percent by 1990, at rate that had more than doubled, to 25 percent, by the time the Netherlands enacted its same-sex marriage law in 2000. Unlike the experience of the Scandinavian countries, however, the nonmarital birth rate has continued to climb in the Netherlands, by about two points a year, to 31 percent in 2003. This is a trend worth following. On the basis of the Scandinavian experience, the social factor most likely contributing to this rising nonmarital birthrate is the incidence of women working outside the home, which has been increasing dramatically at the same time. We offer this explanation as a hypothesis for quantitative researchers to pursue.

Reading the data quite imaginatively, Kurtz argues that the *campaign* for same-sex marriage in the Netherlands, which started right after the Danish Registered Partnership Act was adopted in 1989, caused or contributed to the big upsurge in nonmarital births.[47] His account is slanted in three important ways. To begin with, Kurtz's line of argument, where everything "bad" is "caused" by gay people's assertion of equality rights, greatly overstates the salience and conceivable effect of gay rights debates in Europe. The "campaign" for same-sex marriage in the early 1990s consisted of a few lawsuits brought by a handful of lesbian and gay activists. That campaign had virtually no public visibility. Only a tiny number of straight people, and a minority of gays, would even have been aware that lesbians and gay men were seeking the right to marry, and there is no evidence this campaign influenced the public's thinking about different-sex marriage. This argument exposes Kurtz's lavish understanding of social causation. Even if the public had been aware of, or even engaged in, the same-sex marriage debate earlier in the 1990s, it is hard to see how the mere presence of a debate demoralized straight couples so much that they stopped getting married and started having children outside of marriage.[48]

Second, Kurtz misses a significant way in which the Netherlands' same-sex marriage experience was different from that of Scandinavia and the United States. Many Dutch people would have been aware of Parliament's adoption of a registered partnership law in 1997—but mainly because the Netherlands, unlike the Scandinavian countries, offered the new institution to straight as well as gay couples. Since 1998, when the new law took effect, a majority of the partners registering under this law have been different-sex couples. To the extent that Dutch couples have been influenced by legal developments, it is this universal feature of the new institution that is significant, for it introduces more institutional competitors for marriage. In addition, because the 1997 law allowed couples to dissolve their partnership by mutual consent, without expensive divorce proceedings, it presented a less-committed alternative for straight couples. It is at least conceivable that the Dutch partnership law would contribute to declining interest in marriage—but only because it offered nonmarital options to straight couples, and not because it gave lesbian and gay couples more equal treatment.[49]

Kurtz's third, and most serious, distortion is his claim that the campaign for same-sex marriage denigrated marriage as an institution. He says: "All participants in the debate—the gay community as well as the political left, center, and right—took gay marriage to signify the replacement of marriage by a flexible and morally neutral range of relationship options."[50] That is untrue. From Professor Kees Waaldijk, the drafter of the legislation, to the Netherlands Association for the Integration of Homosexuality (COC), the main gay rights group, to the parliamentary sponsors, the supporters of the same-sex marriage law were united around the primary argument of equal treatment for lesbian and gay couples. Their secondary argument was that lesbian and gay couples would benefit from having a more formal, state-supported institution to express *and* to reinforce their commitment to one another and to the children many such couples were raising. (Traditionalists opposed to same-sex marriage pinned their hopes on arguments within the lesbian and gay community about whether "marriage" was too old-fashioned a goal for their movement, but Waaldijk's procommitment group had its way.) These were their public justifications for the 2000 same-sex marriage statute, and the public justifications reflected their private goals. If their underlying goal had been to denigrate marriage, as Kurtz says, the coalition would have sweetened the partnership legislation. Instead, supporters faulted it for lacking the commitment and family features of civil marriage.[51]

For now, we urge caution in reading evidence from the Netherlands. Does the experience of other countries in Europe have *any* lessons for the defense-of-marriage argument? The most cogent evidence is that assembled by Badgett. She examined the nonmarital birth rate in the eight countries that gave formal state recognition to lesbian and gay partnerships in the 1990s. The average nonmarital birth rate in these eight countries was 36 percent in 1991, and it rose to 44 percent in 2000. One would expect this to be a much sharper increase than that found in European countries not recognizing lesbian and gay unions—but Badgett found their average nonmarital birth rate rose from 15 percent in 1991 to 23 percent in 2000, a similar eight-point increase.[52] Note that countries with high rates of cohabitation and nonmarital births are the ones most likely to recognize lesbian and gay unions, consistent with our observations in this book.

Like evidence from the Netherlands, Badgett's European survey needs to be read cautiously. Most important, Badgett's survey did not formally account for the various cultural, sociological, and even legal differences among the countries; in econometric terms, she did not report analyses that considered the possible effect of the availability of contraceptives and abortion, the portion of women working outside the home, and other possibly influential variables. In addition, Badgett's survey, as reported, was not correlated with the precise years when specific countries recognized lesbian and gay unions. Most of the European countries recognizing same-sex partnerships did so in the late 1990s, and so examining their cohabitation rates for the entire decade may distort the findings.

Larger Normative Problems with a Focus on Children Born "Out of Wedlock"

A broader critique of the defense-of-marriage objection to same-sex marriage examines its normative assumptions. Closely following sectarian and natural law attacks on same-sex marriage, the work of theorists like Gallagher and empiricists like Kurtz assumes that "marriage" is the only proper institution for state support of relationships and family; therefore, any falling away from marriage is a calamity for children and society as well as couples. Likewise, such intellectuals use the term "out-of-wedlock births" in a disparaging manner. In the policy literature, there is an intense and unresolved debate over whether marriage improves people's welfare and whether children are best raised in a marital household. There is irony in Gallagher's and Kurtz's reliance on that literature to disrespect same-sex marriage. If marriage makes married straight men happier, wealthier, and more stable, as much of the literature claims, why should it not have the same or similar effects for married gay men or married lesbians? Early empirical studies have found that cohabiting gay and lesbian couples derive great satisfaction from their relationships. Under traditionalist logic, they should be even happier if they could marry. Wouldn't marriage cement their relationships and lower the odds of breakup, at least marginally?[53]

Likewise, traditionalists maintain that children raised by single parents are much worse off than children raised by married parents. Stanley Kurtz has cited and praised Gunilla Weitoft's thesis, promulgated in 2003, which finds that "lone parenthood" in Sweden is statistically associated with health problems for the single parents and educational, health, and economic deficits for children raised by single parents. Her thesis treats a child's parents as "partnered" if they were *either* married or cohabiting. Weitoft found that children raised by two cohabiting *or* married parents have better health, education, and employment prospects than children raised by "lone parents" (including parents living with a partner unrelated to the child). She offers two reasons for this phenomenon; each is applicable to cohabiting as well as married partners. One reason is that two parents will offer greater economic resources than lone parents will (ordinarily), and that translates into enormous advantages for children. A second reason is that lone parents suffer from role overload—they simply do not have the emotional energy needed to accommodate jobs, children, and other life responsibilities without the help of adult partners.[54] Both of these reasons suggest that the hundreds or thousands of children being raised in lesbian and gay households in Scandinavia (and the United States) would be advantaged if they had two legal parents rather than just one. This argument mirrors the findings of the Swedish Commission on Children in Homosexual Families, which recommended that adoption and assisted reproduction be opened up to committed same-sex couples (as discussed in chapter 3). This was also Bodil Stavad's intuition. She wanted children all her life, but was unwilling to have children until she had a life partner, Britt Pedersen, who was committed to her and to the family project.

Drawing from Weitoft's thesis, we wonder why the state is not right to encourage these couples to stay together, and why same-sex marriage (or registered partnership) would not be a good idea, considering its benefits for the children. Dismissing this possibility, many social conservatives believe that lesbian and gay relationships cannot generate the mutuality and commitment that heterosexual relationships can generate.[55] This is the kind of sectarian assumption that should be subjected to real-world examination, lest it be a vehicle for importing antigay prejudice and stereotyping into public policy. Reread our accounts of the salvation Jean Luscher found in her partnership with Diana Skovgaard (introduction); the productive partnership Jack Baker and Mike McConnell formed in 1967 (chapter 1); the historic partnership of Axel and Eigil Axgil (chapter 2); the frisky delight Peer Toft and Peter Mols have in their marriage (chapter 3); the families with children and committed parents that Bodil Stavad with Britt Pedersen and Kirsten Jepsen with Birgitte Haase have celebrated (chapter 3); the Disneyesque romance that Johnnie and Lars Fledelius discovered in their life together (chapter 4); and the secure bear cave that Per Kjær and Barry Winter have built together (this chapter). Anyone who believes that gay people cannot create the same kind of committed union that straight people enjoy have not talked to real couples in Scandinavia (and more likely, they haven't talked much to gay couples at all). If it is true that marriage is good for the spouses and their adoptive and biological children, why isn't that a good reason to recognize same-sex marriages? Shouldn't lesbian and gay couples, and their adoptive as well as biological children, have the same kind of state support?

Setting the foregoing irony aside, we have a deeper concern, namely, that fetishizing one institution risks displacing attention from the well-being of human beings in society. What is so magical about "marriage"? What's in a name? Barry Winter and Per Kjær are happy as clams that they are registered partners, and many Scandinavians consider registered partnership to be the same as marriage. Conversely, what we now call "marriage" is very different from "traditional marriage," which had a legal monopoly on sex and procreation (feature 1 earlier), which required that sexual activities between the spouses should be procreative (feature 2), and from which was hard, if not impossible, to exit (feature 3). If cohabitation had stronger limitations on exit and gave greater protection to financially dependent partners and children, we could see cohabitation as a superior institution for the mutual commitment and rearing of children that Kurtz assumes for "marriage."

Revisit traditionalist rhetoric about "out-of-wedlock births" in Scandinavia. Many American readers will assume that "out-of-wedlock births" are unwanted children produced by immature or unready mothers and fathers. That is most frequently the case when teenagers have children. But these connotations are less apt in the context of Scandinavia. Couples who have chosen to spend their lives together without a marriage certificate often plan for an otherwise traditional family structure, including children. Thus, "out-of-wedlock births" in Scandinavia are typically children who are wanted by their parents. While the rate of nonmarital births in Sweden, for example, is higher than the rate in the United States, the rate of teenage pregnancy is much lower. Scholars estimate that the rate of "unwanted" births in Sweden is half the rate of this country.[56] Telling evidence that out-of-wedlock children are wanted by their parents to create a traditional family is the incredibly low number of Scandinavian children available for adoption. As we discussed in chapter 3, only about twenty-five Danish children are available for adoption each year in the entire country. (The vast majority of adopted children, over 90 percent, come from poorer countries.)

Thus, Scandinavian couples who have children, regardless of their marriage status, generally do so because they want them. They go through the careful process that Kirsten Jepsen and Birgitte Haase did before they had their daughter Maia. A marriage certificate (or a registration, as in Kirsten and Birgitte's case) is not seen as a prerequisite to creating a traditional family relationship in these countries, particularly because the financial benefits of marriage (including those that accrue to children of married couples) are not denied to children of unmarried couples, as they may be in other countries as "punishment" for not establishing a government-approved form of family relationship. A difference between Scandinavian marriage and cohabitation is the relative difficulty of exiting marriage, which ought to produce longer lived unions, which in turn might benefit children raised by two parents rather than just one. But recall that few "defenders of marriage" seriously advocate abolition of cohabitation regimes. And recall, too, that what the United States and Scandinavia call "marriage" is much more like cohabitation than "traditional marriage" in this regard. No-fault divorce makes modern marriage much easier to exit—yet "marriage advocates" usually disclaim any intention of revoking this liberalization either.

Consider a broader perspective. Regardless of any connection to same-sex marriage, it is a fact that Danish and Swedish children are now—and have long been—more likely to be raised by nonmarried couples than American children are. Is this, per se, bad? Not necessarily, especially if you accept the Weitoft thesis that "lone parenthood" is not as good for parents and children as a partnered arrangement, whether married or not. Children in Denmark and Sweden (and the Netherlands) are much more likely to be raised by their parents than American children. In the United States, 26.5 percent of the households with children were headed by single mothers or fathers in 2001. In Denmark, only 18.4 percent of the households with children were headed by single parents in 2001. In Sweden, the figure was 23.1 percent in 2000. (In the Netherlands, the first country to recognize same-sex marriages in modern times, single parents were raising just 13.0 percent of all children in 2001.) Children in these same-sex marriage or partnership countries are much less likely to be raised by teenage parents than children in the United States. In a family values irony, American rates of divorce, nonmarital births, and single parenting are highest in the South, the part of our country most resistant to state recognition of same-sex unions. What Gunnar Andersson said in 2002 remains true today, especially in those parts of the country most enraged by same-sex marriage: "The USA stands out as an extreme case with its very high proportion of children born to a lone mother, with a higher probability that children experience a union disruption of their parents than anywhere else, and with many children having the experience of living in a stepfamily."[57]

Also, it appears that Swedish and Danish children are much more likely to be raised by their two biological parents than by nonparents or blended families (which include a stepparent). According to Weitoft, 70 percent of Swedish seventeen-year-olds live with their two biological (married or cohabiting) parents. Six percent are living with two parents, one of whom is a biological parent and the other a stepparent. Twenty-four percent are living with single mothers or fathers. In Denmark, seventy-eight percent of households with children are headed by the children's married (sixty-one percent) or cohabiting (seventeen percent) parents. Only two percent of Danish households are ones where children are not living with their parents, and eighteen percent are single-parent households. The "end of marriage" trumpeted by traditionalists does not mean that children are being raised by single parents or by strangers.

The Scandinavia-bashing of public voices like Santorum, Bork, and Kurtz is a most one-sided, and incorrect, reading of what is going on in these countries. Consider another angle. Forget about the Weitoft study, and assume for the sake of argument that in both the United States and Scandinavia a child is better off being raised by two married rather than cohabiting parents. Scandinavian children are more likely to be raised in cohabiting households. Most American readers then assume that the average child is much better off in the United States than in Sweden, for example. That assumption is not necessarily correct either.

A child born in Sweden in 2001 is half as likely to die before the age of five than a child in the United States. That child is likely to live 2.2 (if a girl) or 3.0 (if a boy) years longer than a child born in the United States. If present numbers hold up, that child, if a female, is half as likely to become pregnant before the age of eighteen and half as likely to have an abortion as her counterpart in the United States. The Swedish child is much less likely to contract sexually transmitted diseases, and vastly less likely to be exposed to HIV, the virus that causes AIDS. (The rate of HIV infection among Americans aged fifteen to forty-nine is 0.6 percent, six times the Swedish rate of 0.1 percent.)[58]

The Swedish child born in 2001 is less likely to attempt suicide as a teenager.[59] If the Swedish teenager finds herself with erotic feelings for people of the same sex, she is much less likely to commit suicide, to become depressed, and to be subject to antigay violence than an American teenager. If a female, the Swedish child or teenager is much less likely to be raped or sexually harassed by a close relative, classmate, or stranger. As she approaches adulthood, she faces many more career opportunities and is less likely to be paid a fraction of what a man is paid for the same work.

A society with a relatively low marriage rate, a relatively high divorce rate, and a relatively large number of nonmarital births can do quite well for the children who grow up (and apparently flourish) in it. For reasons such as this, some traditionalists' judgmental attitudes toward Scandinavia in general and Sweden in particular are not shared by less sectarian but equally conservative commentators. A more broadly learned account is afforded by Judge Richard Posner, a jurist in Chicago who is the most distinguished judicial appointment of the late President Reagan. A militant economic conservative, Judge Posner is viscerally hostile to the Swedish welfare state. But he is also a serious empiricist. On the basis of the facts, Posner concludes

> that we have much to learn from the Swedish approach to sex, considered as a whole: Some combination of aggressive and explicit sex education from an early age, provision of contraceptives to teenagers, conditioning generous maternity and child-welfare benefits on the mother's having established herself in the job market, solicitous attention to fetal and neonatal health needs, and an end to discrimination against homosexuals may be the essential elements of a realistic (and inexpensive) program for dealing with our national blights of teenage pregnancy, teenage parenthood, and sexually transmitted AIDS.[60]

And it appears we may have much to learn from the Scandinavian experience with "gay marriage," as well.

CHAPTER 6

Drawing Lines
Scandinavian Lessons for
the American Marriage Debate

Birgitte Haase, Kirsten Jepsen, and their daughter, Maia.

Judge Robert H. Bork is one of our leading conservative legal intellectuals. Like other traditionalists, he believes that the Constitution must be interpreted to follow the "intent" of its framers. Under such a philosophy, there is no constitutional right to privacy. Not only do women have no fundamental right to secure abortions, but romantic couples have no rights to buy or use contraceptives, and interracial couples have no right to marry one another. So not only is *Roe v. Wade* (1973), the famous abortion decision, wrongly decided but so is *Griswold v. Connecticut* (1965), which invalidated a law barring married couples from using contraceptives. *No* judge was willing to say that in 1987—except Bork, when he was nominated by President Ronald Reagan to be an associate justice of the U.S. Supreme Court. His candor about a popular constitutional principle cost Bork his seat on the Court.[1]

Since the end of his judicial career, Bork has become America's conservative constitutional conscience. Few issues have consumed his attention more than gay rights. When he returned to the Yale Law School after service as solicitor general in the 1977–78 school year, he was the most fervent faculty opponent of a student proposal that the Law School not lend its recruitment services to employers who discriminate against lesbian and gay applicants. On the bench, Bork's most influential opinion was *Dronenberg v. Zech* (1984), which defended the constitutional discretion that the armed forces, in his view, should have to imprison homosexual sodomites and exclude them from service, and gave the most lucid explanation for why the exclusion of homosexuals is a good policy. His book *Slouching toward Gomorrah* (1996) suggests that the rights of sexual minorities are central to his fear that judicially recognized constitutional rights are leading America to a horrible Judgment Day.[2]

Not only does Judge Bork believe homosexual couples have no federal constitutional right to either privacy or equal treatment, but he also believes the Constitution should be amended to preempt any *state* constitutional right to equal treatment, such as the Vermont and Massachusetts Supreme Courts recognized in 1999 and 2003, respectively. Hence Bork helped draft the Federal Marriage Amendment, described in chapter 1. In May 2004, he defended his position in a national debate held at the new Constitution Center in Philadelphia. Reflecting the evolution of discourse discussed in chapter 1, Bork did not primarily rely on natural law (marriage by definition is one man, one woman), slippery slope (gay marriage will lead to incestuous marriages and polygamy), or stamp-of-approval arguments to oppose same-sex marriage. He mainly relied on defense-of-marriage arguments. Reflecting the new international version of the defense-of-marriage argument, he invoked the Scandinavian experience: registered partnerships have destroyed marriage in Sweden and Denmark, he maintained, and there is no reason not to expect the same consequence in the United States.[3]

One of us (Eskridge) participated with Judge Bork in the debate and responded with a summary of the information reported in chapter 5: marriage was in decline long before Scandinavia recognized same-sex unions; some of the indicia of marital decline reversed themselves or stabilized under the new regime of registered partnerships; Scandinavian children are more likely to be raised by their biological parents than American children. To the extent that law has played any role in Scandinavia, it was cohabitation recognition and no-fault divorce that undermined marriage—inducing couples to cohabit rather than marry and driving divorce rates up. The serious defender of marriage should demand reconsideration of previous state liberalizations for straight couples, not prevent new couples for joining the institution. The defense-of-marriage argument is a lavender herring.[4]

Bork did not respond to this analysis. Nor did the Scandinavian evidence seem to matter to those in the hall who already opposed same-sex marriage—or to the hundreds of same-sex marriage supporters in the hall. They applauded the fact that we had a statistical answer for the Scandinavian twist on the defense-of-marriage objection, but we could have said almost anything—or nothing—and they would have dismissed the objection. In recent correspondence, we supplied the same information to Jack Baker and Mike McConnell, the gay couple who first sought public recognition of their union as a civil marriage (chapter 1). Now sixty-four years old, these men have been life partners since March 10, 1967. What did they think about the Danish law and its consequences, we asked? They responded: "Know nothing about it." They do not follow this and other international developments. We noted that the law gives almost all the same rights and benefits of marriage. To which they said: "Anything 'almost all' is a non-starter. . . . Never compromise on your birthright," that is, your right to marry the person you love. They see themselves as pioneers unwilling to compromise constitutional principle, and the most articulate defenders of same-sex marriage agree with them: accept no substitutes. In 2004, just before the Philadelphia debate, Baker and McConnell filed suit in United States federal court, seeking to require the Internal Revenue Service to treat them as a properly married couple.[5]

So here's an irony about the same-sex marriage debate in this country. Supporters as well as opponents of same-sex marriage are usually driven by their normative precommitments, and not by the facts or the lessons of experience. This is just as true for intellectuals as for ordinary people. Arguments such as those we pursue in this book have the potential to change people's minds, but in the short term, few minds are changed. Each side cheers its own advocates.

In the longer term, however, such evidence ought to have greater bite. The United States needs to get beyond the unyielding stances of both Robert Bork and Jack Baker. A particularly receptive audience is the new generation of Americans. The large majority of these are openly heterosexual but not homophobic. They have known openly lesbian and gay persons as relatives, teachers, shopkeepers, celebrities, neighbors, and public officials. Many know committed same-sex couples. Most of them would like to marry, and they value discourse that looks to the future of fundamental institutions such as marriage. We urge these Americans to read our book with care and then evaluate our basic points as they observe the continuing evolution of marriage, family, and gay rights in our society.

Another audience that should be receptive to our account is that of older Americans whose views about lesbian and gay relationships have evolved. Some have evolved in a particularly public way, none more than those of Lynne Cheney. The chair of the National Endowment for the Humanities during the Reagan Administration, Cheney is an outspoken cultural conservative and author of a blistering attack on the theories of relativism prominent in the humanities. She also authored an explosive novel, *Sisters* (1981), set in Wyoming of the 1880s. Women have voted in Wyoming since 1869, and the novel depicts the strong-willed freedom such women claimed. They also claimed romance, as this steamy passage suggests for one female couple: "Let us go away together, away from the anger and imperatives of men. There will be only two of us, and we shall linger through long afternoons of sweet retirement. In the evenings I shall read to you while you work your cross-stitch in the firelight. And then we shall go to bed, our bed, my dearest girl." (This was perfectly legal, by the way. There was no sodomy law in Wyoming until the 1890s.)[6]

The author of *Sisters* is also the mother of a lesbian daughter, Mary Cheney, who is partnered. While we do not have access to Lynne Cheney's private evolution, it appears that she and her conservative husband, vice-president Richard Cheney, have moved in their thinking. They not only oppose Bork's Federal Marriage Amendment (in spite of the president's support) but they affirmatively favor state recognition of civil unions for lesbian and gay couples. This is not self-serving sympathy on their part, for Lynne Cheney is one of the toughest-minded policy analysts in Washington. We believe that her prounion, and potentially promarriage, stance is a consequence of her attention to the facts: lesbians and gay men are decent citizens; they form committed relationships that work well for them and contribute to the larger family and community. Hence the state ought to recognize them.[7]

So younger Americans and even some older ones who have come to know lesbian and gay couples ought to listen to their stories and evidence about them with care. But what use does the Scandinavian experience have for those Americans—promarriage as well as antimarriage—who have already made up their minds? Surprisingly, the Scandinavian experience is rich in cautionary lessons for those Americans as well. The experience suggests that genuine defenders of traditional marriage, such as Bork, should beware of scapegoating gay people, for this is a strategy that itself undermines marriage. Genuine defenders of same-sex marriage, such as Baker and McConnell, should beware of all-or-nothing strategies and should consider the time for *equality practice* that many straight people of good faith (such as the Cheneys) need before they can agree to equal marriage rights for gays. Both sides would profit from a central lesson of Scandinavian political culture—the desirability of incremental change to accommodate both minority needs and majority reservations, the principled nature of some compromises, and the ultimate goal of mutual respect.

Lessons Scandinavia Offers for Traditionalists

Robert Bork's Danish counterpart is Jann Sjursen, the former chair (1990–2002) of Denmark's Christian People's Party (CPP).[8] A thoughtful intellectual who is an important conservative political figure, Sjursen spoke to one of us (Spedale) in 1997 about Denmark's experience with registered partnership, which he and his party firmly opposed in 1989. Unlike Bork, Sjursen supports legislation prohibiting antigay discrimination in employment and public accommodations. His argument against same-sex marriage avoids gay-bashing, for his position is that "marriage should hold precedence in legislation before other sorts of partnerships—not only in relation to homosexual partnerships, but also 'paperless' heterosexual domestic partnerships." Sjursen speaks without rancor or emotionalism on an issue that remains important to him, and he generously concedes that the Registered Partnership Act of 1989 has been "an 'icebreaker' to make people more accepting of homosexual families."[9] Once lesbian and gay couples have come out of the closet as *couples* and as *families*, the sensible conservative ought to accommodate their needs, to some extent.

Our conversation with Sjursen suggests three lessons that principled conservatives ought to consider in the same-sex marriage debate. First, they should avoid scapegoating gay people. Second, they should focus on strategies for defending marriage that address the deep reasons for its decline. Third, conservatives should understand that lesbian and gay couples, including those raising children within their committed unions, are here to stay. They are not a passing social phenomenon, and governmental policy should be responsive to their needs, and to the needs of at least a million children being raised in their households.

Hold the Line? Avoid Scapegoating

The most important lesson that Scandinavian conservatives, such as Sjursen, would offer to American conservatives, such as Bork or the Cheneys, is that tradition and, especially, Christianity are not well served by scapegoating a minority group. Sjursen and many of his CPP colleagues are facing the fact that marriage is in decline for reasons having little to do with homosexuality. Fewer people are getting married, more couples are having and raising children outside of marriage, and a lot of spouses are divorcing. These were the trends throughout the twentieth century, and the trends became dramatic in most countries after the 1960s. The decline of marriage has been driven by heterosexuals. Straight women and men have turned from marriage to cohabitation, for social as well as personal reasons. They want to walk out of unhappy marriages, and they do so in unprecedented numbers.[10]

Although marriage has continued to exercise considerable romantic and aspirational appeal, couples today demand more choices and freedoms than their parents or grandparents had. They want the option of living together in a sexual relationship before getting married; they want the option of cohabitation rather than marriage, but without giving up lucrative insurance and other fringe benefits provided by employers; they do not want the state to enforce sexual fidelity rules; they want opportunities to exit unsuccessful marriages without much bother. Throughout Western civilization, the law has accommodated freedom of choice for these heterosexual couples. In the United States and Scandinavia, sex and cohabitation outside marriage are no longer crimes, nor is adultery in most jurisdictions; cohabiting couples receive many of the benefits once reserved for marriage; divorce no longer requires a showing of fault. Anyone could have predicted that these changes in the law would encourage, and perhaps speed along, the decline of marriage. And so they have in Scandinavia and the United States. Some Scandinavians and Americans realize that the free choice regime they have created for straight couples has changed a cherished institution and is hurting children, increasing numbers of whom are now raised (especially in America) in single-parent or stepparent households. This realization creates both anxiety and guilt.[11]

Along comes the possibility of gay marriage—and all of a sudden concerned citizens have a group they can blame besides themselves: homosexuals. From their point of view, gay marriage becomes the Maginot Line the enemy shall never be allowed to cross. If the Line holds, the institution of marriage can be saved, and maybe its defenders can start rolling back their own selfish liberalizations. (The historical Maginot Line was a series of forts France constructed after World War I to protect its northeastern border against invasion by Germany, its historic enemy.) Under this account, the defense-of-marriage argument is less concerned with the factual consequences of same-sex marriage than with holding the Line. This is, ultimately, why so many traditionalists believe unverified, perhaps implausible, empirical claims. Judge Bork, for example, readily admits that straight people are responsible for the decline of marriage but still insists, without any evidence, that gay marriage would force marriage across the line that would destroy it altogether.[12]

Former secretary of commerce William Bennett put it most eloquently in a 1994 speech to the Christian Coalition. "I understand the aversion to homosexuality," held by religious traditionalists, he stated, but he cautioned them that it is no-fault divorce and not homosexual rights that have imposed the greatest harms upon children. Nonetheless, he argues that gay marriage remains a much greater threat than high divorce rates: "In society at large and even in law, divorce is still acknowledged to be a fracturing of the marriage ideal. It declares that a couple has fallen short of a norm that we still believe to be right, valuable and worthy of our respect. By contrast, proponents and supporters of same-sex marriage want to redefine the norm itself." Bennett seems genuinely unaware that no-fault divorce has fundamentally altered the "norm itself," for the ease of divorce has both formally revoked and practically undermined the norm of mandatory (no-exit) lifetime commitment that characterized "traditional marriage" for most of American history.[13]

We respectfully urge such persons to reconsider. The traditionalist who values the mutual commitment features of marriage for life, who places the long-term welfare of children above the immediate needs of their parents, and who respects history is precisely the person who should reject this kind of thinking. If a traditionalist wants to hold the Line, it is already too late. A strategy of holding the Line easily evolves into a strategy of *scapegoating*, or displacing the blame for one's mistakes onto outsiders. In the hands of some well-meaning traditionalists, and most vicious ones, the defense-of-marriage objection to same-sex marriage has become a mechanism for blaming gay people for a longstanding social phenomenon (the decline of marriage) driven by the pleasure-seeking choices of straight couples. Scapegoating comes naturally to human beings, but it is a thoroughly unproductive way of handling serious social problems.

Among the least attractive features of scapegoating is its unfairness. It apportions blame in the wrong place and is therefore contrary to America's fundamental principle of responsibility. One of the early lessons we teach our children is that they ought not avoid personal responsibility by shifting blame. So if John hits his brother Marky, it is no defense for John to say,

"He's such a pervert!" Or this is how Newton will justify his extramarital affairs: "If my wife had not become so unattractive and sick, I wouldn't have cheated on her," implicitly suggesting "It's her fault." This kind of justification is as morally squalid as it is illogical. And Newton is no less a scoundrel if he blames his infidelities on homosexuals. "I guess my moral compass was thrown off so badly by the knowledge my sister is a lesbian, that I forgot about my marital vows."

The unfairness of scapegoating is particularly keen when blame is cast on vulnerable and previously demonized minorities. Americans have blamed blacks for a wide range of social problems, from epidemics of rape and child molestation to crossdressing to urban pollution. Feminists were scapegoats for public fears about women's deviant or public sexuality. Jews have been blamed for assaults on gentile children.[14] As it has become increasingly unacceptable in public discourse to scapegoat Jews, feminists, and African Americans, homosexuals have become America's universal scapegoats— culprits for child molestation panics from 1935 to 1957, the sexual revolution in the 1960s, corruption of the nation's youth in the 1970s and 1980s, and now the decline of marriage. The last to earn social tolerance and state recognition for their relationships, lesbian and gay couples have been the first to bear responsibility for the decline of marriage. This is unfair to gay people.[15]

It is also unfair to traditional family values and to marriage as an institution. In both the United States and Scandinavia, what we call "marriage" today is much more like cohabitation than it is like marriage in 1900. Like cohabiting partners and unlike traditional spouses, couples who are married today typically had sex with one another (and a range of other partners) before moving in together, are under no legal pressure (and only weak social pressure) to be sexually faithful to one another, and can split up (with some expense) and never deal with one another again, unless there are children. American and Scandinavian societies retreated from traditional marriage in the 1970s. Legal liberalizations sought by straight people pressed social practice even further away from the traditional ideal of a couple committed for life and under strong fidelity and support obligations. Both law and social practice have already redefined marriage.[16]

Under this analysis, gay marriage is not the last Line of defense before marriage collapses. Recall that the historic Maginot Line protected France's border with Germany—but Nazi Germany invaded France through a side door, by marching through Belgium. Just as the Maginot Line gave France a deluded sense that it was secure against German attack, so holding the Line against same-sex couples may give traditionalists a deluded sense that marriage is secure. The analogy can be cast even more negatively. Assume no

French fortresses on the German border. But, *after* the Germans invade France and march toward Paris, the French government declares its border with Luxembourg (a tiny country sandwiched between Belgium, France, and Germany) to be the Maginot Line and sends troops to police it. "Luxembourg is our Last Line of Defense—We take our stand here!" What France has done is unfair enough to Luxembourg, but it is insanity for France. Drawing the Maginot Line at the wrong time (after the invasion has occurred) and in the wrong place (where there is no serious threat) not only distracts the defender from the real enemy, and is therefore a major tactical blunder, but is tantamount to surrender. This, we submit, is the mistake made by the defense-of-marriage objection to lesbian and gay unions or marriage.

The acceptance of no-fault divorce, sexual cohabitation, and nonmarital children in Western societies is part of a larger economic and conceptual shift. Not only do adults enjoy a broader array of choices within marriage and other relationships but the nature of marriage and "committed" relationship has changed. It has moved away from a *traditionalist* philosophy demanding self-sacrifice, permanent mutual commitment, and the family as a collective unit—and toward a *consumerist* philosophy of self-satisfaction, mutual cooperation, and the family as a collection of pleasure-seeking individuals. Ours is a society where sex, relationships, and even children are morphing into hedonic goods, that is, sources of pleasure. This development ought to be deeply troubling to traditionalists (including gay traditionalists such as ourselves). The causes contributing to this development are complex and have little to do with homosexuality. To suppose, as Bork and Bennett do, that the best way to stop this trend is to discriminate against homosexual unions is to concede the death of traditional marriage. It would be like France's maintaining a Maginot Line against Luxembourg while the Nazis sip champagne in Paris.

As relative outsiders to this consumerist mentality, we find it remarkable how much religion and social conservatism have accommodated this norm. What amazes us most about the same-sex marriage debate is what traditionalists concede. Most say nothing to challenge the choices available to heterosexual Americans to form cohabiting relationships, to have children outside of marriage, and to walk out of their marriages and turn their backs on commitments that were once understood as lifetime. We challenge our readers to write down the name of every social conservative who has taken the same-sex marriage debate as an occasion to call for a rollback of the legal liberalizations available to heterosexual couples, especially no-fault divorce and stingy child and spousal support awards. Now put a check mark by the name of any person on that list who has seriously introduced and campaigned for proposals to this effect.[17]

Not only do traditionalism and conservatism fail to challenge the law's and society's consumerist approach to marriage and family, but they are in the process of converting. Many traditionalists accept popular liberalizations (such as no-fault divorce, which a good many social conservatives have used to trade in their aging wives for younger ones) and then redefine "tradition" to include the liberalizations and to exclude new groups on the basis of such redefined tradition. This new form of conservativism has emerged as an apologetic political philosophy for American consumerism, shrouding it in the rhetoric of tradition even while protecting it from reforms that would constrain consumer choice. Stanley Kurtz's work exemplifies this phenomenon. He argues against same-sex marriage but insists that "repealing no-fault divorce, or even eliminating premarital cohabitation, are not what's at issue." Moreover, his argument against same-sex marriage rests upon a social science theory insisting that any liberalization of family law is irreversible, a theory that is defeatist from a political point of view and nihilist from a moral one.[18]

A traditionalist philosophy that leaves no-fault divorce and cohabitation untouched is a philosophy that can (retroactively) justify any path that modern marriage might take. With prenuptial agreements added to the mix, marriage itself is becoming a regime for which consumer choice is the core. In that event, there will be less and less space separating marriage, cohabitation, and other less formal arrangements. The next logical step would be for each couple to sit down at a state-provided computer terminal and negotiate the package of benefits and obligations that best fits their needs. As traditionalists and conservatives focus their attention on keeping "homosexuals" out of the institution (and protecting France against Luxembourg), who will be left to object?

Social Conservatives and the Decline of Tradition, Faith, and Marriage

American social conservatives sometimes scapegoat sexual minorities as threats to religious faith itself, but there is another way of understanding the matter. As the Scandinavian experience illustrates, traditionalist religion that sets itself in favor of continued exclusion and pushes hard for continued state discrimination is taking significant risks. One risk is entanglement in politics. Jann Sjursen's party is the *Christian* People's Party (now *Christian* Democrats), and it represents the views of religious traditionalists. A politically engaged church population sacrifices some of its special status in society and risks being perceived as just another "interest group" trying to hijack state apparatus for its own partisan purposes. Partially for this reason, the CPP has not fared well in recent elections. It failed to garner even the 2 percent of the vote needed for representation in Parliament in the 2005 election.[19]

Political scientists worry about the effect of religious mobilization on politics, but we agree with Stephen Carter (another Yale Law School professor) that even more troubling is its effect on religion and faith. Judeo-Christian religions have traditionally emphasized intangible human connections, themes of mercy and compassion, and win-win scenarios where charity enriches both the giver and the needy recipient. Politics represents a shift of emphasis—toward partisan win-lose scenarios where a group deploys the state to exercise power and suppress opposing forces. To be sure, the state and politics sometimes trade in connection, compassion, and win-win proposals—but these features are decidedly not typical of politics. Once religion enters the win-lose games of politics, as happens so frequently, religion loses some of its moral edge. Jesus the Christ emphasized the separation of religious faith from state policy, and He was right.[20]

Another risk is that religious conservatives will place the moral authority of religion on a norm unworthy of it. Throughout the twentieth century, the Church of Jesus Christ of Latter-day Saints and many (white) southern Baptist churches preached that racial segregation was not only proper but was required by God's natural order. This was a squalid norm, and fortunately one that most traditionalist religions—the Roman Catholic Church, African American Baptist churches, the Seventh-Day Adventists, and Orthodox Judaism—rejected. Both the Mormons and the (white) southern Baptists now reject the segregation norm as well. Although fundamentalists based their reversal on "new revelations" from God, it was surely inspired also by those religions' need for survival. If traditional family value philosophies today were openly linked to racial segregation, they would not enjoy nearly the level of support they now have.[21]

This phenomenon of decline-by-association partly explains what has occurred to traditionalists in Norway. Norway's Christian People's Party opposed the registered partnership proposal in 1990–93, but without the relatively measured compassion of MP Sjursen and the Danish CPP before them. Proponents of the law appealed to Norwegians' sense of fairness and humanity: if lesbian and gay couples want to join in committed relationships and even raise children, why shouldn't the state provide institutional regulation? Norway's Ministry of Children and the Family agreed with this analysis. Religious and political traditionalists did not, and there were certainly arguments that could have been respectfully made, arguments like the ones Sjursen has emphasized. Instead, traditionalists responded intemperately on many occasions. In the early stages of the debate, Anders Gåslund, the leader of the Norwegian CPP's youth organization, came out as a gay man and urged fellow traditionalists to support family rights for lesbian and gay couples. Many in the CPP denounced the young man as a traitor and an immoral person, a tactic that struck most Norwegians as un-Christian.[22]

The People's Movement Against the Partnership Law, mobilized in 1992, was potentially an effective mechanism for traditionalists to oppose the bill. Patterned on similar mobilizations in the United States, it sought to demonstrate that large numbers of Norwegians believed that recognition of same-sex relationships did not reflect their vision of community or family. But in public debates or discussions, representatives of the People's Movement often resorted to name-calling and made arguments based upon unfounded stereotypes about lesbians and gay men. When neutral observers noted their many inaccuracies, Norwegians were often left with the impression that the People's Movement was inspired by bigotry and contempt for gay people rather than a truly public spirit. When the People's Movement conducted a prayer vigil in front of the Parliament in Oslo, legislators were offended by their presumptuousness. These people, who were not behaving like Christians themselves, had no standing to preach to Parliament what Christ required of Norway.[23]

The parliamentary debates in Norway had several episodes where traditionalists looked foolish or excessively dogmatic. At one point, an MP suggested that if Jesus Christ were alive today, he would want to encourage lesbian and gay couples to join in mutually loving and committed relationships. The leader of the Norwegian CPP then interjected that his colleague "had a very strange way of interpreting the Master's word!" In the upper chamber, an opponent invoked the fact that Norway would soon host the winter Olympics. "During the Olympics next year we will try to sell Norwegian culture and tradition, Norwegian commodities and services. If anyone believes that this law would be a good commodity to sell under, they ought to think twice." These arguments were neither charitable nor persuasive, and the Olympics appeal was simply comical.[24]

The Norwegian experience illustrates the dilemma faced by Christian and Jewish traditionalists. How does an altruistic but historically grounded religious faith oppose a legal accommodation to a minority group without sounding mean or reactionary? Norwegian traditionalists chose strategies that made the worst of this dilemma, because they sacrificed religious charity without advancing historical principle. Invoking antigay stereotypes and making personal attacks on opponents, traditionalists too often represented their faith in a way that was not attractive. Their reliance on unpersuasive arguments suggested that they were not being candid about their real reasons for opposing equal treatment of lesbian and gay couples. And when

Parliament recognized registered partnerships for same-sex couples, many traditionalists treated it as Armageddon itself.

If so, traditionalists themselves are partly to blame. American social conservatives have correctly observed that the Church in Norway has been discredited, to some extent, by the campaign of Christian fundamentalists against registered partnerships. [25] If American traditionalists insist on scapegoating, they should explore ways in which members of the Church in Norway helped dig its own grave, through intemperate and un-Christian rhetoric and argumentation. In Denmark and Sweden, the Christian People's Parties opposed registered partnerships as well, and with some of the same effects: partnership went through, opponents' predictions of Armageddon were not confirmed, and traditionalist mindsets were discredited. The effect in those other countries was not as dramatic, because their state churches and religious parties were not as culturally powerful as those in Norway and their voices were not as intemperate.[26]

There is another way that religious and social conservatives have undermined traditional marriage in Europe and perhaps also the United States. Traditionalist opposition and the heat of the same-sex marriage debate is now creating a window of opportunity for intellectuals to propose that the state get out of the marriage business altogether. Those proposing the abolition of civil marriage (churches of course could still recognize religious marriages) include not just secular feminists and radical gay theorists but sometimes also traditionalists. Social conservative Douglas Kmiec, the former dean of Pepperdine Law School, has made just such a proposal, albeit one that is limited to Massachusetts. He and his traditionalist allies should realize that there is a growing mainstream heterosexual audience for such a proposal, an audience not limited to one state.[27]

Pluralism Lesson: Lesbian and Gay Families Are Here to Stay, and Need the Protections of Marriage

The biggest lesson American traditionalists should draw from the Scandinavian experience is that lesbian and gay families are now part of the social landscape. They are not going to disappear, and there will be more of them each year. Danish traditionalists have accepted this fact. Whereas opposition to registered partnership was the Danish CPP's main focus in the late 1980s, today it makes no mention of registered partnership whatsoever on the portion of the party's website that sets out its views on various topics. Sjursen even told us that the registered partnership law "has had a [positive] effect on the attitudes that the public has to homosexuals and the homosexual family." Those positive attitudes have encouraged more lesbian and gay Danes to come out to coworkers, family members, and neighbors. Although Sjursen felt that attitudes had not changed as to lesbian and gay families raising children, these attitudes have changed since 1997 (when we interviewed him). Over four hundred couples in registered partnerships in Denmark are raising children born in their relationship. Their social experience fueled demands that Danish law recognize coparenting rights and responsibilities for these same-sex couples, and Parliament agreed to do so in 1999.[28]

The same phenomena are occurring in the United States, even without national recognition for same-sex unions. Partnered since March 10, 1967, Jack Baker and Mike McConnell are approaching their fortieth anniversary. For most of that period, they have been homeowners and good neighbors in Minneapolis and contributing members of society. Since his rebuff by the University of Minnesota in 1971, McConnell has been working for the Hennepin County Library system, where he recently won an award for redesigning the computer network. Although he lost his first case (*Baker v. Nelson*), Baker has practiced law successfully and now advises local companies on how to comply with the law. As a couple devoted to knowledge (McConnell) and the rule of law (Baker), these marriage pioneers have become highly respected members of their community.[29]

Once lonely pioneers, Baker and McConnell now enjoy the company of many other committed same-sex couples, and their numbers are growing each year. The 2000 census reported 594,691 same-sex partner households in the United States, almost a fourfold increase from the 1990 census. The Institute for Gay and Lesbian Strategic Studies estimates that the 2000 census undercounted committed lesbian and gay couples by at least 16 percent, and perhaps as much as 28 percent, a range we consider conservative, even when one factors in possible overcounts. (Because so many same-sex couples remain at least partially closeted, it is impossible to obtain a full count, without the interviewing skills of an Alfred Kinsey.) Fifty-one percent of the households were male, 49 percent female. Same-sex coupled households represented just under 1 percent of all white households, but 1.4 percent of all African American, 1.3 percent of all Latino, and 1.6 percent of all interracial households.[30]

Increasing numbers of these households are raising children. The 1990 census reported that one in five lesbian households was raising children under age eighteen, and about one in ten gay male households. The 2000 census found one in three lesbian households was raising children under age eighteen, and more than one in five gay male households, a significant increase for both groups. The overwhelming majority of children raised in these households were the biological progeny of one parent. Although same-sex couples, like different-sex unmarried couples, tend to live in major metropolitan areas like San Francisco, New York, Washington, D.C., and Atlanta, couples raising children are statistically more likely than childless couples to live in states like Mississippi, Utah, and the Dakotas. In other words, they are relatively more likely to choose child-friendly jurisdictions than gay-friendly ones.[31]

Several reports developed from the census data analyze the ninety thousand same-sex couples reported for California. One-third of the couples have at least one partner who is Latina or Latino. Seventy percent of such couples (aged twenty-five to fifty-five) are raising their own children, a figure much higher than that for different-sex couples as well as other same-sex couples. Overall, same-sex couples in California are raising more than seventy thousand children, including fifty thousand who are the biological progeny of one partner. Most important, the studies found that same-sex couples with children have lower incomes and fewer economic resources than different-sex married couples raising children.[32]

The National Gay and Lesbian Task Force found that 14 percent of the same-sex census couples were African American. They tended to have lower median incomes than other same-sex couples *and* black opposite-sex married couples—but were *more* likely to be raising children within their households. Consistent with the foregoing, studies focusing on couples in Florida, Massachusetts, and New Jersey have reported that same-sex couples raising children are more likely to be racial minority or interracial partnerships and to have lower household incomes and home ownership rates than straight married couples in those states.[33]

These analyses deepen the lesson that traditionalists might draw from the 2000 census. Not only are thousands of LGBT Americans committing their lives to one another but they are committing their partnerships to the bearing and raising of children. To that end, they are making the same kinds of sacrifices Robert Bork and his first wife made for their children—one parent is sacrificing his or her career to stay at home with the children, and both parents are sacrificing sleep to comfort sick infants, educating the children, and making family decisions based upon the needs of the children and not their own convenience. There is every reason to believe, as expert studies have indicated, that lesbian and gay parents are doing a capable job raising these children. But there is also reason to believe that a disproportionate number of them are vulnerable. They are vulnerable because they do not have a lot of money, because they are not white, and because they are homosexual, living in areas where homosexuality, color, and poverty ensure discrimination and even violence. These LGBT people would benefit, modestly at least and sometimes enormously, from the state-assured benefits of marriage (or its legal equivalent).

And so would their children, because civil marriage or its equivalent would reinforce the parents' commitment to one another and, theoretically, improve the odds that the children would be raised by two rather than one parent. Many traditionalists believe it is not in the interests of children to be reared by single parents; there is significant evidence supporting such a belief. Of course, such traditionalists also tend to believe that children are best reared in different-sex households, a belief supported by no reliable social science evidence thus far.[34] At this time, there is no reason to believe that denying lesbian and gay couples marriage rights discourages them from having or adopting children. And the experience in Scandinavia provisionally suggests that same-sex marriage makes it more likely for same-sex couples rearing children to stay together. If civil marriage for those couples would help their children, why not adopt it? Traditionalist Senator Rick Santorum says in his book *It Takes a Family* (2005): "In a compassionate society, adult interests and agendas cannot be allowed to trump the basic needs and rights of children."[35]

What still bothers many traditionalists is the finding that children in same-sex households tend to follow gender roles less rigidly. A few studies have found daughters more aggressive and boys less so than others in their gender cohort. For traditionalists such as Judge Bork, who believe that there are natural gender roles that must be strictly enforced, this could be a strong objection to lesbian parenting and, indirectly, to same-sex marriage. Note, though, that gender roles have varied widely from one generation to the next. What was appropriate masculine conduct in 1850, such as expressing affection for and sleeping in the same bed with other men (as Abe Lincoln did) was not considered masculine conduct in 1950 (when it would have created suspicions of homosexuality). In the new millennium, we have seen the rise of the "metrosexual"—heterosexual men who obsess over their personal grooming and are highly sensitive to fashion trends. Gender roles evolve, and family values conservatives of all orientations ought to have some appreciation for at least one gender reversal in same-sex households. In a random sample conducted by the Urban Institute, one-quarter of the gay male couples rearing children included a father who stays at home and cares for the children, a phenomenon that remains a rarity among straight couples, married or not. One might predict that children of gay male, and perhaps also lesbian, couples would view it as natural that fathers would be nurturing and would sacrifice career opportunities the way mothers have done for the last several generations. This strikes us as an evolutionary path for gender roles that all family-oriented thinkers—straight or gay, conservative or progressive—might applaud.[36]

Lessons Scandinavia Offers for Lesbian and Gay Rights Advocates

While the Scandinavian experience throws cold water on some traditionalist arguments against same-sex marriage, it carries some sobering news for supporters as well. None of the Scandinavian governments recognized registered partnerships until public opinion had turned in their favor, or at least demonstrated that there was not strong opposition among the general population. Public opinion in the United States is not nearly as gay marriage–friendly as that in Scandinavia. Opinion polls conducted by Quinnipiac University, the Pew Research Center, and the Gallup Poll in 2004 all showed about two-thirds of the respondents opposed to state recognition of same-sex marriages. The 2004 elections saw thirteen states (including relatively progay Oregon) vote to amend their state constitutions to limit marriage to one man, one woman. More will follow in the 2006 elections.[37]

This means that gay marriage will not come soon to most of America. Why is that? The moral intuitions that most Americans bring to issues of sexuality, gender, and the law are not formed on the basis of rational policy arguments such as those we have emphasized. Instead, those intuitions are more emotionally driven, and intensely felt. If traditionalists like Bork and Santorum need to understand that lesbian and gay families are here to stay, lesbian and gay marriage activists such as Baker and McConnell need to understand the same thing about Americans whose identity and sense of community are deeply rooted in the strict definition of marriage as one man, one woman.

Since Stonewall (1969), it has been an article of progressive faith that Americans of all sorts who know and admire openly lesbian or gay relatives, coworkers, or teachers will be the most receptive to claims for tolerance and equal treatment for homosexuals. With more Americans on record as lesbian, gay, bisexual, and transgendered (LGBT) than ever before, progressives are optimistic that same-sex marriage will arrive sooner or later. The same-sex marriage debate is throwing cold water on this optimism, for friends of homosexuals will often not go along with marriage-equality claims. For the most dramatic example, consider Senator Santorum. A devout Roman Catholic and father of six children, the darkly handsome Santorum is a pugilistic politician who opposes homosexual marriage and is the leading congressional supporter of Judge Bork's FMA. Yet his communications director, Robert Traynham, a devout Catholic, is an acknowledged homosexual.

When the media outed Traynham, the senator confirmed that he had long been aware of his aide's homosexuality. "Not only is Mr. Traynham an exemplary staffer; he is also a trusted friend and confidante to me and my family," the Senator said publicly. At the same time, his rhetoric has become more temperate. Whereas Santorum's public denunciation of the Supreme Court's 2003 decision striking down sodomy laws seemed to compare homosexual relations to sex with animals, today he says: "the definition of marriage has not ever to my opinion included homosexuality. That's not to pick on homosexuality. It's not, you know, man on child, man on dog." But he remains adamantly opposed to same-sex marriage.[38]

Recall American Eddie Moris and his Danish partner Jens Boesen. They have been together since 1990. Boesen's parents immediately liked Moris and accepted him into their extended family. On the other hand, Moris's parents in California have not accepted Eddie's relationship with Jens. Eddie tried to clear the air with them by writing a twenty-seven-page letter, explaining how he feels as a gay man and the joy he has found with his life partner. The parents never responded. To the best of our knowledge, Mrs. Moris still contributes to ministries seeking to change or de-program gay people's sexual orientation, and hopes that her son will convert to heterosexuality. Like The Antigay Senator and His Homosexual Aide, this Tale of Two Families—the Boesens and the Morises—is a story about how hard it is to change underlying attitudes, particularly when the surrounding culture supports those attitudes.[39] We now explain why this is so.

The Politics of Disgust: Truth, Not Consequences

Supporters of gay rights endorse the harm principle as the foundation for regulating sexual activities: the state should allow individuals freedom to pursue their own happiness and to flourish in their own unique ways, unless their pursuit of happiness and human flourishing tangibly harms their neighbors. The harm principle may have been a cogent argument for repealing criminal sodomy laws,[40] but it has had little traction in the same-sex marriage debate. Even John Stuart Mill's *On Liberty* (1859), the libertarian Bible, draws the line in this way: Mill argued that polygamy should not be a criminal matter but also that the state ought not recognize and encourage polygamous marriages. Modern opponents of same-sex marriage follow Mill: lesbian and gay relationships are no matter for the criminal law, but neither should they receive the recognition and approval of state-sanctioned marriage.[41]

Like Mill's position on polygamy, the stance of Americans rejecting same-sex marriage ultimately rests upon a moral judgment: polygamy (for

Mill) and same-sex marriage (for today's traditionalists) are morally inferior choices, and so should not be encouraged by the state, but they are not so harmful that they should subject participants to criminal sanctions. Adherents believe these stances represent *tolerance* for minority choices, even as they also represent *preference* for majority choices that are, in their widely shared view, morally superior for the individual and, more important, for the community. One may generalize even more broadly: this is the point of civil marriage law. Remaining single and even having sex outside of marriage are not proper objects of criminal sanctions in most of the United States, but the state still encourages sexually active adults to get married. Marriage law reflects a tolerance for remaining single, but a preference for getting married. That preference, in turn, reflects a traditional judgment that people are more deeply fulfilled if they are married and, more important, that they better contribute to community projects—not just replenishing the population but also serving the public good unselfishly. Paraphrasing French philosopher Jean-Jacques Rousseau, the good spouse is a model for the good citizen.[42]

Lesbian and gay rights supporters, including ourselves, have responded with the following kind of argument. The nature and function of civil marriage entail unselfish mutual commitment, aspirationally for the long term. Lesbian and gay couples have the same aspiration; many are raising children together. The benefits of marriage that accrue to different-sex couples as well as their communities are equally applicable to same-sex couples. The good spouse can therefore be a lesbian joined in matrimony with another woman. Accordingly, there is no basis in social utility, or the social function of marriage, to exclude same-sex couples. As we saw in chapter 1, opponents have replied that same-sex marriage cannot fit within the social function of marriage and therefore will actually harm marriage as an institution. Chapters 3–5 suggest that this defense-of-marriage argument lacks foundation and that the experience of Scandinavia strongly undermines it.

Even if we are right about all the foregoing, Mrs. Moris will not change her mind about same-sex marriage. While the debate is not impervious to experience or empirical evidence, for most Americans the debate is about moral truth, not social consequences. Even when the debaters argue about consequences, they are really arguing about truth, and their audience will filter the consequences through moral-truth lenses. Put bluntly, the politics of same-sex marriage involves moral judgments not easily influenced by the facts of social harm. Although chapter 1 demonstrated that public opposition to same-sex marriage had evolved from definitional and stamp-of-approval arguments, to defense-of-marriage arguments, we now observe that the evolution is primarily rhetorical. People still reject same-sex marriage because they just don't see marriage as anything but one man, one woman or because they do not want the state to promote homosexuality or encourage sexual conduct they consider disgusting.[43]

Social psychologists have demonstrated that human judgment is strongly influenced by cognitive stereotypes and emotional prejudices that are resistant to what lawyers consider rational analyses and argumentation. Social intuitionist thinkers say that "moral judgment is caused by intuitive moral impulses and is followed (when needed) by slow, ex post facto moral reasoning." Jonathan Haidt, for example, has found that sexual taboos are particularly susceptible to disgust-driven rather than harm-driven moral reactions. In laboratory experiments, he found that self-identified liberals (whose moral metric is the harm principle) and conservatives (whose moral metric is tradition) had almost the same level of negative reaction to scenarios involving incest and masturbation. The subjects' post hoc justifications differed dramatically, but their bottom-line moral judgments were similar. Interestingly, there was variation between liberal and conservative subjects as to disapproval of consensual homosexual activities, suggesting that the same-sex marriage (and abortion) debates have already created a strong correlation between conservative attitudes and disgust toward homosexual intercourse.[44]

Social scientists and philosophers have thought about this phenomenon from a sociopolitical perspective. Paul Rozin and Martha Nussbaum maintain that our most primordial disgust responses arise out of emotional efforts to humanize our animal bodies and distance ourselves from physical functions that are "reminders of our animal vulnerability."[45] Like prejudices, feelings of disgust are nonrational responses to physical phenomena, yet they may be underlying motivations for our rational discourses. Sexuality is an obvious situs for disgust. Almost anything related to sex is disgusting to some people; some sexual practices are disgusting to almost all people; and many people feel their disgust intensely. Although most adults engage in oral sex, and many in anal sex, a lot of Americans find these activities disgusting. Many more find them disgusting when engaged in by people of the same sex. According to opinion polls in the last generation, most Americans still disapprove of homosexual relations, even though they also seem to recognize that homosexuals are perfectly functional professionals and neighbors.[46]

A *politics of disgust* is one that is driven by such emotional responses. American history is filled with social movements driven by disgust, including the antislavery, temperance, child protection, and human rights movements.[47] A classic politics of disgust, the purity movement, which held sway in most large cities between 1880 and 1920, focused on sexual activities and solicitations of persons the middle class considered morally "degenerate"—female and male sex workers, promiscuous women, crossdressers, and fairies and other gender-bending men. What disgusted middle-class Americans was not just unconventional sex but the public flaunting of it by the targeted classes. The antihomosexual terror of 1935 to 1961 was fueled by these same purity concerns, greatly exacerbated by concerns about sex between adults and minors of the same sex and about external threats (Nazi Germany and then Godless Communism). Openly gay and lesbian persons are among the most natural objects of this kind of politics, because they carry with them three traits that disgust many Americans. They engage in nonprocreative and nonmarital sex, depart from traditional gender roles during sex, and flaunt their unconventional sexuality and gender roles in public (even just by being openly gay or lesbian). Many Americans find any one of these features disgusting; when the three features are combined, the disgust multiplies.[48]

Even after the Supreme Court invalidated consensual sodomy laws in 2003, large numbers of Americans agree with Rick Santorum that oral and anal sex are always immoral (because disgusting) and that consensual sodomy should be criminal. Some of these same Americans do not feel strongly about this issue, however, because they also dislike the invasions of privacy by police that would be required to enforce these laws. So they are at least conflicted. Not so with same-sex marriage. Because they understand same-sex marriage to be a state stamp of approval on homosexual sodomy, and not just a tolerance of it, larger majorities disapprove, and their feelings are more intense. Most of these perfectly sensible Americans are not going to change their minds because gay rights advocates are able to demonstrate that homosexual relationships have been recognized, with no ill effects, in Denmark, Norway, and Sweden.

The Marriage Line and Personal or Community Self-Definition

If the politics of disgust is not enough of a problem for advocates of gay rights, there is an even more challenging way of thinking about the matter. In *Purity and Danger*, anthropologist Mary Douglas famously explored the social implications of disgust. She understands disgust as a matter of *pollution*.[49] Human beings derive emotional as well as intellectual security from familiar patterns, many of which we receive from the surrounding culture. Institutions and practices achieve much of their normative power by their ability to give us a tidy grid in which to organize our thinking about an untidy world. We are emotionally committed not only to our cherished institutions and practices but also to the labels they deploy and the lines they draw. So disgust is a reaction to phenomena and practices that cross lines or do not fit labels. For Douglas, disgust is a reaction that serves the role of *boundary maintenance*.[50] She would treat Rozin's theory of disgust as a specific example of her more general theory. Certain physical phenomena (such as sodomy) are disgusting to many of us because they threaten the boundaries between human being and animal; other phenomena (such as same-sex marriage) are disgusting because they threaten social boundaries and institutional lines.

William Ian Miller adds an important affirmative dimension to the analysis: disgust is constitutive. One's individual identity is, to some extent, created or molded by one's disgusts. "Our durable self is defined as much by disgust as by any other passion . . . It installs large chunks of the moral world right at the core of our identity, seamlessly uniting body and soul and thereby giving an irreducible continuity to our characters." And so is the larger community itself. Disgust is, according to Miller, "especially useful and necessary as a builder of moral and social community. It performs this function obviously by helping define and locate the boundary separating our group from their group, purity from pollution, the violable from the inviolable."[51]

Marriage as a union of one man and one woman is a foundational concept for many human beings and for American society more generally— and the power of marriage may rest in the way it fits with core categories by which we organize our thinking. More than any other social or legal institution, marriage insists upon the binary complementarity of sex and gender: man/woman (yin/yang) is our primordial category, and its key feature is procreative complementarity—when the two human beings fit together, as complements, they can perpetuate the human race. For most religious Americans, marriage is also sanctified by God's approval; it is a sacrament in the Roman Catholic Church and holy in most others. Marriage is the only unpolluted forum for sexual pleasure, because the unitive commitment of marriage cleanses whatever dirtiness (pollution) one feels toward sexual activities. The categories of marriage and man/woman are central to the identities of millions of religious and other traditionalist Americans, and Scandinavians. For them, same-sex marriage is a serious challenge to social boundaries and, indeed, to the warm sense of community felt by a shared commitment to this institution and its tradition.[52]

Seton Hall Law School professor Marc Poirier suggested a most helpful analogy to us. Many Native American cultures consider certain places sacred ground, whose boundaries ought not be encroached by outsiders, or even tribal members except during special occasions. If the government used its eminent domain power to take this land and set up a post office on it, members of the tribe would be disgusted, and furious, because the government had breached a line that was identity-constituting for them and for the tribe itself. For many traditionalists, marriage as one man and one woman is such a sacred communal ground, and proposals to change its boundaries are nothing short of sacrilegious. In short, same-sex marriage is deeply controversial in Western culture because it crosses an important line, traverses a boundary that people have long taken for granted. This makes such proposals triply alarming to many Americans: (1) not only does gay marriage sanction disgusting sodomy and (2) confuse rigid gender roles and conflate the sexes but also (3) it violates categorical lines long central to American law and religious tradition. This theory helps us understand the same-sex marriage debate more deeply.[53]

On the basis of the foregoing analysis, the persistence of certain core arguments against same-sex marriage, introduced in chapter 1, becomes immediately more comprehensible. The natural law argument is a straightforward application of boundary maintenance, and the foregoing theoretical discussion helps us understand how Americans who are not homophobic find it difficult to accept same-sex marriage. It simply does not fit into their cultural script, and it would be difficult to adapt the script, especially when founded in scripture, to accommodate same-sex marriage. This also helps us see why so many religions have become politically invested in the campaign against same-sex marriage. For most Americans, religion is a powerful reassurance because it draws lines, enforces boundaries, insists upon taboos. Opposing same-sex marriage is a perfect opportunity for religions to reassert a primary role in society. If lawyers and judges are waffling on America's commitment to the line between marriage and perversion, then religion stands ready to assume a leadership role again.[54]

Under our analysis, the slippery slope, or Pandora's box, argument against same-sex marriage reveals its awesome power, and several of its linkages to the no-promo-homo argument. There is no logical reason why state recognition of same-sex marriage requires the state also to recognize sexual relationships between multiple partners, blood relatives, or a man and his cat. The power of this slippery slope argument comes not from logic and correct policy but emotion and boundary maintenance. This works at several levels. Advocates opposed to same-sex marriage understand that, in today's society, fewer people are disgusted by homosexual sodomy than in the 1970s, and their disgust is not as intense. Recall Jonathan Haidt's experiment, which also found that everyone remains disgusted by incest. The slippery slope argument seeks disgust by association. If you are not revolted by same-sex marriage, then the advocate runs down the slippery slope until he or she has found something (incest) that does turn your stomach—and warns that society needs to draw the line at gay marriage, to assure that incestuous marriage does not follow. The slippery slope argument also seeks to persuade the audience that they should be disgusted by gay marriage as well. What disgusts people about incest is the sexual mixing of humans who ought not be mixed—the same objection traditionalists have to homosexual intercourse. None of this stuff should be "promoted," which is what gay marriage would do.[55]

The slippery slope argument is most powerful when the audience is anxious that boundaries have already been blurred and cherished institutions are already in decline. The stamp-of-approval argument is most powerful when the homo-anxious audience (e.g., parents of wavering adolescents) believes that homosexuality is starting to saturate public culture. Culturally, these phenomena have helped create and popularize the defense-of-marriage argument. People correctly perceive that marriage is in decline, and many of those people deeply lament the decline. They feel that the decline has occurred because the strict rules of marriage have been relaxed and its clean, religiously inspired lines have been blurred. The blurring of these lines has occurred because Americans want sex for pleasure (not procreation) and do not want to be fettered by permanent obligations. The social group that is the popular embodiment of these fears is homosexuals, who are powerfully and often unconsciously stereotyped as sex-crazed and uncommitted. It seems like a hopeless task to tighten relaxed rules or sharpen blurred lines, and so marriage nostalgia calls for the state to bar the group epitomized by the values that have already undermined marriage (i.e., the homosexuals). Some traditionalists insist that the one-man/one-woman line is the Maginot Line of marriage. Once that Line is crossed or even blurred, marriage is lost. The forces of uncommitted hedonism (epitomized by those homosexuals!) will have prevailed. As Judge Bork put it, "ten years ago, the idea of a marriage between two men seemed preposterous, not something we needed to concern ourselves with. With same-sex marriage a line is being crossed, and no other line to separate moral and immoral consensual sex will hold."[56]

People who accept the foregoing script are the ones who will, mistakenly, find Stanley Kurtz's "empirical" arguments for the Scandinavian twist on the defense-of-marriage objection persuasive—and those people seem to include Kurtz himself. His work is all about boundary maintenance, as if he had read Mary Douglas and then followed her recipe for disgust-based argumentation. Kathleen Kiernan's four-stage model of marriage decline serves as Kurtz's backdrop, for it suggests that once Lines are crossed, a country can never return to a prior regime (a pretty implausible proposition if history is any guide). This allows Kurtz to treat no-fault divorce and heterosexual cohabitation regimes as sunk costs and focus exclusively on gay marriage. Whatever line-crossing no-fault divorce and cohabitation represent, gay marriage is crossing the Big Line, and it will have a domino effect building on the previous liberalizations. As Kurtz sees it, gay marriage will immediately lead to the "end of marriage." Although the Scandinavian experience suggests precisely the opposite, the facts are ultimately irrelevant for most of Kurtz's readers. For Kurtz himself, the "facts" are read, refracted, and (we think) distorted by his precommitment against same-sex marriage and, perhaps too, by some kind of nostalgia for long-departed traditional marriage.[57]

The politics of disgust helps us not only to understand the various arguments against same-sex marriage but also to see how those arguments are interconnected. The natural law understanding of human sexuality as faithfully executed only in the context of procreative (man-woman) marriage is founded upon and fueled by disgust people have for "uncontrolled" sexual activities (by other people, of course) and, especially, homosexual activities. This disgust-driven natural law is, in turn, foundational to the slippery slope, the stamp-of-approval, and the defense-of-marriage arguments. It is therefore no coincidence that Rick Santorum, Robert Bork, and Antonin Scalia—outspoken traditionalist Roman Catholics—are leading public opponents of same-sex marriage. Religious principle underwrites their secular arguments. And, increasingly, secular arguments are creeping into religious principle. Roman Catholic websites no longer rest their case against gay marriage on Scripture, church tradition, and religious precepts alone. They are now loading up Stanley Kurtz's "empirical" articles to "demonstrate" the risks posed to secular society as well. This is a classic example of Steve Goldberg's thesis that religious faith has been "seduced by science" and is gradually losing its distinctiveness in the modern era.[58]

For millions of Americans, the religious as well as the secular arguments are fueled or reinforced by unspoken sexist assumptions, that women's natural destiny and their only deep source of happiness is to be married to a man and bear his children. For most of these and millions more Americans, the arguments against gay marriage are also inspired by antihomosexual prejudice or stereotypes. We should make explicit our distinction between *homo-anxious* Americans, who for religious or other identity-based reasons are anxious about the growing public presence of homosexuality in American culture, and *homophobic* Americans, who for emotional reasons hate homosexuals or harbor inaccurate stereotypes about them. (Admittedly, the line between homo-anxious and homophobic is a thin one.) Not a few Americans are consumed with unreasoning hatred of homosexuals, but it is a mistake to understand bigots as dysfunctional. Instead, prejudice is often functional for the bigot, allowing him or her to construct a stable identity, to process his or her own unacceptable sexual feelings, and to rationalize and exert control over a complex and threatening world. Racism has long been America's all-purpose prejudice, but homophobia runs a close second.[59]

An Incremental Approach to Legal Recognition of Lesbian and Gay Relationships

Given the politics of disgust and boundary maintenance, one might wonder how lesbians, gay men, and bisexuals have ever persuaded legislators or judges to accord them *any* human rights. The lesson of this literature is not that sexual minorities are relegated to permanent second-class status, but instead that such groups will not find immediate and full equality simply by making appeals to reason, justice, and consequences. Such arguments can be persuasive, but are not necessarily so. Instead, gay rights advocates need to understand the politics of disgust/pollution and devise strategies to ameliorate or evade its force. Because they ignored the emotional features of politics and moral norms, gay rights advocates were routed after they won the landmark ruling in *Baehr v. Lewin* (1993), the Hawaii same-sex marriage case discussed in chapter 1. The worst way to deal with a politics of disgust is to win in court without any kind of grassroots effort, which was the case in Hawaii. Beth Robinson and Susan Murray, the gay rights lawyers who won *Baker v. State* (1999) in Vermont, learned from the Hawaii debacle and were able to achieve that state's pioneering civil unions law. Mary Bonauto of the Gay and Lesbian Advocates and Defenders applied a similar strategy in Massachusetts, which brought gay marriage to that state. In an interesting development, civil unions—the American equivalent of Scandinavian registered partnerships—have became a "conservative" alternative to gay marriage in that state and even in Washington, D.C. (Recall the Cheneys.) But gay marriage in Massachusetts has also triggered a nationwide reaction similar to, but less fierce than, the one that followed *Baehr*. The politics of boundary maintenance has been mobilized in America. Interestingly, Scandinavia and Europe have much to teach the Americans about how to deal with this backlash. Most of the lessons arise from the notion that *incrementalism* is necessary and proper.[60]

The leading theorist of the European gay marriage movement has been Professor Kees Waaldijk of the University of Leiden's Faculty of Law. He argues that a Western democracy will not countenance legal recognition of lesbian and gay relationships without an incremental process. Drawing from the experience in Scandinavia and the Netherlands in particular, Waaldijk points to the following pattern. First, the country repeals its consensual sodomy law, which frees gay people from the terror of state police harassment and the stigma of being presumptive criminals. Second, and sometimes long after the first step, the country adds sexual orientation and gay-bashing to its antidiscrimination and hate crime laws; this recognizes gay people's claim to equal citizenship and dignified treatment in the private as well as public sectors. Third, the country accords some state recognition of lesbian and gay relationships, perhaps through provision of insurance benefits to the same-sex partners of government employees, and then extending the benefits and duties entailed in state-recognized cohabitation regimes to same-sex couples.[61] These small steps were the ones Denmark, Norway, and Sweden followed before registered partnerships; Sweden's government has now seated a committee to examine and make a recommendation on extending "full"marriage to lesbian and gay couples, and a newly seated Norwegian Parliament in late 2005 has expressed majority support for a gender-neutral marriage law (a stance which is now supported by approximately sixty percent of the Norwegian population).[62] And of course this is the path the Netherlands and Canada have taken to same-sex marriage.

This step-by-step approach is also the path that Vermont took to civil unions (our analogue to Scandinavian registered partnerships) and Massachusetts to same-sex marriage (following the Netherlands). This also helps us see why the United States is not ready to accept same-sex marriage at the national level. It was not until 2003 that the remnants of sodomy criminalization were swept away, and Congress has never enacted anything close to a national gay rights bill; instead, it enacted DOMA, one of the most sweeping antihomosexual measures in American history. It may take years for the United States to follow Europe, but from a gay rights point of view, a slower process might be a better process. A step-by-step approach is probably a necessary way to overcome the politics of disgust so popular in the United States.[63]

This is not to say we believe that gay and lesbian advocates and their allies should stop fighting for the immediate right to same-sex marriage. Full marriage equality is the ultimate goal of most gays and lesbians in the United States, and it is possible that at least a few states in the short term will be receptive to gender-neutral marriage laws. But just as important, when moderate and conservative policy-makers hear the clamor for equal marriage "right now" from gay and lesbian activists and their supporters, it makes the concept of civil unions a much more palatable compromise (i.e., it becomes the "conservative" option). If activists and their supporters were only to fight for civil unions, they would likely end up with something less than civil unions. Thus we are advocating incrementalism as a best practice, not a strategy.

Human beings rarely change their fundamental attitudes overnight. But one's intuitions grounded upon moral disgust—or at least one's willingness to give vent to or act on them—can change as the culture changes and competing moral intuitions become salient. If you are a man who is sickened by the idea of homosexual intimacy, or a woman who fears its effect on children and the family, you are highly unlikely to support gay marriage. But you might be open to repeal of a homosexual sodomy law, either because its enforcement involves police practices you dislike or because you feel that it is unfair to penalize one small group for engaging in activity widely practiced by heterosexual couples. Over time, sodomy decriminalization and a lessening of public condemnation of homosexuality will embolden some of your gay friends, family members, and coworkers to come out of their closets. You will probably be shocked at first, and you can assimilate them as exceptions to your dislike of "homosexuals," but there is a chance that some of your antigay attitudes will soften. (Certainly, the attitudes of your children will be more favorable.)

Over time, maybe a long period of time, your interaction with gay people might open you up to acquiescing in antidiscrimination laws, for your experience has been that gay coworkers are okay—it is the antigay colleagues who are troublemakers. You may still oppose same-sex marriage, but even this attitude might bend when your daughter, or a close female friend, partners with another woman. Recall the American-Danish couple we described in the introduction, Jean Luscher and Diana Skovgaard. When we first talked to them in 1997, Luscher was going through a difficult period, trying to complete her Ph.D. dissertation, looking for a teaching position, suffering from asthma, and handling her mother's disapproval of her becoming partnered with another woman. Not only did Diana help her through this difficult period but their being registered partners allowed Jean to remain in Denmark and take advantage of that country's health-care services. In September 2000, Jean found a job as a simultaneous interpreter, a profession that draws on her language skills and pays better than college teaching jobs in her field (German studies).[64]

More important, Jean's family has become a part of their lives. Rock-ribbed traditionalist Republicans living in upstate New York, Jean's mother and her two brothers and their wives have accepted Diana into their extended family the way the Skovgaards accepted Jean from the beginning. Mrs. Luscher now displays a photo of Jean and Diana on the same table where she displays her sons' wedding pictures. Mother and daughter are able to talk about the marriage maturely. Jean's younger brother is an officer in the armed forces, and his wife is a strong, athletic woman. One of their children asked Aunt Jean: "Why did you have to go all the way to Denmark to marry Aunt Diana, when you could marry a boy here?" As Aunt Jean pondered her answer, her sister-in-law piped up, "Because Aunt Jean loves Aunt Diana very much!" The nephew was temporarily satisfied with that answer, but has continued to wonder why New York does not follow Denmark in this regard. What is remarkable is that the Luschers, salt-of-the-earth traditionalists, do not view Jean and Diana's marriage as a threat to them, to their children, or to the institution of marriage.[65]

As the Luschers' experience suggests, the most effective response to the antihomosexual politics of disgust is not to simply demonstrate that gay people are normal functioning human beings, nor is it to simply make people acquainted with someone who is lesbian or gay. Certainly, studies do suggest that working with open lesbians and gay men on common projects works against homophobia, sometimes quite powerfully—yet as the Case of the Outed Santorum Aide suggests, this strategy has its limits. Rather, the strongest response to antigay marriage politics is, literally, to domesticate the issue. When Mr. and Mrs. Cheney and Mrs. Luscher learned they had lesbian daughters, whom they loved, they took a step toward toleration of gay people more generally. Recall that family is a great inoculator against the politics of disgust; we are highly unlikely to label our loved ones as disgusting and degraded subhumans. When our loved one starts her own family, and it becomes interconnected with the larger family, then not only does the politics of disgust erode but it can be turned around. As they get older, Jean's nephews and nieces will understand why New York does not accord their union the same respect Denmark does—and some of them may be "disgusted" by what they consider America's intolerance toward same-sex marriage.

Frisind and Equality Practice: Lessons Scandinavia Offers the United States for Debating Same-Sex Marriage

When citizens of a country are evenly but intensely divided over an important issue of public law, democracy itself is at risk. Slavery is the most dramatic historical example of this phenomenon, an example that will remain unique. Like slavery, however, same-sex marriage is a polarizing issue that raises tremendous moral and even identity stakes for public debate. If the issue is handled in such a way that either half of the country feels disrespected, its members might become alienated from the political system altogether. This is another important reason why traditionalists should avoid scapegoating gay people and gay rights advocates should follow an approach that depends on persuading rather than demonizing traditionalists.[66]

A mature, thoughtful democracy handles such highly conflictual issues through a deliberative process that both respects the rights of minorities *and* involves the whole community in the debate. This is very abstract, but we now have some experience in the United States, Canada, and Europe that helps us understand some things to avoid and some things to seek out in a deliberative approach to the same-sex marriage issue. We now suggest some lessons in political economy from the Scandinavian experience. The central lesson is that the democratic process needs to accommodate the most urgent needs of each of the two groups, a process that will require deep and principled accommodation—principally through deliberation within legislatures.

Frisind and the Norm of Mutual Accommodation

A theologian, schoolteacher, and popular author, N.F.S. Grundtvig (1783–1872) is one of the great figures in Danish intellectual history. As we explained in chapter 2, his work is associated with the notion of *frisind*, which can be roughly translated as "open-mindedness." So Grundtvig preached that the Church should not be excessively dogmatic. "The interpretations and constructions of theologians were of less importance than the living community, and this assumed freedom and emancipation from a rigid and authoritarian system." As American fundamentalists know, this approach to Christianity slights the many rules of conduct set forth in Leviticus and other books of the Old Testament, and is at odds with the stringent rules preached by Saint Paul in some of his letters collected in the New Testament. On the other hand, Grundtvig's skepticism of dogma and his emphasis on the human congregation resonate strongly with the New Testament accounts of Christ's teachings. Like Jesus, the Church should be inclusive and nonjudgmental.[67]

Grundtvig applied a similar concept to social and political conduct outside the church. Each individual, he argued, has a moral obligation to respect and value the opinions of others. Such a philosophy does not mean blindly accepting another person's opinion as correct, but does presume that other people have formed their opinions in good faith, that they may be correct, and that their views might have something to teach others. This is *frisind*. Its point of view dominates Danish public life and is an antidote to both the politics of absolute rights, which undergirds the same-sex marriage movement, and the politics of disgust, which undergirds traditionalist opposition to any change in the status quo.

Frisind was the dominant attitude guiding the same-sex marriage debate in Denmark, and something like *frisind* influenced its Scandinavian neigh-

bors. On the one hand, Jann Sjursen of the CPP and most other social conservatives recognized that there were a number of lesbian and gay couples
who were sincerely committed to one another as life partners. Although few
conservatives could bring themselves to support full state recognition of such
relationships, most treated lesbian, gay, and bisexual Danes with respect.
(In our interview with him, Sjursen was gracious, well-informed, and forthcoming, a contrast to the frequently evasive or insulting interactions between American traditionalists and gay people.) For many, respect for fellow
citizens made it hard to treat same-sex marriage as the end of the world.
On the other hand, many Scandinavian supporters of equal rights for lesbian and gay couples recognized that traditionalists were sincerely invested
in the long-held concept of marriage as one man, one woman and refused
to attribute malign "homophobic" motives to their opponents. Many of the
supporters respected the personal desires of traditionalists like Sjursen to
hold the Line on marriage, which these traditionalists devoutly believed
would be wounded by adding same-sex couples.

Mutual efforts to understand one another's position came after years of
study by commissions of Danish public figures reflecting a wide range of
viewpoints. And the result was the fresh idea of *registered partnerships*. The
registered partnership proposal was much more than a simple "compromise," where each side gives up half of its demands so that the group can
resolve a thorny problem. Instead, the philosophy of *frisind* suggested to
each side that it consider *what it is that the other side most values, and then
try to accommodate it without giving up what you most value*. Danish traditionalists most valued the longtime understanding of marriage as one man,
one woman and the special cultural and religious associations of marriage.
Danish lesbians and gay men wanted to associate themselves with that institution because it was so rich in cultural and religious associations, but they
realized this was sacred ground for so many of their compatriots. Conse-
quently, they backed away from demands for same-sex marriage and suggested
an institution—registered partnerships—that met their most important need
(equal treatment by the state) but without directly disrespecting the most
important need of traditionalist Danes. Accordingly, the Danish supporters in Parliament agreed that registered partners would not be entitled to
church weddings, joint custody of children, or even adoption rights. These
were also important symbols for traditionalists who believed that marriage
and only marriage should be associated with the church and families with
children. For this reason, social conservatives found much to praise in the
new institution. Some voted for it in Parliament, though most could not.
But by and large the opponents treated supporters in a dignified and respectful way.[68]

The Danish philosophy and practice of *frisind* is an excellent model for a deliberative democracy whose citizens are deeply divided on an important, identity-constituting issue. Can it be replicated in the United States? On the issue of gay marriage, it is hard to replicate this success story, because our increasingly sexualized and religious culture renders the issue even more emotionally fraught that it is in Europe. Underneath the rational debate, with its ostensible focus on the consequences of same-sex marriage for families, the debaters remain intensely partisan; their identities as gay, fundamentalist, gay-friendly, religiously tolerant are rooted in one position or another in the debate. Such polarized points of view are not easily susceptible to reconciliation. The politics of disgust is particularly strong in the United States, and a large portion of the American population views same-sex marriage as a violation of essential boundaries. At the same time, the gay rights movement is particularly strong in the United States, and a large portion of the American population views same-sex marriage as a constitutional entitlement. Such hard positions, linked to people's identities as traditionalist or gay-friendly, create an atmosphere where open-mindedness and mutual accommodation will not easily occur.[69]

Yet we believe conditions exist for the operation of a mature democratic deliberation in the United States. In contrast to Denmark's national regulation, American family law is the domain of state governments. Accordingly, the same-sex marriage debate should be a normative debate primarily at the state, not the national, level. Nor is it a debate that should be conducted in the courts or popular referenda alone. A very important lesson that the Scandinavian experience has for the United States is that the focus of democratic deliberation should be the legislature. Contrary to the overwhelming academic focus on constitutional rights enforceable through judicial review, the courts are not always the most appropriate forum and should usually not be the exclusive focus. Nor is the initiative or referendum, contrary to the new scholarship touting popular constitutionalism. Indeed, excessive reliance on judicial review by supporters of gay rights, and excessive reliance on popular referenda by opponents, are impediments to American *frisind*.

Replicating the Scandinavian Conditions for Mutual Accommodation: Legislative Deliberation

Liberal constitutionalists in the United States maintain that state laws that deny minority groups fundamental rights violate either the equal protection or due process guarantees of state constitutions and the federal Constitution. In *Loving v. Virginia* (1967), the Supreme Court ruled that state

laws denying different-race couples marriage licenses required a compelling justification under both the equal protection clause (because the discrimination deployed a suspect classification) and the due process clause
(because a minority was being denied a fundamental right). Inspired by
Loving, lesbian and gay couples have been marching to the courthouse for
a generation, seeking similar rulings from state courts. Those couples missed
one of the important lessons of *Loving.*[70]

Virginia's antimiscegenation law first came to the Supreme Court in 1955,
right on the heels of *Brown v. Board of Education.* After remanding the case
to Virginia's Supreme Court (which reaffirmed its statute, notwithstanding *Brown*), the Court ultimately dismissed the appeal. There was no basis
in constitutional principle for ducking the case, but the Supreme Court
rightly feared that striking down such a law risked a firestorm of protest—
not just from the South (already in revolt over *Brown*) but also from the
Midwest and West, and perhaps also the Northeast.[71] Large majorities of
Americans believed that miscegenation was disgusting. Thirty-one of the
forty-eight states had antimiscegenation laws at the end of World War II.
Attitudes changed in the next generation, in large part because more white
Americans associated with people of color in the armed forces and other
public venues. Many Americans who found interracial sex disgusting were
at least ambivalent, and sometimes ashamed, about their feelings. All but
sixteen states (all in the South) had repealed their anti-miscegenation laws
by the time the Supreme Court decided *Loving* in 1967.[72]

One lesson of *Loving* is that the United States Supreme Court will not
interpret the Fourteenth Amendment to require state recognition of same-
sex marriage anytime soon. If the pro–civil rights Warren Court was unwilling to strike down antimiscegenation laws when thirty states still had them,
the conservative Roberts Court is highly unlikely to strike down forty-nine
state laws (all but Massachusetts) that do not recognize same-sex marriages.
A second lesson is that legislatures are sometimes willing to eliminate marriage discriminations on their own, even when many citizens find the new
marriages disgusting. Our account of Scandinavian registered partnerships
suggests that this second lesson applies to lesbian and gay unions. But state
legislative recognition of different-race marriages and Scandinavian recognition of registered partnerships came only after significant educational effort,
and often only after an unexpected window of opportunity opened. Legislative action is far from inevitable, however, as it is much easier for opponents
to block action than for proponents to carry the day in the legislature (especially when it has two chambers, as in most American states and in Norway).

A third lesson is that there are significant advantages, for society but also
for gay people, if government recognition of same-sex unions comes through

legislation rather than judicial decree. The big advantage of a legislated solution over a judicially imposed one is that it is more likely to facilitate mutual accommodation. If the politics of disgust is fully mobilized in a polity against same-sex marriage, as it was in Denmark during the 1970s, no acceptable solution will emerge—exactly as Denmark's Marriage Committee concluded in 1973. But legislatures can create study commissions or charge agencies with gathering information about a social issue, as Denmark's Parliament did in 1969 (the Marriage Committee) and 1984 (the HomoCommission). The purpose of such commissions is not just to educate the legislature and the public about an issue but also to serve as a microcosm for accommodative discussion. For such a process to work, the commission must be composed of well-informed persons with different points of view (therefore, traditionalists and religious leaders as well as lesbian and gay members) who are willing to talk through issues without a spirit of partisanship. Denmark's HomoCommission produced valuable reports that helped create conditions for deep compromise in that country, as did Sweden's Commissions on Homosexuality (1984 report) and on Homosexual Partnerships (1993) and Norway's Ministry of Children and Family Affairs (1992). The Bush administration's 9/11 Commission, chaired by former governor Thomas Kean, is an American exemplar of such a problem-solving, above-partisanship group.[73]

While the Danish HomoCommission had no authority to establish same-sex marriage, legislatures have the capacity not only to implement such big changes in policy but also to calibrate such changes in such a way as to make them more politically acceptable. This was the process of "thoughtful compromise" that occupied the Danish Parliament in 1988 and 1989. Most MPs wanted to accommodate gay people's most urgent need, namely, state recognition of their committed relationships and support of those relationships through the legal benefits and obligations associated with marriage. But most of those same MPs respected the point of view of sincere conservatives and religious leaders, that marriage itself is special and should be reserved for one-man, one-woman couples, as should church weddings. Some MPs also believed that marriage is a unique forum for childrearing and so were reluctant at the time to recognize lesbian and gay families with children. These were not simple matters to work out, and a legislature representing the nation's diversity is a good forum to do it. The result was the highly thoughtful and deeply contemplated compromise embodied in Denmark's Registered Partnership Act of 1989, described in chapter 2.[74]

And indeed, legislators in Scandinavia have demonstrated a willingness to remain thoughtful about the subject. They have amended their partnership acts over time to accommodate the reasonable and defensible arguments regarding children in gay and lesbian families put forward by gay and lesbian groups and their supporters. In Sweden, now that gay and lesbian couples have all of the adoption and insemination/assisted reproduction rights of married couples, and the church has separated from the state, the only real difference between registered partnership and marriage is the name alone—and the Swedish Parliament is now considering making the change from "registered partnership" to "marriage" as well. We see a similar pattern of thinking in Norway, where a new liberal majority in Parliament seated in late 2005 has expressed its support for a gender-neutral marriage law.

Whatever accommodation a legislature adopts would also be seen as more legitimate than one that would be imposed by courts in most states and in the federal system. Although many state judges are elected, federal judges are not elected, and many elected state judges have lengthy terms. A key feature of legislative deliberation is its accountability to the voters. One reason Denmark was willing to recognize registered partnerships in 1989 was the relatively acquiescent feedback its legislators received. Further popular feedback emboldened Parliament to liberalize the registered partnership law in 1999, to allow partners to adopt and to enjoy joint custody over children they are rearing together. These changes were relatively uncontroversial, because lesbian and gay registered partners demonstrated their capacity to form meaningful families.[75]

The advantages of legislative deliberation achieved in the home of *frisind* have been replicated in the United States. In 1999, the California legislature created a statewide institution of *domestic partnerships* for same-sex couples.[76] Lesbian and gay activists were sorely disappointed that few benefits and no obligations were associated with the new institution, but traditionalists were not prepared to concede serious legal consequences for such relationships. In 2000, a large majority in California voted in favor of the Knight Initiative, which added a statutory definition of marriage as one man, one woman and directed judges and other officials not to recognize same-sex marriages from other jurisdictions. Ironically, once couples were able to register at the state level *and* traditionalists were reassured that marriage was reserved for one man, one woman, California was willing to move dramatically toward legal equality. Finding that same-sex couples form "lasting, committed, and caring relationships," the legislature in 2003 extended almost all the rights, benefits, duties, and obligations of married spouses to registered domestic partners. There is a long transition period, so that current domestic partners can adjust their relationships if they do not welcome the new duties and benefits.[77] Immediately after adoption of an accommodation much like Danish registered partnerships, Californians elected as their governor Arnold Schwarzenegger. A Republican macho movie star, who playfully derides his opponents as "girlie men," the nation's beefiest chief executive defended San Francisco's mayor when he handed out marriage licenses to same-sex couples. Schwarzenegger has endorsed the domestic partnership law, but in 2005 vetoed a bill to recognize same-sex marriage.[78]

Do courts have a positive role to play in this debate? For reasons suggested by the *Loving* analogy earlier, the United States Supreme Court is unlikely to have a productive role to play in the near future. Nor do judges have a productive role to play in most states. In states of the South, Great Plains, and Rocky Mountains, judges have no inclination to force same-sex marriage on the populace—and the voters would straightaway amend their state constitutions if they tried. (In many of these states, voters have already amended their state constitutions to head off such judicial rulings.) In states of the Northeast or West Coast, some judges might be inclined to impose same-sex marriage obligations as a matter of state constitutional interpretation. Would this impulse run counter to the lessons we are drawing from the Scandinavian experience?

We think the Vermont Supreme Court got it right in *Baker v. State* (1999), which ruled unconstitutional the state's blanket discrimination against same-sex couples. Chief Justice Jeffrey Amestoy's opinion for the court, however, declined to impose same-sex marriage recognition as the constitutionally required remedy and, instead, requested that the Vermont legislature remedy the discrimination.[79] In January and February 2000, the House Judiciary Committee of the Vermont legislature engaged in a similar process of gathering information about same-sex couples, deliberating about various policy concerns, and making a recommendation to the legislature. Chaired by Republican Tom Little, the committee was composed of five Republicans, five Democrats, and one Progressive. The vice-chair, Bill Lippert, was an openly gay man. The others were married heterosexuals. There were women as well as men, conservatives as well as liberals, Catholics as well as Protestants. The Committee heard from every point of view—including extensive testimony from a wide array of traditionalist law professors and religious leaders, as well as lesbian and gay couples and supporters of same-sex marriage. No one familiar with the process could deny that every committee member listened attentively and sympathetically to all the witnesses. Ultimately, even the most traditionalist members (including all five Republicans) agreed that the state should recognize lesbian and gay families; all but one of the liberal members (including Lippert) agreed that the state was not ready for gay marriage. The Committee proposed creating a new institution, *civil unions.* Like Danish registered partnerships and California domestic partnerships, Vermont civil unions were a new legal form for same-sex couples. Unlike the earlier institutions, civil unions gave same-sex couples all the state benefits and duties of marriage. By narrow but decisive margins, both chambers of the legislature voted for the measure, and Governor Howard Dean signed it into law in May 2000.[80]

The role of the Vermont Supreme Court was important but not final. By invalidating the prior discrimination, the court *reversed the burden of inertia* that thwarted lesbian and gay efforts to achieve equal treatment by the state. By declining to impose its own remedy, the court *deferred to the legislative process,* which was the superior forum to make marriage policy, for the reasons we have articulated. Advocates on both sides were disappointed. Lawyers for the plaintiffs described the court's decision as the worst day of their lives; religious leaders and conservatives decried the civil unions law as tantamount to same-sex marriage. But the public interest was vindicated, and the legislative accommodation has stuck. In exit polling conducted with the 2004 election, the Associated Press told us that 37 percent of Vermonters now favor same-sex marriage, 40 percent prefer civil unions, and only 21 percent favor no formal state recognition of lesbian and gay unions. There are still wounds in Vermont, but even many skeptics have come around to the principle that the state ought to offer lesbian and gay couples the same legal options straight couples enjoy.[81]

The foregoing analysis also helps us understand why the Hawaii Supreme Court's decision in *Baehr* led to such a backlash. Because it was the first time any official statewide organ of government had suggested the possibility of same-sex marriage in the United States, *Baehr* came as a political shock. More than reversing the burden of legislative inertia, *Baehr* seemed to demand same-sex marriage. Few judges could have predicted the firestorm that *Baehr* provoked, or how it immediately polarized the same-sex marriage debate, in both Hawaii and the rest of the country. The Scandinavian experience suggests that the incremental *Baker* approach would have been much more productive. A legislatively created commission of experts delivered a thoughtful report to the Hawaii legislature in 1997, and the legislators were more than capable of deliberating about the issue in a measured, accommodative manner. But the public reaction to judicially imposed same-sex marriage overpowered the legislature's role, and the matter was settled by an acrimoniously contested amendment to the state constitution in 1998.[82]

The Scandinavian and Hawaiian experiences support the approach taken by California, with its domestic partnership statute, and Connecticut, whose legislature in 2005 followed Vermont in adopting civil unions (and without any judicial prodding). These experiences raise some issues regarding the Massachusetts Supreme Judicial Court's decision in *Goodridge v. Department of Public Health* (2003), which followed *Baker* in interpreting the state constitution to invalidate marriage law discrimination but went further than *Baker* or even *Baehr* in directing the state to issue marriage licenses to same-sex couples.[83] Under the circumstances, however, *Goodridge* was somewhere between *Baker* and *Baehr* (and perhaps closer to *Baker* in the end). As an interpretation of the Massachusetts Constitution, *Goodridge* can be overridden by constitutional amendment, just as *Baehr* was. But the people of Massachusetts were more open to same-sex marriage than Hawaiians had been in the 1990s, and the normal process for constitutional amendment in Massachusetts is materially different. It involves three steps: (1) by simple majority of all participating members, the legislature proposes an amendment; (2) at its next yearly session, the legislature (again by majority vote) reaffirms the proposal, which becomes part of the constitution, if (3) a majority of voters ratify it in the next general election. Hence the effect of the *Goodridge* judgment was similar to that of the *Baker* judgment, namely, reversing the burden of inertia and, essentially, remanding to the legislature.[84]

To be sure, *Goodridge* set a higher hurdle than *Baker*: the legislature must act twice, and then be joined by an electoral majority. In light of *Baker*, there was insufficient support for denying lesbian and gay couples *any* state recognition in the Vermont legislature. In March 2004, the Massachusetts legislature voted 105 to 92 to amend the state constitution to limit marriage to one man, one woman *and* to recognize civil unions for same-sex couples, with all the rights and benefits of marriage but not the name or status. Note how the *traditionalist* position evolved, perhaps temporarily, from *Baehr* to *Goodridge*—away from no recognition and toward recognition of civil unions, precisely the accommodation reached in Denmark and Vermont. In 2005, the Massachusetts legislature voted down the proposed amendment, but traditionalists now (2006) support a more sweeping amendment to the state constitution in its place: a citizen initiative has proposed to abolish same-sex marriage, without installing civil unions, in the state constitution; if supported by at least fifty members of two successive sessions of the legislature, well short of a majority, this would be presented to the voters in 2008.[85]

Thus, it remains to be seen what that the Massachusetts constitutional process will produce. But Massachusetts has already contributed one important thing to the American same-sex marriage debate. It has created *conditions for falsification* of arguments made by advocates. No longer must the same-sex marriage debate be conducted in an American empirical vacuum. The experience of Massachusetts with same-sex marriage will be an important reference point for its own constitutional deliberation, as well as that in other states. We would welcome a public vote in Massachusetts, now that its citizens can see the families now recognized by the state. Plus, the advent of same-sex marriage has yielded no disastrous consequences. The sky did not fall on Massachusetts.

Federalism and the Future of Same-Sex Partnerships (Et Cetera) in the United States

The Scandinavian experience also helps us map the course of civil recognition of lesbian and gay partnerships in the United States. The theme for the immediate future is *diversity* among states. States will respond in different ways to the same-sex marriage issue, with most states declining to provide recognition to committed same-sex relationships, and other states providing various forms of recognition (marriage, civil unions, etc.). This diversity is good, and it is workable. The federal government should resist traditionalist demands for a constitutional amendment cutting off state experimentation.[86]

Denmark's recognition of registered partnerships in 1989 put immediate pressure on the other Scandinavian countries to adopt similar institutions, and all have done so. Other European countries have created their own institutions—*pactes civils* (France), life partnerships (Germany), civil partnerships (United Kingdom), and same-sex marriage (Netherlands, Belgium, Spain), among others. Few eastern and southern European states have followed any of these approaches, and many afford no formal recognition of same-sex relationships. At some point, the European Union will impose some uniform requirement upon its member states.[87]

The Scandinavian experience and our equality practice theory suggest the same pattern in the more conservative United States. Table 6.1 and figure 6.1 (following pages) help us see how different U.S. states have responded to gay people's petition to be integrated as full and equal citizens in society.

Group 1: States that had repealed their sodomy laws before the Supreme Court's decision in *Lawrence v. Texas* (2003) and have included lesbians and gay men in their hate crime and antidiscrimination laws are most likely to recognize same-sex unions, as seven states have already done. All of these are on the West Coast or Northeast, whose social and legal regimes have encouraged lesbians and gay men to live their lives out of the closet and to form families.

Group 2: States that had repealed their sodomy laws before *Lawrence* but have not included lesbians and gay men in their hate crime and antidiscrimination laws are less likely to recognize same-sex unions. Most of these states are in the Midwest.

Group 3: A large number of states still have (now unenforceable) sodomy laws on their statute books and do not protect lesbians, gay men, and bisexuals from discrimination or hate crimes. These states, clustered in the

Table 6.1

Gay-Friendly Laws, States of the USA, April 2005

State	Consensual Sodomy No Crime	Sexual Orientation Hate Crime Law	Laws Against Public/ Private Employment Discrimination	Municipalities with Domestic Partnership Registration?
Vermont	1977	1989	1992/1992	Yes
California	1975	1991	1979/1979	Yes
Hawaii	1972	2001	1991/1991	
Dist. of Columbia	1994	1994	1977/1977	Yes
Massachusetts	1974/2002	1996	1989/1989	Yes
Connecticut	1969	1990	1991/1991	Yes
New Jersey	1978	1995	1991/1991	
New York	1980		1983/2002	Yes
Illinois	1961	1991	1996/2005	Yes
Minnesota	2001	1989	1986/1993	Yes
Maine	1975	1995	2005/2005	Yes
Wisconsin	1983	1991	1982/1982	Yes
Oregon	1971	1989	1987/(1998)	Yes
Washington	1975	1993	1985/None	Yes
Maryland	(1999)	2005	1993/2001	
New Hampshire	1973	1997	1997/1997	
Nevada	1993	1989	1999/1999	
Rhode Island	1998	1991	1985/1995	
Delaware	1972	1997	2001/2001	
New Mexico	1973	2003	2004/2004	
Arizona	2001	1997	2003/None	Yes
Pennsylvania	1980	2002	1975/None	
Colorado	1971	2005	2001/None	Yes
Michigan	(1990)		2003/None	Yes
Kentucky	1992	1998	2003/None	
Indiana	1976		2001/None	
Montana	1997		2000/None	
Alaska	1978		2002/None	
Iowa	1976	1992		
Nebraska	1977	1997		
Florida	(1971)	1991		Yes

(continued)

Table 6.1 continued

State	Consensual Sodomy No Crime	Sexual Orientation Hate Crime Law	Laws Against Public/ Private Employment Discrimination	Municipalities with Domestic Partnership Registration?
Georgia	1998			Yes
Missouri	(1999)	2001		Yes
North Dakota	1973			
South Dakota	1976			
Tennessee	1996	2001		
Ohio	1972			
West Virginia	1976			
Wyoming	1977			
Louisiana		1997	2004/None	
Kansas		2002		
Texas		2002		
Alabama				
Arkansas				
Idaho				
Mississippi				
North Carolina				Yes
Oklahoma				
South Carolina				
Virginia				
Utah				

Source: William N. Eskridge, Jr., *Gaylaw: Challenging the Apartheid of the Closet* (Cambridge: Harvard University Press, 1999), 328–37, 356–61, and "Comparative Law and the Same-Sex Marriage Debate: A Step-by-Step Approach Toward State Recognition," *McGeorge Law Journal* 31 (2000): 641–75, updated by David Newman, Yale Law School Class of 2007. See also the updates on www.lambdalegal.org. Dates in (parentheses) in column one mean that the state has not formally repealed its consensual sodomy law but has made some movement in that direction, as by nullifying part of the sodomy law by a lower court decision which essentially leaves the law unenforced. All remaining state sodomy laws were rendered unconstitutional as applied to consensual, private activities by the Supreme Court's decision in *Lawrence v. Texas*, 539 U.S. 558 (2003).

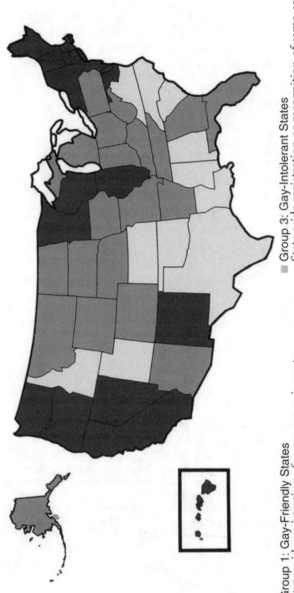

Group 1: Gay-Friendly States
State-wide registration of same-sex unions etc.
now or likely in near future

Group 2: Gay-Tolerant but Gay-Anxious States
State-wide registration or recognition of same-sex
unions etc. possible in near future, but with few
rights/duties

Group 3: Gay-Intolerant States
State-wide registration or recognition of same-sex
unions etc. unlikely in near future

Figure 6.1
State Policies Regarding Lesbian and Gay Citizens

Baptist South and Mormon West, are not likely to recognize same-sex unions. There are relatively few openly gay families in these jurisdictions, and much greater cultural anxiety about the decline of marriage and the unsettling of sexual boundaries.

In the short term, a few states will follow Vermont, Massachusetts, California, and Connecticut (which accord all or almost all the legal rights and duties of marriage available at the state level to same-sex couples) or even Hawaii, New Jersey, and Maine (which accord a limited range of rights and duties to same-sex couples). We should expect those states that do so to be clustered in the West Coast and, especially, the Northeast. (Note the interesting parallel with Scandinavia, which, like the Northeast, is a cluster of states on the northern tier.) It is impossible to predict exactly what accommodation each state will ultimately choose, because that depends upon local political factors and people's perceptions about what is happening elsewhere. For example, because all five West Coast states have laws or constitutional amendments defining marriage as one man, one woman, we should expect the California domestic partnership law or the Vermont civil unions law to be the models for accommodation.[88] The few states adopting same-sex marriage laws will probably cluster in the Northeast, where all three of the states granting *all* the legal rights and duties (Massachusetts, Vermont, Connecticut) are located.

Group 2 states are also not likely to follow Massachusetts in recognizing same-sex marriages. Most midwestern states have statutes or constitutional amendments defining marriage as one man, one woman.[89] In the near future, it is likely that one or more states will provide some limited recognition of same-sex unions—probably along the lines New Jersey followed in its domestic partnership law, which assures employment benefits and a few other rights for registered partners. More ambitious regimes, such as Vermont-style civil unions or California-style domestic partnerships, are possible but not likely in the near future.

Group 3 states will not recognize same-sex marriages or civil unions anytime soon. Almost all the states of the South and West have statutory or constitutional provisions defining marriage as one man, one woman. Many Group 3 states have both statutory and constitutional provisions to that effect.[90] Some of these states might be open to a less ambitious form of recognition, but for most of these jurisdictions the big issue is whether to give any kind of recognition to out-of-state same-sex married or civil-unioned couples who settle in their jurisdictions. As the drafters of DOMA recognized in 1996, a federal requirement that Alabama must recognize same-sex marriages validated in Massachusetts would be politically divisive and an imposition upon accommodations reached in Alabama.

It was not necessary for this DOMA policy judgment to be effectuated in a special federal statute. As Linda Silberman has demonstrated, there is no federal constitutional or statutory obligation for Alabama to give the benefits and obligations of its marriage laws to couples whose lawful marriages in another state are contrary to Alabama's public policy. On the other hand, the fact that neither the Constitution nor federal law requires states to give effect to out-of-state marriages does not mean that no state will do so. States in group 1 might, for some purposes, give effect to Massachusetts same-sex marriages or Vermont civil unions as a matter of their own choice of law principles. In an important precedent, *Langan v. St. Vincent's Hospital* (2003), a New York judge ruled that a partner joined in a Vermont civil union could sue as a "spouse" for wrongful death of his partner under New York law.[91] Under other circumstances, some states in groups 2 and even 3 might do the same. In June 2005, for example, the Iowa Supreme Court upheld a decision by a district court judge in Sioux City, Iowa, approving a divorce for two lesbians who entered into a civil union in Vermont.[92]

Consider the status of a California lesbian couple registered as domestic partners who have joint custody over children they are raising. If the couple moves to Illinois and the biological mother of the children dies, Illinois state courts ought to and probably will recognize the surviving mother as the legal parent of the children. Recognition of a surviving parent, if no legal connection to the child existed, would be unlikely in Alabama, where the courts have sometimes denied even biological mothers child custody rights because of their sexual orientation. But even Alabama courts might respect a California judgment dissolving the lesbian partnership and apportioning joint custody over the children and an equitable division of the partnership assets, as the Iowa court did in regard to the Vermont civil union. Indeed, the full faith and credit clause of the Constitution requires states to give effect to adjudicated *judgments* from other states, even though not to other state statutory or licensing regimes.

Readers of all persuasions may find this array of different family law regimes messy and confusing. However, there is nothing new in this kind of messy interstate diversity. There has never been uniformity among the states as to who can get married. Each state creates its own definition of civil marriage, and there are fifty different definitions. There is even great diversity of rules as to marriages between closely related persons. Eighteen states and the District of Columbia permit first cousins to marry, seven do so under specified conditions, and twenty-five do not validate such marriages. But some and perhaps most of the nonvalidating states will recognize first-cousin marriages validly entered in another jurisdiction. Some will not.[93]

One might wonder how many couples these diverse cousin-marriage regimes affect, but there is an even more dramatic example of our point. For one hundred years, the United States operated under plural regimes governing different-race marriages. Some jurisdictions defined marriage to exclude interracial couples, often going so far as to make this a crime. By no means limited to the South, those jurisdictions took a variety of approaches to what was "different-race." (In Virginia, for example, African Americans could not marry European Americans but could marry Asian Americans.) States followed a variety of choice of law regimes. Some states only allowed marriages to the same race but were willing to recognize different-race marriages validly entered in another jurisdiction. As Andy Koppelman has shown, even most southern states were willing to recognize valid different-race marriages under certain circumstances—circumstances that varied from state to state.[94] This regime certainly created social costs and was ultimately adjudged to be unconstitutional, but during its heyday it was quite functional.

So a regime where different states take different legal stances toward same-sex marriages is where we are heading, and such a regime easily fits within the American tradition of diverse state definitions of marriage. Such a regime also exhibits the virtues of our federalism. One virtue of federalism is that it enables more Americans to express their values through the law. Assume two states, each with one hundred people. Table 6.2 summarizes plausible preference arrays on the issue of same-sex marriage. Large majorities in state 2 do not like them; most state 1 citizens like them fine.

If the decision is made on a national level, the voters would not choose same-sex marriage—leaving ninety citizens very unhappy (twenty in state 2, seventy in state 1). This is democratic, but it is not the best democracy can do, and it is not the American system. Federalism leaves family law decisions to the states, because family law is a matter of intense local variation and emotional commitments. Under the federal arrangement, state 1 will adopt same-sex marriage, and state 2 will not. This satisfies the preferences of 150 citizens, and leaves only 50 citizens very unhappy, a superior result under democratic premises.[95]

Table 6.2
Raw Preferences Regarding Same-Sex Marriage

	State 1	State 2
Same-Sex Marriage Is Good Social Policy	70	20
Same-Sex Marriage Is Disastrous Social Policy	30	80

A second advantage of federalism is that it creates a safety valve for citizens with intense preferences. In our hypothetical, state 1's acceptance of same-sex marriage is a signal that it is a gay-friendly jurisdiction. One might assume that at least some state 2 residents who are gay or who do not want to live in a gay-negative place would relocate to state 1. Correlatively, state 2's stance signals to state 1 citizens who would be miserable living under same-sex marriage that they could relocate there. Although the numbers of people "voting with their feet" would be modest, the democratic payoff is impressive. As the revised scenario suggests (table 6.3), federalism now satisfies 165 people in the two states, with only a total of 35 dissatisfied.[96]

These are arguments against the Federal Marriage Amendment banning same-sex marriages and civil unions. The national Congress should do nothing for the time being. Let federalism take its course, especially on an issue in which people's emotions are so implicated.

This is the short-term solution. What about the longer term? The longer term suggests a third virtue of federalism: the states are laboratories of experimentation. Denmark engaged in a social and even moral experiment when it recognized registered partnerships, and Vermont, Connecticut, and Massachusetts have done the same with regard to civil unions and same-sex marriage. We are confident that Vermont or Connecticut civil unions and Massachusetts same-sex marriages will not have the terrible effects opponents predict. In the many years since Denmark recognized same-sex registered partnerships, thousands of lesbian and gay couples have gained legal recognition of their committed relationships, and both the couples and their society appear to be better off—certainly gay couples, but also straight couples (at least under traditionalist premises). The marriage rate has gone up a little, and the overall divorce rate has fallen. There is no reason to think the experience of Vermont, Connecticut, and Massachusetts will be materially different.

If we are right about that, the social experiment with same-sex unions and marriages will have been a success. Over time, people—especially young people—will notice this. Preferences will change, not only in Vermont (as it becomes proud of what it has done) but also in traditionalist states like Oklahoma (as young people question an antigay policy that turns out to have been oversold). Under this scenario, state 2 will learn something from state 1's suc-

Table 6.3
Preferences after Voting with Their Feet

	State 1	State 2
Same-Sex Marriage Is Good Social Policy	80	15
Same-Sex Marriage Is Disastrous Social Policy	20	85

cessful experiment with same-sex marriage that could not have occurred under a national family law regime. Table 6.4 reflects the foregoing dynamic. Not only would the preferences of the citizens be satisfied but policy itself will be on a sounder footing. By the way, the logic is the same even if we are wrong on the merits. If same-sex marriage proves unsatisfactory and marriage is destroyed for everyone in state 1, then support for it would erode within that jurisdiction, and they might be repealed in state 1, and probably not adopted in other states. Even if there is no clear consequence of state 1's experiment, nothing has been lost. Indeed, under the assumptions of our example, much has been gained, for the local experiment has saved the nation from alienating the citizens of state 2 without sufficient justification.[97]

The social experiment illustrated by tables 6.2–4 suggests a final, and very important, lesson that Americans should draw from the Scandinavian partnership experience. As we showed in chapters 1 and 2, the same-sex marriage debate has been dynamic in both North America and Europe; the arguments have evolved. Building upon chapter 5, this chapter makes the point that family law and the social institution of marriage have been dynamic as well. Even the "traditional marriage" that is being "defended" by social conservatives has been dynamic. This dynamism ought to undermine the confidence of principled conservatives, such as Judge Bork, that gay marriage would "cross the line" separating marriage decline from the end of marriage. It also carries lessons for advocates of equal marriage rights such as ourselves. The same-sex marriage movement, and the traditional family values counter-movement, have contributed to a larger social experiment, whereby Western nations and provinces or states have created new institutions for family formation, such as the French *pactes civils* and British civil partnerships discussed in chapter 2. Given the modest numbers of lesbian and gay couples who have actually married in Massachusetts and the Netherlands or entered into registered partnerships in Scandinavia, the gay rights agenda itself may be revealing the same kind of dynamism the religious right's agenda has already shown. And the struggle for marriage equality is one that will be complicated by the emerging menu of relationship options, for straight as well as lesbian/gay couples, that we explore in the epilogue.

Table 6.4
Preferences over Time if State 1's Experiment Is Successful

	State 1	State 2
Same-Sex Marriage Is Good Social Policy	90	70
Same-Sex Marriage Is Disastrous Social Policy	10	30

I Now Pronounce You . . .
An Emerging Menu of Relationship Options

Jack Baker, the dashing engineer-turned-lawyer, and Mike McConnell, the dimpled librarian who has been Baker's life partner since 1967, are old-fashioned romantics in the midwestern tradition. Each believes the other is his soul mate, his "better half," the one person whose love makes his own life complete. Once you have found your soul mate, Baker and McConnell agree, you ought to commit your lives to one another. The institution within which you should do that—for spiritual, personal, and even civic reasons—is marriage, which they idealize as potentially perfect. Anything else is a cheap imitation. Their view of marriage is in many respects similar to that of Rick and Karen Santorum, also romantics. The passionate senator from Pennsylvania and his even-tempered wife believe themselves to be soul mates. And they see marriage as the only legitimate institution for celebrating and carrying forth their love for one another and raising their six children. They idealize the institution; it makes us better as couples and as individuals.

Where these two couples differ is in how they define this idealized institution called marriage. Baker and McConnell hold it up as a holy grail that lesbian and gay couples should strive to attain. They want the romanticism of traditional marriage to touch and transform the lives of gays in America. The Santorums want the romanticism of marriage to transform and rejuvenate America itself, to rescue America from the moral decay of the last century. They insist that the transformative potential of marriage would be lost if homosexuals were allowed into the romance of marital bliss. They hold up marriage as an institution whose integrity is defined by excluding couples like Baker and McConnell.

The debate between Baker and McConnell, the pioneer couple who brought the first lawsuit seeking equal marriage rights, and the Santorums, leading proponents of the Federal Marriage Amendment against gay marriage, is the debate that called forth this book. It is a debate this book does not settle. Nor have we tried to do so. Our goal has been to illuminate each side's values and fears, even as we try to weed out some of the worst arguments (like the Scandinavian twist on the defense-of-marriage argument). Now we propose one final lesson Scandinavia offers each side of the debate.

Although romance is not dead, it has changed and may, in the old-fashioned sense of the term, be in decline. The same is true of marriage. As the Santorums believe, marriage has, increasingly, focused on consumer choice rather than mutual commitment. As Baker and McConnell believe, the liberalization of marriage has been the consequence of choices made by straights, not gays. But they are wrong to think that the same-sex marriage movement they founded in the United States will not affect marriage. And the Santorums are wrong to think that their unbending opposition to same-sex marriage will save or even help marriage. Consider the logic of this paradox.

An established social fact of the last century is that adults in Western countries have demanded more choices within their romantic relationships, including nonmarital options and opportunities to dissolve unhappy marriages. Responding to this demand, every nation in the postindustrial West has accommodated its family law regime to make it legal for romantic couples to cohabit rather than marry, and almost all of them grant some legal rights and duties to cohabiting couples. The same-sex marriage debate has not contributed to this phenomenon, but it has generated new legal institutions that are fresh rivals to marriage. Here's how. Advocates like Baker and McConnell demand *marriage equality* for lesbian and gay couples. Critics like the Santorums demand *reaffirmation of traditional marriage.* Torn between the equality principle and the integrity of marriage, the political middle has done what the middle usually does—it compromises. The most obvious compromise is to create a new institution, named anything but "marriage," that confers some or most of the legal benefits and duties of marriage to same-sex couples. But different-sex couples often insist on being included, and gay rights advocates are usually amenable, because they have internalized the equality principle. Hence some of the new institutions are open to all couples. Examples include most American domestic partnership registries, registered partnership in the Netherlands, Sweden's cohabitees law, and *pactes civils* in France.

The odd politics of same-sex marriage is part of a larger evolution in the way the state regulates couples. Today in Scandinavia, The Netherlands, France, and Canada—and tomorrow in American jurisdictions as well—couples of all kinds have a *menu of regulatory options* offered by the state. One way to conceptualize that menu is around the degree of unitive commitment expected or entailed in the partners' relationship. Drawing from legal regimes already created in the United States and Europe, the potential menu looks something like the following. We have arrayed the items on this particular menu from lowest to highest level of commitment, and (correspondingly) from least to most like our romantic image of traditional marriage.[1]

1. *Domestic partnership (employment benefits without necessarily much commitment).* Municipal ordinances in the United States have provided a useful model that is being followed by many transnational enterprises. Any employee who is willing to sign a form identifying a significant other (of any sex) ought to be able to add that person to the health-care, life insurance, and other benefits provided by the employer to married employees. Being someone's domestic partner may reflect romantic as well as platonic love, but it reflects a level of commitment only slightly greater (if greater at all) than being a close friend. The emphasis is on employment benefits, but there is some symbolic recognition that the relationship is consequential to both parties and ought to be rewarded with a few benefits. At this level, there is no legal obligation imposed on the domestic partners. They might be highly committed to one another, but that is neither a premise nor an expected effect of state recognition.[2]

2. *Cohabitation (economic obligations as well as more benefits).* Canada and most European countries impose support obligations on and offer some state benefits to couples who have cohabited for a substantial period of time. One can be a domestic partner without living together and with no expectation of a long-term relationship; cohabitation usually suggests both the reality of some legs on the relationship and the expectation for more. The assumption of greater commitment entails greater interdependence, which the state both rewards and obligates. The cohabiting household is treated by the state as a unit for purposes of economic security for each partner. Thus, a cohabitation regime will generally impose duties of support on the couple, especially if there is specialization within the household, where one partner works outside the home and builds up her or his outside earning capacity, while the other partner sacrifices some of hers or his so that the household can run smoothly and children can be cared for properly. European and Canadian laws also provide legal presumptions of joint property ownership and tenancy, family and bereavement leave, and sometimes wrongful death claims as well for cohabiting partners.[3]

3. *Cohabitation-plus (unitive rights as well as economic obligations and benefits).* The arrangement in the previous paragraph is the old version of cohabitation rules. The last two decades have seen them expand, and the compromises entailed in legislative wrangling over same-sex marriage have simulated further innovations. France's *pactes civils*, Germany's life partnership, and Hawaii's reciprocal beneficiaries illustrate a new kind of cohabitation regime. Because the terminology varies so much from one jurisdiction to another, we simply call this *cohabitation-plus*. The regime created by these laws both assumes and creates a greater level of commitment than do domestic partnership or cohabitation. As with domestic partnership, the couple must

register but, unlike domestic partnership, usually has to go through a more formal process of dissolution. As with cohabitation, the state not only imposes duties of mutual support but also provides benefits to encourage the partners' economic unity. What the French, German, and Hawaiian regimes most distinctively add is a wider array of unitive rights, namely, rules treating the partners as coupled and granting them financial and other benefits that reflect their unity in regard to matters like health-care decisions when one partner is incapacitated, organ donations after death, and mandated bereavement or sick leave for one's partner. In an ideal system, cohabitation-plus would also entail rights to enter the host country to be with one's partner. Obviously, this regime signals as well as entails a higher degree of mutual commitment than the first two.[4]

4. *Registered partnerships and civil unions (family rights and obligations as well as unitive rights and economic obligations and benefits).* After or instead of cohabiting, many couples decide to commit to a longer term relationship. Some of those couples want full-fledged state recognition, and the host of rights and obligations like those accorded marriage. The Scandinavian countries and Vermont allow these couples to become registered partners or join in civil unions, respectively. The state will encourage this long-term commitment with employment and other benefits, will help the couple carry out their purposes with the unitive rights and interdependence benefits, will underline the commitment's seriousness with obligations of mutual support and fidelity and with the added difficulty of legal divorce proceedings in the event of a breakup, and will reinforce family ties by giving the partners mutual rights over their adopted or biological children. What the state does not give in these civil union or registered partnership laws is the name *marriage* and its interstate and international portability.[5]

5. *Marriage (the name as well as intangible obligations, unitive rights, and economic obligations and benefits).* The traditional way couples in Western culture commit to a long-term relationship, of course, has been marriage. In the short term, the state will continue to support as well as recognize marriage, with all the rights and duties entailed in registered partnerships and civil unions as well as the trademarked name and the international portability. In the Netherlands and Massachusetts, marriage is open to same-sex couples who choose it, but many of them (as well as some different-sex couples) will choose civil unions, cohabitation(plus), or some other form for ideological reasons. Marriage will continue to be the focal point of family formation, because of its deep history and religious overtones. But under the menu approach now being developed in the West, marriage will have more institutional competitors. And the commitment it signals will continue to be diluted by the possibility of divorce without a showing of

fault. Because the same-sex marriage debate, in the United States especially, has revealed the deeply sectarian features of marriage, there will be increasing demands that the state, which is supposed to be neutral as regards sectarian disputes, should replace marriage with a civil alternative, such as civil unions open to different-sex as well as same-sex couples.[6]

6. *Covenant marriage (all the foregoing, plus it's harder to exit).* No-fault divorce has rendered marriage a less reliable precommitment device. If the state is going to experiment with institutions exacting less commitment from couples than marriage does, why not create (or reestablish) an institution with greater commitment? This is the idea entailed in *covenant marriage:* the state provides all the same rights and benefits of ordinary marriage, plus all the obligations and duties, and makes it harder for couples to dissolve the relationship. Thus, Louisiana's covenant marriage statute requires husbands and wives in unhappy marriages to go through compulsory mediation and a longer waiting period before they can divorce. It remains to be seen how much covenant marriage will increase the durability of marriages, but if these procedural requirements have a significant effect, we should expect to see more experiments in other states, perhaps with stronger commitment procedures. In that event, our culture might recover "traditional marriage" (an institution long ago overtaken by changes in the law) through this new institutional form.[7]

No American state or European nation offers this complete menu of options, and only the Netherlands, Belgium, Spain, Canada, and Massachusetts offer same-sex couples the same menu available to different-sex couples. In 2006, the foregoing menu is just a stylized presentation of the trend in Western family law. The main virtue of the trend is that it permits freedom of choice. Couples get to choose among an array of state regulatory regimes keyed to the level of commitment they want to signal or create. So couples who are uncertain whether they want to live together permanently might choose domestic partnership or cohabitation regimes, which are easy to exit. Committed couples will choose civil union or marriage, which is harder to exit but offers a larger array of legal rights and benefits. Couples rearing children will often choose either (covenant) marriage or civil union.

Relatedly, something like the menu sketched here would facilitate communication about the precise expectations in a relationship. Under a marriage-or-nothing regime, the couple can signal to one another, and to their families and third parties, a mutual commitment to life partnership. (No-fault divorce has considerably weakened this signal.) Providing lower commitment cohabitation-plus institutions would allow couples to signal less commitment than marriage—while providing covenant marriage institutions (perhaps with greater bite) would allow couples to signal more commitment. A woman deciding how much to invest in the relationship receives valuable information when her romantic partner tells her she or he is willing to cohabit but not marry.

The main drawback, for some, is that the menu seems antimarriage. Marriage's monopoly ended decades ago, when Western governments recognized cohabitation regimes, but a menu that includes cohabitation-plus and civil union options will siphon more couples away from marriage. Gay-radicals and some feminists are likely to applaud this development. Gay-liberals such as Baker and McConnell and traditionalists such as the Santorums will not—yet it is they who are now contributing to the expanded menu. Because Baker and McConnell keep trying to enter an institution that the Santorums insist on excluding them from, governments are pressed to create new alternatives to marriage—alternatives that in some cases are becoming competitors. The politics for accommodating both supporters and opponents of same-sex marriage is one that inevitably creates new institutional forms for family recognition. It is not inevitable that these new institutions will be available to different-sex couples as well, but we think most will become universally available over the course of time.

Is this the end of marriage? Not necessarily. It depends on the menu that the state develops. True romantics like the Santorums ought to consider the following legislative proposal in their state, Pennsylvania: recognize same-sex marriages (or civil unions if traditionalists in this state cannot swallow the terminology) in the same legislation that creates a covenant marriage regime with real bite, such as reimposing fault requirements or, better yet, imposing penalties upon the party at fault in a divorce. We close with this irony. Traditional family values Americans like the Santorums greatly outnumber lesbian and gay Americans like Jean Luscher and Jack Baker. Yet traditionalists behave as though they were powerless to influence the evolution of family law in the United States. That is a delusion, unless traditionalists engage in politics purely on an emotional level. A more thoughtful politics, such as the politics seen in Scandinavia, would understand the same-sex marriage movement not as an occasion for reaction but as an opportunity to advance a positive agenda for marriage.

Likewise, gay-liberals ought to understand the opposition to same-sex marriage not simply as the most recent example of gay-bashing in American history but as an opportunity to advance their own positive agenda. If traditionalists decline to work with them, as remains likely in the short term, their allies will be progressives who want the state to offer alternative institutions requiring less formal commitment in return for fewer benefits but some important obligations. The American federal arrangement, where each state is substantially free to create its own family law regime, means that different choice regimes are possible—and probably desirable. As Professor Brenda Cossman and her colleagues have proposed in Canada, one state might consider creating a new nonmarriage regime from scratch. And then sit back and see what works. As our examination of the Scandinavian experience suggests, simple-minded predictions ought not be made, and much can be learned that would enrich our understanding of family, relationships, and even romance in the postindustrial West.[8]

The Danish Registered Partnership Act

WE MARGRETHE THE SECOND, by the Grace of God Queen of Denmark, make it known that:
The Danish Parliament has passed and We give the Royal Assent to the following law:

SECTION 1

Two persons of the same sex may have their partnership registered.

Registration

SECTION 2

(1) Part 1, sections 12 and 13(1) and clause 1 of section 13 (2) of the Danish Marriage Act shall apply in the same way to the registration of partnerships, cf. subsection 2.
(2) The registration of a partnership can only occur if both of the partners, or one of them, has residency here in the country and Danish citizenship.
(3) The rules on the procedure of registration of a partnership, including an examination of whether the conditions for a registration are met, shall be set by the Minster of Justice.

Legal Effects

SECTION 3

(1) The registration of a partnership has, with the exceptions stated in section 4, the same legal effects as the contracting of marriage.
(2) The provisions of Danish law that pertain to marriage and spouses shall apply in the same way to registered partnership and registered partners.

SECTION 4

(1) The provisions of the Danish Adoption Act regarding spouses shall not apply to registered partners.
(2) Clause 3 of section 13 and section 15(3) of the Danish Legal Incapacity and Guardianship Act regarding spouses shall not apply to registered partners.
(3) Provisions in Danish law that contain special rules whereby one of the parties in a marriage is identified by their sex shall not apply to registered partners.

(4) Provisions in international treaties shall not apply to registered partnership, unless the other contracting parties agree to it.

Dissolution

SECTION 5

(1) Parts 3, 4, and 5 of the Danish Marriage Act and Part 42 of the Danish Administration of Justice Act shall apply in the same way to the dissolution of a registered partnership, cf. subsections 2 and 3.
(2) Section 46 of the Danish Marriage Act shall not apply to the dissolution of a registered partnership.
(3) Regardless of section 448c of the Danish Administration of Justice Act, registered partnerships can always be dissolved in this country.

Provisions of Operation, etc.

SECTION 6

This Act comes into force on October 1, 1989.

SECTION 7

This Act shall not apply to the Faroe Islands and Greenland, but may by Royal order be made applicable, either fully or in part, to these parts of the country with such modifications as are required by the special Faroese and Greenlandic conditions.

Given at Christiansborg Castle, this seventh day of June, 1989

Under Our Royal Hand and Seal

MARGRETHE R.

Source: Text of Act no. 372 of June 7, 1989 (translated by Darren Spedale).

Act to Amend the Registered Partnership Act

SECTION 1

Act no. 372 of June 7, 1989 on registered partnership, as amended by Act no. 821 of December 19, 1989 and section 36 of Act no. 387 of June 14, 1995, shall be amended as follows:

1. Section 2(2) is repealed and in its place is inserted:
    "(2) The registration of a partnership can only occur if:
        1) One of the parties has residence here in the country and Danish citizenship, or

2) Both parties have had residence here in the country for the last two years before registration.

(3) Citizenship from Norway, Sweden or Iceland is to be considered as equivalent to Danish citizenship in relation to this (2)1. The Minister of Justice may also set out that citizenship from another country with its own registered partnership legislation, that corresponds to the Danish legislation, may be considered as equivalent to Danish citizenship."

(3) [in the original Act] hereafter becomes (4).

2. In Section 4(1), there is inserted after the first sentence a new sentence: "Nevertheless, a registered partner can adopt the other partner's child, unless such child is an adopted child from another country."

SECTION 2

This Act comes into force on July 1, 1999.

SECTION 3

(1) This Act shall not apply to the Faroe Islands and Greenland, cf. section 2.
(2) This Act may by Royal order be made applicable for the Faroe Islands and Greenland with such modifications as are required by the special Faroese and Greenlandic conditions.

Source: Text of Act no. L70A of May 20, 1999 (translated by Darren Spedale—to change the conditions for entrance into a registered partnership, and stepchild adoption for registered partners).

Official Introduction to the Registered Partnership Act by Its Sponsors in the Parliament of Denmark

The Parliament has in recent years carried out a number of debates and made a number of decisions of consequence to gays and lesbians. Despite disagreement on individual decisions, the debates have revealed a positive opinion toward a social equalizing of gays and lesbians that stretches out over the parties that have carried the individual decisions and bills through.

There is no doubt that these political well-wishers reflect the actual opinion in the population. There is a growing acceptance that gays and lesbians live a life in accordance with their own choices, and that relationships between two people of the same sex, to exactly the same extent as relationships between two people of the opposite sex, are built on love, mutual responsibility and solidarity.

Or, as the founder of LBL, Axel Axgil, wrote in his book "Homofile War Years": "We homosexuals felt neither sick nor criminal. We considered ourselves as people that for one or another reason from nature's side were created differently, but we found that our form of love life could be just as beautiful and full of feelings as for the so-called 'normal' people."

Before the change of public opinion in favor of gay and lesbian cohabitation, there was a century-long development, starting with the 1912 report of the 1905 Commission to Revise the Penal Code, which therein suggested a considerable liberalization of certain laws, and this liberalization—after many attempts—was passed in the new Penal Code of April 15, 1930.

On a previous scale, it was looked at as a considerable accomplishment when Minister of Justice C. Th. Zahle, in connection with the bill, said that "when payment is not offered, and when there is not found an abuse of young people, the relationship may not be said to concern the legal authorities."

This statement marked the political decision-makers' acceptance of relationships between two persons of the same sex. Gays and lesbians considered it as an important step in the right direction, because it implied that persecution on the grounds of homosexuality was impermissible.

But there was no discussion of a true equalizing of relationships between two persons of the same sex and two persons of the opposite sex. This is partially due to the fact that there was no understanding [of gay relationships] in either the population or among politicians, and partially because most gays and lesbians considered these ideas unrealistic, so long as they had enough to do with fighting off persecution and discrimination. Only in the more visionary moments was there discussed true equalization.

Furthermore, the position of the Minister of Justice at that time was not quite in accordance with the opinions of the population and the other authorities on this issue. With the background of a questionable [legal] judgment in 1936, the concept of "payment" was interpreted to mean any material offering, from a visit to a restaurant to a cigarette. Presumably not in accordance with Zahle's intentions, there occurred a widening discrimination of gays and lesbians up until the end of the sixties, when especially MP Else Merete-Ross and Ministers of Justice K. Axel Nielsen and Knud Thestrup are remembered for initiatives that stopped the disgraceful treatment of gays and lesbians.

Since then there has been, both in the population and among political decision-makers across party lines, a quite important change of opinion, which makes it possible to create further legal initiatives in order to equalize relationships between two persons of the same sex with relationships between two persons of the opposite sex.

The change of opinion has already been demonstrated on several occasions:

1) In 1984 the Parliament voted to seat a commission for the enlightenment of the lives of gays and lesbians in society.
2) In 1986 the Parliament voted for equality in inheritance taxes between two people of the same sex and married couples.
3) In 1987 the Parliament voted to widen the existing antidiscrimination law to include, among others, gays and lesbians.

Furthermore, the Interior Minister at the time, Knud Enggaard, and the Parliament's Communal Committee in the beginning of 1987 woke a considerable international awareness with a visit to Holland's organization for gays and lesbians in connection with a research visit to fight against the illness AIDS, and the Danish organization, LBL, to a rising degree has gained recognition as, among other things, a coworker in the Danish fight against AIDS.

The above-named Commission for the Enlightenment of the Situation of Homosexuals in Society published its report in January 1988 (number 1127:1988). At the same time the Social Democrats, the Socialist People's Party and the Radical Left introduced their bill into the Parliament, the Law on Registered Partnership.

The present bill, which with the exception of the Date of Operational Effect is identical with the bill introduced into the previous Parliament, is built to a substantial degree on the suggestions and evaluations of the large minority in the Commission that have been set out on the subject of registered partnership.

2. *The Bill's Goal*

Past the obvious need for equality between two equal forms of cohabitation, which has become of interest over the development of several years, there are several other goals with the bill.

(1) A social acceptance of relationships between two persons of the same sex expressed through specific lawmaking will secure for the partners in such a relationship the same legal guarantees, the same rights and the same responsibilities as apply to married couples.

(2) A partnership institution will secure better opportunities for gays and lesbians to live a life in accordance with their own desires and own choices. This is not least of importance for young people, for whom it is a notoriously difficult and lengthy process to come to a decision in accordance with their feelings and needs, when they additionally will include irrational considerations such as society's and their entourage's reactions in their deliberations.

(3) A formal acknowlegement through explicit legislation will improve the opportunities for long-lasting and permanent relationships between two people of the same sex, since the existence or just the feeling of a negative reaction from society's side is known to work against the durability of a long-term relationship in a negative way.

(4) A partnership institution is a basis to secure two people of the same sex in a permanent relationship the same rights as married couples in relation to other legislation, for example housing law, pension law, and immigration law, and thereby hinder a series of burdening situations.

(5) The possibility for two people of the same sex to choose to enter a formalized partnership means that, in the same way as two people of the opposite sex, they have two options: a formalized [partnership] and a nonformalized one.

Although the bill does not originate from the dangerous situation regarding the sickness AIDS, it has increased interest in its passage. Even without the occurrence of this illness would the passage of a partnership institution be relevant.

But it can of course not be denied that the illness has given occasion for focusing on the collective life situation of gays, such as doctor [and HIV-specialist] Henrik Zoffmann on several occasions has given expression to: that a better life situation, changed opinions and less pressure on permanent relationships between two people of the same sex could reduce the number of casual relationships between gay men and thereby contribute to the fight against the disease's spread.

It is the opinion of the bill's sponsors that this assessment is correct, but in consideration of the other weighty—and non–time based—arguments for the bill, this can only be considered a positive extra advantage to its passage.

3. International Perspectives

Denmark already has a good reputation among gays and lesbians in foreign countries. Despite some difficulties, Denmark is one of the few countries in the world where it is possible for gays and lesbians to have a decent life.

It is assumed, presumably correctly, that such a marked qualitative step forward for all gays and lesbians such as the passage of a proper partnership institution with rights and responsibilities will not, at the present point in time, be passed in other countries than Denmark.

Over a large part of the world, the Parliament's discussion of the present bill will be looked upon with a great deal of interest, since Denmark with its passage will be the first country to take the first step in—at least in Western Europe—an unavoidable development.

In connection with ILGA's (International Lesbian and Gay Association) annual conference, which in 1986 took place in Denmark, many foreign participants expressed hope that the Parliament would pass a partnership bill, since that will improve the situation for their work [for gay and lesbian rights]—not just in reference to achieving corresponding provisions [in other countries], but also regarding the achievement of rights, which Denmark has for many years considered expected human rights. There continues to be a number of countries, even in Europe, where homosexuality is not permitted, or where there is legal authority for discrimination on the grounds of homosexuality.

It is the opinion of the sponsors of the bill that passage of the current bill, by virtue of the power of example, will work for the human rights of gays and lesbians in many countries around the world.

4. The Central Contents

COMMENTS ON THE BILL AS A WHOLE

The bill provides for the transfer of all of the legal rights of marriage to registered partnership, apart from the exceptions that are listed in the bill and appear in these comments.

The bill's sponsors have chosen to use the description "registered partnership," which is partially grounded in the fact that a short name is desirable, and partially because LBL has for many years used this description for a registration process for homosexual pairs, which is why the description is already well known, at least among homosexuals.

Entrance into registered partnership is not restricted to homosexuals, since a condition of this would be set out a definition of what a homosexual relationship contains. Such a definition is presumably neither possible nor desirable. People of the same sex without sexual relations to each other who fulfill the conditions that are set out for the entrance of a registered partnership, will thereby be covered by the bill.

The bill does not contain a demand for cohabitation between the people that want to be registered. The Marriage Act also does not provide for a demand that spouses, either before or during marriage, must live together.

The bill's sponsors are aware that there are a number of provisions in laws related to marriage, that shall apply to registered partnership that use expressions like "husband," "wife," and so on. For example can be named Sections 1, 11, and 26 of the law on marriage's legal effects. The bill's sponsors find it unnecessary to change the words in all such provisions, but find that the problem can be solved by analogy or by a special translation of the concerned provisions.

Nevertheless, it will be necessary to change the provisions in laws related to marriage, where there are conditions placed concerning an earlier marriage, cf. the simultaneously introduced bill on the law of changing of the Marriage Act, Inheritance Act, the Penal Act and the Act on taxes of Inheritance and Gifts. (The changes which follow the passage of a registered partnership bill.)

COMMENTS TO THE BILL'S INDIVIDUAL PROVISIONS

To Section 1

It has been stated that only two persons of the same sex may enter into registered partnership. As discussed in the general comments there is no demand that the two people have a sexual relationship to each other or live together. On the other hand, it follows from this provision that registered partnership only concerns couples. A group of people, for example members of a collective, cannot use the provisions to enter into, for example, mutual inheritance rights. There are furthermore placed additional conditions on the two people, since they must both fulfill the conditions that apply for the entrance of marriage, cf. Comments to section 2.

To Section 2

Clause 1 transfers the conditions for marriage and the rules for the examination of such to apply to registered partnership, however with the exceptions that result from section 2 clause 2.

This means, among other things, that persons under 18 years of age may not enter into registered partnership without the county's and parent's permission. The indispensable prohibition in the Marriage Act's section 6 is also transferred, so that registered partnership cannot be entered into between relatives in a direct upper or lower line or between siblings, but is permissible between cousins. Furthermore the prohibition on bigamy is transferred, cf. Marriage Act section 9, plus the conditions for divorce in the Act's section 10.

The bill further contains that the provisions on church and civil weddings do not apply to registered partnership.

The Minister of Justice is authorized to lay down further rules for the procedures of a partnership's registration, cf. Clause 3.

Clause 2 contains special rules pertaining to the need for the partners' ties to Denmark.

Chapter 1 of the Marriage Act on the conditions for marriage and Chapter 2 on weddings place no demand that a Danish marriage can only be entered into if one or both of the partners has a domicile in Denmark or is a Danish citizen.

Naturally the couple must be in Denmark for the wedding, but there is nothing to prevent that foreign citizens get married here in the country, even if one or both of them resides in a foreign country. In consideration of the examination that the conditions for marriage are fulfilled, the partners must nevertheless stay here in the country a few days before the wedding, while the examining authorities handle the case.

A transfer, at this point, of the above-named rules on the entrance into marriage will only lead to the possibility that completely foreign pairs can enter into registered partnership here in this country, without the registration being of any meaning in their homeland. The bill's sponsors find this consequence undesirable. The registration therefore only ought to find application in situations where at least one of the partners has a residence in Denmark.

In regards to registration it is commented that the bill's sponsors are concerned about rules that would permit Danish diplomats to conduct registrations in foreign countries, which would with a transfer of Danish marriage law be possible under the Marriage Act's section 22. The assumption here is that the concerned country would permit a foreign authority to conduct registrations of homosexuals on their territory. Such permission will presumably not be given.

As a consequence of the fact that section 22 of the Marriage Act will not apply, visa applicants who wish to come to Denmark to enter a registered partnership ought to receive such a visa, even if visas are usually not given to applicants from the concerned country.

Clause 3 authorizes the Minister of Justice to lay down further rules on the entrance into registered partnership.

To Section 3

Section 3 contains the bill's central provision, according to which all of the legal effects of marriage are transferred to registered partnership with the exceptions listed in section 4.

The provision also means that partners in a registered partnership have mutual maintenance obligations, that the Marriage Act's provisions on property apply, that the partners have the right of inheritance from one another, and that the rules on joint taxation and social welfare for spouses also apply.

Suggestions [as] to possible necessary lawmaking [as a result of these provisions] are assumed to be worked out by the Minister of Justice under the bill's deliberations, so that the additional legislation can be passed by the Parliament along with the present bill.

To Section 4

The provision means that the rules in the Adoption Act regarding spouses' ability to jointly adopt a foreign baby, as well as stepchild adoption, do not apply to people who have entered into a registered partnership.

To Section 5

Clause 1 means that the rules in the Marriage Act on annulment, separation and divorce, including the rules on the terms for separation and divorce and changing of these conditions, find application with the dissolution of a registered partnership.

Clause 2 is a consequence of the fact that the rules on church weddings do not apply to registered partnerships. It is therefore found necessary to exempt the provisions in Section 43, clause 1, point 2 of the Marriage Act, which among other things establishes that mediation in connection with a separation or divorce can be done by a priest. Mediation in connection with the dissolution of a registered partnership will hereafter take place through the county [offices], where there can be set down further provisions pursuant to the present provision's section 4. Furthermore section 46 of the Marriage Act concerning parental custody over children in connection with separation or divorce is excepted.

Clause 3. It will, in the opinion of the bill's sponsors, be most appropriate to permit the dissolution of the partnership in Denmark of all Danish registrations regardless of the partners' residence at the point of separation or divorce.

Source: Comments to the bill may be found in the Parliamentary Record in conjunction with the introduction of the Registered Partnership bill on November 22, 1988. (Translated from Danish by Darren Spedale.)

Registered Partnerships in Scandinavia

(A) Registered Partnerships (RPs) in Denmark, 1990–2005

Year	Number of Registered Partnerships[1]	Number of Persons Living in an RP (Male/Female)	Number of Living Persons Whose RPs Have Been Dissolved (Male/Female)[2]
1990	296	640 (518/122)	1 (1/0)
1991	663	1,435 (1,102/333)	14 (6/8)
1992	851	1,891 (1,400/491)	48 (26/22)
1993	986	2,228 (1,602/626)	105 (67/38)
1994	1,078	2,481 (1,777/704)	184 (105/79)
1995	1,191	2,760 (1,898/862)	264 (162/102)
1996	1,308	3,011 (2,050/961)	357 (210/147)
1997	1,433	3,301 (2,194/1,107)	435 (255/180)
1998	1,531	3,541 (2,275/1,266)	540 (322/218)
1999	1,679	3,833 (2,384/1,449)	628 (375/253)
2000	1,829	4,192 (2,556/1,636)	714 (410/304)
2001	1,992	4,544 (2,722/1,822)	813 (467/346)
2002	2,166	4,956 (2,895/2,061)	908 (519/389)
2003	2,315	5,262 (3,024/2,238)	1,049 (570/479)
2004	2,468	5,577 (3,147/2,430)	1,169 (625/544)
2005	2,641	5,953 (3,235/2,718)	1,263 (681/582)

Source: Statistics Denmark, Denmark's national statistical office; based on tables drawn from its website, www.statbank.dk.

1. The number of registered partnerships listed by Statistics Denmark does not equal the number of persons listed as living in a registered partnership. This is due to the fact that Statistics Denmark does not include persons living outside of Denmark in its count of couples, but is more inclusive in its count of individuals. (Information received by Dorthe Larsen of Statistics Denmark.) Thus, the actual number of couples in registered partnerships is more closely reflected in the number of individuals, meaning that approximately 3,000 couples were living in registered partnerships in 2005.
2. This number does not include persons who divorced a registered partner and later entered a new registered partnership.

(B) Registered Partnerships in Norway, 1993–2004

Year	Registered Partnerships Contracted (Male/Female Partnerships)	Cumulative Number of Partnerships Contracted
1993	156 (115/41)	156
1994	133 (86/47)	289
1995	98 (64/34)	387
1996	127 (80/47)	514
1997	117 (74/43)	631
1998	115 (71/44)	746
1999	144 (82/62)	890
2000	154 (78/76)	1044
2001	185 (108/77)	1229
2002	183 (105/78)	1412
2003	204 (116/88)	1616
2004	192 (107/85)	1808

Source: Statistics Norway. Note that Statistics Norway only counts the number of partnerships where the elder partner is residing in Norway, so these numbers will be somewhat undercounted. Also note that Norway's statistics website reports the number of partnerships *contracted* annually as compared to the number of existing partnerships. According to Statistics Norway, there were 1,275 sets of existing registered partnerships as of January 1, 2005, 130 of which were couples with children.

(C) Registered Partnerships in Sweden, 1995–2004

Year	Swedish Partnership Registrations (Male/Female)	Swedish Registered Partner Dissolutions (Male/Female)
1995	665 (498/167)	None
1996	319 (201/118)	None
1997	262 (158/104)	None
1998	250 (158/92)	61 (45/16)
1999	287 (154/133)	80 (42/38)
2000	357 (218/139)	101 (53/48)
2001	381 (195/186)	105 (43/62)
2002	422 (212/210)	92 (47/45)
2003	497 (240/257)	57 (31/26)
2004	567 (285/282)	58 (30/28)

Source: Hans Ytterberg, drawing from statistics compiled by the Swedish government; Turid Noack of Statistics Norway.

APPENDIX 4

Demographic Information for Denmark

(A) Marriage and Divorce, 1901–2004

Year	Population	Marriages	Divorces	Marriage Rate (per 100,000)	Divorce Rate (per 100,000)
1901	2,449,540	17,603	376	718.6	15.3
1925	3,434,555	25,786	1,889	750.8	55.0
1950	4,281,275	38,838	6,868	907.2	160.4
1960	4,585,256	35,897	6,682	782.9	145.7
1970	4,937,579	36,376	9,524	736.7	192.9
1971	4,950,598	32,801	13,401	662.6	270.7
1972	4,975,653	31,073	13,134	624.5	264.0
1973	5,007,538	30,813	12,637	615.3	252.4
1974	5,036,184	33,182	13,132	658.9	260.8
1975	5,054,410	31,782	13,264	628.8	262.4
1976	5,065,313	31,192	13,064	615.8	257.9
1977	5,079,879	32,174	13,383	633.4	263.5
1978	5,096,959	28,763	13,072	564.3	256.5
1979	5,111,537	27,842	13,044	544.7	255.2
1980	5,122,065	26,448	13,593	516.4	265.4
1981	5,123,989	25,411	14,425	495.9	281.5
1982	5,119,155	24,330	14,621	475.3	285.6
1983	5,116,464	27,096	14,763	529.6	288.5
1984	5,112,130	28,624	14,490	559.9	283.4
1985	5,111,108	29,322	14,385	573.7	281.4
1986	5,116,273	30,773	14,490	601.5	283.2
1987	5,124,794	31,132	14,381	607.5	280.6
1988	5,129,254	32,080	14,717	625.4	286.9
1989	5,129,778	30,894	15,152	602.2	295.4
1990	5,135,409	31,513	13,731	613.6	267.4
1991	5,146,469	31,099	12,655	604.3	245.9
1992	5,162,126	32,188	12,981	623.5	251.5
1993	5,180,614	31,638	12,971	610.7	250.4
1994	5,196,642	35,321	13,709	679.7	263.8
1995	5,215,718	34,736	12,976	666.0	248.8
1996	5,251,027	35,953	12,776	684.7	243.3
1997	5,275,121	34,244	12,774	649.2	242.2

(continued)

(A) *Marriage and Divorce, 1901–2004* (continued)

Year	Population	Marriages	Divorces	Marriage Rate (per 100,000)	Divorce Rate (per 100,000)
1998	5,294,860	34,733	13,141	656.0	248.2
1999	5,313,577	35,439	13,537	667.0	254.8
2000	5,330,020	38,388	14,381	720.2	269.8
2001	5,349,212	36,567	14,597	683.6	272.9
2002	5,368,354	37,210	15,304	693.1	285.1
2003	5,383,507	35,041	15,763	650.9	292.8
2004	5,397,640	37,711	15,774	698.7	292.2

Source: Statistics Denmark, Denmark's national statistical office; based on tables drawn from its website, www.statbank.dk.

(B) *Births, 1970–2004*

Year	Total Number of Live Births	Number of Births Outside Marriage	Percentage of Births Outside Marriage
1970	70,802	7,811	11.0
1971	75,359	9,285	12.3
1972	75,505	10,877	14.4
1973	71,895	12,326	17.1
1974	71,327	13,411	18.8
1975	72,071	15,663	21.7
1976	65,267	15,672	24.0
1977	61,878	16,026	25.9
1978	62,036	17,301	27.9
1979	59,464	18,266	30.7
1980	57,293	19,004	33.2
1981	53,089	18,964	35.7
1982	52,658	20,152	38.3
1983	50,822	20,619	40.6
1984	51,800	21,715	41.9
1985	53,749	23,091	43.0
1986	55,312	24,268	43.9
1987	56,221	25,029	44.5
1988	58,844	26,291	44.7
1989	61,351	28,300	46.1
1990	63,433	29,435	46.4
1991	64,358	29,948	46.5
1992	67,726	31,426	46.4
1993	67,369	31,504	46.8

(continued)

(B) *Births,* 1970–2004 *(continued)*

Year	Total Number of Live Births	Number of Births Outside Marriage	Percentage of Births Outside Marriage
1994	69,666	32,642	46.9
1995	69,771	32,425	46.5
1996	67,638	31,302	46.3
1997	67,648	30,538	45.1
1998	66,174	29,643	44.8
1999	66,220	29,708	44.9
2000	67,084	29,902	44.6
2001	65,458	29,208	44.6
2002	64,075	28,568	44.6
2003	64,599	28,980	44.9
2004	64,397	29,268	45.4

Source: Statistics Denmark, Denmark's national statistical office; based on tables drawn from its website, www.statbank.dk.

(C) *Households with Children,* 1980–2005

Year	Single Males	Single Females	Married Couples	Cohabiting Couples	Consensual Unions	Registered Partnerships	Not Living with Parents
1980	13,017	85,594	582,621	53,472	NA	0	24,890
1981	13,751	88,804	570,672	58,781	NA	0	24,353
1982	14,408	91,198	554,829	63,708	NA	0	23,277
1983	15,018	93,582	536,843	69,466	NA	0	22,449
1984	15,325	94,282	519,617	73,673	NA	0	21,634
1985	15,361	94,804	502,413	76,997	NA	0	20,225
1986	15,732	94,718	489,036	81,289	NA	0	19,110
1987	16,020	95,296	479,401	85,114	NA	0	18,408
1988	16,072	96,591	470,933	88,578	NA	0	17,076
1989	16,302	99,395	461,120	90,870	NA	0	16,522
1990	16,218	101,184	449,144	21,759	72,836	10	15,603
1991	16,129	101,872	438,654	21,460	77,132	27	14,991
1992	15,745	102,327	430,216	21,422	81,598	41	14,550
1993	15,526	103,695	422,374	21,023	85,274	46	14,225
1994	15,207	104,363	413,745	20,681	88,803	49	14,117
1995	15,035	104,500	410,883	20,081	90,612	59	14,148
1996	14,609	104,841	411,957	20,041	92,915	81	14,350
1997	14,589	104,783	411,432	19,820	93,841	91	14,383

(continued)

(C) Households with Children, 1980–2005 (continued)

Year	Single Males	Single Females	Married Couples	Cohabiting Couples	Consensual Unions	Registered Partnerships	Not Living with Parents
1998	14,788	104,122	410,373	19,753	95,116	106	14,675
1999	14,931	102,873	410,960	20,155	96,050	150	14,812
2000	15,244	103,316	412,704	21,192	95,525	176	15,328
2001	15,840	104,202	414,657	22,165	95,546	220	15,919
2002	16,399	106,680	416,611	23,171	94,986	266	16,494
2003	17,073	110,286	418,013	22,642	94,496	294	16,753
2004	18,052	113,734	417,838	22,464	94,635	338	16,568
2005	18,882	116,515	418,126	22,704	93,556	401	16,513

Source: Statistics Denmark, Denmark's national statistical office; based on tables drawn from its website, www.statbank.dk.

Demographic Information for Norway

(A) Marriage and Divorce, 1961–2004

Year	Population	Marriages	Divorces	Marriage Rate (per 100,000)	Divorce Rate (per 100,000)
1961	3,609,800	24,142	2,411	668.8	66.8
1962	3,638,918	24,070	2,400	661.4	66.0
1963	3,666,537	24,096	2,414	657.2	65.8
1964	3,694,339	25,005	2,500	676.8	67.7
1965	3,723,168	24,185	2,533	649.6	68.0
1966	3,753,012	27,680	2,627	737.5	70.0
1967	3,784,539	29,154	2,830	770.3	74.8
1968	3,816,486	29,441	3,012	771.4	78.9
1969	3,847,707	29,630	3,029	770.1	78.7
1970	3,875,763	29,370	3,303	757.8	85.2
1971	3,903,039	29,510	3,602	756.1	92.3
1972	3,933,004	28,596	3,878	727.1	98.6
1973	3,960,613	28,141	4,500	710.5	113.6
1974	3,985,258	27,344	4,949	686.1	124.2
1975	4,007,313	25,898	5,409	646.3	135.0
1976	4,026, 152	25,389	5,648	630.6	140.3
1977	4,043, 205	24,022	5,912	594.1	146.2
1978	4,058,671	23,690	6,063	583.7	149.4
1979	4,072,517	23,055	6,442	566.1	158.2
1980	4,085,620	22,230	6,467	544.1	158.3
1981	4,099,702	22,271	6,937	543.2	169.2
1982	4,114,787	21,706	6,974	527.5	169.5
1983	4,128,432	20,803	7,473	503.9	181.0
1984	4,140,099	20,537	7,781	496.1	187.9
1985	4,152,516	20,221	8,090	487.0	194.8
1986	4,167,354	19,873	7,813	476.9	187.5
1987	4,186,905	20,285	8,342	484.5	199.2
1988	4,209,488	20,806	8,689	494.3	206.4
1989	4,226,901	19,950	9,163	472.0	216.8
1990	4,241,473	21,123	10,055	498.0	237.0
1991	4,261,732	19,065	10,164	447.4	238.5
1992	4,286,401	18,627	10,106	434.6	235.8
1993	4,311,991	18,741	10,805	434.6	250.6

(continued)

(A) Marriage and Divorce, 1961–2004 (continued)

Year	Population	Marriages	Divorces	Marriage Rate (per 100,000)	Divorce Rate (per 100,000)
1994	4,336,613	19,866	10,795	458.1	248.9
1995	4,359,184	20,981	10,183	481.3	233.6
1996	4,381,336	22,478	9,836	513.0	224.5
1997	4,405,157	22,933	9,813	520.6	222.8
1998	4,431,464	22,349	9,213	504.3	207.9
1999	4,461,913	23,456	9,124	525.7	204.5
2000	4,490,967	25,356	10,053	564.6	223.8
2001	4,513,751	22,967	10,308	508.8	228.4
2002	4,538,159	24,069	10,450	530.4	230.3
2003	4,564,855	22,361	10,757	489.9	235.6
2004	4,591,910	22,354	11,045	486.8	234.2

Source: Statistics Norway.

(B) Births, 1976–2004

Year	Total Number of Live Births	Number of Births Outside Marriage	Percentage of Births Outside Marriage
1976	53,474	5,824	10.9
1977	50,877	5,903	11.6
1978	51,749	6,150	11.9
1979	51,580	6,729	13.0
1980	51,039	7,392	14.5
1981	50,708	8,169	16.1
1982	51,245	9,041	17.6
1983	49,937	9,616	19.3
1984	50,274	10,687	21.3
1985	51,134	13,203	25.8
1986	52,514	14,673	27.9
1987	54,027	16,705	30.9
1988	57,526	19,407	33.7
1989	59,303	21,588	36.4
1990	60,939	23,503	38.6
1991	60,808	24,844	40.9
1992	60,109	25,801	42.9
1993	59,678	26,526	44.4
1994	60,092	27,581	45.9
1995	60,292	28,690	47.6
1996	60,927	29,435	48.3

(continued)

(B) *Births, 1976–2004* (continued)

Year	Total Number of Live Births	Number of Births Outside Marriage	Percentage of Births Outside Marriage
1997	59,801	29,133	48.7
1998	58,352	28,573	49.0
1999	59,298	29,100	49.1
2000	59,234	29,368	49.6
2001	56,696	28,194	49.7
2002	55,434	27,890	50.3
2003	56,458	28,218	50.0
2004	56,951	29,252	51.3

Source: Statistics Norway.

(C) *Households with Children, 1974–2004*

Year	Married Households with Children	Cohabiting Households with Children	Cohabitants as Percentage of Partnered Households with Children
1974	550,859	NA	NA
1977	547,676	NA	NA
1980	535,934	NA	NA
1982	527,408	NA	NA
1984	514,396	NA	NA
1987	487,458	NA	NA
1989	466,335	35,218	7.0
1991	404,110	47,084	10.4
1993	382,861	59,561	13.5
1995	370,220	72,468	16.4
1997	365,559	80,699	18.1
1999	358,781	89,507	20.0
2000	356,913	92,692	20.6
2001	354,251	92,597	20.7
2002	350,805	95,837	21.5
2003	348,815	98,048	21.9
2004	346,096	101,302	22.6

Source: Statistics Norway.

APPENDIX 6

Demographic Information for Sweden

(A) Marriage and Divorce, 1850–2004

Year	Population	Marriages	Divorces	Marriage Rate (per 100,000)	Divorce Rate (per 100,000)
1850	3,482,541	26,267	100	754.2	2.9
1900	5,136,441	31,478	405	612.8	7.9
1925	6,053,562	37,419	1,748	618.1	28.9
1950	7,041,829	54,222	8,008	770.0	113.7
1960	7,497,967	50,149	8,958	668.8	119.5
1970	8,081,229	43,278	12,943	535.5	160.2
1971	8,115,165	39,918	13,540	491.9	166.8
1972	8,129,129	38,636	15,179	475.3	186.7
1973	8,144,428	38,251	16,021	469.7	196.7
1974	8,176,691	44,864	26,802	548.7	327.8
1975	8,208,442	44,103	25,383	537.3	309.2
1976	8,236,179	44,790	21,702	543.8	263.5
1977	8,267,116	40,370	20,391	488.3	246.7
1978	8,284,437	37,844	20,317	456.8	245.2
1979	8,303,010	37,300	20,322	449.2	244.8
1980	8,317,937	37,569	19,887	451.7	239.1
1981	8,323,033	37,793	20,198	454.1	242.7
1982	8,327,484	37,051	20,766	444.9	249.4
1983	8,330,573	36,210	20,618	434.7	247.5
1984	8,342,621	36,849	20,377	441.7	244.3
1985	8,358,139	38,297	19,763	458.2	236.5
1986	8,381,515	38,906	19,107	464.2	228.0
1987	8,414,083	41,223	18,426	489.9	219.0
1988	8,458,888	44,229	17,746	522.9	209.8
1989	8,527,036	108,919	18,862	1277.3	221.2
1990	8,590,630	40,477	19,357	471.2	225.3
1991	8,644,119	36,836	20,149	426.1	233.1
1992	8,692,013	37,173	21,907	427.7	252.0
1993	8,745,109	34,005	21,673	388.8	247.8
1994	8,816,381	34,203	22,237	387.9	252.2
1995	8,837,496	33,642	22,528	380.7	254.9
1996	8,844,499	33,784	21,377	382.0	241.7

(continued)

(A) Marriage and Divorce, 1850–2004 *(continued)*

Year	Population	Marriages	Divorces	Marriage Rate (per 100,000)	Divorce Rate (per 100,000)
1997	8,847,625	32,313	21,009	365.2	237.5
1998	8,854,322	31,598	20,761	356.9	234.5
1999	8,861,426	35,628	21,000	402.1	237.0
2000	8,882,792	39,895	21,502	449.1	242.1
2001	8,909,128	35,778	21,022	401.6	236.0
2002	8,940,788	38,012	21,322	425.2	238.5
2003	8,975,670	39,041	21,130	435.0	235.4
2004	9,011,392	43,088	20,106	478.1	223.1

Source: Statistics Sweden

(B) Births, 1990–2002

Year	Total Live Births	Births to Married Women	Births to Single, Divorced, Widowed Women	Ratio of Births Married/Nonmarried Women
1990	123,938	65,690	58,248	53/47
1991	123,737	64,108	59,629	52/48
1992	122,848	62,077	60,771	51/49
1993	117,998	58,509	59,489	50/50
1994	112,257	54,330	57,927	48/52
1995	103,422	48,653	54,769	47/53
1996	95,297	43,949	51,348	46/54
1997	90,502	41,557	48,945	46/54
1998	89,028	40,370	48,658	45/55
1999	88,173	39,422	48,751	45/55
2000	90,441	40,404	50,037	45/55
2001	91,466	40,710	50,756	45/55
2002	95,815	42,137	53,678	44/56

Source: Hans Ytterberg, drawing from statistics compiled by the Swedish government.

NOTES

INTRODUCTION

1. McConnell's account of growing up in Norman and of the assault on Joe Clem is taken from Ken Bronson, *A Quest for Full Equality*, manuscript, May 18, 2004.

2. The quotations in text are from *Webster's New International Dictionary of the English Language*, 2nd ed. (Springfield, Mass.: G. & C. Merriam, 1961), 1733. Antihomosexual attitudes in Norman are documented by the Norman Human Rights Commission, *Community Attitudes on Homosexuality and about Homosexuals—A Report on the Environment in Norman, Oklahoma* (1978), discussed in Brief *Amicus Curiae* of the American Association for Personal Privacy [et al.], *Board of Education v. NGTF* (U.S. Supreme Court, Docket No. 83–2030), 32–36.

3. Bronson, *Quest for Full Equality*, 2–3(quoting Jack Baker); Howard Erickson [a.k.a. Lars Bjornson], "New President Greeted by 'So What,'" *Advocate*, May 12, 1971, p. 6.

4. *Baker v. Nelson*, 191 N.W.2d 185, 186 (Minnesota Supreme Court, 1971), appeal dismissed, 409 U.S. 810 (U.S. Supreme Court, 1972). For a history of definitional arguments against same-sex marriage, and some early responses, see William N. Eskridge, Jr., *The Case for Same-Sex Marriage: From Sexual Liberty to Civilized Commitment* (New York: Free Press, 1996), 89–104.

5. For a greater discussion of the definitional objections to same-sex marriage, see chapter 1.

6. For a general discussion of the history and content of the law, see chapter 2.

7. Darren Spedale spent 1996 and 1997 in Denmark on a Fulbright fellowship for the purposes of researching the Scandinavian partnership laws. In addition to the interviews with couples and extensive archive research, he also interviewed activists involved in lobbying for the legislation, members of Parliament connected to the legislation, Scandinavian sociologists, and Danish legal experts, among others. He has presented the results of his research at several universities and conferences, and remains active in following the legal developments related to the Scandinavian partnership laws.

8. Interview by Darren Spedale with Diana Skovgaard and Jean Luscher, Copenhagen, May 1997. Follow-up interview March 2005.

9. Leading articulations of the defense-of-marriage objection to same-sex marriage include the *House Judiciary Committee Report for the Defense of Marriage Act of 1996*, see House Report No. 104–664 (June 1996), 2, 12–15, reprinted in 1996 U.S. Code Congressional and Administrative News 2905, 2915–18; C. Sydney Buchanan, "Same-Sex Marriage: The Linchpin Issue," *University of Dayton Law Review* 10 (1985): 541–67; Teresa Stanton Collett, "Should Marriage Be Privileged? The State's Interest in Childbearing Unions," in Lynn

Wardle et al., eds., *Marriage and Same-Sex Unions: A Debate* (Westport, Conn.: Praeger, 2003), 152–61; Maggie Gallagher, "Normal Marriage: Two Views," in Wardle et al., *Marriage and Same-Sex Unions*, 13–24.

10. Chapter 2 also reports, in detail, the registered partnerships debates in Norway and Sweden and, more summarily, the debates elsewhere in Europe and in Canada. See also Robert Wintemute and Mads Andenaes, eds., *Legal Recognition of Same-Sex Partnerships: A Study of National, European, and International Law* (Oxford: Hart, 2001).

11. Darren Spedale conducted interviews with twenty-four sets of registered partners as part of his research in Scandinavia. For a more detailed description of the interviews, see chapter 3.

12. See chapter 4 for a greater discussion of the benefits of registered partnerships.

13. Stanley Kurtz, "The End of Marriage in Scandinavia," *Weekly Standard*, February 2, 2004. The Scandinavian twist on the defense-of-marriage argument was the main evidence adduced in Congress to support the Federal Marriage Amendment. See chapter 1, which sets forth the Senate debate, as well as House Committee on the Judiciary, *Legal Threats to Traditional Marriage: Implications for Public Policy: Hearing before the Subcommittee on the Constitution of the House Committee on the Judiciary*, 108th Congress, April 22, 2004.

14. Much of the analysis in chapter 5 is drawn from the demographic tables in appendices 4–6.

15. "Robert's Rules of Order," interview by Peter Robinson with Robert Bork, *Uncommon Knowledge*, interview no. 811 (filmed July 16, 2003), available at www.uncommonknowledge.org/800/811.html (viewed August 2005).

16. Drawing from the 2000 census data and empirical follow-ups by private research foundations, chapter 6 documents the number of lesbian and gay households, as well the proportion raising children.

CHAPTER 1

1. Ken Bronson, *A Quest for Full Equality*, manuscript, May 18, 2004, 4–5.

2. Don Kelley, "Homosexuals Should Get Rights," *Los Angeles Collegian* (student newspaper of Los Angeles City College), March 3, 1971, p. 2. See also Kay Tobin and Randy Wicker, *The Gay Crusaders*, 2nd ed. (New York: Arno Press, 1975), 133–55.

3. "Two Girls Held after Marriage to Each Other," November 1947, newspaper article, "Marriage and Relationships" file, Lesbian Herstory Archives, Brooklyn. On the antihomosexual terror after World War II, see William N. Eskridge, Jr., *Gaylaw: Challenging the Apartheid of the Closet* (Cambridge: Harvard University Press, 1999), 57–97; David K. Johnson, *The Lavender Scare: The Cold War Persecution of Gays and Lesbians in the Federal Government* (Chicago: University of Chicago Press, 2004).

4. Harry Hay, "Preliminary Concepts: International Bachelors' Fraternal Order for Peace and Social Dignity" (1950), reprinted in *Radically Gay: Gay Libera-*

tion in the Words of Its Founder, ed.Will Roscoe (Boston: Beacon Press, 1996), 63–76.

5. Donald Webster Cory, *The Homosexual in America: A Subjective Approach* (New York: Greenberg, 1951), chap. 13, "Love Is a Wonderful Thing." For other contemporary examples of homosexual men's impermanent sexual encounters, see Gore Vidal, *The City and the Pillar* (New York: Dutton, 1948), 277; Donald Vining, *A Gay Diary, 1946–1954* (New York: Pepys Press, 1980).

6. Cory, *Homosexual in America,* 231. The quotation is a rhetorical question in Cory's book, but the answer is indicated by Cory's argument that American society should work toward elimination of all its "discriminatory attitudes" toward homosexuals and their unions; 231–33.

7. E. W. Saunders, "Reformers' Choice: Marriage License or Just License?" *One, Inc.* 1, 8 (August 1953): 10–12.

8. "DOB Questionnaire Reveals Some Comparisons between Male and Female Homosexuals," *Ladder* 4, 12 (September 1960): 4–25. See also Gene Damon, "Lesbian Marriage," *Ladder* 2, 11 (August 1958): 12–13.

9. Jody Shotwell, "Gay Wedding," *Ladder* 7, 5 (February 1963): 4–5; Donald W. Cory and John LeRoy, "Homosexual Marriage," *Sexology* 29 (1963): 660–61.

10. Julie Lee, "Economics of Gay Marriage," *Ladder* 13, 7–8 (April–May 1969): 12–15.

11. Compare Martha Shelley, "On Marriage," *Ladder* 13, 1–2 (October–November 1968): 46–47 (quotation in text), with L.B. from Cleveland, Correspondence, *Ladder* 13, 3–4 (December 1968–January 1969): 39 (responding to Shelley).

12. "U.S. Homophile Movement Gains National Strength," *Ladder* 10, 7 (April 1966): 4 (quoting the conference's resolutions).

13. *Loving v. Virginia,* 388 U.S. 1 (U.S. Supreme Court, 1967).

14. Michael Grieg, "Lesbian 'Partners': Gay Married Life," *San Francisco Chronicle,* July 15, 1970, pp. 1, 30 (Los Angeles marriages); "Lesbians Ask Court to Permit Marriage," *San Francisco Chronicle,* November 11, 1970 (Kentucky marriage).

15. Jurisdictional Statement, 7, *Baker v. Nelson,* 409 U.S. 810 (U.S. Supreme Court, 1972) (Docket No. 71–1027).

16. Ibid., 11–12 (Wetherbee's fundamental right-to-marry argument to require state recognition of same-sex marriages), 16–18 (Wetherbee's sex-discrimination argument). Both arguments are further developed, in light of more recent Supreme Court case law, in William N. Eskridge, Jr., *The Case for Same-Sex Marriage: From Sexual Liberty to Civilized Commitment* (New York: Free Press, 1996), 123–52 (fundamental right to marry), 153–82 (sex and sexual orientation discrimination).

17. "Gay Revolution Comes Out," *Rat,* August 12–26, 1969, p. 7 (interview with members of the GLF in counterculture newspaper) (first quotation in text); Ralph Hall, "The Church, State and Homosexuality: A Radical Analysis," *Gay Power,* no. 14 (1970?) (second quotation in text). See also Martha Shelley, "Gay Is Good," in *Out of the Closets: Voices of Gay Liberation,* 2nd ed., ed. Karla Jay and Allen Young (New York: New York University Press, 1992) (reprint of 1st ed., 1972), 31–34. On gay radicalism generally, see Alice Echols, *Daring to Be*

Bad: Radical Feminism in America 1967–1975 (Minneapolis: University of Minnesota Press, 1989); Donn Teal, *Gay Radicals* (New York: Stein and Day, 1971); Tobin and Wicker, *Gay Crusaders.*

18. Demanded by the National Coalition of Gay Organizations, State, Number 8 (February 1972). Federal demand number 4 was: "Elimination of tax inequities victimizing single persons and same-sex couples."

19. *Baker v. Nelson*, 191 N.W.2d 185 (Minnesota Supreme Court,1971), appeal dismissed, 409 U.S. 810 (1972). For lists of the judicial decisions rejecting same-sex marriage claims, see Eskridge, *Case for Same-Sex Marriage*, 232–33 n. 24. For attorney general opinions to the same effect, see 232 n. 23. State laws enacted to make it explicit that marriage is one man, one woman include 1975 Virginia Statutes, chap. 644; 1977 California Statutes, chap. 339; 1977 Minnesota Statutes, chap. 441.

20. On the urgent gay agenda items in the early 1980s, see Randy Shilts, *And the Band Played On: Politics, People, and the AIDS Epidemic* (New York: St. Martin's Press, 1987).

21. Interview by William Eskridge, Jr., with Matt Coles, New York, December 29, 2004; Raymond O'Brien, "Domestic Partnership: Recognition and Responsibility," *San Diego Law Review* 32 (1995): 163–220.

22. Thomas Stoddard, "Why Gay People Should Seek the Right to Marry," *OUT/LOOK*, autumn 1989, pp. 8–12; Paula Ettelbrick, "Since When Is Marriage a Path to Liberation?" *OUT/LOOK*, autumn 1989, pp. 8–12.

23. Stoddard, "Right to Marry," 12; Nan D. Hunter, "Marriage, Law, and Gender: A Feminist Inquiry," *Law and Sexuality* 1 (1991): 9–30.

24. Ettelbrick, "Marriage a Path to Liberation," 11–12. This normalization argument is developed in greater detail by Ruthann Robson, "Assimilation, Marriage, and Lesbian Liberation," *Temple Law Review* 75 (2002): 709–820; Michael Warner, "Normal and Normaller: Beyond Gay Marriage," *Gay Liberation Quarterly* 5 (1999): 119–71.

25. Eskridge, *Case for Same-Sex Marriage*, 1–6, 153–72 (Baehr and Dancel lawsuit in Hawaii); 100–104 (Dean and Gill lawsuit in the District of Columbia). With the support of GAYLAW, Eskridge served as Dean and Gill's attorney at the trial and appellate levels.

26. Cheshire Calhoun, *Feminism, the Family, and the Politics of the Closet: Lesbian and Gay Displacement* (New York: Oxford University Press, 2000), 107–15. See also Morris Kaplan, *Sexual Justice: Democratic Citizenship and the Politics of Desire* (New York: Routledge, 1997).

27. *Baehr v. Lewin*, 852 P.2d 44 (Hawaii Supreme Court, 1993). For analysis of the decisions in the case, see Eskridge, *Case for Same-Sex Marriage*, 130–31, 153–72.

28. Andrew Koppelman, "Interstate Recognition of Same-Sex Marriages and Civil Unions: A Handbook for Judges," *University of Pennsylvania Law Review* 153 (2005): 2143.

29. For the public reaction in Hawaii and the rest of the country, see William N. Eskridge, Jr., *Equality Practice: Civil Unions and the Future of Gay Rights* (New

York: Routledge, 2002), 22–42; David Orgon Coolidge, "The Hawaii Marriage Amendment: Its Origins, Meaning and Fate," *Hawaii Law Review* 22 (2000): 19–118. On DOMA, Public Law No. 104–199, 110 Stat. 2419 (1996), see Andrew Koppelman, *The Gay Rights Question in Contemporary American Law* (Chicago: University of Chicago Press, 2002).

30. "Lesbians Ask Court to Permit Marriage," *Louisville Chronicle,* November 11, 1970 (Miller quotation in text); Eric Pianin, "Hearing Held on Women's Bid to Wed," *Louisville Times,* November 12, 1970 (Hallahan quotation).

31. *Jones v. Hallahan,* 501 S.W.2d 588, 589 (Kentucky Supreme Court, 1973); see also *Singer v. Hara,* 522 P.2d 1187 (Washington Court of Appeals), review denied, 84 Wash. 2d 1008 (Washington Supreme Court, 1974) (also rejecting a same-sex marriage challenge based solely on the traditional definition of marriage).

32. *Baker v. Nelson,* 191 N.W.2d 185, 186 (Minnesota Supreme Court, 1971), appeal dismissed, 409 U.S. 810 (U.S. Supreme Court, 1972) (first quotation in text); Bronson, *Full Equality,* 26 (account of oral argument in *Baker v. Nelson*); Genesis 2:24 (Revised Standard Version) (second quotation in text).

33. Bronson, *Full Equality,* 10–11 (firsthand account of the regents' revocation of McConnell's job offer); *McConnell v. Anderson,* 451 F.2d 193 (U.S. Court of Appeals for the Eighth Circuit, 1971), cert. denied, 405 U.S. 1046 (U.S. Supreme Court, 1972) (overturning trial court decision that had declared the regents' action unconstitutional).

34. Bronson, *Full Equality,* 24–25, 34. Before applying for the license a second time, McConnell legally adopted Baker, who legally changed his name to Pat Lyn McConnell; 23.

35. Grace Lichtenstein, "Homosexual Weddings Stir Controversy," *New York Times,* April 27, 1975, p. B61; "Colorado Gays Marry," *Gay Blade,* May 1975, p. 1.

36. 1975 Opinions of the Attorney General of Colorado (finding no authorization for same-sex marriage in Colorado law), confirmed in *Adams v. Howerton,* 486 F.Supp. 1119 (U.S. District Court for the Central District of California, 1980), affirmed on other grounds, 673 F.2d 1036 (U.S. Court of Appeals for the Ninth Circuit, 1982).

37. Congregation for the Doctrine of the Faith, Declaration *persona humana* (Rome: Vatican, December 29, 1975) (quotation in text); Didi Herman, *The Antigay Agenda: Orthodox Vision and the Christian Right* (Chicago: University of Chicago Press, 1997) (fundamentalist Protestant embrace of the same antihomosexual readings of scripture as that developed in the Vatican pronouncements). For exposition of Roman Catholic natural law, see Germain Grisez, *Living a Christian Life* (Quincy, Ill.: Franciscan Press, 1993). Catholic natural law principles are applied to condemn same-sex marriage in Pope John Paul II, *Letter to Families* (Rome: Vatican, February 2, 1994), and Congregation for the Doctrine of the Faith, *Considerations Regarding Proposals to Give Legal Recognition to Unions between Homosexual Persons* (Rome: Vatican, June 3, 2003).

38. *Howerton,* 486 F.Supp. at 1123.

39. John Finnis, "Law, Morality, and 'Sexual Orientation,'" *Notre Dame Law Review* 69 (1994): 1049–69; Robert George and Gerard Bradley, "Marriage and the Liberal Imagination," *Georgetown Law Journal* 84 (1995): 301–20. See generally Robert George, *In Defense of Natural Law* (Princeton: Princeton University Press, 1999), especially chaps. 8, 9, and 15.

40. Bronson, *Full Equality*, 18 (debate between Baker and Ticen).

41. 1977 Minnesota Statutes, chap. 441. For a recent critique of same-sex marriage largely along slippery slope or Pandora's box lines, see William J. Bennett, *The Broken Hearth: Reversing the Collapse of the American Family* (New York: Doubleday, 2001), 112–13, 135–36.

42. *Dean v. District of Columbia*, Docket Number CA 90–13892 (District of Columbia Superior Court, December 30, 1991) (slip opinion quoted in text), affirmed, 653 A.2d 307 (District of Columbia Court of Appeals, 1995); Eskridge, *Case for Same-Sex Marriage*, 15–50 (short version of the "History of Same-Sex Marriage" submitted to Judge Bowers in *Dean*).

43. The District's Court of Appeals unanimously accepted the District's argument that the Council intended for marriage to be limited to heterosexuals, and (over Judge Ferren's dissent) that this was a reasonable judgment. *Dean*, 653 A.2d 307.

44. Richard A. Posner, *Sex and Reason* (Cambridge: Harvard University Press, 1992), 311–13 (quotations in text).

45. Skovgaard and Luscher interview.

46. Kevin Sack, "Albany GOP Grappling with Gay Rights," *New York Times*, February 6, 1993, p. 23 (Senator Kuhl); *Congressional Record*, 103d Cong., 1st sess., 1993, 139, pt. 12: 17031 (Senator Lott).

47. House Judiciary Committee Report for the Defense of Marriage Act, see House Report No. 104–664 (June 1996), reprinted in 1996 U.S. Code Congressional and Administrative News 2905–47; *Congressional Record*, 104th Congress, 2d sess., 1996, 142, pt. 12: 22,451 (Senator Coates).

48. *Congressional Record*, 104th Congress, 2d sess., 1996, 142, pt. 12: 16,976 (July 11, 1996) and 17,079 (July 12, 1996) (Representative Canady, same language each day).

49. The best review of the scientific theories and evidence as to what causes homosexuality is Edward Stein, *The Mismeasure of Desire: The Science, Theory, and Ethics of Sexual Orientation* (New York: Oxford University Press, 1999). On the dire effects of antigay cultural signals on gay and bisexual youth, see Teemu Ruskola, "Minor Disregard: The Legal Construction of the Fantasy That Gay and Lesbian Youth Do Not Exist," *Yale Journal of Law and Feminism* 8 (1996): 269–332.

50. William N. Eskridge, Jr., "No Promo Homo: The Sedimentation of Antigay Discourse and the Channeling Effect of Judicial Review," *New York University Law Review* 75 (2000): 1327–1411. On Save Our Children, see Dudley Clendenin and Adam Nagourney, *Out for Good: The Struggle to Build a Gay Rights Movement in America* (New York: Simon and Schuster, 1999), 291–330.

51. Harvey Mansfield, "Saving Liberalism from Liberals," *Harvard Crimson*, November 8, 1993 (first quotation in text); Hadley Arkes, "Closet Straight," *National Review*, July 5, 1993, p. 43 (second quotation in text). See generally "The Homosexual Movement: A Response by the Ramsey Colloquium," *First Things*, March 1994, p. 16.

52. *Romer v. Evans*, 517 U.S. 620 (U.S. Supreme Court, 1996); *Congressional Record*, 104th Congress, 2d sess., 1996, 142, pt. 12: 16,972 (Representative Coburn); 22,447 (Senator Byrd).

53. House Judiciary Committee Report, 12–15, reprinted in 1996 U.S. Code Congressional and Administrative News 2916–19.

54. Congressional Record, 104th Congress, 2d sess., 1996, 142, pt. 12: 17,070 (Representative Barr).

55. The argument in text originated with C. Sydney Buchanan, "Same-Sex Marriage: The Linchpin Issue," *University of Dayton Law Review* 10 (1985): 541–67. See also John Witte, Jr., *From Sacrament to Contract: Marriage, Religion, and Law in the Western Tradition* (Louisville, Ky.: Westminster John Knox Press, 1997); Teresa Stanton Collett, "Should Marriage Be Privileged? The State's Interest in Childbearing Unions," in *Marriage and Same-Sex Unions: A Debate*, ed. Lynn Wardle et al. (Westport, Conn.: Praeger 2003), 152–61; Maggie Gallagher, "Normal Marriage: Two Views," in Wardle et al., *Marriage and Same-Sex Unions*, 13–24. Many authors who lament the decline of marriage-as-an-altruistic-space make no negative inferences about gay marriages, however. See, e.g., Margaret Brinig, *From Contract to Covenant: Beyond the Law and Economics of the Family* (Cambridge: Harvard University Press, 2000).

56. Eskridge, *Equality Practice*, 39–40 (the Hawaii campaign against same-sex marriage); Coolidge, "Hawaii Marriage Amendment," 19–118; Kevin Clarkson et al., "The Alaska Marriage Amendment: The People's Choice on the Last Frontier," *Alaska Law Review* 16 (1999): 213–68 (the Alaska campaign).

57. *Baker v. State*, 744 A.2d 864, 881 (Vermont Supreme Court, 1999) (opinion for the Court by Amestoy, C. J.) (quotation in text). Justices Dooley, 889–97, and Johnson, 897–912, fully agreed with the court's invalidation of the discrimination but disagreed as to rationale and (for Justice Johnson) the remedy for the discrimination.

58. *Goodridge v. Department of Public Health*, 798 N.E.2d 941 (Massachusetts Supreme Judicial Court, 2003), reaffirmed, 802 N.E.2d 565 (2004).

59. James C. Dobson, *Marriage under Fire: Why We Must Win This War* (Sisters, Ore.: Multonomah, 2004) (synthesizing the Genesis definition of marriage and the defense-of-marriage arguments).

60. California Domestic Partner Rights and Responsibilities Act of 2003, 2003 California Statutes, chap. 421 (expanding California's 1999 domestic partnership law to provide almost all the same rights and duties of civil marriage to registered partners).

61. Interview by Darren Spedale with Eddie Moris and Jens Boesen, Copenhagen, May 1997.

62. Moris and Boesen interview (quotations in text).

63. See chapter 3 for a brief account of the recognition of same-sex marriages in the Netherlands, Canada, and Spain in particular.

64. For an important endorsement of same-sex marriage as a goal of the LGBT rights movement, see Evan Wolfson (of Lambda), "Crossing the Threshold: Equal Marriage Rights for Lesbians and Gay Men and the Intra-Community Critique," *New York University Review of Law and Social Change* 21 (1994–95): 567–615.

65. Kees Waaldijk, "Small Change: How the Road to Same-Sex Marriage Got Paved in the Netherlands," in *Legal Recognition of Same-Sex Partnerships: A Study of National, European, and International Law,* ed. Robert Wintemute and Mads Andenaes (Oxford: Hart, 2001), 437–64. Wintemute and Andenaes's landmark book is a collection of the papers presented at the 1999 conference.

66. *Halpern v. Attorney General,* Docket Nos. C39172 and C39174 (Ontario Court of Appeal, June 10, 2003); Brief of *Amici Curiae* International Human Rights Organizations and Law Professors (authored by William Eskridge and Robert Wintemute), in *Advisory Opinions to the Senate* (on the acceptability of civil unions, rather than marriage, as the state-recognized institution for same-sex couples), 802 N.E.2d 565 (Massachusetts Supreme Judicial Court, 2004) (No. 09163).

67. See generally Yuval Merin, *Equality for Same-Sex Couples: The Legal Recognition of Gay Partnerships in Europe and the United States* (Chicago: University of Chicago Press, 2002).

68. Ingrid Lund-Andersen, "The Danish Registered Partnership Act, 1989: Has the Act Meant a Change in Attitudes?" in Wintemute and Andenaes, *Legal Recognition of Same-Sex Partnerships,* 417–26.

69. Darren Spedale, "The Sky Hasn't Fallen: It's Been Nine Years Since Denmark Passed Registered Partners Law Allowing Gays to 'Marry,'" *Honolulu Star-Bulletin* (October 24, 1998). Available at http://starbulletin.com/98/10/24/editorial/special.html (viewed September 2005).

70. The claim in text was first made by Darren Spedale, "Nordic Bliss: The Danish Experience with 'Gay Marriage'" (draft circulated summer 1999), manuscript, chap. 3. Although unpublished, the manuscript was widely circulated and its claims reported and endorsed in, among others, Eskridge, *Equality Practice,* 175; Evan Wolfson, *Why Marriage Matters: America, Equality, and Gay People's Right to Marry* (New York: Simon and Schuster, 2004), 220–21.

71. Compare *Lawrence v. Texas,* 539 U.S. 558, 567–72 (U.S. Supreme Court, 2003) (majority opinion, relying on European constitutional court decisions that found consensual sodomy laws inconsistent with a constitutional privacy right), with 598 (Scalia, J., dissenting) (denouncing majority's reliance on "foreign" sources), and 602–3 (arguing that majority would require America to follow Canada in recognizing same-sex marriage).

72. Stanley Kurtz, "The End of Marriage in Scandinavia," *Weekly Standard,* February 2, 2004 (arguing against Spedale's findings). See also Kurtz, "The Mar-

riage Mentality: A Reply to My Critics," *National Review Online* (2004), available at www.nationalreview.com/kurtz/kurtz200405040841.asp (viewed July 2004); Kurtz, "Dutch Debate: Despite a Challenge, the Evidence Stands: Marriage Is in Decline in the Netherlands," *National Review Online* (2004), available at www.nationalreview.com/kurtz/kurtz200407210935.asp (viewed July 2004).

73. House Committee on the Judiciary, *Legal Threats to Traditional Marriage: Implications for Public Policy: Hearing before the Subcommittee on the Constitution of the House Committee on the Judiciary*, 108th Congress, 2d sess., April 22, 2004, 14–16 (testimony of Stanley Kurtz) (first quotation in text); Stanley Kurtz, "Marriage Mentality" (second quotation); Kurtz, "Slipping toward Scandinavia," *National Review Online* (2004), available at www.national review.com/kurtz/kurtz20040202917.asp (viewed July 2004).

74. See, e.g., Kathleen Kiernan, "The Rise of Cohabitation and Childbearing outside Marriage in Western Europe," *International Journal of Law, Policy, and the Family* 15 (2001): 1–21; Kurtz, "Marriage Mentality" (applying the Kiernan model).

75. National Constitution Center, *Same-Sex Marriage: Do We Need a Federal Marriage Amendment?* (May 21, 2004) (statements of former Judge Robert Bork), available at www.constitutioncenter.org/visiting/PublicPrograms/Program Archives/DoWeNeedaFederalMarriageAmendment.shtml (viewed June 2005); Rick Santorum, *It Takes a Family: Conservatism and the Common Good* (Wilmington, Del.: ISI Books, 2005), 27–38; Russell Shorto, "What's Their Real Problem with Gay Marriage? It's the Gay Part," *New York Times Magazine*, June 19, 2005, pp. 34–41, 64–67 (quotation in text, 66).

76. Senate Committee on the Judiciary, *What Is Needed to Defend the Bipartisan Defense of Marriage Act of 1996: Hearing before the Subcommittee on the Constitution of the Senate Committee on the Judiciary*, 108th Congress, 1st sess., September 2003 (statement of Maggie Gallagher). For a nuanced view of the empirical studies of lesbian couples raising children, see Judith Stacey and Timothy Biblarz, "(How) Does Sexual Orientation of Parents Matter?" *American Sociological Review* 66 (2001): 159–78.

77. The revised version of the FMA voted on by the Senate on July 14, 2004, reads: "Marriage in the United States shall consist only of the union of a man and a woman. Neither this Constitution, nor the constitution of any State, shall be construed to require that marriage or the legal incidents thereof be conferred upon any union other than the union of a man and a woman." S.J. Res. 30, 108th Cong., 2d Sess. (introduced March 22, 2004).

78. *Congressional Record*, 108th Congress, 2d sess., 2004, 150, no. 95: S7921 (daily edition July 12, 2004) (Senator Cornyn). For other senators making the Scandinavian version of the defense of marriage argument, ibid., no. 94: S7886 (July 9) (Senate Majority Leader Frist); ibid., no. 95: S7905 (Senator Allard), S7908 (Senator Santorum), S7926 (Senator Brownback); ibid., no. 96: S7967 (July 13) (Senator Inhofe), S8088 (Senator McConnell). Senator Allard inserted Kurtz's leading on-line article into the *Congressional Record*, S8003–7.

79. *Congressional Record*, 108th Congress, 2d sess., 2004, 150, no. 96: S7962 (July 13) (Senator Durbin, Democrat of Illinois), S7962 (Senator Clinton, Democrat of New York) (quotation in text).

80. *Congressional Record*, 108th Congress, 2d sess., 2004, 150, no. 95: S7906–8 (July 12) (Senator Santorum), S7926 (Senator Brownback) (quotation in text); ibid., no. 96: S7967 (July 13) (Senator Inhofe).

81. For the Senate vote rejecting the FMA, 48 to 50, see *Congressional Record*, 108th Congress, 2d sess., 150, no. 97: S8124 (daily ed. July 14, 2004). For debate in the House, compare ibid., no. 121: H7923–24 (daily ed. Sept. 30, 2004) (Rep. DeLay, invoking the experience of Scandinavia and the Netherlands to support the defense-of-marriage argument), with ibid., H7913–15 (Rep. Frank, providing a detailed rebuttal). The House vote, 227 to 186 (short of the two-thirds majority needed to propose a constitutional amendment), is reported, ibid., H7933-34.

82. Eleven states passed referenda in the November 2004 elections: Arkansas, Georgia, Kentucky, Michigan, Mississippi, Montana, North Dakota, Ohio, Oklahoma, Oregon, and Utah. Louisiana and Missouri passed referenda earlier in 2004.

83. Doug Grow, "Gay-Marriage Pioneers, Again," *Star Tribune* (Minneapolis), May 20, 2004, at 2B (describing the new Baker and McConnell lawsuit; quotation in text). Judge Joan Ericksen dismissed Baker and McConnell's complaint on January 3, 2005.

CHAPTER 2

1. On the Axgils' lives and gay activism, see Axel Axgil and Helmer Fogedgaard, *Homofile Kampaar* (Homophile Years of War) (Copenhagen: Grafolio Press, 1985) (in Danish). Also drawn from Axgil's unpublished manuscript *Mit Liv Som Bøsse* (My Life as a Gay Man), first draft dated August 15, 2004 (forthcoming) (in Danish). Note that much of Darren Spedale's research was conducted in the Danish or Norwegian languages.

2. While each of the Nordic nations has its own unique story, many of the arguments raised for and against registered partnership in Denmark were raised in public debates in the other Nordic countries, and therefore our discussion of the public debates in Denmark will also to a large extent apply to the other Nordic countries as well. This also holds true for the discussions in chapter 3 in regard to church weddings, adoption, and artificial insemination.

3. According to Wilhelm Von Rosen, a gay Danish historian, the early part of the twentieth century was a period when "homosexuality had become a loathed, but recognized part of Danish society—something that was not wanted, but had to be recognized as a reality which could not be removed by improved morality, nor (yet) cured by medical interference." From his book *Månens Kulør: Studier I Dansk Bøssehistorie* (The Color of the Moon: Studies in Danish Gay History) (Copenhagen: Rhodos Press, 1993) (in Danish). See also Kenneth Elvebakk, director, *Den Hemmelige Klubben* (The Secret Club) (Norway, 2004)

(documentary depicting antihomosexual attitudes in Norway, Denmark, and Sweden after World War II).

4. In a nutshell, the postwar years in Denmark saw a growth in the undesirable elements that accompany a growing industrial society, including increased crime, materialism, premarital sex, and the disintegration of the family unit (i.e., mother, father, children) as the basic family structure. In response, many sought out others to blame for this deterioration of family values, and the homosexual was one of the main culprits. It was easy to blame gay men, in part, for social problems, as gay men were in no position to become visible or to answer the charges. Thus the urban homosexual became a symbol of all that was wrong and immoral with industrialization, and was used as a scapegoat for many of the modern problems plaguing Danish society in this new age.

5. According to the Ugly Law, enacted in 1961 (Criminal Law 225, sec. 4), not only was the prostitute liable for criminal charges but the person hiring the prostitute was liable for charges as well if the prostitute was under twenty-one. (Previously the one paying was only liable if the prostitute was under eighteen.) The police applied the Ugly Law not only for clear-cut cases of homosexual prostitution but also against gay men who made any kind of present (such as a pack of cigarettes) to a man under the age of twenty-one. Thus, police often set up traps for gay men, and waited outside gay bars to see if a gay man left with a young man who might be under twenty-one. Often these couples were followed by the police for miles, in hopes of seeing any exchange of goods or small change between the two. If any such exchange was seen, an arrest was quickly made. See generally Axgil and Fogedgaard, *Homofile Kampaar*, available at www.sitecenter.dk/zauritsbureau/hjemmeside2/ (in Danish, viewed September 2005). Parliament repealed the law in 1965.

6. "Homosexuelle Ligestilles I Boligkøen" (Homosexuals Equalized in the Housing Queue), *Vennen*, February 1966, p. 51.

7. See, as examples, Ingemar Axlid, "Det Homofile Ægteskab: Vi Blæser På Hvad Folk Siger" (Homophile Marriage: We Don't Care What People Say), *Vennen*, May 1966, 11; Martin Elmer, "Det Homofile Ægteskab" (Homophile Marriage), *Vennen*, March 1967, 7–8; and Per Henri, "Det Homofile Ægteskab: Elleve År, Der Gik Godt" (Homophile Marriage: Eleven Years and Going Well), *Vennen*, April 1967, 20–22.

8. For example, in September 1966, Elmer arranged a meeting with Danish minister of justice Axel Nielsen, to whom he expressed his concerns over the inability of gay couples to marry, and suggested a parliamentary solution. Minister Nielsen, although considered sympathetic to the situation of gay couples, told Elmer that the time was not yet right to approach parliament with a suggestion to legalize gay marriage in any form. Instead, he focused on the inheritance problem, and suggested that the surviving partner could get some inheritance tax relief from the Ministry of Finance on an individual basis. See "Københavns Rådhus Sagde Nej Til At Vie Dem" (Copenhagen's Town Hall Said No to

Marrying Them), *Vennen,* December 1966, p. 7. Also "Siden Sidst" (Since Last Time), *Vennen,* November 1966, p. 2.

9. On the political background of the Danish Marriage Committee, see David Bradley, *Family Law and Political Culture (Scandinavian Laws in Comparative Perspective)* (London: Sweet and Maxwell, 1996), 125–26.

10. For an excellent insider's analysis of the political history of the Danish registered partnership law, see Bent Hansen and Henning Jørgensen, "The Danish Partnership Law: Political Decision Making in Denmark and the National Danish Organization for Gays and Lesbians," in *The Third Pink Book—A Global View of Lesbian and Gay Liberation and Oppression,* ed. Aart Hendriks, Rob Tielman, and Evert van der Veen (Buffalo: Prometheus Books, 1993), 86–99; 90.

11. "Partnerskab" (Partnership), *PAN-Bladet,* June 1974, p. 6.

12. *Ægteskab 1: Ægteskabs Indgåelse* (Marriage 1: Entrance into Marriage), Government Report no. 691 (Copenhagen: Danish National Information Service,1973). See generally Bradley, *Family Law and Political Culture,* 126–28, 151–52, for the political context of the Marriage Committee's work.

13. *Samliv Uden Ægteskab 1* (Cohabitation without Marriage 1), Government Report no. 915 (Copenhagen: Danish National Information Service, 1981).

14. *Kommission Til Belysning Af Bøssers og Lesbiskes Situation I Samfundet* (Commission on the Enlightenment of Gays' and Lesbians' Situation in Society), *PAN-Bladet,* annual report, 1983, p. 7. On the political context for the HomoCommission, see Bradley, *Family Law and Political Culture,* 152–53.

15. As Dorte Jacobsen, a lawyer for LBL, explains of the AIDS crisis: "It turned out, time after time, that many responsible politicians had no knowledge of our way of living, and thereafter, as their knowledge became greater [due to the crisis], their opinions now changed to understand how our human rights for a long time had been trampled on, and [there was now] an acknowledgement that a long line of injustices that had been placed on gays and lesbians must now be addressed." From her unpublished article entitled "Partnerskabsloven, Historien" (The History of the Partnership Law), archives of the LBL, Copenhagen.

16. *Homosexuelle og Arveafgift* (Homosexuals and Inheritance Tax), Government Report no. 1065 (Copenhagen: Danish National Information Service, 1986).

17. *Homosexuelles Vilkår* (The Circumstances of Homosexuals), Government Report no. 1127 (Copenhagen: Danish National Information Service, 1988). See generally Bradley, *Family Law and Political Culture,* 152–54. Bent Hansen, one of the main architects of LBL's strategy to pass the partnership law, has suggested that the minister of justice who seated the HomoCommission chose its members in such a way as to ensure the defeat of the partnership proposal within the commission. See Hansen and Jørgensen, "Danish Partnership Law," 92–94.

18. *Homosexuelles Vilkår,* 122–25.

19. Mads Bue Johnsen, "Registreret Partnerskab" (Registered Partnership), *PAN-Bladet,* January 1988, p. 3.

20. First reading of the registered partnership bill (L 183) in Parliament, March 16, 1988; at pp. 8355–8398 of the Parliamentary Record. Here, at 8355–8358 (Ninn-Hansen).
21. Ibid., 8355–8398. The most amusing argument against the bill came from an MP in the Conservative Party named Kristen Poulsgaard. In his remarks on the bill, he stated that almost half of all men "have a tendency to want to live together man to man" and that passage of the law would have the result of up to 45 percent of Danish men choosing to live together. "Is that what we want?" he asked. "With this bill we are moving in that direction"; 8369.
22. Ibid., 8369 (Ebba Strange).
23. A poll in June 1988 by the AIM polling institute (the Danish branch of AC Nielsen) found that 57 percent of all Danes were in favor of the bill's passage. This surprised many of the bill's opponents, who felt that the majority of Danes were opposed to the legislation. And it contradicted the argument of several legislators who stated that they wouldn't create laws that went against the will of the general public. See "Parteret Registerskab" (Parted Registership), *PAN-Bladet,* June 1988.
24. First reading of the registered partnership bill (L 117) in Parliament, December 15, 1988; at pp. 4290–4310 of the Parliamentary Record. As the bill was re-introduced into Parliament as a new bill after the political crisis, it was given a new bill number and had a new first reading.
25. Ibid., 4298 (Jane Oksen).
26. Ibid., 4301 (Peter Duetoft).
27. LBL to Legal Committee, January 24, 1989, Archives of the Ministry of Justice, Copenhagen.
28. Our account of the rhetoric in popular opposition comes from a series of newspaper clippings on the registered partnership law, Archives of the newspaper *Kristeligt Dagblad,* Copenhagen.
29. Rolf Chr. Slot-Henriksen, "En Lovs Konsekvenser" (A Law's Consequences), *Kristeligt Dagblad,* March 1, 1989. At least one group, Pas På Børn (Look Out for Children), wrote a letter to the Legal Committee warning that the bill would open the doors in Denmark to pedophiles to enter the country as part of a partnership. Pas På Børn to Legal Committee, April 14, 1989, Archives of the Ministry of Justice.
30. The petition was sent to the Legal Committee by priest Jørgen Glenthøj along with a cover letter, April 15, 1989; Archives of the Ministry of Justice.
31. See discussion hereafter on why Denmark was the first country to recognize same-sex unions.
32. Second reading of the registered partnership bill (L 117) in Parliament, May 23, 1989; at pp. 10464–85 of the Parliamentary Record.
33. Ibid., 10473–74 (Inger Stilling Pedersen).
34. Ibid., 10475 (Margrete Auken).
35. Ibid., 10478 (Kristen Poulsgaard).
36. Ibid., 10479 (Peter Duetoft).

37. Third reading of the registered partnership bill (L 117) in Parliament, May 26, 1989; at pp. 10823–40 of the Parliamentary Record.
38. Ibid., 10835 (Inger Stilling Pedersen).
39. Ibid., 10835 (Inger Stilling Pedersen). No public referendum ever took place.
40. Ibid., 10827 (Ebba Strange).
41. Ibid., 10828 (Bjørn Elmquist).
42. Olav Wendelborg, "Dette Har Vi Ventet På Så Længe" (That for Which We Have Waited So Long), *PAN-Bladet,* June 1989, p. 4.
43. Law no. 372 of June 7, 1989.
44. For a discussion of the legal effects of marriage and partnership, see Linda Nielsen, "Family Rights and the 'Registered Partnership' in Denmark," *International Journal of Law and the Family* 4 (1990): 297–307.
45. Chapter 1 recounts the vigorous national reaction in the United States to the possibility of same-sex marriage raised by the Hawaii Supreme Court's decision in *Baehr v. Lewin* (1993). While our discussion here focuses specifically on Denmark, the relationship between religion, culture, and citizenship is quite similar in Sweden, and to a lesser extent in Norway as well.
46. For an excellent overview, in English, of Grundtvig's influence on Denmark, see Steven M. Borish, *The Land of the Living: The Danish Folk High Schools and Denmark's Non-Violent Path to Modernization* (Nevada City: Blue Dolphin, 1991). It is estimated that over the course of his lifetime, Grundtvig's writings added up to the equivalent of approximately 120 volumes; 160.
47. "N.F.S. Grundtvig," in *Denmark,* ed. Thomas Sehested and Carsten Wulff (Copenhagen: Royal Danish Ministry of Foreign Affairs, Department of Information, 2002); available at www.ambwashington.um.dk/en/menu/InformationaboutDenmark/Culture/Literature/N.F.S.Grundtvig.htm (viewed September 2005).
48. Ibid.
49. Ibid.
50. See generally Borish, *Land of the Living.* There are presently about one hundred folk high schools around Denmark, with approximately 2 percent of the Danish population taking a course of study at one of them in any given year.
51. Parliamentary remarks to the debate on Law No. 224 of June 4, 1969.
52. See the second reading of the bill (note 32), at 10476 (Inger Stilling Pedersen). See also the first reading of the bill (note 24) at 4300–4301, in which MP Dorte Bennedsen, also a priest, responded to a theological criticism of the bill as follows: "Nobody can speak on behalf of the [Lutheran] Church. They can speak on their own behalf, but the fact that they happen to be a priest doesn't change a thing."
53. The Danish colony of Greenland also has passed its own registered partnership law, mirroring the Danish law.
54. On Nordic cooperation and parallel movement, especially in the field of family law, see Bradley, *Family Law and Political Culture.* Similarly, gay and lesbian organizations in Scandinavia have had a long history of collaboration. The

Norwegian Society of 1948 was basically established in conjunction with the Society of 1948 in Denmark, and Sweden joined in soon thereafter in 1950 with the creation of RFSL. Furthermore, there is a joint-action organization, the Nordic Council for Homosexuals, that has been in existence since the early 1980s. This Nordic Council offers gay and lesbian activists throughout the Nordic countries the opportunity to share ideas, strategies, and advice with one another.

55. Population, marriage, divorce, and birth trends are documented in appendices 4 (Denmark), 5 (Norway), and 6 (Sweden).

56. Gerd Brantenberg, "Norge Har Fået Ligehed For Loven" (Norway Has Gotten Equality in the Law), *PAN-Bladet*, February 1972, p. 7.

57. *Rapport fra Partnerskapsgruppas Arbeid 1988–1993* (Report from the Partnership Group's Work, 1988–1993) (in Norwegian), Archives of the LLH, Oslo, 5.

58. *The Norwegian Act on Registered Partnerships for Homosexual Couples* (English summary), Report from the Ministry of Children and Family Affairs (Oslo, August 1993), 17.

59. *Rapport fra Partnerskapsgruppas Arbeid 1988–1993*, 5.

60. Ibid., 13. According to the report: "In reality it was taken from the Danish Parliament which decided which law the gay movement in Norway should fight for. When the Danish parliament on the 26 of May, 1989, said yes to the bill on registered partnership, it decided the issue [for Norway], as far as DNF was concerned"; 10.

61. The resolution, a copy of which was sent to the government, read as follows: "DNF-48 calls on the government to prioritize its work in laying out a bill for a partnership law. The Partnership Group will continue/intensify its work to convince [the responsible] government agency and government minister to go in for our principles. A discussion of another suggestion is as of today nonexistent." Ibid., 11.

62. Ibid., 14–20.

63. Ibid., 20. Additional information on "Deep Throat" from an interview by Darren Spedale with Kjell Erik Øie, former chairman of LLH and one of the main architects behind LLH's partnership strategy, Oslo, May 1997.

64. Ibid., 24.

65. Ibid., 30–32. Also from Øie interview.

66. Ibid.

67. *The Norwegian Act on Registered Partnerships for Homosexual Couples* (English summary), 9.

68. Ibid., 22–23.

69. Ibid., 10.

70. Ibid., 11.

71. Ibid., 36.

72. Ibid., 11.

73. Ibid., 13.

74. Inge-Lise Paulsen, "Til Lykke Norge" (Congratulations Norway), *PAN-Bladet*, Anniversary Edition, 1993, p. 11.

75. Øie interview.
76. Ibid.
77. Act No. 40 of April 30, 1993. Regarding the ceremony, see Søren Skov, "Kun Homofile—Første Par Registreret I Oslo" (Only Homophiles—First Couple Registered in Oslo), *PAN-Bladet,* September 1993, p. 3.
78. Sweden even passed legislation in 1987 allowing for "the internment of HIV-positive persons if the Office of Disease Control deemed that an individual was likely not to heed instruction regarding safe sex." Jens Rydström, "The Ombudsman for Gays and Lesbians: The Swedish Welfare State and its Tolerance of Deviation." *Swedish Institute,* March 2000, available at www.sweden .se/templates/cs/Article____2297.aspx (viewed September 2005).
79. SFS 1987:232.
80. Interview by Darren Spedale with Stig-Åke Petersson, former chairman of RFSL and secretary of Sweden's 1977 Parliamentary Commission on Homosexuality, Stockholm, June 1997.
81. "Homosexuelle Ligestilles I Boligkøen" (see note 6).
82. The Swedish Parliament's resolution may be found at the following Parliamentary record location. 1973: LU20, p. 116.
83. *Homosexuella och Samhället* (Homosexuals and Society), Statens Offentliga Utredningar, The State Public Publisher (SOU), 1984: 63.
84. Ibid.
85. Ibid.
86. Ibid.
87. The Homosexual Cohabitees Act is Act 813 of 1987.
88. SOU 1993: 98.
89. Ibid., English summary, 21.
90. Ibid., 28–29.
91. Ibid., 28–29.
92. Ibid., 30. The "church weddings" issue has changed in context in Sweden, as the Swedish Church was separated from the state in 2000. Nevertheless, the Swedish government continues to play some role in the Swedish Church, including the collection of voluntary church dues.
93. Ibid.
94. Ibid., 33–34.
95. Petersson interview.
96. Sweden has in recent years eliminated its restrictions on adoption and assisted reproduction services for same-sex couples. See chapter 3 for a discussion of the Swedish reforms.
97. For example, in 1983 a march to the Icelandic Embassy by LGBT activists was held in Copenhagen to protest the fact that Icelandic gays and lesbians were being prohibited by many media outlets in Iceland from using classifieds or other public forums to advertise LGBT activities—such outlets stating that such announcements went against public decency. "Til Islands Ambassadør" (To the Ambassador of Iceland), *PAN-Bladet,* June 1983, p. 4.

98. Interviews by Darren Spedale with Gudni Baldursson, the first chairperson of Samtokin '78, and with Lana Eddudottir, former chairperson of Samtokin '78, Reykjavik, July 1997.

99. Iceland does have a Christian Democratic Party, a new party similar to those fundamentalist parties in the other Nordic countries, which took part in national elections in 1995 and 1999—however, it only won a total of 0.19 percent and 0.27 percent of the votes in those elections, respectively.

100. Eddudottir interview. As was not the case in other Nordic countries, registered partnership had the government's support soon after its introduction. As there had been little discussion about the registered partnership law prior to its introduction, the government's positive attitude toward the legislation had a positive effect on the mainstream Icelander's view of the legislation. According to Lana Edudottir, "most Icelanders had never thought about the issue—but when they heard the prime minister and other prominent people saying 'Yes, this is a good thing,' then Icelanders thought, 'Yes, of course this is a good thing—I just hadn't thought about it.'"

101. Eddudottir interview.

102. Act No. 87 of June 12, 1996. The Icelandic partnership law was amended in 2000 to permit stepchild adoption by the registered partner of the biological parent.

103. Private memo on the Finnish Registered Partnership Law, by Hannele Lehtikuusi, former chairperson of SETA, written early 1997. This law barring encouragement of homosexual activity remained on the books until June of 1998, when it was repealed; private memo, Helsinki, p. 5.

104. Interview by Darren Spedale with Hannele Lehtikuusi, Helsinki, August 1997.

105. Ibid.

106. Lehtikuusi, private memo, 1.

107. Ibid., 1–4.

108. Act 950/2001. Like Iceland, Finland has come a long way in a short time, in regard to acceptance of gays and lesbians by mainstream society. The president of Finland since 2000, Tarja Halonen, once held the position of chairperson of SETA. While not homosexual, she was very involved with SETA's work to change attitudes about gays and lesbians. While this fact was well known among Finns, she was nonetheless elected by a majority of voters in the 2000 presidential election. See "Tarja Halonen and Gay Rights," available at www.helsinki.fi/%7Eeisaksso/tarja.html (viewed September 2005).

109. The best introduction to country-by-country efforts to persuade parliaments and courts to accord equal marriage rights to lesbian and gay couples remains Robert Wintemute and Mads Andenaes, eds., *Legal Recognition of Same-Sex Partnerships: A Study of National, European, and International Law* (London: Hart, 2001), which is (unfortunately) partially outdated for important developments in Portugal, the United Kingdom, and Canada. The best recent survey is Kees Waaldijk, *More or Less Together: Levels of Legal Consequences of Marriage, Cohabitation, and Registered Partnership for Different-Sex and Same-Sex*

Partners, a Comparative Study of Nine European Countries (2005), available at www.ined.fr/publications/collections/dossiersetrecherches/125.pdf (viewed August 2005). See also Eskridge, *Equality Practice,* 86–126; Yuval Merin, *Equality for Same-Sex Couples: The Legal Recognition of Gay Partnerships in Europe and the United States* (Chicago: University of Chicago Press, 2002).

110. Decision 14/1995, Constitutional Court of Hungary, March 13, 1995, essentially ratified and codified by the Hungarian Parliament's Act of 1996: XLII Law 1-3 (May 21, 1996). For speculation about the motivations of the judges and legislators (i.e., to impress the European Union with how liberal Hungary is), see Lilla Farkas, "Nice on Paper: The Aborted Liberalization of Gay Rights in Hungary," in Wintemute and Andenaes, *Legal Recognition of Same-Sex Partnerships,* 563.

111. *El-Al Israel Airlines v. Danilowitz,* Israel High Court of Justice 721/94, 48 Piskei-Din 749 (May 4, 1994), analyzed in Aeyal M. Gross, "Challenges to Compulsory Heterosexuality: Recognition and Non-Recognition of Same-Sex Couples in Israeli Law," in Wintemute and Andenaes, *Legal Recognition of Same-Sex Partnerships,* 391–414; *National Coalition for Gay and Lesbian Equality v. Minister of Homes Affairs,* Constitutional Court of South Africa (December 2, 1999), analyzed in Eskridge, *Equality Practice,* 107; *M. v. H.,* Supreme Court of Canada, 171 D.L.R.4th 577 (March 18, 1999), decision and responsive legislation analyzed in Eskridge, *Equality Practice,* 107–12.

112. *Vilela v. Weil,* Cour de cassation, Chambre civile 3e, Decembre 17, 1997, Bull. Civ. 1997.III.151, No. 225, Dalloz.1998, Jur.111 (court decision refusing to provide property benefits for same-sex couples), analyzed in Daniel Borrillo, "The 'Pacte Civil de Solidarite' in France: Midway between Marriage and Cohabitation," in Wintemute and Andenaes, *Legal Recognition of Same-Sex Partnerships,* 475–92; Hoge Raad (Dutch Supreme Court), RvdW 1990, nr. 176 (October 19, 1990), analyzed in Kees Waaldijk, "Towards Full Equality in Dutch Law for Same-Sex Partners and Their Children," information brochure no. 6 (Amsterdam: Dutch Association for the Integration of Homosexuality COC, July 1998).

113. The Netherlands's Registered Partnership Law consists of Act of July 5, 1997 and Act of December 17, 1997, analyzed in Kees Waaldjik, "How the Road to Same-Sex Marriage Got Paved In the Netherlands," in Wintemute and Andenaes, *Legal Recognition of Same-Sex Partnerships,* 437–64. Whereas marriage in the Netherlands can only be dissolved by a court, registered partnerships can be dissolved without a court if both partners agree on a plan of dissolution (which includes disposal of assets, etc.). If such agreement cannot be reached, however, the parties to a registered partnership will use the court system for dissolution of a registered partnership, along the lines of divorce in a traditional marriage.

114. The French PaCS statute is Loi no. 89-462, November 15, 1999, analyzed in Borrillo, "'Pacte Civil de Solidarité' in France."

115. The legislative history of the French PaCS legislation can be viewed at www.legifrance.gouv.fr/html/frame_codes_lois_reglt.htm (viewed November 1, 2000). The quotations in text are taken from Borillo, "Pacte Civil de Solidarité."

116. Code civile, new article 515-1 (added by PaCs statute, defining PaCs); new article 515-4 (defining mutual support obligations for couples joined in a PaCs).

117. On the German life partnership law, see Gerald Pilz, "The Details of the Registered Partnership in Germany," in *ILGA-Europe Euroletter,* no. 84 (November 2000), available at www.qrd.org/qrd/www/orgs/ILGA/euroletter (visited August 2005). On Portugal's de facto unions, see Miguel Freitas, "The New Portuguese Law on Same-Sex Unions," *ILGA-Europe Euroletter,* no. 88 (May 2001).

118. "UK Government: Landmark Civil Partnership Law Receives Royal Assent," *M2 Presswire,* November 19, 2005 (describing UK's Civil Partnership Law), with further information referenced to www.dti.gov.uk (viewed August 2005); Sue Leeman, "British Government Says Same-Sex Partnerships Will Begin in December," *Associated Press,* February 21, 2005 (government plans for implementing partnership legislation).

119. The referendum passed with 58% of the national vote. For more information, see the website of the Swiss Federal Department of Justice and Police at http://www.ofj.admin.ch/e/index.html (viewed November 2005). Also "Gay Couples Win Partnership Rights" on the website of swisspolitics.org at http://www.swisspolitics.org/en/news/index.php?page=dossier_artikel&story _ id = 5845155&dossier_id=80 (viewed November 2005).

120. For more information on the New Zealand law, see the website dedicated to information on the Civil Union Act at http://www.civilunions.org.nz (viewed November 2005). The Australian state of Tasmania became the first Australian state to recognize civil unions in the beginning of 2004, while other Australian states offer lesser recognition of same-sex couples. See "Australia's First Civil Unions" on 365Gay.com at http://www.sodomylaws.org/world/australia/ ausnews003.htm (viewed November 2005). In March 2004, a court in the Brazilian state of Rio Grande do Sul enacted civil unions for same-sex couples in that state, granting gay and lesbian couples a number of marriage rights in areas like inheritance, child custody, insurance benefits and pensions. See "Brazilian Go-Ahead for Gay Unions" on the website of the BBC at http:// news.bbc.co.uk/1/hi/world/americas/3534959.stm (viewed November 2005). And in Argentina, initiatives in Buenos Aires and Rio Negro grant same-sex couples recognition and certain benefits.

121. As the Netherlands does not have a state church, church weddings were not an issue that needed to be addressed by Parliament. Furthermore, there is no legislation prohibiting artificial insemination in the Netherlands, as discussed earlier.

122. See Text of Dutch Law on Adoption by Persons of the Same Sex, summary and translation by Professor Kees Waaldijk (January 11, 2001), available at http://ruljis.leidenuniv.nl/user/cwaaldij/www/ (viewed May 2001) (quotation in text).

123. Waaldijk, "Same-Sex Marriage," 447.

124. Ibid.

125. Like the Dutch law, paternity rights of the partner of a new mother in Belgium are not assumed on the child's birth. However, Belgium has not yet allowed same-sex couples any adoption rights (including stepchild adoption), and therefore lags behind the Netherlands on issues of the rights of same-sex partners with children in such families.

126. Tim Naumetz, "158–133: MPs Approve Gay Marriage," *Ottawa Citizen*, June 29, 2005 (background of gay marriage legislation in Canada).

127. "Spanish Parliament Approves Gay Marriage," *Agence France Presse*, June 30, 2005 (quotations in text).

128. Tracy Wilkinson, "The World: A Long Road from Fascist Era to Gay Marriage," *Los Angeles Times*, July 18, 2005 (quotation in text).

129. See Kees Waaldijk, "The Law of 'Small Change': How the Road to Same-Sex Marriage Got Paved in the Netherlands," in Wintemute and Andenaes, *Legal Recognition of Same-Sex Partnerships*, 437–64, as well as Eskridge, *Equality Practice*, 147–58, 188–96.

130. M. V. Lee Badgett, "Predicting Partnership Rights: Applying the European Experience to the United States," draft, March 31, 2005. We are grateful to Professor Badgett for sharing this paper with us, and for the valuable theorizing in this work.

131. The "model" suggested in text is a synthesis of the past regulatory efforts approach suggested in Waaldijk, "Small Change," and Eskridge, *Equality Practice*, and the social factors approach suggested in Badgett, "Predicting Partnership Rights."

CHAPTER 3

1. For the purpose of analyzing the social effects of same-sex unions, Darren Spedale conducted extensive in-person interviews with twenty-four sets of registered partners throughout Denmark. The couples, including fourteen male and ten female couples, were chosen to reflect a diverse set of demographic backgrounds, including geographic location, age, education, occupation, and nationality. Ages of the individuals interviewed are given as of the time the interview was conducted. Most of these original interviews were conducted in 1997, and many of them have been supplemented by follow-up interviews with the couples in 2005.

2. Interview by Darren Spedale with Peter Mols and Peer Toft, Copenhagen (quoting Mols), November 1997.

3. Statistics Denmark, the statistical branch of the country's bureaucracy, the source of our data on the number of registered partners, is not able to provide information regarding the number of partnerships contracted each year.

4. The number of Danes in a marriage also includes individuals whose status is married but separated, as Statistics Denmark does not separate the latter couples out of the category.

5. For statistical analysis, we have compiled available information regarding the demographics of registered partners in Denmark, Norway, and Sweden. Unless otherwise indicated, the sources of our data are public statistics aggregated and maintained by Statistics Denmark, Statistics Norway, and Statistics Sweden, the statistical branch of each country's bureaucracy. These state organizations record vital statistics regarding residents in their respective countries in several fields that are useful to our analysis.

   While these three countries have methods of recording data that are very similar to one another, there are some slight differences in both the manner of recording data between the countries that we shall point out as applicable. In addition, there are certain types of information that are recorded by one country that may not be recorded by the others. Because reporting times differ between these three countries, our data regarding registered partnership from each of these countries are as follows unless otherwise noted: Denmark, 1989–2003; Norway, 1993–2001; Sweden, 1995–2002.

6. No one knows exactly what percentage of a country's adult population is lesbian or gay, but the leading European studies suggest 2–3 percent. See John DeLamater, "Review: The NORC Sex Survey," *Science*, October 20, 1995, pp. 501–3 (reviewing recent studies in the United States and Europe).

7. The survey of 812 Danes was conducted in Danish using on-line polling technology. The nonrandom sample of respondents was solicited via gay and lesbian publications throughout Denmark; 91.6 percent of respondents classified themselves as gay or lesbian, 6.7 percent as bisexual, and 1.6 percent as heterosexual; 96.4 percent of respondents declared themselves as having a Danish nationality, 1.8 percent of another Nordic nationality, and 1.8 percent of a non-Nordic nationality.

8. In our on-line survey, 77.3 percent of the 764 respondents to this question stated that "registered partnership" and "marriage" were about the same; 18.7 percent stated that they were not; and 3.9 percent were unsure; 78.9 percent of all respondents stated that they used words such as "marriage" and "spouse" to describe those in registered partnerships.

   We hypothesize, however, that the recent growth in the number of countries that offer "marriage" as opposed to "registered partnership" is likely to have the effect of increasing the distinction among Scandinavians between the two, and is likely to heighten the demand for "marriage" in the near future.

9. In our on-line survey, 76.2 percent of the 576 respondents who had never been in a registered partnership stated that they would enter into a registered partnership if they found "the right person"; 5.6 percent said they would not; 18.2 percent were unsure. Those in the latter two categories were asked if they would get married if the registered partnership law were changed to full and equal marriage; 18.9 percent said yes, 32.3 percent said no, and 48.8 percent responded that they were unsure.

10. Mols and Toft interview (quoting Mols).

11. Interview by Darren Spedale with Anne-Vibeke Fleischer and Elisabeth Bjerre Knudsen, Copenhagen, July 1997 (quoting Fleischer).

12. Interview by Darren Spedale with Uffe Størner and Kaj Kristensen, Frederikshavn, Denmark, September 1997 (quoting Størner).

13. Interview by Darren Spedale with Birgitte Haase and Kirsten Jepsen, Haderslev, Denmark, October 1997.

14. For Danish registration after 1999, see appendix 3A. For Swedish registration after 2002, see appendix 3C.

15. Sentiments that registered partnership is too tied to patriarchal marriage were often expressed in gay and lesbian publications. See Vivi Svensson, "Lesbiske— BRYD med det Registrerede Partnerskab" (Lesbians—Break Away From Registered Partnership), *PAN-Bladet*, December 1989, p. 4.

16. Fleischer and Knudsen interview (quoting Fleischer).

17. Compare Nan D. Hunter, "Marriage, Law, and Gender: A Feminist Inquiry," *Law and Sexuality* 1 (1991): 9–30, who argues that same-sex marriage may undermine rigid gender roles within different-sex marriages as well.

18. Mols and Toft interview.

19. Toft and Mols interview (quoting Toft).

20. Interview by Darren Spedale with Claus Rasmussen and Niels Andersen, Kaas, Denmark, August 1997 (quoting Andersen).

21. We can do little more than speculate about the number of gay people or gay relationships, because the Scandinavian governments do not keep statistical information on persons who classify themselves as gay or lesbian, and no studies have been conducted to calculate the number of same-sex couples living together in these countries.

22. On the relatively greater number of sex partners for gay men, see, e.g., Anne M. Johnson, "Social and Behavioural Aspects of the HIV Epidemic—A Review," *Journal of the Royal Historical Society* (Statistics in Society), series A, 151 (1988): 102. See also Jonathan Rauch, *Gay Marriage: Why It Is Good for Gays, Good for Straights, and Good for America* (New York: Times Books, 2004), 138–58, for a sober and fact-based analysis of the "gay men are wildly promiscuous" trope. For the way registration as partners has changed the attitudes of some gay men in Denmark, see chapter 4.

23. According to the Vital Statistics Information Manager for the Vermont Department of Health, 4611 female couples and 2072 male couples joined in civil unions between July 2000 and December 2003. See www.healthyvermonters.info/hs/stats/VSB2000/io4.htm, and subsequent years (viewed February 15, 2006).

24. The data and percentages of registered partners discussed in text are taken from appendices 3A–C, which report registration information for Denmark, Norway, and Sweden.

25. For the AIDS epidemic in Denmark, see Lennholm Bo, "HIV I Norden: Danmark ärt drabbat men Finland har en unlikt," *Äkartidningen* 89 (1992): 1908–10. For the terrifying path of AIDS in the United States, partially repli-

cated in Europe, see Randy Shilts, *And the Band Played On: Politics, People, and the AIDS Epidemic* (New York: St. Martin's Press, 1987).

26. Data drawn from Statistics Denmark. In 2003 (the most recent year available), men in the private sector earned an average of 229.93 Danish crowns per worked hour, while women earned 197.79 Danish crowns per worked hour.

27. Gunnar Andersson, Turid Noack, Ane Seierstad, and Harald Weedon-Fekjær, "The Demographics of Same-Sex 'Marriages' in Norway and Sweden," in *Same-Sex Couples, Same-Sex Partnerships and Homosexual Marriages—A Focus on Cross-National Differences*, ed. Marie Digoix and Patrick Festy (Paris: Institut National d'Études Démographiques, 2004), 247–66; 254 (point in text), available at www .ined.fr/publications/collections/dossiersetrecherches/124.pdf (viewed August 2005). Also see the journal *Demography* for an updated version of this article.

28. Interview by Darren Spedale with William Waite and Ken Nielsen, Copenhagen, June 1997 (quoting Nielsen).

29. For an example of women's less dogmatic approach to an exact sexual orientation, compare Robin West, "Sex, Reason, and a Taste for the Absurd," *Georgetown Law Journal* 81 (1993): 2433 (reviewing Richard Posner, *Sex and Reason* [1992] and expressing the view that she had no view about her exact sexual orientation), with Richard A. Posner, *Overcoming Law* (Cambridge: Harvard University Press, 1997), 573 (expressing shock that West would not know her Kinsey number).

30. For the greater gender parity in recent years in Denmark, Norway, and Sweden, see appendices 3A–C. Kees Waaldijk of the University of Leiden provided us with data for Iceland. In the first three years of registration (1997–99), twenty-nine of the fifty-six Icelandic partnerships were female.

31. Danish statistics from Statistics Denmark. Swedish statistics from Andersson et al., "Demographics of Same-Sex 'Marriages' in Norway and Sweden," 254.

32. Mols and Toft interview (quoting Mols).

33. Mols and Toft interview (quoting Toft).

34. Andersson et al., "Demographics of Same-Sex 'Marriage' in Norway and Sweden," 254.

35. For historical examples of May-October male romances, see, e.g., Kenneth J. Dover, *Greek Homosexuality* (London: Duckworth, 1978) (pedagogical but sometimes romantic attachments between older and younger men in ancient Greece); Bret Hinsch, *Passions of the Cut Sleeve: The Male Homosexual Tradition in China* (Berkeley: University of California Press, 1990) (May-October male relationships in China); Charley Shively, *Calamus Lovers: Walt Whitman's Working Class Camerados* (San Francisco: Gay Sunshine, 1987) (Whitman's male relationships were with younger, less educated, working-class men).

36. Danish statistics from Statistics Denmark; Swedish and Norwegian statistics from Andersson et al., "Demographics of Same-Sex 'Marriage' in Norway and Sweden," 254. Sweden has a greater number of urban areas outside of Stockholm—including Gothenburg and Malmo—than does Norway, so if

other such large urban areas were taken into account, the Swedish number would be more along the lines of the Norwegian number.

One might also assume that, of the people not counted by national statistical agencies because of their status as foreign nationals, most live in urban areas. This follows from an assumption that the majority of gay couples in which one is a foreigner live in urban areas.

37. Andersson et al., "Demographics of Same-Sex 'Marriage' in Norway and Sweden," 254.

38. From the report *Registreret Partnerskab, Samliv og Velsignelse* (Registered Partnership, Cohabitation and Blessings) (Aarhus, Denmark: Diocese of Aarhus, 1997). This study was prepared by the church committee investigating church blessings for registered partnerships; 34. The figures for the general population are drawn from the 1995 Danish census, while those for registered partners are drawn from the report. There is no reason to believe that the general population statistics and those of registered partners have changed significantly since that time. We note, however, that these figures are not controlled for a possible age effect between the compared groups.

39. Andersson et al., "Demographics of Same-Sex 'Marriage' in Norway and Sweden," 254.

40. Ibid., 255.

41. Ibid.

42. *Registreret Partnerskab, Samliv og Velsignelse*, 35.

43. The breakup data for registered partnerships are taken from Statistics Norway and Statistics Sweden.

44. Andersson et al., "Demographics of Same-Sex 'Marriage' in Norway and Sweden," 258–61. Although some have supposed that many of the early-registering couples may have been caught up in the excitement about the possibility of marriage, and therefore might be at greater risk of a divorce, the data do not bear this out. Overall, those who entered into registered partnership in the first year of its existence in Norway or Sweden had about the same likelihood of divorce as those who registered in later periods. The "pioneering" male couples in Norway and Sweden were at a slightly higher risk of divorce relative to those who entered the institution later, but female couples were less likely than later registrants to be at risk of divorce.

45. Ibid., table 3.

46. Ibid., table 3.

47. The "what is best for the child" language comes from the UN Convention on the Rights of the Child, to which the Scandinavian countries are signatories. Article 3 of the Convention states: "In all actions concerning children, whether undertaken by public or private social welfare institutions, courts of law, administrative authorities or legislative bodies, the best interests of the child shall be a primary consideration." On the basis of this article, consider the following language from the Swedish Report from the Commission on the Situation of Children in Homosexual Families: "The best interest of the child should

guide all considerations concerning adoption. No other interests may be put before or regarded as equally important as the consideration of the best interest of the child." *Children in Homosexual Families, Summary,* Report from the Commission on the Situation of Children in Homosexual Families (Stockholm: Swedish Government Official Reports, SOU 2001:10), English summary, p. 20.

48. However, in respect to the Danish "what is best for the child" policy, surviving nonbiological parents could eventually obtain legal rights over the child. If the biological parent in the partnership should die, and both the registered partner and the other biological parent desired to obtain custody of the child, it would be up to the child authorities to decide what is best for the child. For example, if the child had lived his or her whole life with the two partners and recognized them as his or her two parents, this would strongly support the efforts of the registered partner to obtain custody, even if the other biological parent had legally retained custody since the child's birth. However, in such a situation where the other biological parent still had custody, the registered partner would have had to make a strong case to convince the authorities to let him or her obtain custody.

  If the biological parent died, and nobody else had legal custody of the child, the case for the registered partner to obtain custody would have been easier. In addition, a biological parent with sole custody can write up a "child testament" to be applied in the case of his or her death, in which he or she points out who he or she wishes to have custody of the child in the case of his or her death or incapacitation. This document is nevertheless not legally binding, and could be rejected if the authorities feel that it would not be in the child's best interest.

49. Statistics available on the website of the Danish National Board of Adoption, www.adoptionsnaevnet.dk/regler/default.htm.

50. Linda Nielsen, "Family Rights and the 'Registered Partnership' in Denmark," *International Journal of Law and the Family* 4 (1990): 305. Additional information on government policy from interview by Darren Spedale with Jonna Waage, civil servant at the Denmark Ministry of Justice, Copenhagen, August 1997.

51. Of the 370 respondents under age thirty who were surveyed in our poll of Danish gays and lesbians, 339 responded to the question "If you don't have children, are you planning to have children?" They responded as follows: 27.4 percent, "yes, either as a single parent or in a relationship"; 37.5 percent, "yes, but only in a relationship"; 18 percent, "no"; 14.2 percent, unsure; 2.9 percent, wanted to consider other options (e.g., a gay man fathering a child with a lesbian woman).

52. Haase and Jepsen interview (quoting Haase).

53. Haase and Jepsen interview (quoting Jepsen).

54. Haase and Jepsen interview (quoting Jepsen).

55. Mols and Toft interview (quoting Mols).

56. On the biological and legal complications for gay men wanting to have biological children, see John Robertson, "Gay and Lesbian Access to Assisted Reproductive Technology," *Case Western Reserve Law Review* 55 (2004): 323–72.

57. Mols and Toft interview (quoting both Toft and Mols); Haase and Jepsen interview (quoting Haase).

58. See the debate on Bill L70, in its second reading on May 18, 1999. The text of the debate may be found online at the Denmark Parliament's website at www.folketinget.dk (in Danish). The bill, as passed on May 20, 1999, and effective as of July 1, 1999, also expands the eligibility for entry into a registered partnership to include citizens from countries with similar marriage or marriage-equivalent legislation for same-sex couples. It also opens up eligibility for a couple where neither has the requisite citizenship but both have lived in Denmark for at least two years prior to registration.

59. Ibid.

60. Ibid.

61. Ibid.

62. Stian Sigurdsen, "Stedbarns Adopsjon" (Stepchild Adoption), located on LLH's website at www.llh.no/Jus+Law/Adopsjon/?module=Articles;action =Article.publicShow;ID=241 (viewed September 2005).

63. *Children in Homosexual Families, Summary*, Report from the Commission on the Situation of Children in Homosexual Families (Stockholm: Swedish Government Official Reports, SOU 2001:10), 4 (quotation in text).

64. Ibid., 6–7.

65. Ibid., 9–10.

66. Ibid., 13.

67. Ibid., 17–18.

68. Ibid., 18–19.

69. Swedish law 2002:603, amending the Registered Partnership Act, June 13, 2002.

70. Extensive information on the history of assisted reproduction services for lesbians in Denmark is located on LBL's website, available at www.lbl.dk. Norwegian law is worded in a similar manner: "Assisted reproduction may only be carried out on women who are married or cohabit with a man in a marriage-like relationship." The Norwegian Biotechnology Law, Section 2-2; Law No. 2003-12-05-100, effective as of Jan 1, 2004.

71. Law No. 460 of June 10, 1997.

72. Haase and Jepsen interview (quoting Haase).

73. Interview by Darren Spedale with Steffen Jensen, former member of the Executive Board of LBL and member of the Board of the International Lesbian and Gay Association, European Region, Copenhagen, August 1999.

74. Bill L53, rejected June 19, 1998.

75. Bill L115 of the 2004–5 legislative session. It had its first hearing on April 27, 2005.

76. Interview by Darren Spedale with Margrete Auken, Copenhagen, August 1997.

77. Magnus Korkala, "Lesbian Couples Get Right to Insemination at Swedish Hospitals," press release from Swedish Parliament, May 24, 2005.

78. Martin Strecker-Adel, "God Is My Shepherd (and Knows I'm a Homo)," *PAN-Bladet, Guide to Gay Denmark*, 1995, p. 4.

79. Mols and Toft interview (quoting both Toft and Mols).
80. Interview by Darren Spedale with Lars Henriksen and Jan Lorenzen, Farm near Holstebro, Denmark, July 1997 (quoting Henriksen).
81. Henriksen and Lorenzen interview (quoting Henriksen).
82. Anderson and Rasmussen Interview (quoting Anderson).
83. From the *Registreret Partnerskab, Samliv og Velsignelse*, 36. For background, see note 38.
84. Interview by Darren Spedale with Ivan Larsen, an openly gay priest who has been one of LBL's main activists on the subject of church blessings for same-sex couples, Copenhagen, June 1997. Larsen and his partner also served as grand marshals for New York City's Gay Pride Parade in 1990, in honor of the opening up of same-sex "marriage" in Denmark.
85. For other examples, see Strecker-Adel, "God Is My Shepherd," 4.
86. "Voldsom Debat om Kirkelig Velsignelse af Homopar" (Violent Debate Over Church Blessings of Homosexual Couples), *PAN-Bladet*, February 1995, p. 4.
87. For examples of gay-friendly readings of the Bible that are just as learned as the gay-hostile readings emphasized by some traditionalists, see, e.g., Derrick Sherwin Bailey, *Homosexuality and the Western Christian Tradition* (London: Green, 1955); Eugene F. Rogers, Jr., *Sexuality and the Christian Body: Their Way unto the Triune God* (New York: Blackwell, 1999), 17–60. For a learned response to such gay-friendly readings, see Bernadette J. Brooten, *Love between Women: Early Christian Responses to Female Homoeroticism* (Chicago: University of Chicago Press, 1996). See especially Brooten's reading of Romans 1:19–32, 215–302.
88. Fleisher and Knudsen interview (quoting Fleisher).
89. *Registreret Partnerskab, Samliv og Velsignelse*, 100–101.
90. Ibid., 54.
91. Ibid., 101.
92. Ibid., 88–99.
93. Ibid., 101.
94. Interview by Darren Spedale with Peter Mols and Peer Toft. October 2005 (quoting Mols).

CHAPTER 4

1. This account is taken from an interview by Darren Spedale with Lars and Johnnie Fledelius, Copenhagen, January 1997.
2. Ibid. (quoting Johnnie Fledelius).
3. The "mocking burlesque" language is from Hadley Arkes, "Closet Straight," *National Review*, July 5, 1993, p. 43. Chapter 1 outlines the stamp-of-approval objection in some detail.
4. On the policy goals of civil marriage, see David Chambers, "What If? The Legal Consequences of Marriage and the Legal Needs of Lesbian and Gay Male Couples," *Michigan Law Review* 95 (1996): 447.

5. Fledelius and Fledelius interview (quoting both Lars and Johnnie Fledelius).

6. The survey of 812 Danes was conducted in Danish using on-line polling technology. 775 respondents answered this question. The question was "What was, or would be, your PRIMARY reason for entering into a registered partnership?" In addition to this 49 percent, an additional 39.5 percent responded "to demonstrate my commitment to my partner"; 1.3 percent responded "to demonstrate my commitment to others in my community"; 1 percent responded "to support the passage of the registered partnership law in Denmark"; and 9.2 percent gave a variety of other responses. See chapter 3, note 7, for a more detailed description of the survey methodology.

7. Interview by Darren Spedale with Jean Luscher and Diana Skovgaard, Copenhagen, May 1997; telephone interview by William Eskridge and Darren Spedale with Jean Luscher and Diana Skovgaard, New Haven, Connecticut, March 2005.

8. This account is taken from an interview by Darren Spedale with Niels Andersen and Claus Rasmussen, Kaas, Denmark, August 1997.

9. Ibid. (quoting Rasmussen).

10. On Danish inheritance law, see Linda Nielsen, "Equality and Care in Danish Family Law and Law of Inheritance," in Børge Dahl et al., *Danish Law in a European Perspective* (Copenhagen: GadJura, 1996), 179–83.

11. Interview by Darren Spedale with Peer Toft and Peter Mols, Copenhagen, November 1997.

12. 1997 Luscher and Skovgaard interview (quoting Luscher).

13. Interview by Darren Spedale with Lars Henriksen and Jan Lorenzen, Holstebro, Denmark, July 1997. On Danish tax law, and its various effects on married or partnered couples, see Jan Pedersen, "Danish Tax Law and International Tax Law," in Dahl et al., *Danish Law*, 329–40.

14. See chapter 3 for statistics on transnational couples who have registered as partners.

15. 1997 Luscher and Skovgaard Interview (quoting Luscher). On Danish healthcare benefits, see Ruth Nielsen, "Danish Labour Law in a Period of Transition," in Dahl et al., *Danish Law*, 360–61.

16. See, e.g., The Danish Law on Patient's Rights, Law no. 482 of July 1, 1998.

17. On pension law generally, see Kirsten Ketscher, "The Danish Social System," in Dahl et al., *Danish Law*, 302–7.

18. Interview by Darren Spedale with Per Kjær and Barry Winter, Aalborg, Denmark, February 1997 (quoting Kjær).

19. Interview by Darren Spedale with Anne-Vibeke Fleischer and Elisabeth Bjerre Knudsen, Copenhagen, July 1997 (quoting Fleischer).

20. 2005 Luscher and Skovgaard telephone interview (quoting Luscher).

21. Interview by Darren Spedale with Eva Fog and Gunna Højgaard, Copenhagen, April 1997 (quoting Højgaard).

22. See the introductory comments to the legislation in appendix 2 (quotation in text). For an important sociological survey demonstrating the power of in-

terpersonal commitment for American same-sex couples, see Kathleen E. Hull, *Same-Sex Marriage: The Cultural Politics of Love and Law* (Cambridge: Cambridge University Press, 2006).

23. Interview by Darren Spedale with William Waite and Ken Nielsen, Copenhagen, June 1997 (quoting Nielsen).

24. Interview by Darren Spedale with Deborah Kaplan and Anne Jespersen, Copenhagen, April 1997 (quoting Kaplan).

25. See note 6 for other responses to this question.

26. Fog and Højgaard interview (quoting Fog).

27. Ibid.

28. Fleischer and Knudsen interview (quoting Fleischer).

29. Ibid. (quoting Fleischer).

30. Fledelius and Fledelius interview (quoting Lars Fledelius).

31. E.g., the 1977 antigay campaign spearheaded by Anita Bryant in response to passage of a sexual orientation antidiscrimination ordinance in Dade County, Florida. For information on Bryant see http://en.wikipedia.org/wiki/Anita_Bryant (viewed September 2005).

32. See William N. Eskridge, Jr., *The Case for Same-Sex Marriage* (New York: Free Press, 1996), 120; Tomas Philipson and Richard A. Posner, *Private Choices and Public Health: The AIDS Epidemic in an Economic Perspective* (Cambridge: Harvard University Press, 1993), 179–80. For a recent, and most rigorous, analysis, see Christina Muller, "An Economic Analysis of Same-Sex Marriage," German Working Papers in Law and Economics, 2002, article 14, available at www.bepress.com/gwp/default/vol2002/iss1/art14 (viewed July 2005).

33. Interview by Darren Spedale with Uffe Størner and Kaj Kristensen, Frederikshavn, Denmark, September 1997 (quoting Størner).

34. Luscher and Skovgaard interview (quoting Luscher).

35. One of our male couples located in Copenhagen. No names are associated with this quotation for privacy reasons.

36. Thomas S. Dee, "Forsaking All Others? The Effects of 'Gay Marriage' on Risky Sex," National Bureau of European Research, working paper 11327 (May 2005), available at www.nber.org/papers/w11327 (visited July 2005). See 14–15 (syphilis rates much lower for countries recognizing same-sex marriage), 23–25 (lower rates not explained by other variables); 15 (gonorrhea rates); 15 (HIV-infection rates).

37. See chapter 3 for a statistical analysis of the growth of same-sex couples with children in Denmark.

38. *Children in Homosexual Families, Summary,* Report from the Commission on the Situation of Children in Homosexual Families (Stockholm: Swedish Government Official Reports, 2001), 10.

39. Haase and Jepsen interview.

40. *Children in Homosexual Families, Summary,* 10. For an empirical study supporting the Commission's finding and demonstrating that "lone parents" have great difficulties raising children, see Gunilla Ringbäck Weitoft, *Lone*

Parenting, Socioeconomic Conditions and Severe Ill-Health (Stockholm: Center for Epidemiology, 2003), which we discuss in chapter 5.

41. Kjær and Winter interview (quoting Kjær).

42. Fledelius and Fledelius interview (quoting Lars Fledelius).

43. Interview by Darren Spedale with Eddie Moris and Jens Boesen, Copenhagen, May 1997 (quoting Jens Boesen).

44. Moris and Boesen interview (quoting both Moris and Boesen).

45. Størner and Kristensen interview (quoting both Størner and Kristensen).

46. Ibid. (quoting Størner).

47. 1997 Luscher and Skovgaard interview (quoting Luscher).

48. 2005 Luscher and Skovgaard telephone interview (quoting Luscher).

49. Ibid. (Luscher).

50. Kaplan and Jespersen interview (quoting Kaplan). For a similar account, see, e.g., interview by Darren Spedale with Palle Heilesen and Otto Bygsø, Copenhagen, March 1997 (quoting Heilesen): "Some people did see our relationship differently after we got married, and we didn't expect that. But I felt the difference—some saw our getting married as a special thing. So in their minds, even if you have been living together for eight or nine years, it might still not be serious—but now that you have the paper, it's serious, in their view."

51. 1997 Luscher and Skovgaard interview (quoting Luscher).

52. Kaplan and Jespersen interview (quoting Jespersen).

53. Moris and Boesen interview (quoting Moris).

54. Heilesen and Bygsø interview (quoting Heilesen).

55. Ibid.

56. Henriksen and Lorenzen interview (quoting Henriksen).

57. Ibid.

58. Mols and Toft interview (quoting Mols).

59. On the generous state financial support for the elderly, the disabled, the infirm in Scandinavian countries, see, e.g., Kirsten Ketscher, "The Danish Social System," in Dahl et al., *Danish Law*, 293–326.

60. Under Danish law, for example, single parents in financial need are likely to qualify for higher levels of state aid in recognition of the needs of the child. If a couple is married, however, the state authorities will take the financial condition of both parents into account in determining the state's offer of aid. Furthermore, if a couple has been married and later divorces, the noncustodial parent will still be considered responsible for the financial welfare of his or her child, and be required to make child support payments. See Nielsen, "Danish Family Law," 185–88.

61. For example, Chris Sidotti, Australia's human rights commissioner, and Marta Suplicy, at the time a member of Brazil's legislature and later Mayor of São Paulo, requested information regarding the structure and effect of the Scandinavian partnership laws.

62. Ove Carlsen, "Gay Pride i New York—Med To Danskere i Spidsen" (Gay Pride

in New York—with Two Danes Heading the Procession), *PAN-Bladet*, August 1990, 4.

63. See chapter 3 for data on registered partnerships involving citizens of the Nordic nations and noncitizens from another country.

64. Interview by Darren Spedale with Andre Oriveira and Jan Nørmark, Copenhagen, August 1997 (quoting Oriveira).

65. See appendix 2 for the introductory comments in Parliament to the legislation.

66. Dee, "Forsaking All Others," 14–15 and 19–24 (effect of same-sex marriage on syphilis rates); 15, fig. 1 (HIV-infection rates in the recognition and nonrecognition countries).

67. Denmark began mandatory reporting of new HIV infections in August 1990. In the last five months of that year, eighty cases of MSM were reported in Denmark. On the basis of this number of approximately sixteen new infections per month it has been estimated that the total number of new HIV infections of MSM in 1990 were about 190. For Danish HIV infection statistics, see the Statens Serum Institut (National Serum Institute) website at www.ssi.dk.

68. Norwegian statistics taken from HIVNetNordic at www.hivnetnordic.org/stats/nor/stats_hiv_eng_no.html. For information on the initiation of mandatory HIV reporting in each of the Nordic countries, see Andrea Infuso, Françoise F. Hamers, Angela M. Downs, and Jane Alix, "HIV Reporting in Western Europe: National Systems and First European Data," *Eurosurveillance Monthly*, February 2000, pp. 13–17. Available at www.eurosurveillance.org/em/v05n02/0502–221.asp (viewed September 2005).

69. Swedish HIV infection reports before 1988 are reported as an aggregate number rather than on an annual basis; for the purposes of clarity we therefore take the annual reported numbers from 1988. We note, however, that the number of reported annual HIV infections in Sweden before 1988 (887 in total), appear to be higher on an annual basis than in the years we report. For Swedish HIV statistics see the website of the Swedish Institute for Infectious Disease Control, www.smittskyddsinstitutet.se. Swedish HIV statistics of MSM available at www.smittskyddsinstitutet.se/upload/4552/HIV_total_ smittväg_ kön_1988–2004a.xls (viewed September 2005).

70. The Swedish HIV statistics are somewhat skewed by two particularly high-infection years of 1988 (159) and 1989 (141). However, even if these are removed, the annual HIV infection rate from 1990 to 1994 is 108.4, producing a 31 percent decrease in the number of HIV infections for MSM in the pre- to post-partnership periods.

71. Interview by Darren Spedale with Bent Hansen, Copenhagen, September 1997.

72. See the Congressional Record for September 10, 1996, page S10110, for Senator Byrd's comments during the DOMA debate regarding the potential costs of same-sex marriage.

73. Correspondence between the United States General Accounting Office and Senator Bill Frist, dated January 23, 2004. Available online at http://www.gao.gov/new.items/d04353r.pdf. (viewed November 2005).

74. The reports by the National Gay and Lesbian Task Force used the states of Oregon and Massachusetts as case studies. See Terence Dougherty, "Economic Benefits of Marriage Under Federal and Oregon Law," National Gay and Lesbian Task Force Policy Institute (2004). Available online at http://www .thetaskforce.org/downloads/OregonTaxStudy.pdf (viewed November 2005). Also, see Terence Dougherty, "Economic Benefits of Marriage Under Federal and Massachusetts Law," National Gay and Lesbian Task Force Policy Institute (2004). Available online at http://www.thetaskforce.org/downloads/ EconomicCosts.pdf (viewed November 2005).

75. Report of the Congressional Budget Office, "The Potential Budgetary Impact of Recognizing Same-Sex Marriages," dated June 21, 2004. Available online at http://www.cbo.gov/showdoc.cfm?index=5559&sequence=0 (viewed November 2005).

76. M. V. Lee Badgett et al. "Counting on Couples: Fiscal Savings from Allowing Same-Sex Couples to Marry in Connecticut," Policy Study by the Williams Project of the UCLA School of Law and the Institute for Gay and Lesbian Strategic Studies at the University of Massachusetts- Amherst (March 2005). Available online at http://www.iglss.org/media/files/ct_marry.pdf (viewed November 2005).

77. M. V. Lee Badgett, "The Fiscal Impact on the State of Vermont of Allowing Same-Sex Couples to Marry," Technical Report from the Institute for Gay and Lesbian Strategic Studies at the University of Massachusetts–Amherst (October 1998). Available online at http://www.iglss.org/media/files/techrpt981 .pdf (viewed November 2005).

78. M. V. Lee Badgett and R. Bradley Sears, "Equal Rights, Fiscal Responsibility: The Impact of AB 205 on California's Budget," Policy Study by the Williams Project of the UCLA School of Law and the Institute for Gay and Lesbian Strategic Studies at the University of Massachusetts- Amherst (May 2003). Available online at http://www.iglss.org/media/files/wppolicystudy.pdf (viewed November 2005).

CHAPTER 5

1. This account is taken from an interview by Darren Spedale with Barry Winter and Per Kjær, Aalborg, Denmark, February 1997.

2. Ibid. (quoting Kjær).

3. Ibid. (quoting Winter).

4. Landmark publications developing the Scandinavian twist on the defense-of-marriage objection include Rick Santorum, *It Takes a Family: Conservatism and the Community Good* (Wilmington, Del.: ISI Books, 2005), 28–39; Stanley Kurtz, "The End of Marriage in Scandinavia," *Weekly Standard*, February 2, 2004; Kurtz, "Slipping toward Scandinavia," *National Review Online* (2004), available at www.nationalreview.com/kurtz/kurtz20040202917.asp.; National Constitution Center, *Same-Sex Marriage: Do We Need a Federal Marriage*

Amendment? (May 21, 2004) (statements of former Judge Robert Bork), available at www.constitutioncenter.org/visiting/PublicPrograms/Program Archives/DoWeNeedaFederalMarriageAmendment.shtml (viewed in June 2005). See generally Senate hearings conducted by Senator John Cornyn, another leading advocate of the Scandinavian twist, House Committee on the Judiciary, *Legal Threats to Traditional Marriage: Implications for Public Policy: Hearing before the Subcommittee on the Constitution of the House Committee on the Judiciary*, 108th Congress, April 22, 2004, as well as the Senate debate on the Federal Marriage Amendment on July 12, 2004 (described in chapter 1).

5. Richard A. Posner, *Sex and Reason* (Cambridge: Harvard University Press, 1992), surveying social science evidence for family trends in Scandinavia and emphasizing the role of the welfare state in discouraging marriage. See generally Linda Nielsen, "Equality and Care in Danish Family Law and the Law of Inheritance," in Børge Dahl, et al., eds., *Danish Law in a European Perspective* (Copenhagen: GadJura, 1996), 167–70 (evolution of Danish family law), 175–79 (no-fault divorce rules), 183–84 (cohabitation rules).

6. The Danish statistics discussed in text are derived from the demographic data in appendix 4A.

7. The Danish statistics discussed in text are derived from the demographic data in appendix 4A. Stanley Kurtz argues that the declining Danish divorce rate is a result of the weakness of marriage; because so few Danes were getting married in the 1980s and 1990s, he maintains, fewer Danes were getting divorced. As figure 5.1 reveals, however, many more Danish couples were getting married in the 1990s than in the 1980s—yet the divorce rate in 1989–2003 has been lower than the rate in the 1980s.

8. The Danish statistics discussed in text are derived from data reported in appendix 4C.

9. The Norwegian statistics discussed in text are derived from the demographic data in appendix 5A.

10. The Norwegian statistics discussed in text are derived from the demographic data in appendix 5C.

11. Another way of analyzing the data in appendix 5C is to consider the ratios between the number of married couples (with and without children) to the number of cohabiting couples (with children). The ratios for each year are as follows: 1989–95, 4 percent; 1991–93, 5 percent; 1993–92, 7 percent; 1995–90, 8 percent; 1997–90, 9 percent; 1999–90, 10 percent; 2001–90, 10 percent; 2002–89, 10 percent; 2003–89, 11 percent; 2004—89, 11 percent. As we say in the text, the trend toward cohabiting couples raising children has slowed down considerably.

12. The Swedish statistics discussed in text are derived from the demographic data in appendix 6A.

13. Stanley Kurtz suggests that Sweden's 1987 Homosexual Cohabitees Law (and not just the 1994 Registered Partnership Law) contributed to Sweden's decline of marriage. But the 1987 law did not siphon off any potentially married couples. More important, the Homosexual Cohabitees Law was immediately followed

in 1989 by the largest marrying cohort in Sweden's history. Changes in Swedish pension law fueled the 1989 marriage-bulge, but that bulge corrupts the post-1989 marriage trends and precludes any sure conclusions about possible effects of the Homosexual Cohabitees Law. Finally, the Homosexual Cohabitees Law does not fit Kurtz's argument that same-sex marriage delinks marriage from procreation and parenting. If anything, the law supported the link between marriage and procreation: lesbian and gay couples, who cannot procreate among themselves, got cohabitation as their only option, while straight couples, who can procreate among themselves, had the additional option of marriage.

14. The data discussed in text can be derived from the demographic information for Sweden in appendix 6A. Changes in Swedish family law, especially no-fault divorce, are discussed in David Bradley, *Family Law and Political Culture (Scandinavian Laws in Comparative Perspective)* (London: Sweet and Maxwell, 1996), 65–67 (divorce), 74–79 (property rights after divorce).

15. Changes in Danish family law are laid out in Nielsen, "Equality and Care in Danish Family Law," 170, 175–79 (divorce); 183–84 (cohabitation), as well as Bradley, *Family Law and Political Culture,* 155–60 (cohabitation allowed and regularized by judicial decisions). The Danish statistics discussed in the text are derived from the demographic data in appendices 4A and 4C.

16. Kathleen Kiernan, "The Rise of Cohabitation and Childbearing outside Marriage in Western Europe," *International Journal of Law, Policy, and the Family* 15 (2001): 1–21; 3 (quotation in text).

17. All four of the countries in which young (25–29 years old) women were likely to be single or cohabiting rather than married (Denmark, Sweden, Finland, France) have recognized same-sex partnerships; in a middle group of countries, with as many married as cohabiting young women, most have recognized such partnerships (Netherlands, Belgium, Germany, and Great Britain this year) while one other has not (Austria); in the bottom grouping, with very few cohabiting couples (Ireland, Spain, Portugal, Greece, Italy), only one (Spain) has recognized same-sex partnerships. Ibid., 5 (fig. 1).

18. *Congressional Record,* 108th Congress, 2nd sess., 2004, 150, no. 95: S7921 (daily ed. July 12, 2004) (statement of Senator Cornyn, supporting the Federal Marriage Amendment); Stanley Kurtz, "The End of Marriage in Scandinavia," *Weekly Standard,* February 2, 2004, both describing and drawing from the four-stage model developed in Kathleen Kiernan, "Partnership Formation in Western Societies," in *Encyclopedia of the Social and Behavioral Sciences,* ed. Neil J. Smelser and Paul B. Baltes (Amsterdam: Elsevier, 2001), 11902–6.

19. Maggie Gallagher, "A Reality Waiting to Happen: A Response to Evan Wolfson," in Lynn D. Wardle, et al., eds., *Marriage and Same-Sex Unions: A Debate* (Westport, Conn.: Praeger, 2003), 11 (first quotation in text); House Committee on the Judiciary, *Legal Threats to Traditional Marriage,* 14–16 (testimony of Stanley Kurtz) (second quotation, emphasis added). See also Kurtz, "End of Marriage": "The separation of marriage from parenthood was increasing; gay marriage has widened the separation. . . . Instead of encouraging a society-

wide return to marriage, Scandinavian gay marriage has driven home the message that marriage itself is outdated, and that virtually any family form, including out-of-wedlock parenthood, is acceptable."

20. The account in text, and the quotations, are taken from interview by Darren Spedale with Bodil Stavad and Britt Pedersen, Rødovre, Denmark, September 1997.

21. Ibid. (quoting Pedersen).

22. Michael Sokolove, "The Believer," *New York Times Magazine*, May 22, 2005, p. 6 (first Santorum quotation in text); Santorum, *It Takes a Family*, 34 (second Santorum quotation); Maggie Gallagher, "Reality Waiting to Happen," 12 (the essential goal of marriage is other-regarding) (third quotation). Stanley Kurtz makes a similar point in "The Marriage Mentality: A Reply to My Critics," *National Review Online* (2004), at www.nationalreview.com/kurtz/kurtz200405040841.asp (viewed August 2004).

23. For examples of lesbian and gay couples whose unions have been altruistic in the traditional sense, see, e.g., William N. Eskridge, Jr., *Equality Practice: Civil Unions and the Future of Gay Rights* (New York: Routledge, 2002) (stories of the three Vermont lesbian and gay couples who sued for equal marriage rights); Ellen Lewin, *Recognizing Ourselves: Ceremonies of Lesbian and Gay Commitment* (New York: Columbia University Press, 1998) (profiles of various lesbian and gay couples, their commitment ceremonies, and their understanding of the collective nature of their relationship); Eric Marcus, *Together Forever: Gay and Lesbian Marriage* (San Diego: Greenhaven Press, 1998) (interviews with forty long-term lesbian and gay couples); Suzanne Sherman, ed., *Lesbian and Gay Marriage: Private Commitments, Public Ceremonies* (Philadelphia: Temple University Press, 1992) (interviews with twenty-four lesbian and gay couples); Merle James Yost, ed., *When Love Lasts Forever: Male Couples Celebrate Commitment* (Cleveland: Pilgrim Press, 1999).

24. Kjær and Winter interview (quoting Kjær).

25. The quotations in text are taken from interview by Darren Spedale with Gunna Højgaard and Eva Fog, Copenhagen, April 1997.

26. *American Community Survey, 2002*, available at www.gaydemographics.org/USA/ACS/2002/index.htm (visited July 2005); Stephanie Armour, "Gay Parents Cheer a Benefit Revolution," *USA Today*, January 10, 2005 (quoting Gary Gates of the Urban Institute).

27. The inspirational story of Steve Lofton and Roger Croteau is based upon a telephone interview by William Eskridge with Stephen Lofton, May 2005. See also *Lofton v. Secretary of Department of Children & Family Services*, 358 F.3d 804 (U.S. Court of Appeals for the Eleventh Circuit, 2004), rehearing en banc denied, 377 F.3d 1275 (2004), especially Judge Birch's decision for the Court, Judge Barkett's dissenting opinion from the full Court's denial of en banc rehearing, and Judge Birch's response to Judge Barkett's dissent.

28. On the monopoly American law accorded marriage for Americans who wanted to be sexually active and to rear children, see Nancy F. Cott, *Public Vows: A*

History of Marriage and the Nation (Cambridge: Harvard University Press, 2000), 126–31 (national campaign to standardize monogamy after Civil War). See also 32 (states gave few rights to children born outside of marriage), 160 (enforcement of adultery laws).

29. On the illegality of abortion almost everywhere by 1900, see James C. Mohr, *Abortion in America: The Origins and Evolution of National Policy, 1800–1900* (New York: Oxford University Press, 1978) (abortion made a crime almost everywhere by 1900); Dorothy McBride Stetson, *Women's Rights in the USA: Policy Debates and Gender Roles* (New York: Garland Press, 1997), 109–10. On the illegality of contraceptives, see 69 (contraceptives illegal in most state by 1900; mailing them was a federal crime under the Comstock Act). On the illegality of sodomy, see William N. Eskridge, Jr., *Gaylaw: Challenging the Apartheid of the Closet* (Cambridge: Harvard University Press, 1999), 328–37 (appendix A1); 17–34 (expansion of state definitions of what constituted sodomy, and of enforcement efforts).

30. On the presumption that a child born within a marriage was the progeny of husband and wife, see Homer H. Clark, Jr., *Law of Domestic Relations in the United States,* 2nd ed. (St. Paul, Minn.: West, 1988), 151–52. On the marriage preference for adoption, see Bryan Paul Gill, "Adoption Agencies and the Search for the Ideal Family, 1918–1965," in *Adoption in America: Historical Perspectives,* ed. E. Wayne Carp (Ann Arbor: University of Michigan Press, 2002), 162–70. On the difficulty of divorce, see Cott, *Public Vows,* 106–7; Stetson, *Women's Rights,* 195. On the tender years doctrine and the practice of vesting children with the mother, see Clark, *Domestic Relations,* 259, 787; Stetson, *Women's Rights,* 202, 209.

31. On the Scandinavian legal regime regulating marriage and divorce in 1900, see Bradley, *Family Law and Political Culture,* 3–9 (although more liberal than the family law elsewhere in Europe, the Scandinavian countries required proof of fault as the basis for divorce, and other features similar to American law in 1900); Nielsen, "Equality and Care in Danish Family Law," 167–70 (evolution of Danish family law, 1850–1950).

32. Sweden has been the pioneer in ending marriage's monopoly on romantic relationships and child-rearing. Excellent sources include Bradley, *Family Law and Political Culture,* 95–109, 252–58 (comparing Sweden's individualistic approach with the more fragmented approach followed by its neighbors); Mary Ann Glendon, *The Transformation of Family Law: State, Law, and Family in the United States and Western Europe* (Cambridge: Harvard University Press, 1989), 273–77. See also Bradley, *Family Law and Political Culture,* 155–63 (Denmark), 209–17 (Norway); Nielsen, "Equality and Care in Danish Family Law," 169–70, 183–84 (Denmark). For almost as thoroughgoing liberalization in the United States, see Jana B. Singer, "The Privatization of Family Law," *Wisconsin Law Review* 1992: 1443–1568.

33. Bradley, *Family Law and Political Culture,* 239–40; Singer, "Privatization," 1453. See also Posner, *Sex and Reason,* 333–34, suggesting that the United States and

Sweden followed essentially the same path of sexual liberalization outside of marriage.

34. On the ease of divorce and, effectively, fewer obligations on the part of divorced fathers, see as Roderick Phillips, *Putting Asunder: A History of Divorce in Western Society* (Cambridge, England: Cambridge University Press, 1988); Bradley, *Family Law and Political Culture*, 64–72 (Sweden), 129–37 (Denmark), 177–92 (Norway); Nielsen, "Equality and Care in Danish Family Law," 174–79 (Denmark); Singer, "Privatization," 1474–78 (United States). On the state's taking up most child-support obligations, see Bradley, *Family Law and Political Culture*, 119–24 (Sweden), 169–73 (Denmark), 233–37 (Norway).

35. Marriage constrains the choices spouses can make about their sex lives, sharing of money and resources, and so forth. In all three countries, the state now gives couples some of the legal benefits of marriage (like employee benefits) without undertaking the obligations of marriage, allows married spouses to exit the institution much more easily, and prohibits penalties on children born outside of marriage. (Sweden and Denmark have gone further on the first point but not the second and third.) The results are predictable. In all three countries, the incidence of marriage is lower today than it was fifty years ago, the incidence of divorce is higher, and more children are born and raised outside of marital families.

36. Robert H. Bork, "The Necessary Amendment," *First Things* 145 (August–September 2004): 17–21 (quotations in text); "Robert's Rules of Order," interview by Peter Robinson with Robert Bork, *Uncommon Knowledge*, interview no. 811 (filmed July 16, 2003), available at www.uncommonknowledge.org/800/811.html (viewed August 2005). See also Robert H. Bork, *Slouching toward Gomorrah: Modern Liberalism and American Decline* (New York: Regan Books, 1996), positing a general theory of cultural decline in the United States so long as Americans do not overcome liberalizing moves such as cohabitation, gay rights, etc.; Stanley Kurtz, "Unhealthy Half Truths: Scandinavia Marriage *Is* Dying," *National Review Online*, May 25, 2004, available at www.nationalreview.com/kurtz/kurtz200405250927.asp (viewed June 2004), arguing that sexual cohabitation, nonmarital children, and gay marriage are "mutually reinforcing" trends that, working together, are proving fatal to marriage.

37. The quotations in text are taken from the Fog and Hojgaard interview.

38. Kurtz, "End of Marriage."

39. See Maggie Gallagher, "Normal Marriage: Two Views," in Wardle et al., *Marriage and Same-Sex Unions*, 13–24. On the harms to children when parents break up, see, e.g., Sara McLanahan and Gary D. Sandefur, *Growing Up with a Single Parent: What Hurts, What Helps* (Cambridge: Harvard University Press, 1994); Judith Wallerstein, et al., *The Unexpected Legacy of Divorce: A Twenty-Five-Year Landmark Study* (New York: Hyperion, 2000) (in-depth study of nonrandom sample over time); Sharon K. Houseknecht and Jaya Sastry, "Family 'Decline' and Child Well-Being: A Comparative Assessment," *Journal of Marriage and the Family* 58 (August 1996): 726–39, a particularly

nuanced comparative study of the United States, Sweden, West Germany, and Italy. The evidence is more impressionistic, but persuasive to most, that cohabiting couples are less likely to stay together than married couples. E.g., E. J. Graff, *What Is Marriage For? The Strange History of Our Most Intimate Institution* (Boston: Beacon Press, 1999), 143.

40. Kurtz, "End of Marriage."

41. On the soaring nonmarital birth rate in Scandinavia, see Bradley, *Family Law and Political Culture*, 108–9 (Sweden), 162–63 (Denmark).

42. The Denmark statistics discussed in text are taken from appendix 4B.

43. The Denmark statistics are derived from data reported in appendix 4C.

44. The Norway statistics discussed in text are derived from the data in appendix 5B.

45. M. V. Lee Badgett, "Will Providing Marriage Rights to Same-Sex Couples Undermine Heterosexual Marriage? Evidence from Scandinavia and the Netherlands," presented to the Council on Contemporary Families and the Institute for Gay and Lesbian Strategic Studies (July 2004), available at www.iglss .org/media/files/briefing.pdf (viewed October 2004).

46. The Sweden statistics discussed in text are derived from data reported in appendix 6B.

47. Stanley Kurtz, "Going Dutch? Lessons of the Same-Sex Marriage Debate in the Netherlands," Weekly Standard, May 2004, available at www.weekly standard.com/Content/Public/Articles/000/000/004/126qodro.asp (viewed October 2004).

48. Explaining why same-sex marriage initially wasn't on the radar in Denmark during discussions of antidiscrimination laws, Professor Kees Waaldijk reports that the media dismissed the possibility, and it was traditionalist opponents who created some visibility in the mid-1990s. "How Holland Did It—Discussion and Visibility Is Key in Ending Marriage Discrimination," interview by Kevin Bourassa and Joe Varnell with Professor Kees Waaldijk, June 8, 2002, available at www.same sexmarriage.ca/advocacy/turin/KeesWaaldijk_2002.htm (visited August 2005).

49. On the predominance of different-sex couples taking advantage of Dutch registered partnerships, see Council of Europe, "Demographic Yearbook 2003," available at www.coeint/T/E/Social%5Cohesion/Population/Demographic %5FYear%5FBook/2003_Edition/04%20Country%20Data/Membe r%20States/ Netherlands/Netherlands%20%20General %20PAge.asp#TopOfPage (viewed July 2005).

50. Kurtz, "Going Dutch?"

51. Bourassa and Varnell Interview with Waaldijk. The leading traditionalist website, opposed to same-sex marriage, says nothing about any gay-liberal desire to weaken marriage and, to the contrary, pinned its hopes on anticommitment voices within the lesbian and gay community. Hans van Velde, "The Long Road to Civil Marriage: From Trial Process to Reality," in *No Gay Marriage in the Netherlands*, available at www.gaykrant.nl/index.php?id=222 (viewed August 2005).

52. M. V. Lee Badgett, "Did Gay Marriage Destroy Heterosexual Marriage in Scandinavia?" *Slate,* May 20, 2004, available at www.slate.msn.com/id/2100884 (viewed August 2004).

53. Social scientist Lawrence Kurdek studied 239 straight married couples, 79 gay male unmarried couples, and 51 lesbian unmarried couples over a five-year period. He found that the quality of the relationship and partner happiness was about the same for the married straight and the unmarried gay male couples—and significantly higher for the unmarried lesbian couples after five years. See Kurdek, "Relationship Outcomes and Their Predictors: Longitudinal Evidence from Heterosexual Married, Gay Cohabiting, and Lesbian Cohabiting Couples," *Journal of Marriage and the Family* 60 (1998): 553–68.

54. Gunilla Ringbäck Weitoft, *Lone Parenting, Socioeconomic Conditions and Severe Ill-Health* (Stockholm: Center for Epidemiology, 2003).

55. E.g., Teresa Stanton Collett, "Recognizing Same-Sex Marriage: Asking for the Impossible?" *Catholic University Law Review* 47 (1998): 1261–62. Compare Stanley Kurtz, "What Is Wrong with Gay Marriage," *Commentary,* September 2000 (arguing that it is the "complementarity" of men and women that assures stability in marriage; because couples of the same sex are not "complements," same-sex marriage is an oxymoron), with William Eskridge, correspondence, *Commentary,* December 2000, p. 5 (responding to Kurtz: the lived experience of thousands of committed lesbian and gay couples raising children is testimony to the fact that same-sex couples can and do enjoy stable and productive relationships).

56. Elise F. Jones, *Pregnancy, Contraception, and Family Planning Services in Industrialized Countries,* app. B (New Haven: Yale University Press, 1989), 243.

57. Gunnar Andersson, "Children's Experience of Family Disruption and Family Formation: Evidence from Sixteen FFS Countries," *Demographic Research* 7 (August 2, 2002): 359 (quotation in text). Our source for children being raised in single-parent homes is Clearinghouse on International Developments in Child, Youth, and Family Policies, Columbia University, table 2.17a, "Single-Parent Households, 10 Countries, Selected Years, 1980–2002" (as updated May 2004), available at www.childpolicyintl.org/contexttabledemography/table 217a.pdf (viewed August 6, 2005). For a higher estimate of the number of American children raised by single parents, see Andrew Hacker, "Gays and Genes," *New York Review of Books,* March 27, 2003. On the South's high incidence of divorce and nonmarital children, see chapter 6.

58. The facts in this paragraph are taken from the World Resources Institute's Earth Trends tables for each country, available at www.earthtrends.wri.org (viewed June 2004). Most of the generalizations made in text for Sweden also apply to Norway and Denmark.

59. The rate of adult suicides in Sweden is higher than that of the United States, but the gap has narrowed since 1970. According to the World Health Organization's Mental Health Country Reports and Charts (Geneva: World Health Organization, 2003), the Swedish suicide rate was 22.3 per 100,000 in

1970, compared with 11.5 in the United States. The American rate rose in the 1970s-1990s but fell back to 10.7 in 1999. The Swedish rate has steadily declined and was 13.8 in 1999.

60. Posner, *Sex and Reason,* 441 (quotation in text).

CHAPTER 6

1. For Judge Bork's repeated rejections of a constitutional right of privacy, and of the Court's decisions in *Griswold v. Connecticut,* 381 U.S. 479 (1965), and *Roe v. Wade,* 410 U.S. 113 (1973), see Senate Committee of the Judiciary, *Hearings on the Nomination of Robert H. Bork: Hearings before the Senate Committee of the Judiciary,* 100th Congress, 1st sess., 1987, 184–85, 3547–49, as well as 3896–3910 (post-hearing letter from Judge Bork, strongly reiterating his views). On the public rejection of Bork's nomination, see Ethan Bronner, *Battle for Justice: How the Bork Nomination Shook America* (New York: Norton,1989).

2. Derek B. Dorn, "Sexual Orientation and the Legal Academy: The Experience at Yale," Yale Law School supervised analytical paper, June 2002, 142–77 (detailed account of Professor Bork's intense opposition to the student proposal, ultimately accepted by an overwhelming faculty vote in 1978, to decline assistance to employers who discriminate against lesbian and gay students); *Dronenberg v. Zech,* 741 F.2d 1388 (U.S. Court of Appeals for the D.C. Circuit, 1984) (Bork, J.), an analytical defense of criminalizing homosexual sodomy that was a blueprint for the Supreme Court's decision in *Bowers v. Hardwick,* 478 U.S. 186 (1986); Robert H. Bork, *Slouching toward Gomorrah: Modern Liberalism and American Decline* (New York: Regan Books, 1996), 112–15, denouncing the Supreme Court's willingness to interpret the Constitution to protect minorities, including homosexuals, in *Romer v. Evans,* 517 U.S. 620 (1996).

3. National Constitution Center, *Same-Sex Marriage: Do We Need a Federal Marriage Amendment?* (May 21, 2004) (statements of former Judge Robert Bork), available at www.constitutioncenter.org/visiting/PublicPrograms/Program Archives/DoWeNeedaFederalMarriageAmendment.shtml.

4. Ibid. (statements of Professor William N. Eskridge, Jr., Yale Law School). As he said at the Philadelphia debate, Eskridge is proud to serve on the same faculty as Judge Bork and was honored to have had the opportunity to debate the judge.

5. Jack Baker to William N. Eskridge, Jr., February 23, 2005, questions and answers, answer no. 1 (first quotation in text); answer no. 2 (second quotation in text). For other supporters of equal marriage rights who reject advocating for "marriage-lite" or even civil unions, see, e.g., Jonathan Rauch, *Gay Marriage: Why It Is Good for Gays, Good for Straights, and Good for America* (New York: Times Books, 2004), 29–54, 89–90 ("Accept No Substitutes"); Evan Wolfson, *Why Marriage Matters: America, Equality, and Gay People's Right to Marry* (New York: Simon and Schuster, 2004), 123–44, 159–87.

6. Lynne Cheney, *Sisters* (New York: Signet, 1981); this book is not easily avail-able, even in major libraries, so the quotation in text was taken from the sum-mary in www.usatoday.com/life/books/news/2004–04–03–cheney-book_x. htm. An example of her rigorous conservativism is Lynne V. Cheney, *Telling the Truth: Why Our Culture and Our Country Have Stopped Making Sense— and What We Can Do about It* (New York: Simon and Schuster, 1995).

7. Rick Klein and Brian C. Mooney, "GOP Hardens Stand against Gay Marriage; Platform OK'd after Cheney Splits on Issue," *Boston Globe*, August 26, 2004, p. A1 (quoting Dick Cheney in opposition to the Federal Marriage Amend-ment); Carolyn Lochhead, "Faced with Dissension in Its Ranks, GOP Retreats on Gay Marriage Vote," *San Francisco Chronicle*, July 14, 2004 (quoting Lynne Cheney as saying "people should be free to enter into the relationships that they choose" and "that when it comes to conferring legal status on relation-ships, that is a matter left to the states"). See also "Where They Stand," *De-troit Free Press*, October 20, 2004 (citing Dick Cheney's "personal support" for civil unions); Tamara Lipper and Evan Thomas, "Cheney Family Values," *Newsweek*, July 26, 2004.

8. The party's name was changed to Christian Democrats in 2003.

9. The account and quotations in text are taken from an interview by Darren Spedale with Jann Sjursen, Copenhagen, September 1997.

10. On American marriage trends since World War II, see Andrew J. Cherlin, *Marriage, Divorce, Remarriage*, rev. ed. (Cambridge: Harvard University Press,1992); Steven Mintz and Susan Kellogg, *Domestic Revolutions: A Social History of American Family Life* (New York: Free Press, 1998). On Scandina-vian trends, see David Bradley, *Family Law and Political Culture (Scandina-vian Laws in Comparative Perspective)* (London: Sweet and Maxwell, 1996).

11. On the liberalizing legal revolution in marriage law, exclusively at the behest of straight people who want freedom of choice, see Bradley, *Family Law and Political Culture* (Denmark, Norway, Sweden); Jana Singer, "The Privatization of Family Law," *Wisconsin Law Review* 1982: 1443–1568 (United States); Hans Ytterberg, "From Society's Point of View, Cohabitation between Two Persons of the Same Sex Is a Perfectly Acceptable Form of Family Life: A Swedish Story of Love and Legislation," in Robert Wintemute and Mads Andenaes, eds., *Legal Recognition of Same-Sex Partnerships* (London: Hart, 2001), 427–37.

12. "The Maginot Line," in I.C.B. Dear and R.R.D. Foot, *The Oxford Companion to World War II* (Oxford: Oxford University Press, 1995), 709. For Bork's view on the decline of marriage: "If legislatures want to approve civil unions, it's up to them. I would oppose that but it's up to them. But marriage itself is too impor-tant I think to be sacrificed in the way that homosexual marriage would do. Now it must be said that heterosexuals have already done enormous damage to the marriage with their laws about no-fault divorce and that kind of thing so that the whole blame for the damage to the current situation of marriage and the family is certainly not to fall on homosexuals. But this would be a decisive step I think." "Robert's Rules of Order," interview by Peter Robinson with Robert

Bork, *Uncommon Knowledge*, interview no. 811 (filmed July 16, 2003), available at www.uncommonknowledge.org/800/811.html (viewed August 2005).

13. William J. Bennett, *Broken Hearth: Reversing the Moral Collapse of the American Family* (New York: Doubleday, 2004), 135–36 (quotation in text).

14. For historical examples of Anglo-American society blaming minorities for sexual "perversions" and assaults, see, e.g., Irving C. Rosse, "Sexual Hypochondriasis and Perversion of the Genetic Instinct," *Journal of Nervous and Mental Disease* 17 (1892): 795 (African Americans introduced crossdressing and other perversions into America); James Weir, "The Effects of Female Suffrage on Posterity," *American Naturalist* 24 (September 1895): 815–25 (feminists have created a boom in lesbianism and female perversions).

15. On the scapegoating of homosexuals, see William N. Eskridge, Jr., *Gaylaw: Challenging the Apartheid of the Closet* (Cambridge: Harvard University Press, 1999).

16. On the continuing evolution of marriage as an institution in the United States, see Nancy F. Cott, *Public Vows: A History of Marriage and the Nation* (Cambridge: Harvard University Press, 2000); E. J. Graff, *What Is Marriage For? The Strange Social History of Our Most Intimate Institution* (Boston: Beacon Press, 1999).

17. One of the few activists against same-sex marriage who has even criticized no-fault divorce is Maggie Gallagher, whose Institute for American Values has focused on actual threats to marriage at the same time it has opposed same-sex marriage. E.g., Maggie Gallagher, *Can Government Strengthen Marriage? Evidence from the Social Sciences,* report (New York: Institute for American Values, 2004). Contrast Lynn D. Wardle, "Is Marriage Obsolete?" *Michigan Journal of Gender and Law* 10 (2003): 189–235, which provides accurate diagnoses for the decline of marriage but does not advance a proposal to reform no-fault divorce, even though large majorities of Americans support reforms making it harder to divorce, and "Robert's Rules of Order" (candidly agreeing that no-fault divorce etc. have caused the decline of marriage but proposing nothing to remedy that problem).

18. Stanley Kurtz, "The End of Marriage in Scandinavia," *Weekly Standard*, February 2, 2004 (quotation in text), reprinted in *Congressional Record*, 108th Congress, 2nd sess., 2004, 150, no. 96: S8003–07 (daily ed., July 13, 2004). For other examples of such a defeatist attitude that scapegoats gay people rather than addresses underlying problems, see, e.g., Bennett, *Broken Hearth*; Russell Shorto, "What's Their Real Problem with Gay Marriage? It's the Gay Part," *New York Times Magazine,* June 19, 2005, p. 34.

19. See, e.g., "The Blocher Factor," *Economist*, February 14, 2004, which describes how one "blameless" CPP minister was "boot[ed] out" of what had been understood as a permanent cabinet seat for the CPP after the party received fewer votes than the populist right-wing People's Party in the 2003 election.

20. Stephen L. Carter, *God's Name in Vain: The Wrongs and Rights of Religion in Politics* (New York: Basic Books, 2000). See also Steven Goldberg, *Seduced by Science: How American Religion Has Lost Its Way* (Chicago: University of

Chicago Press, 1999), which powerfully argues that religion is losing its distinctive contribution to human flourishing by absorbing secular scientific arguments and proofs.

21. See, e.g., Jerry Falwell, *Strength for the Journey: An Autobiography* (New York: Simon and Schuster, 1987), 290–99, for an account of aggressive (white) Baptist support for racial segregation, and a confession for today's audience that such support was misguided. Contrast David L. Chappell, *A Stone of Hope: Prophetic Religion and the Death of Jim Crow* (Chapel Hill: University of North Carolina Press, 2004), which demonstrates the power of black Baptist preachers and congregations, as well as many mainstream white Protestant and Catholic ones, in the struggle against apartheid.

22. See chapter 2 for a detailed discussion of the movement of Christian fundamentalists in Norway against the registered partnership legislation. Our account of Anders Gåslund comes from the report of the Norwegian Partnership group of LLH. See chapter 2, note 57.

23. Ibid.

24. Inge-Lise Paulsen, "Til Lykke Norge" (Congratulations Norway), *PAN-Bladet*, (Anniversary Edition 1993), p. 11.

25. Contrast Stanley Kurtz, "Slipping toward Scandinavia," *National Review Online* (2004), available at www.nationalreview.com/kurtz/kurtz2004 0202917.asp., which argues that registered partnerships have undermined traditional marriage by discrediting organized religion in Norway.

26. A poll in June 2005 found the Norwegian Christian Democrats to be the second most unpopular political party in Norway. See Agnar Kaarbø, "Christian Democrats Unpopular," *Aftenposten*, June 17, 2005. Available at www.aften posten.no/english/local/article1062152.ece (viewed August 2005).

27. Douglas W. Kmiec and Mark S. Scarberry, "Massachusetts Alternatives," *National Review Online*, February 11, 2004 ("One overlooked possibility is for the commonwealth to temporarily get out of the new marriage business altogether"). For a blue-ribbon commission's report urging that the Canadian government get out of the marriage business entirely, see Brenda Cossman and Bruce Ryder, *The Legal Regulation of Adult Personal Relationships: Evaluating Policy Objectives and Legal Options in Federal Legislation*, research paper prepared for the Law Commission of Canada, May 2000, available at www.lcc .gc.ca/research_project/00_regulations_1–en.asp (viewed August 2005).

28. Sjursen interview (quotation in text).

29. Letter from Baker to Eskridge.

30. Tavia Simmons and Martin McConnell, *Married Couple and Unmarried-Partner Households: 2000* (Washington, D.C.: U.S. Census Bureau, February 2003). For the undercount analysis, see M. V. Lee Badgett and Marc A. Rogers, *Left Out of the Count: Missing Same-Sex Couples in Census 2000* (Amherst, Mass.: Institute for Gay and Lesbian Strategic Studies (IGLSS), 2003).

31. Simmons and McConnell, *Married Couple and Unmarried-Partner Households*, 10–11.

32. M. V. Lee Badgett and R. Bradley Sears, *Same-Sex Couples and Same-Sex Couples Raising Children in California: Data from Census 2000* (Amherst, Mass.: IGLSS and Williams Project, May 2004); Gary Gates and R. Bradley Sears, *Latino/as in Same-Sex Couples in California: Data from Census 2000* (Amherst, Mass.: Williams Project, May 2005).

33. Alain Dang and Somjen Frazer, *Black Same-Sex Households in the United States: A Report from the 2000 Census* (Washington, D.C.: NGLTF Policy Institute, October 2004); Michael Ash, et al., *Same-Sex Couples and Their Children in Massachusetts: A View from Census 2000* (Amherst, Mass.: IGLSS, February 2004); Jason Cianciotto and Luis Lopez, *Hispanic and Latino Same-Sex Households in Florida: A Report from the 2000 Census* (Washington, D.C.: NGLTF Policy Institute, 2005); Gary Gates and Jason Ost, *A Demographic Profile of New Jersey: Gay and Lesbian Families* (Washington, D.C.: Urban Institute, July 2004).

34. The best survey of the social science evidence is Judith Stacey and Timothy Biblarz, "(How) Does the Sexual Orientation of Parents Matter?" *American Sociology Review* 66 (2001): 159–72, which concludes that children raised in same-sex households show few differences from those raised in different-sex married households.

35. Rick Santorum, *It Takes a Family: Conservatism and the Common Good* (Wilmington, Del.: ISI Books, 2005), 38.

36. Stacey and Biblarz, "Does the Sexual Orientation of Parents Matter"; Ginia Bellafonte, "Two Fathers, with One Happy to Stay at Home," *New York Times,* January 12, 2004.

37. The polling information by Quinnipiac, Pew, and Gallup are reported on www.PollingReport.com, which we visited in December 2004. Eleven states passed referenda constitutionally barring recognition of same-sex marriages in the November 2004 elections: Arkansas, Georgia, Kentucky, Michigan, Mississippi, Montana, North Dakota, Ohio, Oklahoma, Oregon, and Utah. Louisiana and Missouri voters had adopted similar constitutional amendments earlier in 2004.

38. On Santorum's traditionalist philosophy and opposition to same-sex marriage and previously intemperate antigay rhetoric, see Michael Sokolove, "The Believer," *New York Times Magazine,* May 22, 2005, pp. 56–63, 70–71. Santorum's defense of his homosexual aide and kinder, gentler antigay-marriage rhetoric are reported in Lou Chibbaro, "Santorum Defends Outed Gay Staffer," *Washington Blade,* July 22, 2005, p. 12 (first Santorum quotation in text); Steve Goldstein, "Gay-Rights Opponent Santorum Stands by Outed Aide," *Philadelphia Inquirer,* July 16, 2005 (second quotation).

39. Interview by Darren Spedale with Eddie Moris and Jens Boesen, Copenhagen, May 1997.

40. See American Law Institute, Model Penal Code, *Commentary* (Philadelphia: ALI, 1962) (libertarian justification for decriminalizing consensual sodomy, fornication, adultery). Some enthusiasts have interpreted *Lawrence v. Texas,* 539 U.S. 558 (2003), where the Supreme Court invalidated consensual sodomy

laws, as a constitutionalization of the harm principle. For reasons that follow in the text, we are most dubious.

41. John Stuart Mill, *On Liberty and Other Writings* (Cambridge, England: Cambridge University Press, 1989), 91–93. Mill's position on polygamy is echoed in natural law philosopher John Finnis's position on gay marriage: don't make it a crime, but don't promote it with state recognition. See Finnis, "Law, Morality, and 'Sexual Orientation,'" *Notre Dame Law Review* 69 (1994): 1049–69.

42. Applying Rousseau's romantic understanding of marriage and citizenship to the same-sex marriage debate is Walter Berns, "Marriage Anyone?" *First Things,* April 1996, p. 13. For a similar point by Hegel, see Maura Strassberg, "Distinctions of Form or Substance: Monogamy, Polygamy, and Same-Sex Marriage," *North Carolina Law Review* 75 (1997): 1557.

43. The phenomenon described here is strikingly similar to that which Dan Kahan has identified for the criminal law generally: everyone argues that the criminal sanction serves deterrent purposes, but no one really seems to change his or her mind on the basis of empirical evidence. See Kahan, "The Secret Ambition of Deterrence," *Harvard Law Review* 113 (1999): 413–500.

44. Jonathan Haidt, "The Emotional Dog and Its Rational Tail: A Social Intuitionist Approach to Moral Judgment," *Psychological Review* 108 (2001): 814 (quotation in text); Haidt, "Sexual Morality: The Cultures and Emotions of Conservatives and Liberals," *Journal of Applied Psychology* 31 (2001): 191–221 (experiment described in text). See also Joshua Greene and Jonathan Haidt, "How (and Where) Does Moral Judgment Work?" *Trends in Cognitive Sciences* 6 (2002): 512–23 (neutral bases for social intuitionist theory of how we form moral judgments). We first learned of this literature from Courtney Megan Cahill, "Same-Sex Marriage, Slippery-Slope Rhetoric, and the Politics of Disgust: A Critical Perspective on Contemporary Family Discourse and the Incest Taboo," *Northwestern University Law Review* 85 (2005): forthcoming.

45. Paul Rozin, "Disgust," in *Handbook of Emotions* (2000): 642 (quotation in text); Martha C. Nussbaum, *Hiding from Humanity: Disgust, Bodies, and the Law* (Princeton: Princeton University Press, 2004), 89 (drawing from Rozin's work and exploring the way disgust emotions "polic[e] the boundary between ourselves and nonhuman animals, or our own animality").

46. The American Enterprise Institute compiled polling data on gay rights from 1973 through 2004. Although staggering majorities oppose most antigay employment discriminations, including the armed forces' exclusion of homosexuals, most Americans (58 percent in a 2002 University of Chicago poll) continue to disapprove homosexual relations. As late as January 2004, Gallup found a small plurality in favor of making consensual homosexual relations illegal.

47. The classic account of a disgust-driven social movement is Joseph R. Gusfield, *Symbolic Crusade: Status Politics and the American Temperance Movement,* 2nd ed. (Champaign: University of Illinois Press, 1986).

48. On the disgust-driven moral panics of the last 150 years, see Philip Jenkins, *Moral Panic; Changing Concepts of the Child Molester in Modern America* (New

Haven: Yale University Press, 1998) (cyclical interest in regulating sex with children, driven by disgust as well as harm principle); David J. Pivar, *Purity Crusade: Sexual Morality and Social Control, 1868–1900* (Westport, Conn.: Greenwood Press, 1973); Ruth Rosen, *The Lost Sisterhood: Prostitution in America*, 1900–1918 (Baltimore: Johns Hopkins University Press, 1982).

49. Mary Douglas, *Purity and Danger: An Analysis of the Concepts of Pollution and Taboo* (London: Routledge and Kegan Paul, 1966). Compare Nussbaum, *Hiding from Humanity,* 91, which situates Douglas's theory as an account of "taboos and prohibitions," and not "disgust" per se. Nussbaum prefers Rozin's theory as an account of disgust, but makes some modifications to it which, she says, are consistent with the spirit of Rozin's theory.

50. Douglas, *Purity and Danger*, 123–24; see also Pierre Schlag, "The Aesthetics of American Law," *Harvard Law Review* 115 (2002): 1061–65, which discusses the law's obsession with classifications and grids; Cahill, "Politics of Disgust," which applies Douglas's social pollution idea to incest taboos.

51. William Ian Miller, *The Anatomy of Disgust* (Cambridge: Harvard University Press, 1997), 194–95 (first quotation in text); 250–51 (second quotation). See also Dan M. Kahan, "The Anatomy of Disgust in Criminal Law," *Michigan Law Review* 96 (1998): 1621–57 (excellent review of Miller's book); Joseph R. Gusfield, "On Legislating Morals: The Symbolic Process of Designating Deviance," *Southern California Law Review* 56 (1968): 54–73.

52. The classic statement of the complementarity of the sexes is the natural law–inspired document issued by the Congregation for the Doctrine of the Faith, per Cardinal Josef Ratzinger (now Pope Benedict XVI), "Considerations Regarding Proposals to Give Legal Recognition to Unions Between Homosexual Persons" (Rome: Vatican, June 3, 2003). Secular statements that seem quite similar include Robert H. Bork, "The Necessary Amendment," *First Things* 145 (August–September 2004): 17–21 (arguing that crossing the gender line with same-sex marriage would be "nuclear"); Stanley Kurtz, "What Is Wrong with Gay Marriage," *Commentary*, September 2000, p. 35 (arguing that the "complementarity" of the sexes is what makes marriages stable and augurs against same-sex marriage).

53. Professor Marc Poirier's brilliant analogy between fundamentalists' concept of marriage as one man, one woman and Native Americans' preservation of sacred areas was suggested at a workshop on draft chapters of our book, sponsored by Professor Nan Hunter (the convenor) and Professor Suzanne Goldberg (the host) at Columbia Law School in June 2004.

54. For an excellent introduction to the cyclical nature of religious moralism in American public culture, from the Puritans (1690s) to the Comstockerites (1870s) to the religious right (1980s), see James Morone, *Hellfire Nation: The Politics of Sin in American History* (New Haven: Yale University Press, 2003).

55. Cahill, "Politics of Disgust," focuses on the incest taboo and demonstrates how it is the key to slippery slope arguments against gay marriage.

56. Bork, "Necessary Amendment" (quotation in text). See also Bennett, *Broken Hearth*, 112–13, 135–36 (similar argument).

57. For a trivial but telling example, Kurtz concedes that the portion of Scandinavian children born outside of marriage has been steadily rising for a generation, but exhibits great alarm that the rate did not reach 50 percent in Norway until registered partnerships were recognized. See Kurtz, "Slipping toward Scandinavia." Crossing the 50 percent mark is like crossing the sound barrier, a kind of point of no return, from Kurtz's point of view. Although he seizes on the 50 percent mark as totalizing in Norway, he then forgets about it for the other countries. Sweden reached the 50 percent mark before its registered partnership law was enacted; Denmark has never reached that benchmark.

58. Goldberg, *Seduced by Science*. For examples of Roman Catholic Church reliance on Kurtz's "empirical" studies of Scandinavian partnerships, see, e.g., Catholic Educator's Resource Center, available at www.catholiceducation.org/directory/Current_Issues/Marriage_and_Family/more5.html (viewed July 2005), which highlights Kurtz, "End of Marriage."

59. For a brilliant argument that prejudice serves psychological functions for the bigot, and that homophobia is our most all-purpose prejudice, see Elisabeth Young-Bruehl, *The Anatomy of Prejudices* (Cambridge: Harvard University Press, 1996).

60. On post-*Baehr* learning curve for lawyers advocating gay marriage, see Eskridge, *Equality Practice*, chaps. 1–2.

61. Kees Waadijk, "Small Change: How the Road to Same-Sex Marriage Got Paved in the Netherlands," in Wintemute and Andenaes, *Legal Recognition of Same-Sex Partnerships*, 437–64.

62. Two recent national polls in Norway have demonstrated support of at least sixty percent of the population for a gender-neutral marriage law. See Geir Arne Bore, "Seks av ti positive til homo-esteskap" (Six of Ten in Favor of Gay Marriage), Dagsavisen, April 20, 2005. Also Espen Lokeland-Stai, "Ja til homo-ekteskap" (Yes to Gay Marriage), Klassekampen, September 3, 2005.

63. See generally William N. Eskridge, Jr., "Comparative Law and the Same-Sex Marriage Debate: A Step-by-Step Approach to State Recognition," *McGeorge Law Review* 31 (2000): 641–72.

64. The information in this and the next paragraph in text is taken from telephone interview by William Eskridge and Darren Spedale with Jean Luscher and Diana Skovgaard, New Haven, Connecticut, March 2005.

65. Ibid. (quotations in text).

66. See Robert Dahl, *A Preface to Democratic Theory* (New Haven: Yale University Press, 1957); Adam Przeworski, *Democracy and the Market: Political and Economic Reforms in Eastern Europe and Latin America* (New York: Oxford University Press, 1991).

67. On Grundtvig and his philosophy of *frisind*, see "N.F.S. Grundtvig," in *Denmark*, ed. Thomas Sehested and Carsten Wulff (Copenhagen: Royal Danish

Ministry of Foreign Affairs, Department of Information, 2002) (quotation in text), available at www.ambwashington.um.dk/en/menu/Informationabout Denmark/Culture/Literature/N.F.S.Grundtvig.htm (viewed September 2005).

68. For the dignified nature of the debate in Denmark, see chapter 2 of this book.

69. See Louis Michael Seidman and Mark V. Tushnet, *Remnants of Belief: Contemporary Constitutional Issues* (New York: Oxford University Press, 1996). Compare, for example, Dudley Clendenin and Adam Nagourney, *Out for Good: The Struggle to Build a Gay Rights Movement in America* (New York: Simon and Schuster, 1999), which traces the rise of an aggressive, equality-demanding gay rights movement, with Oran P. Smith, *The Rise of Baptist Republicanism* (New York: New York University Press, 1997), which traces the rise of an aggressive line-drawing and moralistic religious fundamentalism.

70. *Loving v. Virginia*, 388 U.S. 1 (U.S. Supreme Court, 1967), discussed in chapter 1.

71. *Naim v. Naim*, 87 S.E.2d 749 (Virginia Supreme Court, 1955) (reaffirming the constitutionality of its miscegenation law after *Brown*), appeal dismissed, 350 U.S. 985 (U.S. Supreme Court, 1956); Alexander H. Bickel, *The Least Dangerous Branch: The Supreme Court at the Bar of Politics* (New Haven: Yale University Press, 1962), 174 (explaining the Court's *Naim* disposition).

72. On the twentieth-century history of miscegenation laws, including the repeal of most of them after *Naim* and before *Loving*, see Randall Kennedy, *Interracial Intimacies: Sex, Marriage, Identity, and Adoption* (New York: Pantheon, 2003), 244–80.

73. For information on the various government reports and their contents, see chapter 2.

74. On the notion of "deep compromise," whereby different normative visions work out a principled accommodation, rather than just "splitting the baby," see Henry S. Richardson, *Democratic Autonomy: Public Reasoning about the Ends of Policy* (New York: Oxford University Press, 2002), 143–61. On the virtues of legislative deliberation, see, e.g., Jeremy Waldron, *Law and Disagreement* (New York: Oxford University Press, 1999).

75. See our discussion of the 1999 amendment to the Registered Partnership Act in chapters 2–4.

76. 1999 California Statutes chap. 588.

77. California Domestic Partner Rights and Responsibilities Act, 2003 Cal. Statutes chap. 421 (A.B. No. 205), §1(b) (legislative finding, quoted in text); §4(a) (extending almost all benefits and duties of marriage to domestic partners). The main exceptions to the equal-benefits-and-duties principle are the following: domestic partners are not eligible for the public employee long-term care benefits set forth in Cal. Govt. Code § 21661; a surviving domestic partner is not protected from a property tax reassessment of a jointly owned home after the death of one partner (Proposition 13 protects surviving spouses from such reassessments); domestic partners who are childless, have been together for five years or fewer, have no support obligations to one another, and satisfy stated debt and real property restrictions can dissolve their relationship

by jointly filing a notice of termination with the secretary of state. See new California Family Code § 299(a). Otherwise, domestic partnerships can be dissolved only by going through formal divorce proceedings; § 299(d).

78. Jessica Garrison, "Wigging Out over Governor's 'Girlie Men' Remark," *Los Angeles Times*, July 26, 2004 (Schwarzenegger's description of his Democrat opponents in the legislature as "girlie men"); Carla Marinucci, "Governor, Newsom Campaign to Safeguard Local Tax Funds: Schwarzenegger Declares Democrat 'A Very, Very Strong Mayor,'" *San Francisco Chronicle*, October 26, 2004 (instead of dismissing San Francisco Mayor Gavin Newsome as a "girlie man" for his handing out marriage licenses to same-sex couples, the nation's biggest muscled governor responded, "I think this is the right way to go . . . let the courts decide and let the people decide").

79. *Baker v. State*, 744 A.2d 864 (Vermont Supreme Court, 1999). All five justices agreed that the state's discrimination against same-sex couples violated the common benefits clause of the Vermont constitution. Justice Denise Johnson dissented from the majority's refusal to insist on same-sex marriage as the required constitutional remedy.

80. For detailed accounts of the Vermont legislature's deliberations leading to the Civil Unions Act, see William N. Eskridge, Jr., *Equality Practice: Civil Unions and the Future of Gay Rights* (New York: Routledge, 2002), 57–82; David Moats, *Civil Wars: A Battle for Gay Marriage* (Orlando, Fl.: Harcourt, 2004); Michael Mello, *Legalizing Gay Marriage* (Philadelphia: Temple University Press, 2004), an excellent account by a straight Vermonter who supports same-sex marriage as a matter of principle. See also Greg Johnson, "Vermont Civil Unions: The New Language of Marriage," *Vermont Law Review* 25 (2000): 15–41.

81. For disappointment with civil unions on both sides of the issue, see Mello, *Legalizing Gay Marriage*, 48–68, which reproduces dozens of letters written by ordinary citizens to their legislators and to newspapers during the legislative debates in 2000. See also Michael Mello, "For Today I'm Gay: The Unfinished Battle for Same-Sex Marriage in Vermont," *Vermont Law Review* 25 (2000): 188–212 (similar).

82. *Baehr v. Lewin*, 852 P.2d 44 (Hawaii Supreme Court, 1993) (holding the same-sex marriage exclusion to be a sex discrimination the state must justify), on remand, 1996 WL 694235 (Hawaii Circuit Court, First Circuit, December 1996) (declaring the exclusion unconstitutional), vacated as *Baehr v. Miike*, 994 P.2d 566 (Hawaii Supreme Court, 1999) (dismissing the constitutional challenge in light of a 1998 amendment to the state constitution). For background and the divisive debate in Hawaii, see Eskridge, *Equality Practice*, 22–42; David Orgon Coolidge, "The Hawaii Marriage Amendment: Its Origins, Meaning, and Fate," *Hawaii Law Review* 22 (2000): 19–118.

83. *Goodridge v. Department of Public Health*, 798 A.2d 941 (Massachusetts Supreme Judicial Court, 2003), reaffirmed in *Opinions of the Justices to the Senate*, 802 N.E.2d (Massachusetts Supreme Judicial Court, 2004), which opined that the legislature could not satisfy the Massachusetts constitution by creating a sepa-

rate-but-equal regime of civil unions for same-sex couples. The commonwealth started issuing marriage licenses to same-sex couples on May 17, 2004.

84. Excellent analyses of *Goodridge* and its aftermath include Jennifer Levi, "To-
ward a More Perfect Union: The Road to Marriage Equality for Same-Sex
Couples," *Widener Law Journal* 13 (2004): 831–58; Mary L. Bonauto, "*Goodridge*
in Context," *Harvard Civil Rights–Civil Liberties Law Review* 40 (2005): 1–69.
Focusing on the first proposed constitutional amendment is Lawrence
Freidman, "The (Relative) Passivity of *Goodridge v. Department of Public
Health*," *Boston University Public Interest Law Journal* 14 (2004): 1–23.

85. See Pam Belluck, "A New Challenge to Same-Sex Marriages," *New York Times*,
June 17, 2005, p. A16, which describes the new proposed constitutional amendment in Massachusetts.

86. The federalism theme for the same-sex marriage debate was first explored by
Andrew Koppelman, *The Gay Rights Question in Contemporary American Law*
(Chicago: University of Chicago Press, 2002), and Eskridge, *Equality Practice*,
115–20, 231–42. See also the subsequent iteration of these arguments in Rauch,
Gay Marriage, 172–91.

87. For maps of European diversity in recognizing same-sex unions, see Kees
Waaldijk, *More or Less Together: Levels of Legal Consequences of Marriage,
Cohabitation and Registered Partnership for Different-Sex and Same-Sex Part-
ners, a Comparative Study of Nine European Countries* (2005), available at
www.ined.fr/publications/collections/dossiersetrecherches/125.pdf (visited
July 24, 2005).

88. Alaska and Hawaii have statutes limiting marriage to one man, one woman
and constitutional amendments allowing the legislature to do so. In 2004,
Oregon's voters amended the state constitution to define marriage as one man,
one woman. California and Washington have statutes (also adopted by the
voters) to the same effect. For up-to-date surveys of marriage non-recognition statutes and constitutional amendments, see www.lambdalegal.org.

89. Ohio and Michigan have both statutory and constitutional provisions defining marriage as one man, one woman. Illinois, Indiana, Iowa, and Minnesota
have statutes to that effect. For the current status of these laws, see www
.lambdalegal.org.

90. Arkansas, Georgia, Kentucky, Louisiana, Missouri, Mississippi, Montana,
North Dakota, Oklahoma, and Utah have both statutory and constitutional
provisions defining marriage as one man, one woman. Nebraska and Nevada
have constitutional provisions to that effect. Alabama, Arizona, Colorado,
Florida, Idaho, Kansas, North Carolina, South Carolina, South Dakota, Ten-
nessee, Texas, Virginia, and West Virginia have statutes to that effect. For the
current status of these laws, see www.lambdalegal.org.

91. *Langan v. St. Vincent's Hosptial*, 2003 WL 21294889 (New York Supreme Court,
2003) (appeal pending). For application of the full faith and credit clause to
same-sex marriages or unions, see Linda Silberman, "Can the Island of Hawaii Bind the World? A Comment on Same-Sex Marriage and Federalism

Values," *Quinnipiac Law Review* 16 (1996–97): 191–208, who demonstrates that the clause does not *require* interstate recognition of such marriages but does require interstate recognition of judgments.

92. Frank Santiago, "Iowa Judge's Ruling In Lesbian Divorce Case Will Stand," *Des Moines Register* (June 17, 2005), available at http://desmoinesregister.com/apps/pbcs.dll/article?AID=/20050617/NEWS01/50617001/1001/NEWS (viewed September 2005).

93. See Martin Ottenheimer, *Forbidden Relatives: The American Myth of Cousin Marriage* (Urbana, Ill.: University of Illionois Press,1996); Brett McDonnell, "Is Incest Next?" *Cardozo Women's Law Journal* 10 (2004): 337–50.

94. Koppelman, *Gay Rights Question;* Andrew Koppelman, "Same-Sex Marriage, Choice of Law, and Public Policy," *Texas Law Review* 76 (1998): 921–1001.

95. Table 6.2 is adapted from the federalism analysis first espoused by Gordon Tullock, "Federalism: Problems of Scale," *Public Choice* 6 (1969): 19–29.

96. Voting with their feet models, which inspire table 6.3, originate with Charles Tiebout, "A Pure Theory of Local Expenditures," *Journal of Political Economy* 64 (1956): 416–24.

97. On states as laboratories of experimentation, see *New State Ice Co. v. Liebmann,* 285 U.S. 262, 311 (U.S. Supreme Court, 1932) (Brandeis, J., dissenting); *FERC v. Mississippi,* 456 U.S. 742, 788 (U.S. Supreme Court, 1982) (O'Connor, J., dissenting).

EPILOGUE

1. The menu of options is based upon William N. Eskridge, Jr., *Equality Practice: Civil Unions and the Future of Gay Rights* (New York: Routledge, 2002), 121–26.

2. On domestic partnerships, see chapter 1, and especially Raymond O'Brien, "Domestic Partnership: Recognition and Responsibility," *San Diego Law Review* 32 (1995): 163–220.

3. On cohabitation regimes in Canada and Europe, see the essays in Robert Wintemute and Mads Andenaes, eds., *Legal Recognition of Same-Sex Partnerships: A Study of National, European, and International Law* (Oxford: Hart, 2001).

4. On Hawaii reciprocal beneficiaries, see Eskridge, *Equality Practice,* 22–25. On French *pactes civils,* see Daniel Borrillo, "The 'Pacte Civil de Solidarite' in France: Midway between Marriage and Cohabitation," in Wintemute and Andenaes, *Legal Recognition of Same-Sex Partnerships.* See generally Kees Waaldijk, *More or Less Together: Levels of Legal Consequences of Marriage, Cohabitation, and Registered Partnership for Different-Sex and Same-Sex Partners, a Comparative Study of Nine European Countries* (2005), available at www.ined.fr/publications/collections/dossiersetrecherches/125.pdf (visited August 2005).

5. On Scandinavian registered partnership laws, and their evolution, see chapter 2. On Vermont civil unions, see Eskridge, *Equality Practice,* 57–82. We note,

however, that there is already some international portability for registered partnerships within Scandinavia and the Netherlands; it is likely that this portability will expand, at least within Europe.

6. For a proposal that Massachusetts should now get out of the marriage business, see Douglas W. Kmiec and Mark S. Scarberry, "Massachusetts Alternatives," *National Review Online*, February 11, 2004.

7. Louisiana Code sec.229, 272; Joel Nichols, "Louisiana's Covenant Marriage Law: A First Step toward a More Robust Pluralism in Marriage and Divorce Law?" *Emory Law Journal* 47 (1998): 929–1001. For other covenant marriage laws, see Arizona Statutes §25–901 et seq. 2001 Arkansas Acts 1486.

8. For an important analysis suggesting that the state disassociate itself from sectarian marriage, see Brenda Cossman and Bruce Ryder, *The Legal Regulation of Adult Personal Relationships: Evaluating Policy Objectives and Legal Options in Federal Legislation*, research paper prepared for the Law Commission of Canada, May 2000, available at www.lcc.gc.ca/research_project/00_regulations_1–en.asp (viewed August 2005).

INDEX